KT-486-745

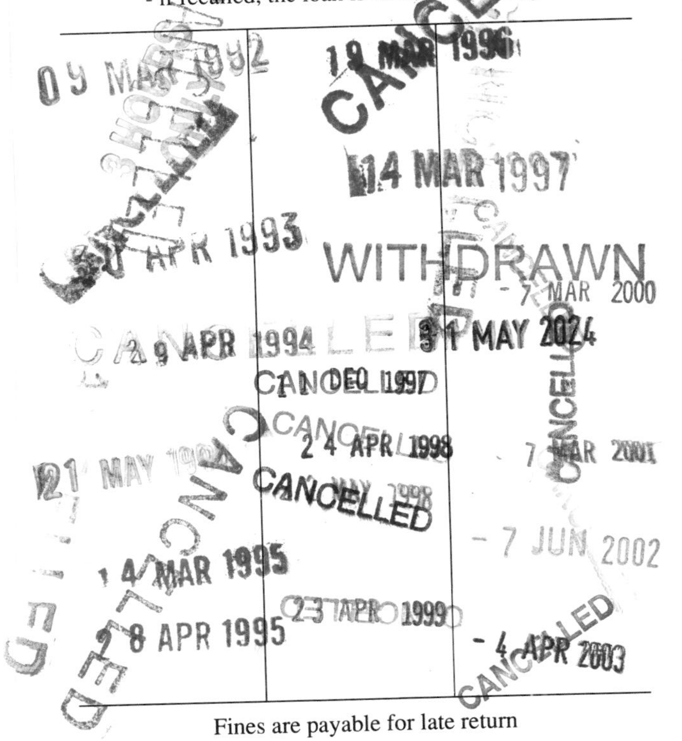

100 years of WIMBLEDON

The Final Tie will be Played on Monday, July 16, at 3.30 p.m.

Postponed to Thursday, July 19, at 4.30 p.m.

LAWN TENNIS CHAMPIONSHIP,

OPEN TO ALL AMATEURS.

FIRST PRIZE.—The GOLD CHAMPION PRIZE, value 12 guineas, with a Silver Challenge Cup, value 25 guineas (presented by the Proprietors of *The Field*).

SECOND PRIZE.—The SILVER PRIZE, value 7 guineas.

THIRD PRIZE.—Value 3 guineas.

	Winners of 1st ties.	*Winners of 2nd ties.*	*Winners of 3rd ties.*	*Winner of 4th tie.*	
Mr. H. T. Gillson					
Mr. Spencer Gore	Gore				
Mr. R. D. Dalby		Gore			
Mr. Montague Hankey	Hankey				
Mr. J. Baker			Gore		
Mr. J. W. Trist	Baker.........				
Mr. E. N. Langham		Langham ...			
Mr. C. F. Buller.........	Langham ...				
Mr. H. Wheeler.........				Gore	
Mr. L. R. Erskine......	Erskine				Gore 1st prize
Mr. H. C. Soden		Erskine			
Mr. J. Lambert	Lambert ...				
Mr. B. N. Akroyd......			W. Marshall (a bye) 2nd prize		
Mr. G. Nicol	Akroyd				
Mr. W. C. Marshall ...		W. Marshall			
Mr. F. D. Jackson......	W. Marshall				
Mr. F. W. Oliver					
Major Battye	Oliver				
Mr. Julian Marshall ...		J. Marshall.			
Capt. Grimston	J. Marshall.		Heathcote ... 3rd prize		
Mr. C. G. Heathcote ...					
Capt. G. F. Buxton ...	Heathcote—a bye ______				

The Official Score will be posted on the Notice Board in the Pavilion after each tie.

Lawn Tennis Championship

1877

100 years of WIMBLEDON

Lance Tingay

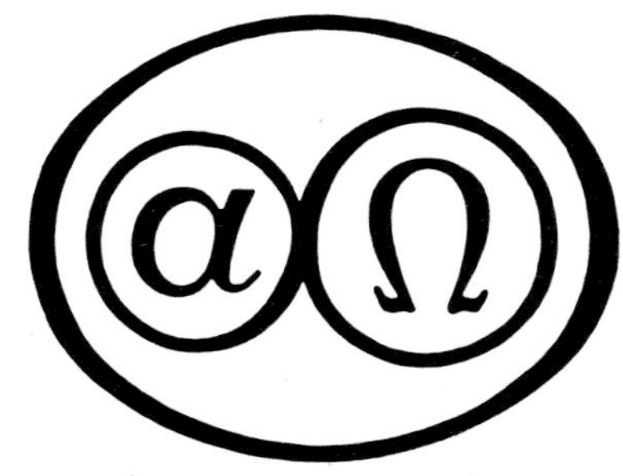

GUINNESS SUPERLATIVES LIMITED
2 CECIL COURT, LONDON ROAD, ENFIELD, MIDDLESEX

ACKNOWLEDGEMENTS

Photography: Gerry Cranham
Historical pictures supplied by the Popperfoto picture agency and Michael Searle

Editor: Alex Reid
Designer: David Roberts

ISBN 0 900424 71 0

The official history of the Wimbledon Lawn Tennis Championships published with the approval of the All England Lawn Tennis and Croquet Club by Guinness Superlatives Ltd, 2 Cecil Court, London Road, Enfield, Middlesex

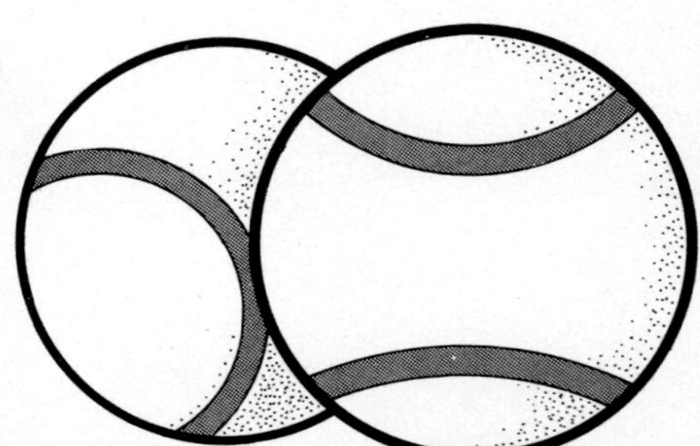

Printed in Great Britain at the University Press, Oxford by Vivian Ridler, Printer to the University

CONTENTS

FOREWORD

by HRH The Duke of Kent, GCMG, GCVO

As President of the All England Lawn Tennis and Croquet Club I am very happy to maintain a close family connection with what is as much a British institution as a sporting event, the Lawn Tennis Championships.

My association is deep rooted, having begun in 1907 when my grandfather, then the Prince of Wales and later King George V, became President. After World War I he and Queen Mary were regular attenders at the Championships both at the old Worple Road ground and the new one in Church Road. They performed the opening ceremony at the Church Road ground in 1922, and in 1926 presented the commemorative medals to past Champions on the fiftieth anniversary of the Championships. In that year also my uncle, then the Duke of York and later King George VI, competed in the Championships. In 1930 my father became President and was succeeded in 1943 by my mother, Princess Marina, Duchess of Kent, who held the office for the next twenty-five years.

In the nine years since I became President profound changes have occurred in the rules governing the Championships, yet during this time not only has Wimbledon maintained the standards of organisation for which it is famous, but the quality of play has actually improved.

As Wimbledon approaches the Centenary of the Lawn Tennis Championships, I know it is the ambition of all connected with the All England Club that the Championships should remain not just one of the highlights of the summer, but the premier Lawn Tennis Tournament of the world.

I welcome this history of the first hundred years and I am confident that ambition will be fulfilled.

Edward

York House
St. James's Palace
London S.W.1

PREFACE

by Air Chief Marshal Sir Brian Burnett, GCB, DFC, AFC
Chairman of The All England Club and Chairman of the Committee of Management of the Championships

Those concerned with the organisation of The Lawn Tennis Championships will be astonished to learn on reading Lance Tingay's account that the first Tournament, which began on 9 July 1877, was only mooted at a Committee meeting of The All England Club just 37 days before, on 2 June.

Between 1877 and 1977 the event has grown to proportions undreamed of by the worthy Dr Henry Jones and his colleagues who organised the first lawn tennis tournament at Wimbledon. The story of its growth is not only the story of a tournament, which has provided the keenest competition between the world's finest players over the century; it is a history of the game itself and a tribute to Major Walter Clopton Wingfield, MVO (1833–1912), the founder of lawn tennis.

Today it takes rather more than 37 days to prepare for the Championships! And the Committee of Management responsible for what is acknowledged to be the world's outstanding lawn tennis championship is confronted with many complex problems. It is inevitably bedevilled by the political bothers that beset the organisation of the game throughout the world, and we sometimes envy our early predecessors.

Nevertheless, when it comes down to it, the purpose of the Wimbledon Championships from year to year is clear enough. It is to have the best players of the world in competition against each other in conditions that are as good as can be devised. Lawn tennis is a fascinating sport. It is more than a mere athletic pursuit. It is a matter of artistry to a high degree. For that matter it is also a matter of psychology. It is also one of the few great sports where the ladies and men can play not only alongside each other but also together in mixed doubles.

Wimbledon's aim has always been to provide the best, and the Championships have become not only one of the highlights of the London summer scene but a tradition acknowledged throughout the world. We hope to maintain that tradition and we are proud of our one hundred years at Wimbledon. We hope that our descendants will in due course be proud of another century.

In the following pages Lance Tingay records the first one hundred years. He has seen a good deal of it, every day, in fact, of every Championship since 1932. Since 1952 he has been lawn tennis correspondent to the *Daily Telegraph*. I am sure all tennis players will be grateful to him for the diligence and devotion with which he has produced this excellent history of our great Championships which sets standards for other sports to match. I strongly commend it to all lovers of the game.

PRESIDENTS OF THE ALL ENGLAND CLUB

1907–9	HRH The Prince of Wales, KG, KT, KP, GCSI, GCMG, GCIE, GCVO, ISO
1911	A. W. Gore
1912–14	Lord Desborough, KCVO
1915–20	H. Wilson Fox, MP
1921–9	H. W. W. Wilberforce
1930–42	HRH The Prince George (later Duke of Kent), KG, GCVO
1943–68	HRH Princess Marina, Duchess of Kent, CI, GCVO, GBE
1969–	HRH The Duke of Kent, GCMG, GCVO

HISTORY

MILESTONES

1868 23 July. Formation of the All England Croquet Club.

1875 25 February. Lawn tennis added to the activities of the All England Croquet Club.

1877 14 April. Change of name, from the All England Croquet Club to The All England Croquet and Lawn Tennis Club.

1877 The first Lawn Tennis Championships staged.

1884 Women's singles and men's doubles events introduced into the Lawn Tennis Championships.

1913 Women's doubles and mixed doubles events introduced as full Championship events.

1922 The All England Club opens its new ground in Church Road.

1968 The first meeting open to all classes of players, the distinction between amateurs and professionals having been abolished. Prize money paid for the first time.

1
GENESIS & THE HARROVIAN ERA *(1877-1880)*

There is a tradition that the Lawn Tennis Championships were begun to raise money to repair a pony roller. After one hundred years the same pony roller, albeit no longer hauled by a pony but in splendid working order, may be seen in a corner of the Centre Court at Wimbledon. It stays there not only because it is still in use but because it is too wide to be taken out through any of the exits.

Whatever the motive behind its foundation the first Lawn Tennis Championship began on Monday, 9 July 1877, at 3.30 pm. It was a warm, sunny day and ten matches were played, this comprising the entire first round of the men's singles, the only event. There is no record of who struck the first ball in the world's first lawn tennis championship. It could have been the first champion, Spencer William Gore; his name had come out in the top bracket of the draw and his would have been the logical match with which to begin.

This was a year which could be taken as the quintessence of the Victorian age. As from 1 January Queen Victoria, a dour widow for some sixteen years, had

The Centre Court's oldest inhabitant – the pony roller

been Empress of India; the papers in midsummer were full of war news from the Balkans; the annual military manœuvres occupied Wimbledon Common; Anthony Trollope had just brought out the last chapters of *The American Senator* in *Temple Bar*; on that happy Monday in July, Gore, an old Harrovian of 27, beat a man called H. T. Gillson by 6–2 6–0 6–3 and the game of lawn tennis had taken the first vital step in transforming itself into a sport. How had it come about?

The All England Croquet and Lawn Tennis Club had been known as such only since 14 April 1877 when a special general meeting approved the change. It was founded as the All England Croquet Club and, indeed, at its inception lawn tennis did not exist. That was on 23 July 1868 when a meeting was held in the offices of *The Field*, then as now a notable sporting magazine, in the Strand. The chairman of the meeting was J. H. Walsh, the 57-year-old editor of *The Field* who had begun his career as a doctor. The gentlemen with him were Captain R. F. Dalton, Mr J. H. Hale, Rev A. Law, Mr J. H. Clarke Maddock and Walter Jones Whitmore.

These croquet enthusiasts (the year before Whitmore had become the first recorded champion) agreed on the formation of the All England Croquet Club with an entrance fee of one guinea and a yearly subscription of the same amount. Whitmore was appointed honorary secretary and Maddock the honorary treasurer. They met again on 6 August when Mr E. B. Mitchell was put on the committee, 38 members elected and £5 approved for expenses in finding a suitable ground. On 5 November a life membership was created for ten guineas and Whitmore, Hale and Walsh made themselves such. On 20 November William Whitmore Jones also became a life member. The subsequent history of Wimbledon was bedevilled by the inevitable confusion between the croquet champion, Jones Whitmore, and Whitmore Jones, not to mention one Henry Jones who was the most important figure of all.

So far the All England Croquet Club had members, confusion over names that might have existed in a Welsh valley, but no ground. At a committee meeting on 30 January 1869 there was even a gloomy suggestion that the club should be wound up. On 3 June there was some kind of row with Whitmore who wanted to resign and asked for his life membership money to be returned. On that date the club had credits of £89 5*s* and debits of £44 16*s* 4*d*, making a credit balance of £44 8*s* 8*d*. On 8 July Henry Jones was made auditor. On 24 September the Earl of Essex was made president. Daniel Jones was made a member; he was a brother of Henry. Maddock reported that he had found a promising site for a ground in Wimbledon; it was offered by Alfred Dixon on a lease for a rental of £50 the first year, £75 the second and £100 the third. There were four acres between Worple Road and the London and South Western Railway.

By the end of 1869 the affairs of the All England Croquet Club had progressed smoothly. The lease of the ground was approved; £1 was laid out to provide for the right to have a gate from the club to the footpath by the side of the railway; the row with Jones

The first champion, Spencer Gore

Whitmore had gone off the boil and he was talking to the All England Club in his capacity as secretary of the National Croquet Club; a donation fund of £600 was available and of this £495 was spent, including £425 which was the tender for laying out the ground and building a gardener's cottage and pavilion. The building sub-committee comprised Henry Jones, Maddock and Walsh.

And so into 1870. Early in the year the All England Club and the National Croquet Club agreed on a joint code of rules. At a committee meeting on 7 April the appointment of a gardener at a wage of 4*s* a day was agreed. The new club was almost ready for occupation. There was one snag that had to be resolved. Wimbledon at that time was a fast-growing community, like all areas near London served by the railway, but it had not lost its rural charm entirely. The secretary was 'requested to give notice to the person farming the field on the west of the ground to make his fence good so as to keep his cattle and swine from trespassing on the club ground'. On 24 June the 36th committee meeting of the All England Croquet Club was held. It took place on the club ground for the first time. A little later that summer the Croquet Championships were staged and for that and the next four summers nothing but the click of croquet mallet and ball was heard in Worple Road. Financially there were difficulties; at the end of 1873 a fund was raised to clear the club debt, with Walsh contributing £10 and Henry Jones £5.

There seem to have been complaints from time to time about the smoothness of the lawns, of which there were twelve, laid out in three terraces. The pony roller made its appearance. It was kindly presented to the club by Walsh. The club, equally kindly, made his daughter a life member.

None the less croquet, the delight of curates, the permissive outlet for Victorian young ladies who could then flirt daringly, was to be ousted as the supreme British garden-party pastime. Lawn tennis was in the process of evolution. In 1872 Major Harry Gem had founded the Leamington Lawn Tennis Club, the first of its kind, after playing his version of the game on the lawn of J. B. Perera's home in Edgbaston, Birmingham, in the 1860s.

More vitally for the future of the infant game, Major Walter Clopton Wingfield had, on 23 February 1874, patented (or, rather, entered a patent application) 'A New and Improved Portable Court for Playing the Ancient Game of Tennis' which he marketed under the name of 'Sphairistike'. The patent application lapsed on 2 March 1877 but Wingfield seems to have sold his invention most successfully. Before 1874 was out the new game was known across the lawns of Britain; croquet went 'out' and the newfangled 'sticky' or 'lawn tennis' was 'in'. It is clear, looking back across more than ten decades, that no All England Club member was more aware of the trend than Henry Jones.

Above: An early 'Sphairistike' racket

Left: 'Sphairistike' as visualised in Major Wingfield's pamphlet

The debt owed by lawn tennis to Major Gem has long been acknowledged and so, too, the greater debt owed to Major Wingfield. Doctor Jones has not had his due as a pre-eminent creator of what lawn tennis has become. I call him Doctor Jones because he was Henry Jones, MRCS, FSA born in London on 2 November 1831, eldest son of Henry Derviche Jones, surgeon. He was at King's College School, Wimbledon, from 1842 to 1848 and at St Bartholomew's Hospital until he qualified in 1852. He practised medicine near Soho Square until 1869 when, having begun writing on whist in 1857, he gave up to become a full-time writer on games. As 'Cavendish' he was widely known and wrote extensively in *The Field*. It was ironic that when he died, on 10 February 1899, the fortunes of Wimbledon were at a low ebb and his obituaries ignored his outstanding role in lawn tennis.

Major Wingfield, 'inventor' of lawn tennis

On 25 February 1875 the All England Club had its 104th committee meeting. Mr C. F. Dalton, Mr R. Gray, Mr James D. Heath, Dr H. Jones, Mr J. H. Walsh, Dr Murray and Colonel Busk, who was in the chair, were present. Henry Jones proposed and Mr Dalton seconded a motion, duly approved, 'that one ground be set apart for lawn tennis and badminton during the ensuing season'. A sub-committee was appointed comprising Jones, Heath and Dalton and in due course an expenditure of £25 was approved. On 24 June, on the proposition of Jones, it was agreed 'that MCC laws of lawn tennis be adopted'.

The MCC code was issued on 29 May, not quite four weeks earlier, after that body had convened a meeting of interested parties in an effort to bring some sort of order to the varying rules under which the game was played. Between 21 March 1874 and 15 May 1875 *The Field* gave many columns to the controversy on the best way to play. The size of the court, its shape, the weight of the balls, all these were the subject of differing opinions. The authority assumed by the MCC was logical enough since it was the governing body of both tennis and rackets, from which the new game was derived. Under the MCC code the court had retained its hourglass shape favoured by Major Wingfield. Scoring, as in all the rival codes, was as in rackets.

During 1876 the All England Club devoted itself increasingly to the new game. Four more courts were brought into use and at the annual general meeting on 29 June it was agreed to have a committee member whose only interest was lawn tennis. George Nicol was appointed.

And so to the happenings of 1877. There was no doubt a good deal of preliminary lobbying but the events, when they did occur, came about with astonishing rapidity. The change of name to the All England Croquet and Lawn Tennis Club had formally taken place on 14 April. It was at a committee meeting as late as 2 June—it was, incidentally, the 125th committee meeting—that approval was given for a motion proposed by J. H. Walsh and seconded by Bonham Carter Evelegh. (The latter, then 34 years old, seemed to belong more to croquet than lawn tennis. He was croquet champion in 1877, again in 1879 and for the third time in 1899; but he was also destined to become referee of the Lawn Tennis Championships and of many other tournaments.)

The motion was 'that a public meeting be held on July 10th and following days to compete for the Championships in lawn tennis, and that a sub-committee composed of Messrs J. Marshall, H. Jones and C. G. Heathcote be appointed to draw up rules for its management'.

That, let it be noted, was less than six weeks away. In the event Monday, 9 July was the starting date, anyway. This three-man committee, of which Jones became the secretary, had much to do. Indeed, no lawn tennis committee at any time can have had occasion to take such momentous decisions as did this pioneer trio—or have such little time to bring them about! Heathcote was a barrister who later became stipendiary magistrate at Brighton and, incidentally, an authoritative historian of the early game. He was one of the competitors at the inaugural meeting. So, too, was Julian Marshall, an old Harrovian who had been rackets champion at school. Marshall, like Heathcote, was also a tennis player; more than that he was the authoritative historian of that venerable sport and his *Annals of Tennis* was in 1877 in the course of publication.

It would be foolish to extrapolate modern problems back one hundred years to the organisation of the first championships; for all its fashionable success, lawn tennis in 1877 was a long way short of being a high-powered sport, belonging largely to the vicarage lawn. In any case, the administrative problems of the first lawn tennis tournament had the precedent of the croquet meeting to follow. What was unique for the committee was its necessary concern with the very fundamentals of the sport whose championship it was promoting. How was the championship lawn tennis to be played? This, as it happened, was a matter to which Henry Jones had given assiduous attention. He had the sort of critical mind which saw rules and regulations not as minutiae but as the life-blood of what they served.

The first announcement about the new tournament was in *The Field* of 9 June.

The All England Croquet and Lawn Tennis Club, Wimbledon, propose to hold a lawn tennis meeting, open to all amateurs, on Monday, July 9th and following days. Entrance fee, £1 1*s* 0*d*. Two prizes will be given—one gold champion prize to the winner, one silver to the second player.

Henry Jones
Hon Sec of the Lawn Tennis sub-committee.

Henry Jones was appointed as referee of the meeting on 15 June. The following day *The Field* expanded its announcement, adding 'also a Silver Challenge Cup, value 25 guineas, will be given by the Proprietors of *The Field*, to be competed for annually on conditions to be laid down by the committee of the AEC and LT Club'.

The notice added further 'the matches will be played in accordance with the following laws. Each match will be the best of five sets, without advantage sets except in the final tie.'

This was no humdrum announcement. It was in fact revolutionary, the first public intimation of the momentous decision taken by the committee; they had decided on tennis and not rackets scoring.

Of all the controversy about the best way to play lawn tennis, whether a fault should be taken, whether a let was permissible, into which court the ball should be served and so on and so forth, the question of scoring seems to have risen not at all. Universally the rackets method was in operation. Gem used it at Leamington. Wingfield had it in his patented version. So did Hales with his Germains Lawn Tennis, which had been sold like that of Wingfield. The MCC code had included rackets scoring unquestioningly. In such only the server—'hand in'—could score, until he lost a rally and became 'hand out'. Each game comprised 15 points up.

The first advocacy of tennis scoring appears to have been in a letter to *The Field* on 24 June 1876. Such scoring, the writer declared, 'renders every ace important'. The writer, who was supported by Julian Marshall, was, it need hardly be stressed, the ubiquitous Henry Jones.

The hourglass shape of the court was abandoned. Under the MCC rules it was 24 ft *7·32 m* wide at the net, 30 ft *9·14 m* at the baseline. Jones and his colleagues decreed a rectangular court, 78 ft *23·77 m* in length, which was no change, but uniformly 27 ft *8·23 m* in width.

On 30 June, incidentally, the regulations that were being laid down for the championships were also being written into the rules of the club. It was then resolved that in the future no courts should be laid out for lawn tennis except to the dimensions of 26 yd *23·77 m* by 9 yd *8·23 m* or, in the case of the four-handed game, 'as at Prince's' 26 yd *23·77 m* by 12 yd *10·97 m*.

The height of the net was laid down as 5 ft *1·52 m* at the posts, 3 ft 3 in *0·99 m* at the centre. This differed from the MCC rules which had the same height at the posts but 4 ft *1·22 m* at the centre. The service line, 26 ft *7·92 m* from the net, was retained at that figure.

Some of the rules laid down by Messrs Jones, Marshall and Heathcote were amended in the course of the following years. They shortened the distance of the service line from 26 ft *7·92 m* to 22 ft *6·71 m* in 1878 and to its current 21 ft *6·40 m* in 1880. The height of the net became 4 ft 9 in *1·45 m* at the posts, 3 ft *0·91 m* at the centre, in 1878; in 1880 it came down to 4 ft *1·22 m* at the posts and in 1882 to 3 ft 6 in *1·07 m*. With those amendments the basic rules of 1877 have pertained to this day.

The vital reforms made by Henry Jones and his colleagues were twofold. The hourglass court made no sense and they abolished it. The even tenor of rackets scoring was replaced by the inherently more interesting tennis method with its spells of heightened drama. One may speculate what kind of course lawn tennis would have followed had it, like badminton, allowed the server to go on serving until the rally was lost and one suspects it would have been different. There will be many who think that of all the inspirations from Wimbledon's pioneer committee that of tennis scoring was the greatest.

The Times of Friday, 6 July printed its first notice:

> Next week at the All England Croquet Club Ground a Lawn Tennis Championship Meeting will be held. The ground is situated close to the Wimbledon Station on the South-Western Railway, and is sufficiently large for the erection of 30 "courts". On each day the competition will begin at 3.30, the first ties, of course, beginning on Monday. The Hon. Sec. of the meeting is Mr. J. H. Walsh, while Mr. H. Jones will officiate as referee. The entries are numerous.

There were, in fact, 22. The '30' courts was wrong. The All England Club at Worple Road had space for 12 courts. How many were marked out for the 1877 meeting is not known but 5 would have been ample.

It was not made clear in *The Times* that play was planned for the first four days only. The prospectus had made it clear that 'if the Matches are not finished on Thursday, play will be adjourned over Friday and Saturday (the Eton and Harrow Match being fixed for those days), and will be resumed on Monday July 16th'. To later generations this deferment of lawn tennis to another sport has tended to bring surprised comment. It did no more than recognise the social realities of the age and it was some years before Wimbledon acquired sufficient *haut ton* to ignore the cricket occasion which then ranked as one of the highlights of the social calendar.

The draw was made on Saturday, 7 July, timed for 3.30 pm and the name of Mr H. T. Gillson was the first to be drawn. It was followed by that of Spencer Gore, who, whatever his talents and skill, ranks as a lawn tennis immortal, not only as the first champion of Wimbledon but consequently as the first champion of lawn tennis anywhere. And let Mr Gillson be remembered also. His appearance in the lawn tennis world was fleeting but none the less as first in the draw he was the number one tournament player for all time.

The rackets depicted here, some old, some not so old, are housed in the museum at Wimbledon

Indeed, there is a touch of immortality about all the challengers who dared put their untried skill to the test, even the one who should have done but did not. That was Mr C. F. Buller who was absent when called upon to play on the Monday; Mr F. N. Langham, a Cambridge tennis blue of 1861 and 1862, was given a walkover. Mr Buller was an old Etonian and was known as a formidable rackets player, notable for a flamboyant style. Since the whole tenor of the first Wimbledon tended to be rackets players proving themselves better than the tennis men it seems a shame that Mr Buller was unable to show his prowess in the infant game.

It is worth making a note of the Wimbledon 'firsts' —Gillson, first in the draw, Buller, the first to concede a walkover. It is not on record who actually struck the first ball. The first man to play five sets, and this on the opening day, was Julian Marshall, one of the organising trio. He came from behind to beat a Captain Grimston after losing the first two sets. His committee colleague, Heathcote, may have been the first to win a love set, though it could have been B. N. Akroyd who started with two love sets against George Nicol, the All England Club committee member whose sole interest was lawn tennis.

As far as can now be ascertained that opening Monday, 9 July 1877, went off without a hitch. The whole of the first round was complete, ten matches in all plus the walkover. There were spectators, who paid one shilling each, but their number was unrecorded. It is safe to assume that Henry Jones, the referee, was as active as anyone. A contemporary later wrote of him: 'He was a familiar figure on the ground, clad in white flannel, a white helmet on his head, bearing a white umbrella with a green lining, and retailing his generally improving reflections to an admiring audience.'

The Times reported these happenings without, however, being very illuminating beyond the comment that this, the first lawn tennis championship, included 'some of the best players in England'. The second day, Tuesday, was, like the first, fine and warm, and one learns that 'the first ties having disposed of the weaker competitors play all round was of a much higher order and attracted more visitors'. The field was now eleven men and one need not be an expert mathematician to see that the draw was getting complicated.

Five matches were played in the second round on the Tuesday and Gore, now on top of the draw, lost a set to Montague Hankey, a Cambridge tennis blue of 1862. L. R. Erskine, who, two years later was to become All England doubles champion at Oxford with H. F. Lawford, beat J. Lambert 6–2 6–1 retired. Poor Lambert! One wonders what happened to him. At least he was another Wimbledon 'first' in retiring and he seems never to have appeared again.

Julian Marshall, who was 41 years old, survived another five setter, this against F. W. Oliver. It is curious that the only five-set matches played in 1877 were both won by the same man. Heathcote, at the bottom of the draw, was given a bye into the third round. There were now six survivors.

On Wednesday, the weather still good, it was observed that 'some good play was exhibited, especially between Mr Erskine and Mr W. Marshall'. William Marshall, not to be confused with Julian, was a Cambridge tennis blue of 1870, 1871 and 1872 and he beat Erskine 6–5 5–6 6–4 6–1. (Advantage sets were then decreed only for the final.) As for Julian Marshall he was beaten 6–3 6–3 6–5 by his committee colleague Heathcote but he 'had a heavy fall, or probably the result would have been closer as he is a brilliant player'. Gore survived in four sets against F. N. Langham, another of the old Cambridge tennis blues.

For Thursday, when the sun still shone, there were, then, three survivors, Gore, William Marshall and Heathcote and by modern practice a curious state for the semi-final round. This, though, was before the neat restriction of all byes to the first round. Clearly one player had to have a bye through to the final. The system was to work upwards from the bottom but since Heathcote had already had a bye it was given to Marshall. Starting at 4 pm Gore beat Heathcote 6–2 6–5 6–2. Just William Marshall stood between him and the Wimbledon championship. Gore, who was a surveyor by profession, was 27 years old and lived on the edge of Wimbledon Common, doubtless welcomed the break for the Eton and Harrow match as much as anyone. He was himself an old Harrovian and had played cricket for his school in 1867, 1868 and 1869. The final was arranged for Monday, 16 July at 4 pm.

The day of Wimbledon's first final was, alas, wet! It was agreed to play three days later, Thursday, 19 July, this time starting at 3.30. And, as it turned out, Thursday was also rather damp and dreary. Even so about 200 spectators turned up paying one shilling each, doubtless accounting for the tradition that the profit from the meeting was £10. Gore and Marshall, unwilling to disappoint them and, perhaps, anxious also to get the tournament finished, agreed to play between the showers. Accordingly the first lawn tennis final in history began an hour late, at 4.30. Gore won easily by 6–1 6–2 6–4 and Marshall was disappointing. With a lead in the third set he marred his own chances by double faulting twice. The first set lasted 15 minutes, the second 13 and the third 20, making 48 minutes in all on a dead and slippery court. None the less, Marshall was not so downcast by his loss that he did not go back on to court and play Heathcote for the second prize, winning 6–4 6–4.

Gore stood as Wimbledon champion. As such he is the doyen of champions for all time. Equally the motif of the game was composed for its hundred years dominance. The volleyer had beaten the baseliner. Gore intimidated Marshall, as he had his other opponents, by his work at the net. Volleying was then a tactic that had not penetrated the game to any real degree and, indeed, was considered by some to be unsporting. Even so, Gore's victory was hailed as a win for the rackets style over the tennis style.

Spencer Gore, then, took the champion's gold prize and had for a year the silver challenge cup valued at 25 guineas. He did not exalt in his triumph.

On the contrary he wrote, fifteen years later:

> That anyone who has really played well at cricket, tennis, or even rackets, will ever seriously give his attention to lawn

tennis, beyond showing himself to be a promising player, is extremely doubtful; for in all probability the monotony of the game as compared with others would choke him off before he had time to excel in it.

When the championship was finished Henry Jones was not idle. Yielding nothing to modern statisticians he gathered all his score cards to analyse the results of his rule making. He found that of the 601 games played during the tournament 376 were won by the server and 225 by the receiver, a preponderance of five to three or, when the more even sets were picked out, by nine to five. This, by modern standards, would indicate an astonishing lack of service dominance. There was, though, no overhead serving in 1877, the ball being delivered either underarm or at shoulder height over a high net into a service court 26 ft *7·92 m* in length. The outcome of the analysis was an alteration in the rules in 1878, the length of the service court being reduced to 22 ft *6·71 m* and the height of the net being lowered by 3 inches at all points.

The changes were made after consultation with the MCC. The new rules, issued with the joint authority of the MCC and the All England Club, sold 7000 copies in a few weeks and though rackets scoring was retained as an alternative the more attractive method pioneered at Wimbledon was widely taken up. Rackets scoring was abandoned for good in 1883.

The entry for 1878 was 34, excluding Gore. As champion he had special status. With his quality already proven he was not required to participate in the general hurly-burly and stood aside until the best of the challengers had proved himself. The challenge round system pertained at all the tournaments staged in Worple Road. Apart from Gore seven of the 1877 players entered again. Among the newcomers was Herbert Lawford, destined for future fame. The pattern was much the same as the year before, except that the starting time was put back to 4 pm. There was a round of matches every day from Monday, 8 July to Thursday, 11 July, by which time there were three survivors, Frank Hadow, Lawford and L. R. Erskine. Hadow had not then lost a set and nor was he to do so—to this day he holds a unique position in being the only man never to have lost a set at Wimbledon.

A note of modernity was introduced by the former Cambridge real tennis blue A. T. Myers. He served overhead. The seed he planted proved fruitful.

There were two Hadows in the field, Frank being accompanied by his elder brother, A. A. Hadow, who was put out by Myers in the second round. Both were Harrovians who had excelled at rackets and Frank had taken up coffee planting in Ceylon; after a three-year stint the new game had caught his attention when home on leave. He was 23 years old.

By the end of Thursday, the outstanding match, and the best of the entire meeting, was Erskine's fourth round win over C. G. Hamilton by 6-4 3-6 6-1 3-6 6-5 after trailing 3-5 in the fifth set and being match point down. Erskine later beat Lawford to reach the final, Hadow getting the bye at this stage. In the final Hadow beat Erskine and went on to take the title from Gore in the challenge round. Years afterwards Hadow told his own story:

I felt very fit and well to the break off for the Eton and Harrow match, when I somehow got a touch of the sun and was otherwise ill, with the result that the Saturday, Sunday and Monday I had to keep quiet with ice on my head. On the Tuesday I had to go down to play the final against Erskine, but was fairly fit though feeling pretty cheap, and was glad when it was over and able to get to bed again with a horrible headache, where I remained all the next day. On the following day I had to play Spencer Gore, the previous year's champion. I confess I was not feeling even as well as when playing Erskine, taking a frantic headache with me in the train to Wimbledon, which got worse and worse.

It was not easy to drive down the side lines, like a rackets stroke down the side wall, with the net sagging to the centre from the posts and fastened below the top of each post, instead of being level. I was told the 'lob' had not been introduced before. It was only natural enough though, with a tall, long-legged and long-armed man sprawling over the net, ready to reach over at the ball before it had even reached the net. My attempts to pass Gore, I can remember, with a low hard stroke, when he was at the net, usually failed.

That was all Wimbledon and the lawn tennis world saw of Frank Hadow for 49 years; he was persuaded to attend the jubilee celebration in 1926.

The final score by which Hadow beat Gore, who had a bad wrist, was 7-5 6-1 9-7, these being the first advantage sets played at Wimbledon. Another novelty was a dispute during the course of the challenge round whether it was proper for Gore to reach over the net to make his volleys. There was a halt and discussion before it was ruled legal for him to do so.

The day was very hot and, it seems, there was talk of adjourning the third set at five all for a rest; as it happened a rest interval never became part of the game in the Championships. Henry Jones wrote his decision into the rules as soon as possible and by 1879 it was illegal either to volley the ball before it had passed over the net or, indeed, to touch the net.

The enthralling contest between Erskine and Hamilton was seen by 700 spectators and 'several hundred' watched Hadow take the title from Gore. This was a prosperous meeting. As for serving dominance it was found that of 431 games between evenly matched players 229 were won by the server, 202 by the receiver, and this was held to be satisfactory. Two pioneer champions had made their mark on a scene they did not grace again. Spencer Gore, whose brother became famous as the first Bishop of Birmingham in the early years of this century, died in 1906. Hadow survived until 1946 when he died at the age of 91.

By 1879 lawn tennis had enlarged its world. The Scottish Championships, including a men's doubles, were begun in 1878. In 1879 a significant men's doubles championship was inaugurated at Oxford and the Irish Championships started in Dublin. The last indicated how the game was to go. There were not only men's singles and men's doubles but women's singles and mixed doubles as well. The All England Club, however, still stopped short of this wider horizon. The men's singles entry was 45, of whom 36 were newcomers. They included John Thorneycroft Hartley, a 33-year-old clergyman with a living at Durneston in the North Riding of Yorkshire. He was a tennis player rather than a rackets man and had played for Oxford in 1870. He was—need it be said?—an old Harrovian.

Hartley was a safe player who got the ball back without taking risks and was an unspectacular winner, hardest pressed by Erskine in the second round, winning only by 6–5 in the fifth set. He was described as being more accurate than the hard hitters but a harder hitter than accurate rivals. He made the passing shot a telling stroke. But he had not bargained on being involved in the later stages of the tournament and was still alive as a semi-finalist when he had to retreat home on Saturday to fulfil his Sunday duties as parish priest.

On the Monday morning Hartley had to be up early to drive himself ten miles to Thirsk and entrain for London. He arrived at King's Cross about two o'clock and dashed across town to Wimbledon where he arrived in time for his match against C. F. Parr. Exhausted and hungry he lost the first set when, fortunately for him, it began to rain. Hartley was able to refresh himself with tea and he went back on court to win 2–6 6–0 6–1 6–1.

That put Hartley into the All Comers' Final which, since Hadow was not defending, was the match for the title. It seems that Hadow's absence had brought adverse comment about his reluctance to defend. His brother A. A. Hadow was constrained to write to *The Times* explaining that Frank could not play because he was in Sri Lanka, or Ceylon as it then was.

The finalist against Hartley was the pseudonymous 'St. Leger', who had become the first champion of Ireland not long before. 'He was', wrote Hartley, 'a cheery, wild Irishman, Irish champion and a very pretty player. I think he volleyed more than any of us that year; but there was some weakness I suppose in his play, as being fit and well after a night's rest, I won three sets straight off.' The score in fact was 6–2 6–4 6–2.

'St. Leger' provides a macabre footnote to the history of lawn tennis. He was Vere Thomas St. Leger Goold, younger son of an Irish baronet. In August 1907 he was with his French-born wife, formerly Mlle Violet Girodin, in Monte Carlo. Things evidently went ill. On the 6th of that month they appeared at Nice railway station asking for two trunks to be sent to England. The trunks aroused immediate suspicion and were opened to reveal a dismembered body. It was of a Danish widow, Emma Levin. Both were charged with murder and at their trial Goold wanted to take all the blame. But Mrs Goold was sentenced to death and the unfortunate Goold to life imprisonment. The death sentence was not in fact carried out and Mrs Goold died in Montpelier prison in 1914. Goold died on Devil's Island in September 1909 when he was 55 years old. He had been 25 when he blossomed at Wimbledon.

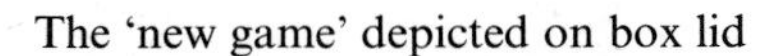
The 'new game' depicted on box lid

The final of 1879 was watched by 1100 spectators. The profits for the two earlier years have not survived in the records but for this year they have. The All England Club made £116 0*s* 4*d*, a not unimportant item in the finances where the over-all balance for the year was 1*s* 10*d*.

In 1879 two interesting names appeared in the draw for the first time. There was E. Renshaw and also W. Renshaw. Neither played, the former giving a walk-over to Sir Victor Brooke and the latter to G. E. Tabor.

In 1880 they did appear and both lost to an Ealing player, O. E. Woodhouse. Wimbledon did not appreciate it then but with their presence neither the meeting nor lawn tennis round the world was to be the same again.

By this time Wimbledon was no longer blazing the trail. The Northern Championships had been established and there was a championship meeting at Prince's Club immediately preceding the event at the All England Club, won by Lawford in an exciting five-set final against E. Lubbock. Changes were made in the rules at the start of the season. The height of the net at the posts was lowered to 4 ft *1·22 m* and the length of the service court reduced to 21 ft *6·40 m*. The entry for Wimbledon was 60. It was the biggest to date. It was not surpassed until 1904. For the first four days the charge for admittance was the original sum of 1*s*. Then it was raised to 2*s* 6*d* which caused a bit of a row, for it was felt that insufficient notice had been given. With so big an entry, which meant spreading the first round out over two days, all twelve courts had to be made ready. It began on Monday, 5 July and ended on Thursday, 15 July but, for all the bustling prosperity, there was again no question of not giving preference to the Eton and Harrow cricket on the Friday and Saturday.

The All Comers' event was won by Lawford without the loss of a set. It was evident that the game was growing up but the expertise involved still apparently belonged to the vicarage lawn. The inordinate length of some of the rallies in the matches of 1880 was a subject of comment and it was held that in an early match between Lawford and Lubbock, who had met in the Prince's final, one rally went on for a record 81 strokes.

Like many other notable champions the Renshaws failed at their Wimbledon debut. They were not unknown for William Renshaw had, in October 1879, won a tournament, partly indoors and partly outside on an asphalt court, in their native Cheltenham, beating Goold in the course of it. And William had taken the Irish Championship with his net play not long before Wimbledon started. In the Championships William fell to Woodhouse in the third round by three sets to one on a damp court on which he could not keep his foothold. In the next round Ernest suffered the same fate. Yet in the doubles tournament at Oxford the twins had carried all before them.

Lawford, notable for his top-spun forehand, triumphed hugely in the All Comers', where he beat Woodhouse in the final, but did not do well in the challenge round against Hartley. It was evidently a war of attrition, the rallies long enough for their length to be counted. One rally of 33 strokes and four exceeding 25 were noted. The technique of the vicarage lawn, so ably represented by Hartley, had its four-set triumph and 1300 spectators watched it. The profit for the All England Club that year was £306 14*s*.

2
THE RENSHAWS (1881-1889)

The year 1881 was hardly less significant for lawn tennis than 1877. In the United States there was the formation of the US Lawn Tennis Association and the institution of the first US Championships at Newport, Rhode Island. At Wimbledon the men's singles was won, from an entry of 48, by a well-to-do 20 year old, William Renshaw from Cheltenham, who with his twin, Ernest, was destined to transform a pastime into a sport. The pacemakers had arrived. They did not invent the overhead service or the smash but they forged these weapons into a standard of precision and excellence earlier players had not dreamed about.

William was the elder twin by 15 minutes and they were posthumous sons of a rich man. A friendly Chancery action had to be arranged to settle the question of their benefiting equally under his will. Both went as day boys to Cheltenham College where they were good cricketers. They took early to lawn tennis, though it is not known precisely how early. They were just 13 years old when Wingfield took out his patent. Cheltenham was one of the first towns to have a covered court.

Indistinguishable one from the other the Renshaws captivated not only by their high playing skill but by their warm personalities. William was clearly the more dominating player because of a greater pace of shot, more boldness of execution and cooler judgement. Ernest had quicker footwork and more delicacy of stroke. William took the ball at the top of the bound, then a striking innovation. 'The Renshaw smash' was for years a descriptive part of the vocabulary of the game.

Ernest got no further in 1881 than the third round where he was beaten by R. T. Richardson, against whom William obtained vicarious revenge in the final of the All Comers'. It was not the only old score paid off by William since in the fourth round, the equivalent of the quarter-final, he put out Woodhouse, conqueror of both himself and his brother the year before. But William's major contest was the semi-final against H. F. Lawford. The Renshaw–Lawford rivalry became the major theme of the decade.

Indeed, 'the Renshaw smash' was rivalled only by the 'Lawford forehand'. This was top spun and taken near the top of the bound. Lawford, who was a Londoner, was a long way from being young and, in 1881 when he had the first of his big Wimbledon clashes against either Renshaw, he was 30 years old. He was hailed as the first of the pace-making baseliners.

In their clash in 1881 William Renshaw beat Lawford 1–6 6–3 6–2 5–6 6–3. His subsequent climb to championship status was unchecked. In the challenge round he would doubtless have beaten the Rev John Hartley easily in any case, but as it was the unfortunate vicar had no chance at all. He was suffering from an attack of 'English cholera' and was beaten 6–0 6–1 6–1 in 37 minutes, the shortest time on record for the men's singles title match. William, under pressure or not, was notable as a man who bustled between the rallies as well as in them.

For the next five years William's high skill contributed to a singular lack of match practice at Wimbledon! He won the next five challenge rounds, the first two in five sets against his brother, and the next three, none of which went beyond four sets, against Lawford. An outstanding business of the All Comers' event was to settle whether Ernest Renshaw or Lawford should challenge the holder and they clashed in three out of the five years.

In 1882, the year the net was brought down to the height it has since maintained, 3 ft 6 in *1·07 m* at the posts, 3 ft *0·91 m* in the middle, Ernest beat Lawford in the fourth round in five sets. In 1883, stressing the gamble of every event when no seeding of any kind took place, they were drawn in the opening round. The match that ensued was perhaps as odd as any in the top-class game, played in a wind blowing straight down the court. The system of changing ends after every odd game had not then come into force. It was possible to change ends at the end of every game or at the end of a set. In this case ends were changed at the end of each set. And the habit still prevailed of playing short sets until the final of the event.

It is on record that Renshaw began playing against the wind, though whether that fact helps to make sense of the extraordinary convolutions of the score is hard to say. Be that as it may, Renshaw led 5–1 in the first set only to lose it 5–6 when Lawford took five games in a row. Renshaw, now playing down wind, took the second set 6–1 and, after changing ends, led

3–0 in the third. Lawford responded by taking six games in succession, Renshaw accordingly losing the set 3–6 and trailing one set to two. Lawford did not stop there. He made it a run of eight games for a lead of 2–0 in the fourth set. None the less, Renshaw's riposte was six games running for the set 6–2 and level pegging at two sets all. In the final set, Lawford, playing downwind, as he had at the start of the match, won five successive games to be 5–0. Faced with this appalling deficit, Ernest Renshaw, 'in despair' as an observer put it, delivered an underarm twisting service. With the spin and the wind the ball bounced wide enough to draw Lawford right out of court. Instead of taking it on the backhand he ran round hoping to make a forehand kill. The tactic failed and Lawford was never the same player for the rest of the match. Ernest Renshaw finished with six games in a row to win by 5–6 6–1 3–6 6–1 6–5.

Lawford was a noted apostle of baseline play. Ernest Renshaw wrote 'taking the ball off the ground will be quite the exception; and in its place there will be far finer and more exciting rallies on the volley than have ever been up to the present'. Lawford responded, 'Perfect back play will beat perfect volleying'.

Yet Lawford was more of a volleyer than his theory seemed to indicate. A keen statistician was at work on that incredible first round match and counted 124 volleys. Renshaw made 97 but the other 27 were played by Lawford. It seems a shame that the same statistician does not appear to have handed down the number of match points Lawford may have had in the course of those last six games.

Ernest, having got over this hurdle, was checked on his way to the challenge round. A little curiously, he lost an opening set to love against Donald Stewart, a good volleyer, in the All Comers' Final. William, beating his brother in five sets, won for the third year running and the original *Field* championship cup outright.

The fame of the Renshaws spread abroad. There was a feeling in the United States that it should be put to some sort of test. To that end the Clark brothers, C. M. and J. S. challenged the Renshaws to a doubles match. The Clarks had previously obtained the consent of the American champions, James Dwight and Richard Sears, against whom they were fairly evenly

Upper, Ernest Renshaw immortalised in porcelain

Lower, William v Ernest Renshaw in 1883

matched, to act as a representative pair. They had two matches at the All England Club in 1883. On 18 July the Renshaws won 6–4 8–6 3–6 6–1 and five days later they won again by 6–3 6–2 6–3. The difference was that while the Clarks played one up at the net and one back, the Renshaws were both up at the net.

Great Britain v America 1883—the Renshaw twins v the Clark brothers on the Centre Court at Worple Road

The year 1884 was something of a milestone. A men's doubles was added to the programme. This was for the trophies that had been played for in Oxford since 1879. The Oxford University Club, finding its event declining from lack of support, offered the cups to Wimbledon. Whether the Oxford event should be regarded as the same as that at Wimbledon is a moot point. What was clearly an innovation was the start of a women's singles, though even this event was originally planned by the London Athletic Club who yielded it to the All England. But neither the doubles nor the women's singles was started in 1884 until the men's singles was completed.

It was a turning-point in the men's singles as well. There was an entry from overseas for the first time. The challengers were the Americans, Sears and Dwight. They were currently US doubles champions and Sears had been US singles champion for the last three years, with Dwight as the runner-up in 1883.

Sears had to withdraw in the first round and Dwight was narrowly beaten (6–1 2–6 6–3 3–6 7–5—this being the first year of advantage sets in every round) by Herbert Chipp in the second. Chipp was an ambidextrous player and afterwards the first secretary of the British Lawn Tennis Association. In the doubles Sears and Dwight lost in the semi-final to the Renshaws. They were roundly beaten 6–0 6–1 6–2. All in all the first American assault on Wimbledon was not strikingly successful.

As he had won the cup outright William Renshaw intended to retire against his brother Ernest in what would have been the third successive challenge round between them. It did not work out like that. Instead, 1884 was the first of three successive challenge rounds in which William checked the ambitions of Lawford. Ernest was unexpectedly beaten in the semi-final by C. W. Grinstead, a talented player making his second and last appearance in the championships and who had lost to him the year before.

Twelve months later Ernest was in the All Comers' Final against Lawford who won from a deficit of two sets to one. Lawford, having beaten one Renshaw in five sets, was in turn beaten in four by the other. This was the closest of the three William Renshaw-

Lawford challenge rounds. William was the victor 7–5 6–2 4–6 7–5 pulling back the fourth set after trailing 0–4, 15–40. He did so by changing his normal role as volleyer. He stayed at the back and Lawford, apparently outgeneralled, lost the match from up at the net.

This was the 'Renshaw boom' at its peak. There were 3500 spectators for the 1885 challenge round. The previous year the South Western Railway had found it worth while to run special trains from Waterloo that stopped just outside the ground. But booming as Wimbledon was with spectator interest, the very expertise of the Renshaws and Lawford had a deterrent effect on competitors. The men's singles entry, which was 60 in 1880, fell in successive years to 48, 28, 23, 28, 23, 23 until, in 1887, it was as low as 16. The surplus for the championship in 1885 was £800.

The 1885 meeting saw a change in the method of the draw. Instead of the byes being distributed through all the rounds until the final, the Bagnall Wild system was adopted with all byes restricted to the opening round, the number being easily calculated by subtracting the number in the draw from the next power of two.

Before William Renshaw had his sixth victory in 1886, with his third challenge round success against the persistent Lawford, his brother Ernest had got no further than the last eight. E. W. Lewis, who beat him after losing the first two sets, was a noted volleyer. He won another five setter in the semi-final against H. W. W. Wilberforce and, meeting Lawford in the final, also went the full distance there.

In 1886 Henry Jones was no longer referee. After nine years, during which time the meeting had grown from garden-party rapture to serious, if still very amateur, sporting business, the worthy doctor gave up. He more than anyone was responsible for the creation of a British institution. He was succeeded as referee by Julian Marshall.

Lawford met with the reward for his diligent efforts at last in 1887, when 36 years old. His chance came when William Renshaw, laid low with tennis elbow, did not defend. It was Lawford's tenth successive challenge and after six years when he had lost only to a Renshaw.

He can hardly be said to have won from a great field. He was but one of sixteen challengers in Queen Victoria's Jubilee year. His victory apparently surprised himself for, in the Irish Championship not long before, Ernest Renshaw had beaten him readily. They met in the All Comers' Final which, for the first time since 1877 was the title match in the absence of the holder. Ernest Renshaw led two sets to one and let the match slip away.

The Renshaw era was not yet finished. It was, though, drawing to an end. Some of the buoyancy was, temporarily, going from the All England Club and the championship meeting. For one thing the club no longer functioned as the legislative authority in the game. It had done so, first in consultation with the MCC and, later, in consultation with a conference of clubs. An attempt had been made to form a national lawn tennis association in 1883 but that had come to naught. In 1888 the Lawn Tennis Association came into being with an inaugural meeting on 26 January at the Freemasons' Tavern in Great Queen Street. William Renshaw was made the first president.

Ernest Renshaw

His attempt that year to win back the championship that he had dominated for so long was a failure. After a close second round match in which he beat H. Grove 5–7 14–12 6–3 6–2 he went out in the third round to an Irishman, Willoughby Hamilton. Known as 'The Ghost', Hamilton was famous for a running forehand, a stroke described for many years as the 'Irish drive'. The frail-looking Hamilton beat William 5–7 7–5 6–4 6–2 and it was left to Ernest to salvage family honour. He did so, first by beating Hamilton 7–5 7–5 5–7 6–3 in the semi-final, then by paying off an old score against Lewis by 7–9 6–1 8–6 6–4 in the final before beating Lawford 6–3 7–5 6–0 in the challenge round.

With Ernest in possession of the singles the former situation of the twins was reversed for 1889. Whilst Ernest stood out William had to undergo the hurly-burly of the All Comers'. He played, and beat, a familiar rival in the semi-final, Lawford, now aged 38 and competing in his twelfth successive Wimbledon in which he had yielded in all but the first three only to a Renshaw. William's final was against the 29 year old H. S. Barlow and a memorable affair.

Barlow, taking the first two sets 6–3 7–5, was within two points of winning the match in three sets but Renshaw won the third 8–6. In the fourth set Barlow led 5–2. He came six times in all within a point of victory and never more dramatically than in the fourteenth game. Renshaw, 6–7 30–40, followed his serve to the net only to have the racket slip from his hand. Barlow had the entire court open for any sort of winner he cared to make. Instead of which he merely dollied back the ball to give Renshaw time to retrieve his racket. Quixotic? Many would just call it sporting. Not that it was the end of the excitement. Renshaw won the fourth set 10–8 only for Barlow to go to 5–0 in the fifth. Renshaw drew level. Barlow still led at 6–5 but Renshaw broke his service in the thirteenth game and took the set 8–6 for the match. Accordingly William, who went on to win the challenge round with a four-set victory over his younger (by fifteen minutes) brother, took his seventh singles championship after being six times within a stroke of defeat. Such knife-edge success was unparalleled until Henri Cochet did the same in 1927.

William Renshaw created one record that was never equalled. He was singles champion seven times, uniquely among men. One cannot, of course, compare it with performances made after the abolition of the challenge round but, none the less, it has reverberated down the years as an incomparable effort that is hardly likely to be surpassed.

William and Ernest Renshaw were equally commanding in the doubles. They put their names on the trophies by winning the event at Oxford in 1880 and 1881. They played through to win the Wimbledon doubles in 1884 and 1885. The following year it became a challenge-round event like the singles and the Renshaws continued to reign supreme. William was out of action in 1887 with his tennis elbow and only then did other names, H. W. W. Wilberforce and P. B. Lyon, appear on the honours roll. The Renshaws came back from the loss of the first two sets in the challenge round when they recovered the title in 1888. They kept their title in 1889, after which they retired. In 1889 they beat Lewis and George Hillyard in the challenge round and it was notable because in two earlier clashes that season they had lost. And what was remarkable about it was that the first of those losses, in Dublin, was the first suffered by the Renshaws as a pair for seven years!

The light with which the Renshaws illuminated lawn tennis faded. The Irish were to take over Wimbledon. But it was not only Wimbledon that thrived under creative Renshaw brilliance but the game at large. They founded the modern game. When they began playing lawn tennis as youngsters in Cheltenham it was virtually pat ball. A decade of dominance, displayed in its most spectacular form at Wimbledon, turned the adjunct to the vicarage lawn into a sport requiring its own high skills that owed nothing to real tennis or to rackets but only to itself. The Americans came to Wimbledon and looked with awe at what the Renshaws were doing and took back what they had learned.

For all that it was not easy going at Wimbledon in the 1890s.

The William Renshaw, All Comers' Challenge Cup

3 THE IRISH INVASION (1890-1896)

Between 1890 and 1896 four men won the singles, Willoughby Hamilton, Wilfred Baddeley, Joshua Pim and Harold Mahony; all except Baddeley were Irish. The peak of Irish domination was 1890 when, with Hamilton the men's singles winner, Pim and F. O. Stoker doubles champions and the obscure Miss L. Rice the best of the women, all champions were from Ireland. But though the Irish can charm the birds from trees they somehow failed to make their magic work at Wimbledon. The 1890s was a period of slump, so much so that in 1895 the meeting recorded its first and only loss, one of £33—and that in a year when socially the event had the boost of its first visit from Royalty, the Crown Princess Stephanie of Austria.

The fourteenth meeting of 1890 marked the start of the 13-year reign as referee of Bonham Carter Evelegh, who took over from Julian Marshall. He was the seconder of the 1877 motion to stage a lawn tennis championship at the All England Club. Despite his zest for lawn tennis he retained his interest in croquet and became champion for the third time in 1899. There was, in 1890, a change of rule about changing ends. Instead of switching at the end of the set or, as was sometimes the case, if the umpire so ruled, at the end of every game, the present rule, a change after every odd game, was brought into operation.

Hamilton's singles championship in 1890 was gained from a field of 30 and he was taken to five sets in his last two matches. In the All Comers' Final against Barlow he was involved in some of those extraordinary see-saws of fortune in which Barlow seemed to specialise. The year before William Renshaw had barely survived the same round and this time Hamilton, leading 2–6 6–4 6–4 4–0, lost six games running and trailed 2–4 in the fifth set before winning it 7–5 with the last two games to love. The challenge round brought the eclipse of the now 29 year old William Renshaw, Hamilton trailing one set to two but then winning 6–1 6–1. This was the end of the glories of the Renshaws; they did not defend their doubles crown.

The entry fell to a meagre 22 in 1891 when Hamilton was sick and did not defend his title. The reign of the Baddeley twins began, a reign hotly disputed and often checked by Pim. Wilfred Baddeley in 1891 was young, light and mobile, a player of vast retrieving powers and concentration. Pim, a doctor, was full of Irish *joie de vivre*, brilliant but less certain. Baddeley is said to have beaten Ernest Renshaw that year in half an hour. Since to play 20 games in 30 minutes is hardly possible the time keeping could have been at fault but it is certain that in the semi-final Baddeley beat his man 6–0 6–1 6–1.

Pim played with the handicap of an injured hand, suffered by falling out of a car in Dublin! He got to the final, won the second set but could not stop the indefatigable Baddeley winning the fourth to love. This was the first of Wilfred Baddeley's three singles championships.

What was remarkable about his victory was the age at which he achieved it. Wilfred Baddeley was aged 19 years 5 months 23 days when he won on 4 July 1891. Among men he stands as the youngest winner of a major singles championship on grass. The year before the winner of the US Championship had set a record for precocity when Oliver Campbell took the singles in Philadelphia. He was 19 years 6 months 9 days old.

Campbell came to Wimbledon in 1892 but, with three other Americans, did not survive the second round. Arthur Gore beat him, remarkably by 6–1 8–6 8–6 after saving the third set from 0–5. Baddeley kept his title and again the key contest was against Pim, this time in the challenge round. Pim won the All Comers' Final against Lewis from two match points. The Baddeley twins, though, did not retain the doubles which twelve months before they had gained from a field of only five pairs, losing to Lewis and Barlow.

Wilfred and Herbert Baddeley were identical twins, impossible to distinguish one from the other. Barlow was reputed to have been once greatly incommoded by this in a doubles when, having found his opponent in the left-hand court to be frail overhead, began lobbing his way to success. It was cut short when, unbeknown to him, the twins switched sides at the end of the set.

Wilfred acquired awesome fame as a player able to go right through the season without ever missing a sitter. He certainly earned the respect of his rivals. For instance, the Wimbledon champion of 1896, Mahony, was moved to write (in 1903) that he 'might fairly be described as the most successful player that ever was . . . his successes were gained against stronger players than other champions had had to meet. His method and generalship were unrivalled.'

Having withstood the challenge of the Irish, Wilfred Baddeley had to give way in 1893. The All Comers' Final was entirely Irish, Pim beating Mahony and then bringing down Wilfred Baddeley in four sets in the challenge round. In the doubles Pim and Stoker won back that title for Ireland also. There was the last echo of the Renshaws. William conceded a walk-over to Ernest in the first round who failed over five sets to Mahony in the second.

The Renshaw dominance extended for the ten years from 1881 to 1890, during which time no title match for the singles was played without the presence of either William or Ernest. The later dominance of the Dohertys had a similar ten-year spell, from 1897 to 1906 when no singles title match was staged without either Laurie or Reggie. There was, as it happened, no gap between their presence at Wimbledon. The year 1893 saw the last of the Renshaws, 1894 brought the first of the Dohertys. In that year Reggie, then aged 19, appeared in the first round, losing to C. H. L. Cazalet. Wimbledon, however, was still short of the Dohertys' reverberating presence. The worthy Dr Pim won for the second time.

Wilfred Baddeley came through to the challenge round, making for the fourth meeting in four years against Pim. In the All Comers' Final, Baddeley had a hollow victory over Lewis, missing only a complete whitewash when Lewis won the fourth game in the second set. In this way Wilfred avenged the defeat his twin Herbert suffered in the round before at the hands of Lewis. In this Lewis won the fifth set from 0–5 with seven games in a row. Pim kept his title with a three-set win, thus making the honours level at two victories apiece so far as their Wimbledon rivalry was concerned.

Pim did not defend in 1895 when the entry was sparse, just eighteen. Wilfred Baddeley won his third singles title after remarkably little play but none the less after being within a stroke of losing it. With the benefit of three retirements he played just two matches. The first was against Barlow, whom he beat in three sets. The second was the title match against W. V. Eaves and proved a long way short of a walkover. Eaves was a noted volleyer and Australian born. Reared in England, he did as much as anyone to foster the growth of the game in its early Australian days before he returned to Britain where he practised as a doctor. Eaves got within one point of becoming Wimbledon champion. He led the industrious Baddeley 6–4 6–2 6–5, 40–30 when he put a lob just over the baseline. The reprieved Baddeley won the match 4–6 2–6 8–6 6–2 6–3. Baddeley's first walkover was against Arthur Wentworth Gore. His second, in the semi-final, was against his own brother, Herbert. The undefended challenge round gave him his third.

Herbert Baddeley had the experience of beating two Dohertys before retiring to his more dominant

The Baddeley twins v the Doherty brothers

brother. One was Reggie. The other, in the round before, was not Laurie but the elder brother of the family, W. V., who had beaten H. A. Nisbet before yielding to Herbert. Unlike his more famous brothers, W. V. Doherty went, not to Cambridge but to Oxford. As a university blue he was reckoned equally as brilliant but he was ordained an Anglican priest and did not pursue the game.

The entry for the men's singles in 1896 was 31, the highest since 1881. It was a signal of the upsurge of Wimbledon's fortune, though it is curious to learn, at this distance, that one way of encouraging entry was to allow members of the All England Club admission to the draw without entrance fee. Clubs affiliated to the Lawn Tennis Association were also allowed to nominate one player without cost. A further boost came with the inauguration of the All England Plate, open to players defeated in the first or second round of the singles. The first winner of this, incidentally, was Arthur Wentworth Gore and the runner-up Laurie Doherty, both destined to find greater fame.

Laurie lost to Cazalet, the man who had beaten his brother two years before. As for Reggie he went down to Mahony. William Larned, then three times a finalist in his own US All Comers' singles but five years away from the first of his seven American championships, was a quarter-final loser to Herbert Baddeley. Mahony won the title that year, dispossessing a not very fit Wilfred Baddeley in a five-set challenge round in which he trailed one set to two. Mahony, who was then 29, was the last of the Irish winners. He had a lively Celtic temperament, poor ground strokes but was a splendid opportunist volleyer. Sadly, he was found dead, when only 38, having fallen off his bicycle at the foot of an Irish mountain in 1905.

The first Doherty final for a title was played in 1896, this the men's doubles challenge round when Reggie partnering Nisbet, unsuccessfully challenged the holders, the Baddeley twins. The Doherty brothers did not play together and Laurie was with R. B. Scott losing to the Allen twins in the semi-final. These Allen twins, much esteemed as humorists and with a reputation as Tweedledum and Tweedledee among spectators, played a fine All Comers' Final against Reggie Doherty and Nisbet for the match was described as the finest doubles ever seen. The Baddeley twins, in winning the doubles, did so for the fourth and last time.

The doubles championships was won four times by the Baddeley twins between 1891 and 1896. Their initial success was from a meagre entry of only five pairs but was notable for their first round (and semi-final!) against Mahony and G. R. Mewburn. This was a long affair, the Baddeleys winning 13–11 4–6 8–6 7–5, a total of 60 games for the four sets. There was a longer match in 1892 in the All Comers' Final where Lewis and Barlow beat Pim and Mahony 8–10 6–3 5–7 11–9 6–1: 66 games in all.

It is curious how twin brothers dominated the early years of Wimbledon. The Renshaws did so from 1881 to 1889, the Baddeleys from 1891 to 1896. Yet if the reign of twins were finished that of brothers was not. With the Doherty brothers, Reginald Frank (Reggie) and Hugh Lawrence (Laurie) Wimbledon entered its most striking period of growth and prosperity.

4 THE DOHERTYS (1897–1906)

When Hugh Lawrence Doherty died on 11 August 1919 *The Times* recorded his passing with more distinction than normally accorded a sportsman. He was given the tribute of a leader. It read:

> Doherty was a great lawn tennis player, many say the greatest that has been; he and his brother maintained for us that cherished supremacy which we have recently lost; but from the national point of view his technical capacity was but one of his recommendations, and not the greatest. With him there was no possibility of 'unpleasant incidents'; he was too true a sportsman to commit an ungenerous act deliberately, too cool to seize in the excitement of the moment an advantage he might subsequently regret. Defeat at his hands lost half its sting, for he was courtesy itself; and if defeat was his own portion he accepted it with the same equanimity which had made it so difficult to bring about. He played an English game in the spirit in which Englishmen think games should be played. He was a typical Englishman, and it is a source of legitimate pride to his countrymen that we can call him so.

His brother, Reginald Frank Doherty, who was two years older, died nine years earlier. Neither was physically robust and, indeed, Reggie once said that he had never had a day in his life when he felt really well. Between them they arrested the decline of Wimbledon, turned a flagging event into one of bursting prosperity, so much so that in due course a new home for the Championships had to be found. At that new home, in Church Road, the south-east entrance is through 'The Doherty Gates'.

The Dohertys were born in Wimbledon itself and went to Westminster School, where Reggie, tall and thin, was a soccer player and Laurie, shorter and more sturdy, an athlete. Family influence had them playing lawn tennis from an early age, Reggie winning a boys' singles in North Wales when he was 14 and Laurie taking a junior singles in Scarborough when 15. Both went to Trinity Hall, Cambridge, where Reggie was an outstanding blue in 1895 and 1896 and Laurie in 1896 to 1898. Oddly they did not play together in the doubles when both were in the side against Oxford in 1896. It was then they acquired their description as 'Big Do' (Reggie) and 'Little Do' (Laurie).

Their early vicissitudes at Wimbledon were recorded in the last chapter. The first triumphant Doherty year was 1897, when for the first time the Championships started in June instead of July. Reggie dominated a field of 31 with *élan*. Whilst his brother failed to match the error-free game of Wilfred Baddeley in the quarter-final, Reggie, who was lucky to get a walk-over from Frank Riseley at that stage, avenged this loss with an easy semi-final victory. He went on to beat Eaves in the final, when Eaves had to retire exhausted in the third set, before putting out Mahony in the challenge round. In so doing he recouped his loss of the year before. Reggie accordingly won without the loss of a set, the first to do so, playing through, since Hadow in 1878. It was another four decades before another man was so dominating.

In doubles the brothers began a majestic reign of ten years when, except on two occasions, their invincibility was not assailed. They dispossessed the Baddeleys in the challenge round and that, so far as Reggie was concerned, meant that in 1898, 1899, 1900 and 1901, the only matches he subsequently had to play in the Championships were the challenge rounds.

There were three Americans competing in 1898, the most prominent being Clarence Hobart. In singles he became the first American and, indeed, the first overseas player to reach the semi-final—the first into the last eight was another American J. F. Talmage in 1894. Laurie Doherty beat Hobart in three sets and went on to win the final against Mahony. The Irishman was at match point at 5–4 in the fifth set which Laurie eventually won 14–12 when he took the last two games to love. The fraternal challenge round brought victory to Reggie in five sets but it was a final without 'bite' and it seems that there were those who wished that the players could have been less 'sporting'. Reggie had a chance to win in four sets; his eventual triumph was by 6–1 in the fifth. In the doubles title match the Dohertys were challenged, quite unsuccessfully, by Hobart in partnership with the British H. A. Nisbet. For the first time a player from overseas had got within one match of a Wimbledon championship.

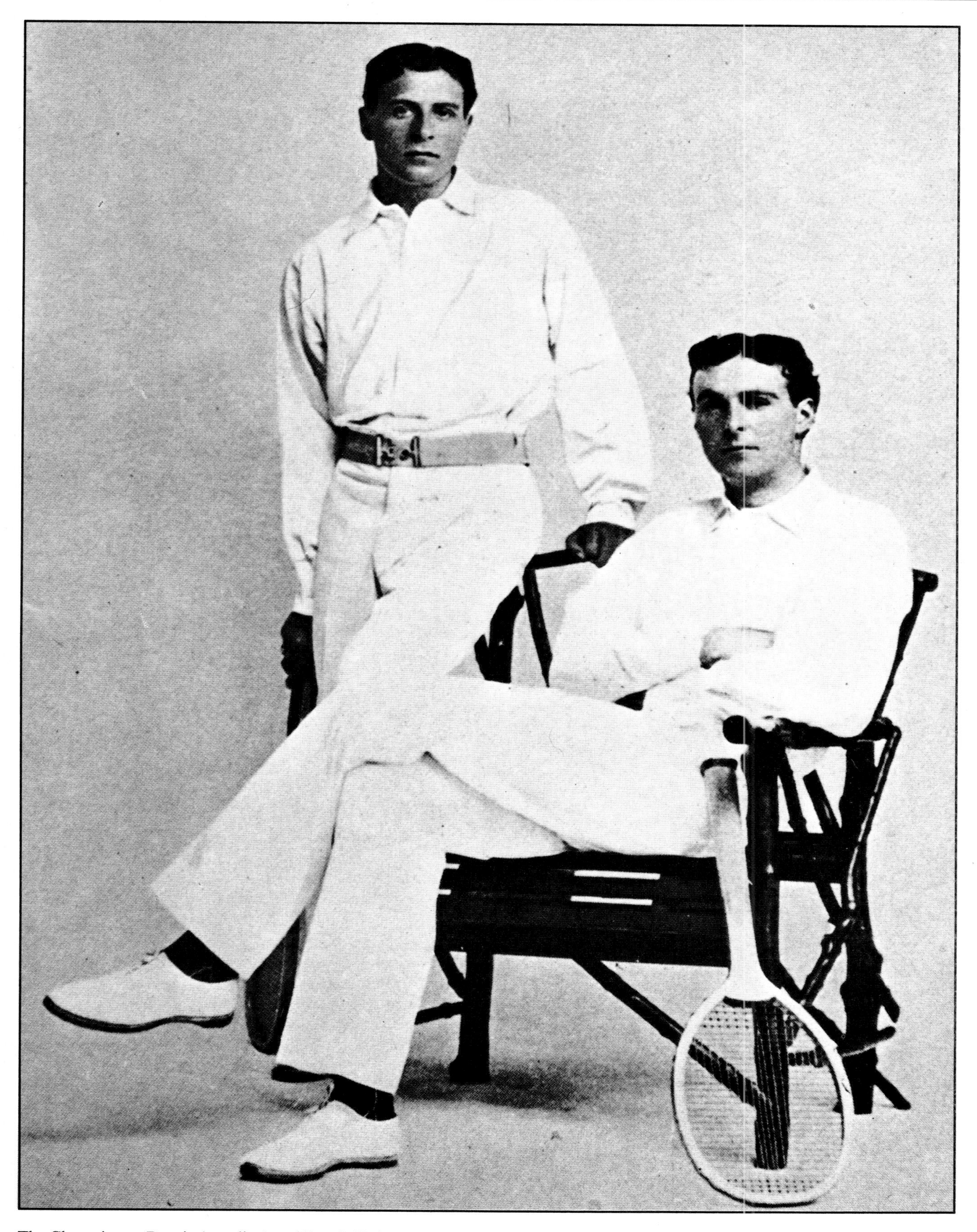

The Champions—Reggie (standing) and Laurie Doherty

Hobart came back in 1899 and was less successful, being beaten by Roper Barrett in the singles quarter-final. He again partnered Nisbet in the doubles and again got to the challenge round, losing once more to the Dohertys in three sets. The intrusion of Roper Barrett on the scene was that of one of Britain's most skilled and lively players, with a penchant for playing under various pseudonyms. He became a member of the first British Davis Cup side in 1900 and, much later, became its most distinguished and successful non-playing captain. At the 1899 Championships Roper Barrett played under the disguise of 'Mr Player' and, in the second round, beat C. G. Allen, one of the famous twins, by 6–0 6–0 6–0. Roper Barrett lost in the semi-final to S. H. Smith, a player from Stroud with a blistering forehand. Smith gained his victory, 8–6 in the fifth, after being within a point of trailing 3–5, at which stage the linesman did not call a ball 'out' because he was not looking! The problem was not new even then. Arthur Gore won the final from Smith and in due course Reggie Doherty beat Gore in the challenge round after losing the first two sets. Laurie Doherty, not being fully fit, did not compete in the singles that year.

'Big Do' acquired his fourth and last singles championship in 1900. His younger brother lost to Gore in the semi-final but Gore in turn lost the final to the forehand blasts of Smith. There was more risk to the Doherty supremacy in the doubles where Roper Barrett took Hobart's place as partner with Nisbet, won a five-set All Comers' Final against Smith and Frank Riseley, and stretched the Dohertys to the limit in the challenge round. The Dohertys were hard pressed to lead two sets to love and they lost the next two. This was the time of the Boer War, and Archdale Palmer, the honorary secretary of the club, was absent at the front. So was W. V. Eaves.

This was the year that the Davis Cup had its inaugural match between Great Britain and the United States in Boston. The British team clearly smacks of a makeshift effort in view of the form at Wimbledon. Neither champion nor challenger was able to make the trip and the Yorkshireman, Ernest Black, who shared the singles with Gore, was never able to number himself among the last eight at Wimbledon. Roper Barrett, who played in the Davis Cup doubles, persisted in his extraordinary habit of cloaking his identity. He appeared as 'Verne' in 1900. The following year it was as 'Dagger' (in 1897 it was A. L. Gydear).

The opening of the twentieth century, 1901, brought triumph at last to Gore and the eclipse of Reggie Doherty. 'Big Do' was showing signs of failing health and when Gore, a steady, persistent and accurate baseliner, forged his way through to the challenge round, the normal Doherty brilliance was tarnished. Gore achieved his first Wimbledon title at his thirteenth attempt, for he played first in 1888. He was then 33 years old and, as it turned out, merely at the start of a remarkable career! Laurie Doherty was beaten this year in the third round by George Hillyard 0–6 4–6 6–1 6–4 6–3. Hillyard, later to become Wimbledon's secretary, having pulled that match round from behind, lost to Gore, the eventual champion, in a dramatic quarter-final. Gore beat Hillyard 6–1 2–6 4–6 8–6 6–2 when, match point down in the fourth set, he had a net cord. In the challenge round Reggie Doherty won the first set 6–4 and led 5–2 in the second before his energy ran out. It was the last singles played by 'Big Do' at Wimbledon.

The doubles occupied a major interest in 1901 because of the challenge, in that event only, of the Americans Dwight Davis and Holcombe Ward, the American champions. The reputation of the American twist service, which had done so much to thwart the British Davis Cup effort the year before, preceded them. Davis and Ward won the All Comers' and became the first overseas players to play a challenge round. The Dohertys resisted their challenge after playing, in effect, seven sets. Level at one set each and nine games all in the third the match was held up by rain and started anew the following day. The Dohertys then won 4–6 6–2 6–3 9–7 after trailing 1–4 in the fourth set.

The Championship meeting was now entering a prosperity it never lost. The reign of the Dohertys was resumed with more magnificence than before with the emergence of 'Little Do' as the dominant exponent. He did so as the international aspect of the meeting began to widen. In 1902 two Belgians, Paul de Borman and W. Lemaire, provided the vanguard of a continental challenge. This was Laurie's seventh challenge and he was 25 years old. He was perhaps lucky to escape defeat in the semi-final against Mahony. The Irishman, volleying authoritatively, won the first two sets and then retired early in the fourth because of exhaustion. Laurie went on to beat M. J. G. Ritchie in a decisive All Comers' Final before robbing Gore of his title in a four-set challenge round. In the doubles, however, the Dohertys were, albeit only temporarily, dispossessed. Their arch rivals, Smith and Riseley, beat them 4–6 8–6 6–3 4–6 11–9, the longest title match played to that time.

There were a couple of Dutchmen in the draw for 1903, T. F. Vreede and A. B. Van Groenen, neither of whom survived the first round. Hobart was over from America again but did not prosper. Frank Riseley, who barely won a 60 games semi-final of the All Comers' singles against his doubles partner Smith by 9–7 in the fifth set, challenged Laurie Doherty without success, not taking a set and being routed 6–0 in the third.

In 1904 the entry rose to an all time high of 62, the preceding peak having been 60 more than twenty years earlier, in 1880 when the game still smacked of the vicarage lawn. The champion of Austria, H. Kinzl, was in the lists. Tony Wilding, a New Zealander at Cambridge, played and lost to Mahony in the first round. The two Belgians were back and de Borman got as far as the semi-final. At two sets all they had played a total of 50 games and Smith retired. Riseley again survived to the challenge round and again did not take a set from the invincible Laurie Doherty, who had, the previous autumn, become the first man from overseas to win the American title.

In 1903 the brothers had won back the doubles from Smith and Riseley without losing a set in the challenge round. Challenged by the same pair in 1904

Laurie Doherty at Worple Road in 1901

they won even more easily against them and they did so again, though with more difficulty, in 1905.

It was in 1904 that all ten courts, as distinct from the Centre Court, were 'dressed' with a surround of canvas 3 ft *0·91 m* high. The suppliers of balls and equipment were now Messrs Slazengers, following a round robin from the players in 1901.

Wimbledon lost its domesticity for ever in 1905. Apart from having its first overseas winner in the women's singles the men's event bristled with international interest. There was a record entry of 71 for the singles and it included three Australasians, Norman Brookes, Wilding (both future champions) and A. W. Dunlop, four top Americans, Beals Wright, William Clothier, William Larned and Holcombe Ward, all of whom had been or were to become US champions. Belgium, Denmark, Sweden and South Africa were also represented. Three overseas men reached the last eight of the singles, Wilding, Brookes and Larned. Brookes beat Riseley, Gore and Smith, and survived brilliantly to challenge for the title. His defeat of Smith in the All Comers' Final was by 7-5 in the fifth set after being a service break behind. The title match against Doherty was hailed as the finest singles yet played at Wimbledon, though Brookes threatened, so far as the score went, only when he led 6-5 in the first set, Doherty winning 8-6 6-2 6-4.

Brookes, a left hander, was then 27. Lawn tennis has been full of great Australian players. Arguably he was the greatest of them all though, by modern standards, a 'late developer'.

The 1905 doubles emphasised the strength of the overseas challenge. Brookes and Dunlop won the semi-final of the All Comers' against the Americans Larned and Clothier. Smith and Riseley were the only British partnership at that stage where they beat the other Americans, Ward and Wright, before putting out Brookes and Dunlop in the final. This was the eighth win out of nine years for Laurie and his brother.

There was a diminution, though only temporary, of the influx from overseas in 1906. This was the last year for the Dohertys. In the doubles they surrendered to Smith and Riseley—it was the fifth successive challenge round between the same pairs—after leading two sets to one. 'Big Do', less robust than ever, was the weak link.

On the other hand, 'Little Do' maintained the Doherty glories in the singles. He won his fifth successive challenge round when, for the third time in four years, he was assailed by Riseley. The latter had had another of his semi-finals against Smith, this time winning in four sets and he beat Gore in the final. Gore had beaten Wilding, then still a Cambridge undergraduate, in the semi-final.

The 29 year old Laurie Doherty came back to Wimbledon no more, at least not as a serious competitor. He retired as unbeaten champion and the brilliance of his glories has shone down the years.

The Renshaws laid the foundation of lawn tennis. The Dohertys built the major structure. It was not only Wimbledon that acquired fame, popularity and prestige by their skill and personality but the game itself. They were idolised everywhere.

One cannot fail to remark on the extraordinary dominance by brothers in the early years of the championships. There were the Renshaws, the Baddeleys and the Dohertys. Out of the first 30 meetings, 1877-1906, their names occupy 20 of the places in the singles honour roll. And of the 25 doubles championships that took place the same names occupy 17.

5
OVERSEAS INCURSIONS (1907-1914)

Wimbledon shed its parochial image for ever in 1907. In that year the Doherty brothers retired from the game as serious competitors and so did Smith and Riseley. It marked the end of the dominance of British men after three decades! A singles title which had never left the British Isles in 30 years was destined to go overseas all but five times out of the next seventy. Despite the absence of reverberating British figures this watershed year was a bustlingly successful one. George Hillyard took over the reigns of control as secretary. The Prince of Wales with his wife came as spectators. This was, of course, the future King George V and Queen Mary, for so long central figures in the Wimbledon scene. There never was a more avid spectator, right up to her death, than Queen Mary. The Centre Court was protected by a tarpaulin cover for the first time. The pony roller continued to give good service.

Two years before Norman Brookes had been the first man from overseas to win the All Comers' singles. He did as much when he came back and since there was no defence in the challenge round he won the championship. He had two difficult rounds, and only two; in the second he met the New Zealander Tony Wilding, his doubles partner and Davis Cup confrère for what was then Australasia, and in the fourth he met the American Karl Behr. He won both matches in the fifth set but was not stretched in any of his five other matches. Arthur Gore got but eight games from him in the title match.

The success of Brookes and Wilding in the doubles was meteoric. There was American opposition in the title match, which, with the retirement of Smith and Riseley, was the All Comers' Final, but Behr and Beals Wright did not even stretch them to advantage sets. In five rounds Brookes and Wilding lost no sets, won 90 games to 24, the easiest 'play through' victory on the books.

The overseas domination was entire for the womens' singles went for the second time to the Californian May Sutton. Not only did the three championships go overseas but even the consolation plate was taken by Wilding. The non-championship mixed doubles went to the Americans, Wright and Miss Sutton. Only the non-championship womens' doubles stayed at home, being won by Connie Wilson and Dorothea Lambert Chambers. It was, incidentally, the last of the non-championship womens' doubles events until 1913.

The Australasian domination at Wimbledon went far beyond the Championships in 1907. Nine days after the end Brookes and Wilding played the United States in the Davis Cup, just winning in the fifth rubber. Four days after they successfully challenged the British Isles for the trophy, winning in the fourth rubber to begin the long run of what was then Australasian but later entirely Australian success.

Brookes did not defend his title in 1908 and his presence was missed. It was spoken of as a dull meeting and, for the first time, there was no challenge round in any of the three events. But if the best Americans and the best Australian were not there the international flavour was well maintained. France had its first representative in the lists and so did India and the plate finalist was a German, Otto Kreuzer, who won, against a South African, Victor Gauntlett.

Gore, 40 years old, won the singles after a long title match against Roper Barrett, who was 34. Barrett beat Wilding in the quarter-final and then M. J. G. Ritchie in the semi. It was evidently a pretty dreary final and Gore, nothing if not brave and persistent, won it in the fifth set after taking the first two and trailing 3–4 in the last. In the doubles the singles finalists were partners but they lost in the last match to Wilding and Ritchie, victors by 9–7 in the fifth set. The official description of the destiny of the doubles title reads oddly. It is: A. F. Wilding and M. J. G. Ritchie (challengers) w.o. A. F. Wilding and N. E. Brookes (holders). It was the only occasion a player walked-over himself to take a championship.

There was a lot of rain in 1909, necessitating a third week. Again the overseas challenge was more impressive in quantity than quality. A German, F. W. Rahe was in the semi-final of the singles but apart from this there was British domination. Ritchie beat Roper Barrett for the right to challenge Gore. Ritchie, who was 38, won the first two sets and led 2–0 against Gore. Having been that close to success he did nothing but retreat and Gore won 18 out of the next 22 games. Gore was 41 years old and Wimbledon singles champion for the third time. This was the 22nd time he had been at Wimbledon, where he first played in 1888. It was not his last effort by any means!

To the regret of some who liked the feel of turf beneath their feet, even when wet, the All England Club, conscious of the mud of the year before, laid asphalt pathways round the courts in 1910. This was Wilding's first year as singles champion and he won from a field of 92. The modernisation of Wimbledon had not then extended to the notion of seeding. There was a chance of the New Zealander going out in the first round where he clashed with Roper Barrett but he overcame this threat after losing the first set. It was an uneven draw for Wilding. He went through the second round for the loss of only one game and in the third round clashed with Ritchie. Here he had a four-set win and was able to sail through the fourth without losing any games at all. In the quarter-final he beat a strong German, Otto Froitzheim, in three sets and he won over the same distance in the semi-final against James Cecil Parke, the Irish Rugby international, who, uniquely, flourished in the top standard of both sports.

The All Comers' Final was against the American Beals Wright, a formidable net rusher who had beaten Wilding in the Davis Cup ties of both 1907 and 1908. The victory was hailed as justifying the dictum that a volleyer could make his skills prevail over the equivalently good ground stroke exponent only in a best of three sets match. Wilding beat Wright after losing the first two sets. The British men's game was now on the defensive. No less than five of the last eight in the singles were from overseas. As for the challenge round, Gore made a valiant but unsuccessful stand against the most talented and admired player from New Zealand. Gore, playing rather out of character, volleyed a lot, led 4–1 in the opening set only to lose five successive games, failed to consolidate a lead at the start of the second set and was eventually beaten in the fourth.

A notable singles champion had begun his reign. Wilding had much the same sort of qualities as Laurie Doherty. He was idolised not only for his fine skill but for his personality. Like the younger Doherty also his highest skill as a singles player flowered later than with some. He was 26 when he won the singles in 1910. In doubles Wilding paired with Ritchie and won back the title they had taken two years before.

The All England Club at Worple Road was now bursting with its own success. The men's singles entry reached three figures in 1911 when Wilding was challenged by 104 players. The assiduous Roper Barrett, 37 years old, survived to do so, though only after recouping the loss of the first two sets in the final to Charles Dixon, a long-standing rival one year older. This exhausting match was played in broiling heat and so was the challenge round where Wilding played what was described as a 'peculiar and uncanny match', trailing one set to two and keeping his title when Roper Barrett retired at two sets all. The doubles went to France, to André Gobert and Max Decugis who got the title with a five-set challenge round win against Wilding and Ritchie; their Wimbledon performance was also remembered for a third round success in three sets against the Germans, Hans Kleinscroth and Friedrich Rahe which was hailed as a vignette of aggressive perfection.

There was a move in 1912 to abolish the challenge-round system and Wilding declared he was prepared to go along with the change. At that time it came to nothing. This year, a wet one, there was an all-French singles semi-final, Gobert surviving a five setter at that stage to reach the final. This, astonishingly, was against the evergreen Arthur Gore and, remarkably, this unique British stalwart won. Gore won the third set from Wilding in the challenge round but had no basic chance of deterring the New Zealander's success. Gore was—and it seems incredible—then 44 years old and competing at Wimbledon for the 25th time! All that and he was within one match of being champion for the fourth time!

This was the last spectacular success of Gore and perhaps the place to set down his unrivalled record of achievements. It was not his last effort in singles by any means. He went on competing and numbered himself among the last eight in singles in 1914. He reappeared after the First World War. When the All England Club moved to Church Road in 1922 he played in the singles then. He went on competing in the doubles. In 1926 he and Roper Barrett beat Louis Greig and HRH The Duke of York (later George VI). His swan song was to lose in the first round in 1927—he and Roper Barrett were beaten 3–6 6–4 12–10 by F. T. Stowe and E. U. Williams—when he was 59 years old, having been at every one of 36 meetings since 1888. He was Britain's first Davis Cup captain in 1900. He was All England Club president in 1911. He was not only the oldest singles winner, 41, but an extraordinarily durable competitor.

Whilst the then 44 year old Gore was making his mature skill felt in the singles in 1912 there was mature skill at work in the doubles. Roper Barrett, 38, and Dixon, 39, dispossessed the French holders, Gobert and Decugis. A year later they thrust back the German challenge of Kleinscroth and Rahe. They had the reputation of being the canniest pair that ever was.

Their success in 1913 gave them a resounding title. Indeed, all Wimbledon titles became grandiose in description in 1913 following the formation of the International Lawn Tennis Federation. They became, with no particular desire from those concerned, the World Championships on Grass. It was accurate but unnecessary. There was also instituted a World Championship on Hard Courts and a World Championship on Covered Courts, the second of which impinged little on the game at large. Hitherto the title accorded Wimbledon was the All England

Championships, though this applied only to the two singles events and the men's doubles. With this accolade from the International Federation, of which Britain but not the United States, was a founder member, the mixed at Wimbledon was changed into a full championship event and the women's doubles reintroduced with championship status. The 'All England' titles for these events had always belonged elsewhere and were not affected. To complete the curious saga of nomenclature I record the fact that when the United States joined the International Federation their tacit condition of membership, the abolition of the world titles, was accepted, and the Wimbledon 'World' titles lapsed after 1923. The 'All England' mixed doubles, alternating between Liverpool and Manchester, lapsed after 1938 and the women's doubles, held in Buxton, died after 1953.

In the men's singles in 1913, where the entry was 116, only one home player, Parke, was in the semi-final of the All Comers'. He was beaten there by a meteoric newcomer from America, Maurice McLoughlin, known as the 'Californian Comet'. He was never there again but he made his mark with a tremendous service. He had to hit through the wiles of Roper Barrett in the first round, which he did 8–6 in the fifth set. He made more simple progress subsequently and beat the Australian Stanley Doust in the final to qualify for a challenge against Wilding. It was assessed as Wilding's finest performance. McLoughlin had a lead of 5–4, 40–30 on his own service in the first set but was worsted by an outright winner against one of his strongest deliveries and never got in front again, Wilding winning 8–6 6–3 10–8.

The attendance for 1913 does not seem to have been recorded but was held as the biggest of all time. Indeed, it seems that McLoughlin's concentration against Wilding was upset by the disturbance of spectators fainting in the crush to see the match. But Wilding was immaculate and it was perhaps his finest hour as a player.

Norman Brookes, who had not played since 1907, came back in 1914. He began with a whitewash win, consumed M. J. G. Ritchie for the total loss of only three games, lost only four in the next round and so arrived against Gore, the other former champion in the event, having lost but six games in nine sets. Gore, pertinacious still, forced the first advantage set against the Australian, but the victorious Brookes went on to beat another British international, Arthur Beamish, to reach the All Comers' Final. There he had his first real match, against Froitzheim whom he beat 8–6 in the fifth after leading all the way. The challenge round brought the eclipse of Wilding and it was the submission of a pupil to his master. Building a lead of 4–0 in the first set, Brookes, an adept volleyer, took the title by 6–4 6–4 7–5 with the exertion of what seemed to many to be a moral supremacy.

Rivals then, they were allies in the doubles and their authority was not seriously threatened. Brookes accordingly gained his fourth Wimbledon championship and Wilding his eighth. Brookes was to impinge on the game for many years. Wilding did not survive the war; he was killed by shell fire at Neuve Chapelle on 9 May 1915, aged 31.

The Championships were now part of the British social and sporting scene. When in 1877 Messrs Jones, Walsh and Heathcote had envisaged their 'Lawn Tennis Championship Meeting' they can hardly have imagined the success they were to be 38 meetings later. Yet as the First World War continued its tragic course the hope was for survival rather than expansion, like all else in Great Britain and elsewhere.

The Challenge Round of 1913, Norman Brookes v Tony Wilding. The last match before the war

6
THE WOMEN TAKE THE COURT (*Women* 1884-1902)

Maud and Lilian Watson

So far as the women were concerned Wimbledon followed after others who led; it was not until 1884 when The Lawn Tennis Championships had existed for seven years as a purely masculine stronghold that the women were seen there. Should upholders of women's liberation wish to give due honour they must do so to the Irish, for the first distaff event was the women's singles (and mixed doubles) at the inaugural Irish Championship meeting in 1879. The first champion was May Langrishe from an entry of seven and it is a shame she missed the first women's action at Wimbledon.

The inauguration of a women's singles championship at Wimbledon seems to have been an afterthought. Early in 1884 it was decided to enlarge the meeting by a men's doubles event for that promoted by the Oxford University Lawn Tennis Club since 1879 had fallen on evil times. The Oxford Club offered the cup to Wimbledon and the decision to stage a championship for the trophy was made on 7 March; the new doubles event was to start the day after the end of the singles and a prospectus giving these details was issued. Nothing was then said about a women's singles. It was not until 21 June that the big decision was made. Henry Jones proposed the motion that ended male dominance at Wimbledon. The committee agreed to stage a women's singles championship at the same time as the men's doubles, with a first prize valued at twenty guineas and a second valued at ten.

The entry was thirteen and included two sisters, Maud, who was the younger, and Lilian Watson. With a third contender, Blanche Bingley, they were dominating. Maud, having beaten Miss Bingley in the semi-final 3–6 6–4 6–2, won an even tougher final against Lilian 6–8 6–3 6–3. That season Maud had already proved her capacity as a champion by beating Miss Langrishe in Dublin. Born in 1863 she was a daughter of the vicarage. Her father, notable as a mathematician, was vicar of Berkswell, near Coventry. Her mother had been a croquet champion and apart from her sister she also had a brother who was said to be a first-class tennis player. She was, wrote N. Lane Jackson in his *Sporting Days and Sporting Ways* nearly fifty years later, 'a true sportswoman, clever, gentle and kind and always a gentlewoman'.

She kept her title in 1885, playing through; neither the men's doubles nor women's singles became challenge-round events until the following year. Maud Watson played Miss Bingley in the final, winning 6–1 7–5. When in 1886 Maud Watson, standing out as champion, played the challenge round it was again for the title against Miss Bingley and Miss Bingley won 6–3 6–3. Thus emerged the first of the women champions of formidable standard of performance. Miss Bingley was then 22 years old and two decades later her name was still being inscribed on the roll of honour; six years after that it was recorded as a semi-finalist. There have been greater women players than Mrs Hillyard, which Miss Bingley became, but none with so stalwart a standard of performance at Wimbledon.

Before Mrs Hillyard made her most striking appearance on the lawn tennis stage she had to wait a while in the wings. In 1887 a little girl from Cheshire sent in her entry. She was born on 24 September 1871. She won the All Comers' event easily, then beat Miss Bingley 6–2 6–0, and thus became Wimbledon champion at her first attempt at the age of 15 years 9 months, an unsurpassed record of precociousness. She was Charlotte Dod, known as Lottie Dod. Her Wimbledon career can be covered simply. She successfully defended in the challenge round of 1888, beating Mrs Hillyard, as Miss Bingley had by then become, 6–3 6–3. She did not compete again until 1891. Then, playing through, she won the title again by beating Mrs Hillyard 6–2 6–1 in the final. In 1892 she successfully defended against Mrs Hillyard's challenge by 6–1 6–1 and did so again in 1893, winning 6–8 6–1 6–4, her only close match. She was never beaten at Wimbledon.

This record of invincibility does not match in any real degree that shown by later champions like Suzanne Lenglen, Helen Wills Moody or Maureen Connolly. Apart from the differing standards of play, the different costumes and the different style, the fields from which Miss Dod emerged as champion were miniscule. Indeed, in 1890—not that Miss Dod was in action that year—the total number of challengers for the women's singles championship was as low as four! None the less, Lottie Dod stands out like a beacon in the saga of Victorian women's sport.

She was, as N. Lane Jackson was to reminisce in 1932, 'more than a lawn tennis champion for she gained a similar distinction at golf and archery. She was captain of the English ladies' hockey team and was, I believe, one of three who passed the diamond test at figure skating. She is now a very clever musician, and I have it on good authority that she is also one of the best bridge players in London.' At hockey she gained her international honours in 1899 and 1900. The British women's golf championship she won at Troon in 1904.

In lawn tennis the remarkable Miss Dod made her mark when only 14 years old. That was at Bath in June 1886 when she played against the Wimbledon champion to bring about the first defeat suffered by Maud Watson since the Edgbaston tournament in 1881, a run of 55 matches without loss.

Miss Dod had one advantage brought about by the fashion and conventions of her time. At the age of 15 she ranked still as a girl. She was permitted—and it seemed she used—a short skirt which would not have been possible had she been four or five years older. The freedom and extra mobility it gave her were factors in her success.

Harry Scrivener, writing in 1902 or thereabouts, described Miss Dod as the '*beau ideal* of what a lady-champion should be. In the matter of play, pure and simple, she was absolutely without a weak point, but on a very hot day and in exceptionally bright sunshine it was just possible (by steady play and much lobbing) to beat her . . . but I am not prepared to say that I have yet seen her equal.' Looking at the old pictures of the incomparable Lottie Dod, invariably wearing a mob cap, she was clearly an entrancing personality.

She was said to have been a better player than Suzanne Lenglen at the same age—and Mlle Lenglen was herself something of a young prodigy. Her forehand drive, it was said also, had the pace of a man's and she volleyed with accuracy. Despite serving underarm she wielded a powerful smash. On serving Miss Dod expressed her own views. She wrote:

> It is doubtful whether ladies gain anything by serving overhand. In the majority of cases they expend a good deal of strength without making the service more difficult than the ordinary underhand; therefore, unless exceptionally good, and performed without undue exertion, I do think ladies' overhand service is a great waste of strength.

But on volleying she was adamant:

> In mixed doubles, it is my opinion that the pair is much stronger where the lady can go up and volley, taking her fair share of the work . . . Ladies doubles would be far more interesting if fought like gentlemen's, on the service line . . . Two good volleyers will beat two good back players or a volley and a back player.

Miss Dod's major glory was her forehand. Said Herbert Chipp 'it was made very quietly and very decidedly, and with absolute freedom; its power and length took one by surprise'. Said G. W. Hillyard 'her greatest strength lay in a particularly fine forehand drive, which was not only accurate but had great pace, and was beautifully placed'. Miss Dod was queen of Wimbledon whenever she went there.

When Miss Dod stepped down after retaining her title in 1888 the way was left clear for Mrs Hillyard to win for the second time. She did not do so easily. The title match was, of course, the All Comers' Final and in this Mrs Hillyard played Helene Rice. Mrs Hillyard won, but only just. The score was 4–6 8–6 6–4 and Miss Rice had three match points in the second set where she led 5–3, 40–15. The following year, 1890, the event reached its nadir so far as numbers were concerned. Miss Dod was not there and Mrs Hillyard did not defend. The entire field was four players. Never was a Wimbledon semi-final place gained so cheaply! It is simple to record that Miss Rice beat Miss M. Steedman 7–5 6–2, that Miss Jacks beat Mrs. C. J. Cole 6–4 7–5 and that in the final Miss Rice beat Miss Jacks 6–4 6–1 to become champion.

Who was Miss Rice? She was a Wimbledon champion shrouded in almost complete obscurity. She was Irish and came from Tipperary. She appeared for the first time in the Irish Championships in 1889 but having flitted across the stage in that year and the next she somehow contrived to vanish. She was born on 21 June 1866 and she died on 21 June 1907 in the place where she was born.

Miss Dod, having come back in 1891, took the title for three years but after 1893 came back no more. The key match in her triumphs was always against Mrs Hillyard and in 1894 that remarkable player was able to reassume an ascendancy that lasted out the century. The record of Blanche Hillyard as an enthusiastic and successful player is awesome. Had it not been for Miss Dod it is obvious she would have won Wimbledon another five times. Instead she had to be content with six.

Blanche Hillyard collected lawn-tennis titles like a bibliophile amassing first editions and if pre-1900 Wimbledon singles titles be regarded as *incunabula* she stands, among women at any rate, as owner of the most valuable library. She was obviously a good match player. Frank Burrow wrote of her as owing

. . . as much of her successes to her unconquerable resolution as to her actual strokes, though her powers of running also had a good deal to do with it. She never volleyed unless forced but her powerful forehand driving, the stroke made at the top of the bound and a little top spin applied, was too much for most of her opponents. Her backhand was purely defensive . . . Unlike the generality of early women players, she served overhand; but it was not a service of any great terrors. One thing that differentiated her from nearly every woman player in the game's history was that she invariably wore white gloves.

A rival, Charlotte Sterry, wrote of her as 'a splendid example of the true fighter. Her persistency and pluck on the court are wonderful; as for her staying power she seems to be able to last for ever. She certainly heads the list of the most victorious in the ladies' singles and is one of the most sporting of them.'

Mrs Hillyard's six Wimbledon championships, the first in 1886 and the last in 1900, were the outcome of a remarkably consistent standard of performance from her entry at the first meeting in 1884 to her submission to Mrs Sterry in the challenge round of 1901. She played fourteen times in that period and every time she competed she either won the title or lost to the champion. Five of her successes were after playing through the draw and only once did she benefit by the relatively cheap way of keeping the title, standing out and successfully defending in the challenge round. That was in 1900 when she thrust back the challenge of Mrs Sterry. The next year she lost to the same player.

That marked the end of Mrs Hillyard's career as a top champion, though it was very far from ending her participation in the game. She was 37 when she lost to Mrs Sterry in 1901 but was none the less back as a Wimbledon competitor in 1905. In 1912 she reached the semi-final. Her last appearance was as late as 1913 when she went out in the second round to Mrs Hannam, then being in her 50th year.

She was noted as a good horsewoman; both she and her husband, George Whiteside Hillyard, a sporting all-rounder, have claim to rank as the most enthusiastic couple the game has known. George Hillyard became All England Club secretary in April 1907 and was there until 1924. Blanche's last tournament success seems to have been to win, with her husband, the All England Married Couple's Championships at Nottingham in 1914, this long-defunct title existing from 1910 until it died for lack of entries after 1923.

Between 1884 and the end of the century there were but five names on the roll of women champions, Maud Watson, Blanche Hillyard, Lottie Dod, the elusive and fleeting Helena Rice and Charlotte Sterry. The last, another of the stalwarts, appeared first as Charlotte Cooper in 1893. At first she filled the same sort of role towards Mrs Hillyard as that player had towards Lottie Dod. Mrs Hillyard won her championships when Miss Dod chose not to appear. Miss Cooper won hers when Mrs Hillyard was absent. That was in 1895 and 1896. In 1901, soon after Miss Cooper had become Mrs Sterry, she denied her former persistent conqueror entry into the twentieth century as a singles champion by winning 6–2 6–2. She was eight years younger.

Charlotte Sterry emerges from the mists of time as an engaging and lively player. She was described as 'a quite unusually strong and active girl, with a constitution like the proverbial ostrich, who scarcely knew what it was to be tired, and never was sick or sorry'. Her outstanding strength was her volleying and she was reputed to have lived at the net. She died only in 1966 and as a nonagenarian flew happily from Glasgow to London to take part in the 75th anniversary celebrations of the Championships.

Though destined in due course to take the championship for the fifth time in 1908 the nimble Mrs Sterry did not sustain her fourth triumph of 1901. The singles winner of 1902 was Muriel Robb, a player with a formidable forehand and who was one of the overhead servers of the time.

By then the women's singles at Wimbledon had started its twentieth-century boom. The entry of 30 in 1901 was a record and it was similarly flourishing a year later. One who made her debut in 1902 was Dorothea Douglass. She reached the semi-final before being beaten by Miss Robb 6–4 2–6 9–7. The latter won the challenge round against Mrs Sterry after a title match unique in the history of the meeting in that it was played twice over. It began in miserable weather conditions and Mrs Sterry won the first set 6–4. She lost the second 11–13 and by then conditions made it impossible to continue. It was decreed that the match should begin afresh the next day and so it was, with Miss Robb the winner by 7–5 6–1. Over all

53 games were played and Miss Robb won three sets to one. Some of the early US women's finals were staged over the best of five sets but this curiosity is the only time it happened at Wimbledon! Miss Robb came from Newcastle and died in 1907, sadly because she was only 28.

In 1900 there was the first hint of the international colour of the women's game at Wimbledon. In Philadelphia the previous summer Marion Jones had won the US women's singles championship for the first time. Incidentally she had in 1898 been the unsuccessful challenger against Juliette Atkinson when the winning score was 6–3 5–7 6–4 2–6 7–5! Miss Jones came to spread her wings, the pioneer international player of her sex. It was an event that made small impression at the time and Miss Jones came and went. Even so the purely domestic character of the women's events at Wimbledon had ended.

Another factor making 1900 something of a landmark was that for the first time there were five events. A women's doubles was initiated in 1899 and the mixed doubles followed one year later. In the case of the mixed there was continuity from that date but the women's doubles ceased from 1907 until 1913. Not until 1913 did these events rate as championships. The other titles at Wimbledon were the 'All England Championships' but in the case of the women's and mixed doubles these had long been pre-empted. The All England Women's doubles championship had been at Buxton since 1885. It continued there until it died in 1953. The All England Mixed title was played for in alternate years in Manchester and Liverpool and ran like that from 1888 to 1938. In 1913 all five events at Wimbledon acquired from the newly formed International Lawn Tennis Federation the resounding, unnecessary and, as it turned out, temporary description as Championships of the World on Grass.

By the end of 1902 the cradle stage of the women at Wimbledon was over. There had been six champions in nineteen years. They still functioned very much as the weaker sex. Even Lottie Dod did not avoid a slightly apologetic air when she wrote: 'There are few games in which ladies and gentlemen can join, therefore it is all the more necessary that ladies should try to improve their play and not spoil the sport for men, as they too frequently do.' Women, though, were moving towards the limelight.

7 DOROTHEA LAMBERT CHAMBERS & THE REST (*Women* 1903-1914)

Dorothea Katherine Douglass, who became Mrs Robert Lambert Chambers, was a parson's daughter from Ealing, who, whatever the merits of the engaging Lottie Dod or the indefatigable Blanche Hillyard, must rank as the greatest of all women players prior to the First World War. It could be that a chubby, entrancing Californian, May Sutton, was, at her peak, the better for a brief period; in due course a Frenchwoman, Suzanne Lenglen, certainly was; but as lawn tennis grew into the twentieth century the achievements of Mrs Lambert Chambers at Wimbledon laid the foundations of what the women's game has since become. She won the singles seven times, four times after playing through; in one year, 1910, when she survived six matches, she won the title with a final tally of 72 games to 16, a standard of superiority surpassed only by Mlle Lenglen and equalled only by Helen Wills Moody.

Her first appearance at Wimbledon was in 1902 when she lost in the semi-final to Muriel Robb. Her last challenge for the singles was in 1920 and in all those years—she did not play in 1909 and 1912—she either won the title or yielded only to the champion of the year. Her final appearance was in 1927 in the doubles. It was her twentieth Wimbledon and she was 48 years old.

She could be called a late developer. Born in 1878 she was 21 before she began winning at lawn tennis. She took the Kent Championship in 1901 and having taken the Wimbledon crown in 1903 her authority became dominating. She was at her peak from 1910 to 1914, that is from the age of 31 to 35.

Frank Burrow wrote of her:

> She both looked, and was, a most determined player. Every stroke was made with a definite purpose; her generalship and tactics were as sound as her driving was superb, and few indeed have been able to induce such a feeling of hopelessness in her opponents as she did . . . She was so far in front of any English woman player that she could probably have given any of them fifteen . . . She had no weak point at all.

The All Comers' Final was the title match in 1903 when Mrs Lambert Chambers won for the first time, after losing the first set to Ethel Thomson, who, as Mrs Larcombe, took the title nine years later. She had small difficulty in keeping it the following year against the challenge of Mrs Sterry. It was only in 1904 that the women's entry exceeded 32 for the first time. But after 1905 the women's events at Wimbledon were never quite the same again.

The 18 year old who intruded with such vehemence that year was born at Plymouth, Devon. None the less, she came from Pasadena, California, and had been a precocious winner of the Southern Californian Championship five years before. In 1904 she had won the US Championship in Philadelphia. She was a chubby lass with twinkling eyes and arrived in England with a letter of introduction from Marion Jones.

Her happy personality was as entrancing, it seems, as that of Miss Jones, her playing skill vastly higher. This was May Sutton, the first overseas player to be inscribed on the roll of Wimbledon champions. She came to Wimbledon to win and win she did, for no one could cope with a forehand drive of 'devastating' strength. To the astonishment of the natives she took a deep breath before each stroke and exhaled with audible effort when she struck the ball. She was not a lightweight (she weighed 11 stone 6 lb *72·6 kg* and had been 15 lb *6·8 kg* at birth) but she was fast of foot. She won the singles without losing a set, though extended to 6–3 8–6 in the All Comers' Final by Connie Wilson who had notably beaten Mrs Hillyard in the round before by 7–5 9–11 6–2. In the challenge round Miss Sutton beat Mrs Lambert Chambers, then still Miss Douglass, by 6–3 6–4. (One may provide a fascinating footnote to this clash. Twenty years afterwards, in 1925, Mrs Lambert Chambers and May Sutton, now Mrs Bundy, faced each other in the Wightman Cup at Forest Hills. For Britain Mrs Lambert Chambers and Ermyntrude Harvey beat Mrs Bundy and Molla Mallory 10–8 6–1. Mrs Lambert Chambers was 46, her old American rival 38.)

Not even with the assistance of the challenge-round system could Miss Sutton keep her title a year later. Or, possibly, it was because of it that the American yielded to Mrs Lambert Chambers in 1906. It always was a debating point, whether or not the challenge round favoured the holder. Some players preferred not to come to a big match 'cold'. Mrs Lambert Chambers won her third Wimbledon singles when she beat Miss Sutton 6–3 9–7 after being 0–4 in the second set. Twelve months later the boot was on the other foot and it was 1905 all over again. Miss Sutton cavorted through the All Comers' and again beat Connie Wilson in the final, this time more easily by 6–4 6–2. In the challenge round her forehand had the pace to subdue Mrs Lambert Chambers, this time 6–1 6–4.

That was two wins in three years, signs of much Californian dominance at Wimbledon. While it lasted the rivalry between the parson's daughter and the British naval captain's daughter (for such was the otherwise very American Miss Sutton) provided the most colourful motif the women had so far had.

In 1908 Mrs Lambert Chambers did not prosper as of old. She clashed with Mrs Sterry in the quarter-final only to be beaten 6–3 7–5. Mrs Sterry went on to win the title against Miss A. M. Morton, there being no challenge round in the absence of Miss Sutton. Twelve months later there was an entry of 34 but the quality was thinner. Mrs Lambert Chambers did not play. Nor did Mrs Sterry. Apparently quite unnoticed there was a Miss Bjurstedt in the draw. She lost in her first match by 6–1 7–5 to a Miss Johnson. She was then Norwegian and six years away from her first American championship success and enduring fame as Molla Mallory. The 1909 Wimbledon champion was Dora Boothby and in the final she beat Miss Morton 6–4 4–6 8–6.

A contemporary account said that it 'was remarkable for its tension and protracted rallies. There have been more scientific, more stroke-varied ladies' finals at Wimbledon but none in which the result hung so long in the balance or in which the combatants showed such hardihood and such resolution.' Miss Boothby acquired her championship status after the longest title match since 1889 (excluding the duplicated effort of Miss Robb and Mrs Sterry 1902.) She was destined to lose her title with brevity a year later and to fail also the year after in the briefest title match of all time.

In 1910 Mrs Lambert Chambers was at her most authoritative to date. In the final of the All Comers' she had her only real contest, this against Miss E. G. Johnson whom she beat 6–4 6–2. For the rest she played no set longer than eight games and beat Miss Boothby in the final 6–2 6–2. Afterwards the only discussion was whether Mrs Lambert Chambers or Lottie Dod was the best woman player ever to be seen at Wimbledon. The title defence for Mrs Lambert Chambers in 1911 was nominal. Miss Boothby came through to challenge her only to fail utterly. Mrs. Lambert Chambers won 6–0 6–0, uniquely a white-wash victory in a singles title match in the championships.

With Mrs Lambert Chambers not defending, the favourites for the title in 1912 were Ethel Larcombe and Mrs Hannam. Their clash in the third round was described as one of the best games ever seen in the event and Mrs Larcombe won 7–5 8–6 after being four times within a point of losing the second at 4–5. There were, though, two former champions in the field, Mrs Sterry and the indomitable Mrs Hillyard. And among the victims of Mrs Hillyard, before she lost in the semi-final to Mrs Larcombe, was an American newcomer, Elizabeth Ryan. In the quarter-final Mrs Hillyard was hard pressed to beat this 20-year-old Californian 3–6 8–6 6–3. A third ex-champion competing was Miss Boothby. Mrs Sterry beat her 6–2 4–6 6–1. Mrs Larcombe beat Mrs Hillyard 6–1 6–0 in the semi-final and went on to win the final against Mrs Sterry by 6–3 6–1. Mrs Larcombe's volleying was famous, though it seems she confounded some by choosing to stick it out against Mrs Hannam from the baseline. Mrs Larcombe won her first and only championship.

Between 1884 and the First World War there were only ten women's singles champions. One can now view the happenings of 1912 with hindsight. Mrs Hillyard, beating Miss Ryan to reach the semi-final, was past holder of six singles. In due course, Miss Ryan was to take no singles but nineteen doubles championships.

There was no title defence in 1913 and as in 1910 the play through for the title was little more than a formality for Mrs Lambert Chambers who never lost more than five games in any of five matches. The lack of final defence was accidental. This was the year when the women's and mixed doubles assumed full championship status following the founding of the International Federation and the grant to Wimbledon of official status as The Lawn Tennis Championships of the World on Grass. There had in fact been a mixed event at the All England Club since 1900 and a women's doubles from 1899 to 1907. By a curious coincidence the upgrading of both events to championship status brought casualties in its train. In the mixed final Mrs Larcombe partnered J. C. Parke to be 6–3 3–5 against Hope Crisp and Mrs Tuckey when Parke miss-hit a smash into his partner's eye. Mrs Larcombe was not only prevented from defending her singles title in the challenge round but kept out of lawn tennis for some weeks. In the women's doubles final

Mrs Lambert Chambers and Mrs Sterry were leading Mrs McNair and Miss Boothby 6–4 4–2 when Mrs Sterry tore a tendon in her leg.

The seventh singles title fell to Mrs Lambert Chambers in 1914. In this halcyon year before the First World War it was hoped that a remarkable 15-year-old French girl, Suzanne Lenglen, who had won the World Hard Court Championship in Paris, would compete but the only French woman challenger was Mlle Broquedis. The total women's singles field was 52, the biggest to that time. Mrs Lambert Chambers was challenged by Mrs Larcombe, was made to work fairly hard before winning 7–5 6–4 and, after an event of no great excitement, took the crown for the seventh time.

It was noteworthy that the All Comers' Final was contested between Mrs Larcombe and Miss Ryan. The American got no further in the singles but with Miss A. M. Morton she won the doubles. It was the first of many.

As for Mrs Lambert Chambers she had come to the end of her career as champion. Her Wimbledon singles record was awesome, eleven challenges and seven victories. She was already 35 years old. And yet this tremendous player, outstandingly the best to date in the women's game, was still to play her most famous match, a contest that marked a turning-point in the development of Wimbledon and women's lawn tennis.

When the curtain of the First World War came down on Wimbledon after 1914 there had been 31 women's singles championships. There had been but 10 champions and 4 of them won 23 titles, Mrs Lambert Chambers (7), Mrs Hillyard (6), Miss Dod (5) and Mrs Sterry (5). Only one champion was not British, though this exception, Miss Sutton, was born in Britain anyway. Subsequent years were vastly different.

Dorothea Lambert Chambers

8
WORPLE ROAD OUTGROWN (1919-1921)

The holocaust and difficulties of the war from 1914 to 1918 did nothing to diminish the growing popularity of lawn tennis as a whole and Wimbledon in particular. Rather it was as if enthusiasm burned more strongly in having had no outlet. That the All England Club had survived was largely due to the personal efforts of Mr H. Wilson Fox, club president from 1915 to 1921. The demand for seats for the 1919 meeting necessitated a ballot. It was touch and go whether selection would not have to be introduced in the men's singles but, as it happened, the entry was precisely 128, the limit set. In the event selection was introduced one year later.

The improvements made just before the war did not suffice to cope with the growing pressure. The stands, holding some 2000, had been enlarged to take 3200. Gross gate receipts in 1912 were £3468. In 1913 the figure was £4555 and in 1914 £7000. In 1919 it was £9390. The first post-war tournament made it evident that the Championships had outgrown its original home and that a move to bigger quarters was necessary.

The most striking happening in 1919 was the appearance of Suzanne Lenglen. Her prodigious exploits are dealt with later. The winner of the men's singles was the Australian Gerald Patterson, a tall 23 year old from Melbourne. He had not been at Wimbledon before. He was a big server and it was mainly on the strength of his serving that he became a champion at his first attempt. The immediate post-war men's standard, all commentators agreed, was not terribly high. It was pointed out that the older players had lost their speed and that the younger had yet to learn their tactics.

Wilding had not survived the war. His Australasian Davis Cup team mate, the adept Norman Brookes, had been luckier and he was at Wimbledon to defend his title. Patterson dynamited his way through the All Comers' event almost without difficulty and he lost a set only in the semi-final to M. J. G. Ritchie. It was in fact the only set lost by the pace-making Patterson. In the challenge round he found his compatriot, Norman Brookes, easy opposition. With seven matches in the All Comers' and the play-off against the holder, Patterson won eight rounds in becoming champion, yet of the 25 sets played he lost only one.

The story in 1920 was much the same. In this case the newcomer was far more striking than Patterson had been. A vibrant personality arrived: 'Big Bill' Tilden from the United States. William Tatem Tilden, from Germantown, Philadelphia, was not a youngster. He was already 27 years old when he came to England

'Big Bill' Tilden, arguably the greatest player of all time

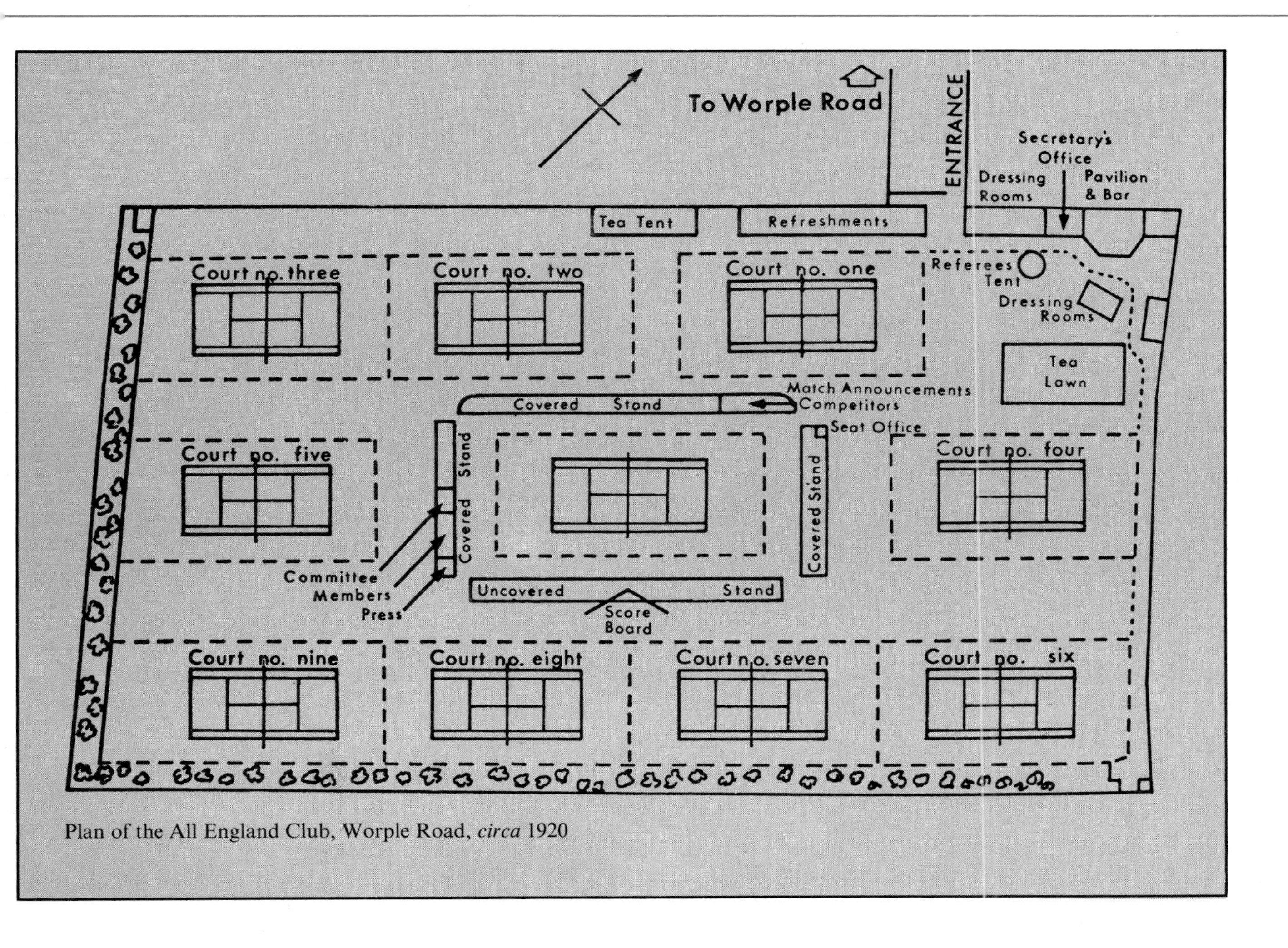

Plan of the All England Club, Worple Road, *circa* 1920

as a member of the American Davis Cup side and markedly a 'late developer'. In June 1920 he was not yet American champion.

The lack of seeding was either unfortunate or exciting, depending on the viewpoint. The two best American players that year were Tilden and William ('Little Bill') Johnston. The three best British were A. R. F. Kingscote, J. C. Parke and A. H. Lowe. The blind draw fell in such a way that only one could get as far as the last eight. It was Tilden. Parke beat Johnston but was put out by Tilden. Kingscote beat Lowe and Tilden in turn beat Kingscote. This fourth-round contest was reckoned the best of the meeting and Tilden won it in five sets.

Tilden waxed in strength as the tournament progressed. His All Comers' Final was against the Japanese Zenzo Shimidzu and Tilden made what seemed almost impudent recoveries against him, winning 6–4 6–4 13–11 after trailing 1–4 in the first set, 2–4 in the second and 2–5 in the third. Tilden's status as Wimbledon champion was in doubt until the third set of the challenge round against Patterson. The Australian, who won the first set, was within a point of leading 3–0 but Tilden, having just reached a drop shot to save the rally, went on to take six consecutive games. Like Patterson the year before Tilden had to win eight matches for his Wimbledon title. He yielded four sets in doing so.

This was the first international success of perhaps the game's greatest player. It was also the first Wimbledon title to be taken by an American man. For good measure in 1920 America won the men's doubles as well, though not with their leading pair, Tilden and Johnson, but with Norris Williams and Charles Garland who beat them.

When in 1921 Tilden defended his singles title it produced a curious climax to the meeting. The challenger was Brian Norton of South Africa, a player who has echoed down the years as a rather controversial figure in the game. During the All Comers' singles Shimidzu beat Randolph Lycett in a unique quarter-final. Lycett, an Anglo-Australian, was a highly talented performer with essentially an individualistic approach. On this occasion this individualism extended to taking on court a supply of champagne and, some said, brandy as well. Be that as it may, it was a long, hard match on a hot day with Shimidzu winning 10–8 in the fifth set after twice being within a stroke of defeat. It seems that Shimidzu and spectators and officials needed to discipline their reactions when Lycett increasingly and distressingly showed the effect of his recourse to stimulants. Shimidzu earned high respect by the polite way in which he allowed his opponent to reel and stagger to his hazy downfall.

The latter stages of the event were exciting all

round. In the semi-finals the Spaniard, Manuel Alonso beat Shimidzu only by 8–6 in the fifth set, watched by what was the biggest crowd to date, and Norton needed five sets to get home against the American Frank Hunter. As for the All Comers' Final, Norton came from two sets behind and 2–5 in the third set to beat an exhausted Alonso.

Three weeks earlier Tilden had undergone a minor operation in Paris. In a lawn-tennis sense he was not fully fit and his only competitive practice prior to the challenge round was in the mixed doubles where, with Molla Mallory, he was beaten in the third round. No one was surprised when Norton won the first set and then the second. Tilden by then looked tired and spent. Even so he began the third set with a hint at last of sparkle.

At the same time a section of the crowd began to shout contemptuous remarks at Tilden. The reaction came not from Tilden but from Norton. He was known to be a friend of Tilden's. Contemporary critics were clear enough on that point. Since in that day and age no reference was made to Tilden's homosexuality the sort of relationship they were hinting at is far from clear. It is certain, though, that Norton, upset, made no real effort to win either the third or fourth sets, which were easily taken by Tilden for the loss of only one game. It became a real match again in the fifth set where Norton had the first vital lead at 4–2. He was brought back to 4 all but none the less was in front again at 5–4, with Tilden serving. The American fell to 30–40 and played a shot which he seemed to think was out but which was assessed by the linesman as having clipped the outside of the line. Norton's return was definitely an error. There was a second match point for Norton but this time Tilden's service winner was emphatic and not returned. With the next two games Tilden kept his championship. It was some years before he came back to Wimbledon.

This was the last year at the old All England Club in Worple Road. The decision to move was made in 1920 when Stanley Peach was commissioned to design the new club in Church Road. The cost, raised by issuing £50 debenture shares which, before being repaid at par, earned not dividends but Centre Court seats, was £140 000. It was a joint venture by the All England Club and the Lawn Tennis Association.

Things were changing. Even prior to the war there was murmuring that the challenge-round system was archaic. Notably the 'new' events, the mixed and women's doubles which only acquired full championship status in 1913, did not adopt it. In 1913 a poll was taken of 142 leading players. Of those who responded 68 were in favour of a 'play through' system and 46 wished to retain the challenge round. Another poll was taken in 1921. On this occasion 91 players voted for playing through and only 27 wanted to retain the challenge round. The challenge-round system at Wimbledon did not survive the move after 1921.

9
CHURCH ROAD & THE FRENCH ERA *(1922-1929)*

The first shots in the first lawn tennis championship at the All England Club in Worple Road, Wimbledon, had been struck on Monday, 9 July 1877 at 3.30 pm. Those in the 42nd tournament at the All England Club in Church Road, Wimbledon, were hit at 2 pm on Monday, 26 June 1922. The first one of all, a service, was on the Centre Court by Leslie Godfree against his British compatriot Algernon Kingscote. Mindful of the significance of the occasion, he retrieved the ball. It would have remained a museum relic to this day had it not been destroyed by moth in the course of time.

The new Wimbledon was bold in its modernity. The main court was known as the 'Centre Court' from the start, not because it was in fact in the centre but because the main court at Worple Road had logically acquired that name, now redolent with nostalgic memories. The peak capacity round the court in Worple Road had been about 7000. It was more or less double that on its new site.

There were many in 1922 who longed for the more cosy atmosphere of the All England Club as it used to be. The concrete structure was raw and harsh, as yet not covered by greenery. Inevitably there were corners where the builders had not finished and their rubbish was an eyesore. Two factors nearly made for disaster. Commander G. W. Hillyard, the club secretary since 1907, had decided on lush Cumberland turf for the Centre Court, entranced by the smoothness to be seen on bowling greens. It was entirely too soft to withstand the harsh wear of lawn tennis. Then there was the weather, the worst and wettest ever known.

It would have been difficult in any case but in that inaugural year protective tarpaulin covers were available only for the main court. The upshot was that fifteen days were required for the meeting instead of the scheduled twelve, the last matches not being staged until the Wednesday of the third week. The second week was the worst; on three successive days only eleven matches could be staged outside the protected Centre Court. One mixed doubles was put on the schedule for four days without getting played and in the end it never was because one of the pairs got tired of waiting and withdrew. Yet despite the miseries and delays the meeting was in no way a failure.

The 128 entries for the men's singles had to be whittled down from 170 applicants. That for the women's was up to 64. King George V and Queen Mary came to open the new ground and continued to pay visits. Queen Alexandra, the Queen Mother, the Prince of Wales and his brother the Duke of York added to the quality of Wimbledon as a royal occasion.

Wimbledon's keenest spectator. Queen Mary in the Royal Box

Some of the happenings during those damp fifteen days were perhaps more significant in retrospect than at the time. Arthur Gore, for instance, was beaten in the first round by an Indian doctor working in England, A. H. Fyzee. He lost 6-2 6-2 6-4. This was the last singles played by Gore, his first having been in

1888 and the championship having fallen to him three times over the years. He was 54 years old. His last singles coincided with the first played by a Frenchman, Jean Borotra, who beat F. H. Jarvis 6–3 6–4 6–4 and was eliminated in the third round by Gerald Patterson 6–0 6–1 6–3. Another Frenchman, Jacques Brugnon, also played for the first time. He lost in the fourth round to Randolph Lycett in four sets. A third Frenchman, Henri Cochet, went out in the same round to James Anderson. A fourth French newcomer, René Lacoste did not survive the first round against Pat O'Hara Wood.

These were all eminently respectable defeats. In view of later events it is worth stressing that Cochet's first victory, against the British W. C. Crawley in the first round, was after losing the first two sets. To indicate that this French quartette was to make a mark at Wimbledon is an understatement. They were to dominate not only Wimbledon but the game at large as no other band of players before or since. That, though, was in the future.

Gerald Patterson became Wimbledon's first men's singles champion after the abolition of the challenge round. 'Big Bill' Tilden did not come back to defend. Indeed, the American men's challenge was meagre. That of Australia, in contrast, was good. The men who played all finals, Patterson and Lycett in the singles, Anderson and Lycett, Patterson and O'Hara Wood in the doubles, O'Hara Wood and Lycett in the mixed, were entirely Australian in the sense that the British-born Lycett had learned the game in Australia and, in fact, declined an invitation to play for them in the Davis Cup in 1911.

Patterson regained the title he took in 1919. He was taken the full distance by Kingscote in the fourth round and by Anderson in the semi-final. He was led 2 sets to 1 by both. But Patterson's big service, despite the slow courts, pulled the big Australian through.

Lycett, having won the doubles the year before with Max Woosnam, took it with Anderson. The event had many peaks of excitement. Lycett and Anderson were eight times within a point of trailing two sets to love in the third round against Percival Davson and Theodore Mavrogordato, winning only after 73 games, 5–7 15–13 6–3 5–7 7–5. The finalists, Patterson and O'Hara Wood, survived their semi-final against Brian Norton and Roper Barrett only by 6–1 3–6 5–7 6–3 15–13 and five match points against them. That was 65 games. As to the title match, Anderson and Lycett won that 3–6 7–9 6–4 6–3 11–9, a total of 64 games and a 2–0 deficit.

The Australian dominance of 1922 was replaced by American in 1923. The big three players from the United States were 'Little Bill' Johnston, Frank Hunter and Vincent Richards. The last, 20 years old, had been known as a 'boy wonder' and won the London Championship immediately before the start of Wimbledon. For the first and only time the acceptances for the men's singles were allowed to go beyond the tidy 128. With 133 players there were 123 first-round byes and, though it did not work out like that, there was a possibility of the champion playing eight matches.

In the event Johnston, with his fine forehand drive, won seven matches for the loss of only one set to make himself champion. He disposed of Richards in the fifth round. The Irish Davis Cup player, Cecil Campbell, who met him in the quarters, was his most successful rival. He met his compatriot Hunter in the final and his precise play brought him an easy victory for the loss of only four games. It was not one of Wimbledon's greatest finals.

The Frenchmen were again over although Cochet was missing. Both Lacoste and Borotra got as far as the last sixteen, Lacoste, after leading 2–0, losing to Campbell and Borotra going out in four sets to the South African Norton. Brugnon was the victim of Richards in round four.

Lycett, astonishingly, won the men's doubles for the third time. It was astonishing because it was with his third different partner, this time the British Leslie Godfree. The final was won against the Spaniards, Eduardo Flaquer and Count de Gomar, on a very hot day after both pairs had survived some exhausting rounds; it was notable for the high proportion of lobbing.

This was the last year the meeting carried the resounding but unnecessary official description as the 'Championships of the World on Grass Courts'. This was the outcome of the formation of the International Lawn Tennis Federation and was first applied in 1913. Its loss was the price insisted on by the United States for at last joining the world's governing body; they were very sensitive about the status of their own national championships. But so far as Wimbledon was concerned the titles had sounded a little vulgar and were discarded without regret.

It was ironic that 1924, the first post-war year when the women's events were not dominated (because of illness) by Suzanne Lenglen, should mark the inception of an unbreakable authority by the men of France which lasted half a dozen glorious years. The 'four musketeers', Borotra, Cochet, Lacoste and Brugnon, embodied the golden age of lawn tennis. Nothing like them existed before. Nothing like them has existed since. All were great players, each in a different way, and all were great personalities. They enraptured Wimbledon.

There were ten years between them. The oldest was Jacques Brugnon, known as 'Toto', a Parisian born in 1895. He was a good, useful singles player at the top level but not more. At doubles he was a genius. Jean Borotra, a Basque, was born in 1898. If anyone can be said to have created the serve-volley game it was he. His volleying was acrobatic and unique. His backhand volley was especially a killer and on the backhand he hit the ball with the same face of the racket as on the other side. He was, I daresay, more popular in Britain than in his own country and nowhere was he more popular than at Wimbledon.

A beret was his insignia. When he donned it, it was a signal that he was hard pressed and about to launch his major effort. It was also a signal for the crowd to rise to their feet and applaud him, even if he were opposed to a British player. Borotra learned to play on the emotions of the crowd as if he were a conductor with an orchestra at his bidding. He used this theatrical ability to help him in his matches. Laurie Doherty would have looked askance at his exhibitionism.

While Borotra was idolised, Cochet, a Lyonnaise born in 1901, was loved, by his opponents as well as the crowd. He was individualistic in his style of play to the *n*th degree. He had hardly any swing back. He merely caressed the ball with abbreviated motion and used the half volley as a routine shot. He looked lazy and half asleep and yet he had a magic touch. He could win brilliantly, breathtakingly; he could equally lose ridiculously to men far below his basic skills.

René Lacoste, a Parisian and the youngest—born in 1905—was the only one of the four that more mundane performers might presume to imitate with profit. His theory—with Lacoste theory tended to come first, with ideas being put into practice after he had studiously worked things out—was based on the superiority of baseline play against the volley. It was more or less an outmoded conception in his day and, among men, would meet with scant support today, but Lacoste made it work. His superb ground-shot control gave him the highest honours in the game.

From 1924 to 1929 the singles at Wimbledon went to none but one of the four musketeers and in only one of the years was the losing finalist from outside that band. The men's doubles went to them three times, first to Borotra and Lacoste and then twice to Cochet with Brugnon. In two subsequent years, Brugnon won with Borotra.

Norman Brookes, 46 years old and a long way from his last success in 1914, was in the lists in 1924. He survived three rounds, including a win against the American, Hunter, before losing to the Belgian Jean Washer. The American challenge that year included Vincent Richards, Norris Williams and Watson Washburn but only Williams got to the last four. Lacoste, after nearly losing in the second round to the Spaniard, Manuel Alonso, put Williams out in the semi-final. Borotra progressed to the final without major travail and, beating Richards in the quarters, brought down the South African, Louis Raymond, in the semi-finals.

The first all-French final went to five sets and yet, of that ilk, was about the quickest ever played. Borotra not only hustled in the rallies with his electric volleying but he hustled between the games. Borotra won 6–1 3–6 6–1 3–6 6–4 and the 42 games lasted only 75 minutes. In modern matches it is a safe estimate that most contests of that distance would occupy 18 minutes in changing ends.

The serve-and-volley tactics of Borotra were spectacular and physically exhausting. It was universally assumed that no man could sustain such tactics over long. Borotra adopted the policy of volleying like a demon for one set, resting for a second, volleying to take the third and then recuperating once more in the fourth in preparation for the renewed onslaught in the fifth. The assumption that it was physically impossible to serve and volley throughout five sets was universal. (Equally it was then assumed that the four-minute mile was impossible. The Australian, Roy Emerson, did more than any player to abolish the illusion in later years just as Roger Bannister shattered the psychological barrier over the four-minute mile.)

Cochet was not at Wimbledon in 1924. In doubles Brugnon paired with Paul Feret but went down in five sets to the eventual champions in the second round. Borotra and Lacoste were in harness but they did not get beyond the first round and the American combination of Williams and Washburn. It was another American pair who won the title, Richards and Hunter, who beat them in the final after Williams had served for the match in the fourth set.

In 1925 the conquest by France was entire. Had Elizabeth Ryan not shared the women's doubles with Mlle Lenglen all five titles would have ended across the Channel. Three out of the last four places in the men's singles belonged to France, the only intruder being the Australian James Anderson. This was the second year of the national seeding whereby up to four players of the same nationality, if nominated by their association, were guaranteed to fall into different quarters of the draw. This seeding could not deter a clash beyond the semi-final and Borotra and Cochet met at that stage. In the round before Cochet involved himself in one of those cliff-hangers which made him so unpredictable and entrancing a player. The American, John Hennessey had the lead two sets to nil.

Against Borotra the dreamy Cochet, despite a better record on hard courts against him, could not sustain a lead of a set and 4–2, 40–15, in the second. The match swung round at this point, Borotra tightening his game enormously and Cochet falling to pieces. In the other semi-final Lacoste, who worried Anderson with a chopped forehand, beat the man who had defeated Brugnon in the round of the last sixteen despite two sets to love against him.

In the Lacoste versus Borotra final the defending champion suffered, as he did throughout his long career, for his foot faulting. As he served he tended to drag his right foot over the baseline. It would be a footfault today. Then, when even to swing over was illegal, it was doubly so. When so checked Borotra usually was at pains to ask the footfault judge to explain his misdemeanour. It almost became a ritual. Borotra also suffered from the application of another of the more esoteric rules. He lost a point in the second set for volleying the ball on the wrong side of the net. Down by two sets to love he recouped in the third set and led 4–1 in the fourth. He failed to sustain the recovery and Lacoste avenged his defeat of the year before. It had been a much slower affair all round.

The men's doubles was close to being an all-French final also. It did not work out like that because Brugnon and Cochet were put out in the semi-final by the Americans Hennessey and Raymond Casey over four surging sets. Borotra and Lacoste replied like true Frenchmen. Crucially they won the second set after trailing 2–5 to lead two sets to nil, a vital insurance as they had to yield both the third and fourth before clinching the title in the ninth game of the fifth.

Borotra, who won the mixed with Mlle Lenglen,

The Jubilee Medallists of 1926. Reading from left to right, *Back Row*: R. T. Richardson, J. T. Hartley, P. F. Hadow, M. J. G. Ritchie, C. P. Dixon, S. H. Smith, F. L. Riseley, R. Lycett, A. W. Gore, H. Roper Barrett. *Middle Row*: Sir H. W. W. Wilberforce, Hon P. Bowes-Lyon, W. Baddeley, H. Baddeley, L. A. Godfree, M. Woosnam, C. E. Weldon, J. Pim, W. J. Hamilton, F. O. Stoker. *Front Row*: Miss M. Watson, Mrs G. W. Hillyard, Miss L. Dod, Mrs A. Sterry, Mrs R. Lambert Chambers, Mrs A. C. Geen, Mrs D. R. Larcombe, Mrs L. A. Godfree

was heavily occupied as a triple finalist. Because of that, the meeting did not finish until the third Monday. This was the first year a qualifying competition was held.

There were celebrations in 1926, the jubilee of Wimbledon. The first meeting was staged just 50 years before. Before the 46th championship meeting got under way ceremonial tribute was paid to the half century of lawn tennis history that was involved.

On a red carpet in the middle of the Centre Court, King George V and Queen Mary held the centre of the stage. The current competitors were massed beyond either baseline. Paraded down the sidelines were the champions, old and new, as many as could be mustered. They were awarded commemorative medals in order of seniority as champions. Pride of place was taken by P. Frank Hadow, the unbeaten champion of the second meeting in 1878. He was 71 and this was the first time he had been back. The first champion, Spencer Gore, had been dead for twenty years. But the first woman champion, Maud Watson, the winner in 1884, was present. She was 63. Jean Borotra, one of the newest champions, made a spectacular late entrance. He had flown from Paris that morning, driven hot foot to Wimbledon, changing on the way, and appeared on the court complete with rackets and ready to play! He justified his extrovert display by his performance.

Lacoste was ill and did not defend his singles. Had he done so it is probable the last four of the men's singles would have been entirely French. As it was France took three of the places, held by Borotra, Cochet and Brugnon and the only intruder was the American Howard Kinsey. The semi-finals were enthralling. The defences of Kinsey, who came from St Louis and who turned professional later in the year, prevailed against Brugnon, but only just. Brugnon was denied five match points in the sixteen games final set. The old and familiar rivals, Borotra and Cochet, had a five setter also and it was Borotra who recouped a deficit, coming from a leeway of two sets to one before winning 7–5 in the fifth. Borotra volleyed happily against the spin of Kinsey in the final and won in three sets to take the singles for the second time.

The men's doubles held special interest. This was the year that the Duke of York, who became King George VI, entered with Wing Commander Louis Greig. They were both in the Royal Air Force. In the first round they were drawn against an old time pair, Gore and Roper Barrett and a good deal of thought was put to its scheduling, for a balance had to be struck between being fair to the participants and satisfying the popular interest aroused by such a contest. It was staged on Court Two, a compromise between being fair to the players and the dangers of holding it on a court without spectator facilities. The future king, a left hander, was outplayed, Gore and Barrett winning 6–1 6–3 6–2. The Duke afterwards confessed to the referee, Frank Burrow, that he feared the Wimbledon standard was rather too good for him. He was neither the first nor the last player to feel like that.

Gore and Roper Barrett were hardly youngsters (58 and 52 in fact and doubles champions nineteen years earlier). They did not go on to win the title and doubtless hardly expected to do so. Cochet and Brugnon were the victors, the most telling opposition being in the last sixteen when they won against Borotra, playing with L. J. Aslangul, by 8–6 in the fifth set. Kinsey was fated to be a losing finalist for the second time. He and Vincent Richards won only one set in the last match, one of humdrum standards.

It is not unreasonable to claim that 1927 was the most momentous year in the history of the game, not only at Wimbledon but elsewhere. The Australian, French and American Championships were all more than normally dramatic. France, beating the United States, won the Davis Cup for the first time. Events at Wimbledon have been a talking point among enthusiasts ever since. It was the first year of full-merit seeding. For the men's singles the order was:

1. R. Lacoste (France)
2. W. T. Tilden (USA)
3. J. Borotra (France)
4. H. Cochet (France)
5. T. Harada (Japan)
6. L. Raymond (South Africa)
7. J. Brugnon (France)
8. J. Kozeluh (Czechoslovakia)

The weather was awful, almost as bad as it had been in 1922. The meeting did not end until the third Tuesday. Yet what a tournament it was!

The return of Tilden was a major point of interest. His dominance of the American game was overpowering or, rather, it had been until the previous year when Cochet beat him at Forest Hills, his first loss in the US Nationals since 1919. At this stage of his career he was still unbeaten in a live singles in the Challenge Round of the Davis Cup. Wimbledon had not seen him since his precarious but successful title defence in the last of the meetings at the Worple Road ground in 1921. He was 34.

A novelty this year was a starting time of 1 o'clock on the opening Monday, the object being to complete all 64 first round men's singles matches. Since the day was fine—the only day that was—this tidy endeavour by referee Frank Burrow worked in copybook fashion.

The seeding was shown to be less than perfect at the same time. The first seeding upset of Wimbledon's history came in the opening round when the Japanese Takeichi Harada was beaten by Pierre Landry of France. The South African Louis Raymond lost to the British George Crole-Rees in round two but all in all the first time seeding was not much amiss and six of the official favourites reached the last eight. It was, for the first time, a last eight without a British player.

The reduction to the last four left Tilden and three Frenchmen, Cochet, Lacoste and Borotra. Cochet had the most adventurous quarter-final. Against the unseeded Frank Hunter of America he lost the first two sets 3–6 3–6. This was a dreamy sort of loss. There was a rain interruption. Cochet then had a dreamy sort of win, taking the next three sets 6–2 6–2 6–3.

The semi-finals poised Cochet against Tilden, Borotra against Lacoste. Cochet's victory over Tilden was a classic episode in the history of the game.

What Cochet did was not only to haul back to victory after losing the first two sets but to recover when the situation was such that a sweeping American victory looked absolutely certain. Tilden's superiority in going to 6–2 6–4 5–1 was complete. At that stage in the third set Tilden had lost only two points in three service games. Cochet was serving in the seventh game and he lost a point to be 15 all. He took the next three points. With the score standing at 5–2 in his favour Tilden had his service to come. Four devastating cannon balls were expected. Instead of which came nothing but American frailty. A strong-armed Tilden was transformed into ineffectiveness. He lost that game to love, and the next and the next. By then the score was five games all and Cochet as much alive as he had seemed dead. When the Frenchman went to 30–0 in the next game he won his seventeenth consecutive point. He came up from 1–5 to 6–5 for the loss of two points only. Cochet won the set 7–5 by taking Tilden's service to deuce.

The victory that never was. The score sheet of the third set of Tilden v Cochet semi-final 1927

EVENT

MATCH Cochet v Tilden

UMPIRE H. T. PARRY

SET No. 3

Game	Received Odds	Servers	Initials	Owed Points Owe 40 30 15	Strokes	Games Won By
1	4,5 sixths	C				T 1-0
2	1,2,3,4,5 sixths		T			T 2-0
3	5 sixths	C				C 2-1
4	2,3,4,5 sixths		T			T 3-1
5		C				T 4-1
6	3,4,5 sixths		T			T 5-1
7	4,5 sixths	C				C 5-2
8	1,2,3,4,5 sixths		T			C 5-3
9	5 sixths	C				C 5-4
10	2,3,4,5 sixths		T			C 5-5
11		C				C 6-5
12	3,4,5 sixths		T			C
13	4,5 sixths					
14	1,2,3,4,5 sixths					
15	5 sixths					
16	2,3,4,5 sixths					
17						
18	3,4,5 sixths					

SET WON BY Cochet 7 GAMES TO 5

The rest of the match was a desperate battle. Tilden double faulted quite a lot. He never again found his earlier sweeping aggressive pressure and though in the fifth set he led 3–2 with his service to come, he had passed the point of no return some time before. Cochet won the match 2–6 4–6 7–5 6–4 6–3 in one hour and forty-five minutes.

For years the question was asked, 'Why did Tilden let Cochet off the hook?'—for that was how it seemed to spectators. It was said that Tilden decided deliberately to spin out the end of the match because he wanted the kudos of a more spectacular finish when the King of Spain would have arrived in the Royal Box. He wrote himself, 'Personally I have no satisfactory explanation. All I know is my co-ordination cracked wide open and I couldn't put a ball in court.'

The other semi-final went the full distance also, this more by tactical design. Borotra beat Lacoste 6–4 6–3 1–6 1–6 6–2. An all-out volleying attack gave Borotra the first two sets. He stayed at the back of the court for the next two. Having thus 'rested' he attacked again and won. It was as simple as that and typical of Borotra's technique.

In the third all-French final in four years Cochet and Borotra brought the meeting to a crescendo of excitement. Borotra was perhaps at his most theatrical, donning a new beret at the end of every set. Cochet, a man who could seemingly play without effort, was at his most tantalising. Borotra, getting an early service break in each, won the first two sets 6–4 6–4. Cochet's ground strokes began to take increasing toll against Borotra at the net. He won the third set from three all. The fourth he took from 2–4. In the fifth Borotra resumed his victory course and led 5–2.

Cochet, serving, was advantage point down in the next game but on this match point Borotra netted his service return a little tamely. At 5–3 Borotra served for the match. At 40–30 he double faulted. Then he reached advantage for a third match point. A volleying exchange ensued and Cochet's first shot, a backhand, was thought by some to be a double hit. The umpire quickly ruled that the ball was good. But a dramatic game was not yet done. Borotra had three more advantage points. He put a volley out. A forehand passing shot from Cochet clipped the line. Borotra volleyed out again. That was six chances Borotra had had in all. He had no more. His momentum slackened. Cochet took the next three games for the loss of three points to win the match 4–6 4–6 6–3 6–4 7–5.

There was never a championship won like that before. Cochet's first singles title was the outcome of 'brinkmanship' of a degree not seen before and not quite to the same extent since. In his last three rounds this genius of a touch player, who gave the impression of playing with his eyes shut, won after losing the first two sets in every match, from 1–5 in the third set of the semi-final and from 2–5 and six match balls in the fifth set of the final.

Franco-American rivalry was the leitmotiv of the singles and America had the worst of it. Franco-American rivalry was equally the climax of the men's doubles. A memorable doubles final marked the extension of the tournament to the third Monday. The holders, Cochet and Brugnon, were challenged by Tilden and Hunter and it was Cochet's fate to be hoist on his own petard. He and Brugnon led 6–1 6–4 and Cochet served for the match at 5–4 in the third set. He had two match points and lost the game. He also dropped his service the next time he served, allowing the Americans to take the set 8–6. Tilden and Hunter went on to win 6–3 6–4. Accordingly the unpredictable Cochet, having won the singles title after being six times within a point of losing it, lost the doubles title having been twice within a point of taking it.

A year later the dominance of the French was stronger than ever. They had five in the last eight. A newcomer was Christian Boussus, who beat Brugnon in the quarters before losing to Cochet in the semi-final. Borotra was another quarter-final casualty. He lost at that stage to Tilden who, as in 1927, alone prevented the French from making a clean sweep of the last four places.

Tilden lost to Lacoste in the semi-final to prove, as the Frenchman had done in the Davis Cup in Philadelphia, that generalship could thwart the big guns of the American. Lacoste had to tax Tilden's stamina and mobility to get his win which was by a score of 2–6 6–4 2–6 6–4 6–3. Lacoste won one game less and seven fewer points than the man he beat.

This was Lacoste's finest spell. Cochet played badly against him in the final and the diligence of Lacoste was rewarded with his second Wimbledon championship. He was not robust and because of ill health he did not play again.

As for the doubles, Brugnon and Cochet won again. The tricolour again flew proudly over Wimbledon. As in 1927 there was no British survivor in the last eight of the men's singles, though H. W. Austin significantly took Lacoste to five sets in the fourth round with ground strokes that were almost as precise and controlled.

There was one more year before the French grip on Wimbledon was relaxed. Borotra had already won the singles twice and so had Lacoste. In 1929 Cochet had his second singles win. It was not, as in 1927, an awesomely breathtaking performance. He showed the cool efficiency of an expert throughout. He played five sets only once, in the third round against the tall, very Irish George Lyttleton Rogers. He tamed Tilden, short of his best that year, in a surprisingly one-sided semi-final. His final victory was over Borotra, also in three straightforward sets. It was Borotra's fifth final in six years.

In the semi-final Borotra beat Austin, the precursor of many a notable battle between them. Austin's fourth-round survival against his fellow Briton, Charles Kingsley, was notable for coming from a 0–40 match point situation in the 11–9 fifth set. This was Austin's fourth challenge and his most successful to date. Even more significantly from the viewpoint of British prestige it was the first challenge by Fred Perry. He won two rounds with some difficulty and lost to a fellow Middlesex player, John Olliff. At that time Perry, was, it seemed, a ridiculously daring performer with a risky forehand taken on the run that screamed for its perpetrator to be beaten.

A notable American pair won the men's doubles, Wilmer Allison and John van Ryn. They beat Tilden and Hunter, 1927 champions, in the semi-final having put out Cochet and Brugnon, the winners of 1926 and 1928, in the round before. Patriotic hopes ran high in the final which was reached by Colin Gregory and Ian Collins and they were not dashed until Gregory lost his service in the ninth game of the fifth set.

It was not then apparent but the dominance of the French at Wimbledon had ceased. For six successive years the men's singles winner was a Frenchman. For five out of the six the losing finalist was French as well. Cochet, Lacoste and Borotra made up the team that so captivated spectators with skill and personality that the period of their domination has come to be known as the golden age of the game. The fourth of the 'Four Musketeers' was Toto Brugnon, whose skill at doubles was legendary and whose attacking lob has probably never been equalled.

Wilmer Allison and John Van Ryn after their doubles triumph in 1929

10
THE THIRTIES: GREAT BRITAIN TRIUMPHANT (1930-1939)

When the Championships began in 1930 it would have been a bold prophet who declared that the years of French domination had ended, that in singles the heroic exploits of the 'musketeers' belonged to the past; it would have been a bolder one to affirm that an American of 37, ten years away from the first of his championships, would win for the third time. That Big Bill Tilden was among the greatest players of all time has always been an acknowledged fact of lawn tennis and he has mostly been graded among the firsts. He was short of his best when he won Wimbledon in 1919 and 1920. His Davis Cup record indicates he was past his best in 1927, the year he returned to Wimbledon. Neither in that year, nor in 1928, nor 1929, could he get beyond the semi-final and a Frenchman.

There was nothing in 1930 to indicate that Tilden might do better. He suffered an unusual setback on his tour of the Riviera early in the year. At the Carlton Club tournament at Cannes he was beaten (9–7 8–6) by the looped drives of Eric Peters. The latter, who many years later was a member of Wimbledon's Management Committee, was the only Englishman to beat Tilden.

Henri Cochet, seeded number one as the defending title holder, and Jean Borotra, who was seeded number three, were the Frenchmen on Tilden's tail. To put it like that is, of course, to exploit hindsight knowledge. Rather it was that Tilden and Borotra were on the tail of the incomparable Cochet, whose manifest genius had been displayed in his own championships not long before. He had beaten Tilden in the final, Tilden having beaten Borotra in the round before.

Such was the expectation at Wimbledon but this was frustrated by the intrusion of the Texan, Wilmer Allison. He was more renowned as a doubles than a singles player but he upset the official seeding in the first round by beating the eighth choice, the Australian, E. F. Moon. He met Cochet in the quarter-finals and won in three sets, playing consistently while his opponent's expected recovery never materialised. Allison's victory momentum was maintained in an all-American semi-final against John Doeg (then third in the US ranking list, four places higher than Allison) and the Texan projected himself into the final unseeded. It was nearly a quarter of a century before any other unseeded man did as well.

The best any Englishman did in 1930 was to reach the last eight. That was achieved by the Yorkshireman, Colin Gregory. To do so he beat Fred Perry, then 21 years old, held by some to be a player of high promise, by others to have a hopelessly suicidal forehand. In the third round Perry beat the Italian, Baron H. L. de Morpurgo, the sixth seed, to record his first substantial success.

Tilden found no problems in beating Gregory and came through to a semi-final against Borotra. It was a clash between the two most dominating personalities in the game. Each was well used to exploiting the mood and tension of the crowd to his own advantage. Tilden had actually tried to make a career in the theatre, without success. Borotra had the knack of being able to impart drama to the simplest situation, like changing ends or walking on to the court. His lawn tennis style was unorthodox. There was no stroke in the game of which Tilden was not the master. But he was 37 years old. Borotra was 31.

There had been six important clashes between them. The first was in the Davis Cup challenge round in 1925 in Tilden's native Philadelphia when, in the opening singles, the tall American was hard pressed to win. Borotra led two sets to one and served for the match at 6-5 in the fourth set. He never got so close again. (As Tilden's genius dimmed with the years, one Frenchman, Cochet proved his mastery—at that stage the current tally was 6-2 in Cochet's favour. Another Frenchman René Lacoste, retired from the game owing to ill health, had also had the better by 6 to 2 of their important meetings.)

But with Borotra, Tilden had been more at ease. Indeed, in matches that mattered he never lost. It was a psychological advantage that clearly helped Tilden enormously in their memorable semi-final, acclaimed as the best match played thus far at the All England Club's new site.

Borotra started meteorically. Forcing a tremendous pace he won the first set 6-0. Undeterred, Tilden kept steadily to the back of the court, knowing that the intensity of the fireworks could not last. He won the second set 6-4. Yet Borotra was a long way short of burning out. He won the third set by the same score. Having thus got the lead again he made a tactical submission of the fourth set after losing two service games and Tilden took it 6-0. In the final set Borotra leaped forward once more. He got to 3-1. He could not maintain the lead. In the eleventh game, Tilden, a cool defender against acrobatic French volleying, broke again to get in front and then served to win at 7-5.

In the meantime Allison took five hard sets to survive against Doeg. The final produced no surprise. Tilden commanded it very much as the senior American. At the age of 37 he was champion for the third time.

Arthur Gore played through to win the men's singles in 1908 when he was 40 years old. Tilden stands as the second oldest champion. One must hail Tilden's performance as the better for it was achieved from a vastly stronger field. He never came back to Wimbledon and this outstanding player retired as champion. He turned professional at the end of the year.

The weight of the American game at the 1930 meeting matched that of the French of 1925 when four and a half titles went across the Channel. Allison and van Ryn took the men's doubles for the second time. The two women's events went to the US. Were it not that the Australian, Jack Crawford, shared the mixed with Elizabeth Ryan all five titles would have belonged to America. A point about 1930, though, was that apart from the mixed doubles, the finalists in the other four events were exclusively American.

As a footnote to the 1930 meeting is added here the curious adventure had by Allison (who won the US singles in 1935) when, later in July, he went with the US Davis Cup side to Paris. A week before losing the challenge round to France (as had also been the American fate in three previous years) the US beat Italy in the Inter-Zone final. Allison's opening singles win against Georgio de Stefani was measured 4-6 7-9 6-4 8-6 10-8. Its remarkable course seems never to have been adequately recorded. Stefani led 5-2 (and also 6-5) in the fourth set. He also led 5-1 (and also 8-7) in the fifth set. The ambidextrous Italian had eighteen match points in all.

Having had its second oldest men's singles winner with Tilden, the Championships had its second youngest with Sidney Wood twelve months later. The 1931 champion was 19 years 8 months old, less than 3 months senior to Wilfred Baddeley whose age was 19 years 5 months when he won in 1891. Wood's unique status as a champion was as the only one to get his title with a walk-over. The other finalist, Davis Cup team mate Frank Shields, hurt his knee in beating Borotra in the semi-final and was withdrawn by the American captain.

In retrospect it can be seen that 1931 was short of being a 'vintage' Wimbledon. Tilden did not defend and nor that year did Helen Wills defend her women's crown. Yet the crowds rose to a record level. One obvious reason was the resurgence of the British game. There were two British men seeded in the singles, Perry at number five and Bunny Austin at number six. Both not only fulfilled their seeding status but another British Davis Cup man, Pat Hughes, was also among the quarter-finalists. A tally of three in the men's singles last eight was better than anything since 1923. It has not been equalled since.

Hughes occupied a quarter-final place that should have been filled by Cochet. This was the year when the Frenchman set a new record for his own unpredictability by being seeded number two and losing in the first round. He won only six games against the British Nigel Sharpe. Austin went out to Shields in the quarter-finals. Hughes lost there to Wood. Perry went through to the semi-finals and lost to Wood in turn. This muscle among the British men was a sign of things to come. Even so all the men champions for 1931 were American and Van Ryn, having won the doubles twice with Allison, paired with George Lott, a rollicking and popular mid-westerner, to take it for the third time.

There was a mystery in 1931. In the first round 'N. van Chim' and 'H. van Giao' appeared neither for the singles nor doubles in which their names were included. Frank Burrow, the referee, later wrote that they were Annamites and that he had proof of their existence. A well-known practical joker of the day, Hubert Winterbotham, a solicitor turned journalist, zealously spread the story that they had last been seen in Ashby-de-la-Zouche asking the way to Wimbledon! Did they in fact exist?

Events in 1932 were captivating. This was the year of Ellsworth Vines. When, in 1913, Maurice McLoughlin appeared at Wimbledon he was called the Californian Comet. Vines was an American meteor who flashed across the sky with such dazzling brilliance that, for about a year, all else in the game appeared in shadow. Vines, like McLoughlin, was a Californian. Like McLoughlin he will be remembered for his service. He will also be remembered for one particular delivery.

This was in the men's singles final against the British Austin. Vines stood 6-4 6-2 5-0, 40-15. Spectators watched him prepare to serve, throw the ball up. So did Austin. The tall Californian swung at the ball and it seemed to disappear. A cloud of dust rose from the service line. On that evidence the linesman assumed the service to be good. Austin did not even swing at the ball. He was unaware whether it whistled by him on the forehand or backhand. Behind him there was the familiar noise of a ball hitting the canvas. The ball flopped to the ground. The umpire called 'Game, set and match and championship' and that was that. It was probably the fastest service ever hit in the history of the game.

Not only Vines's service but his forehand was a spectacular and intimidating stroke. His power was tremendous. It is to be doubted if ever a player hit the ball harder than did Vines in his last three rounds in 1932. He got better as the championships progressed and, having only conceded a couple of sets on the way, he yielded only seven games to the Spaniard, Enrique Maier, in the quarter-final and but six in the semi-final against the Australian, Jack Crawford, before his splendid final effort against Austin.

Vines was 20 years old when he achieved his reverberating success at Wimbledon. It was his debut, probably the most striking of all time. His pace was the upshot of hitting the ball without a trace of spin, leaving no margin for error. Vines was not destined to have long life as a champion but at his peak in 1932 he produced probably the most devasting lawn tennis ever seen.

Cochet contrived another spectacular loss. Seeded first, he yielded to the Scot, Ian Collins, in the second round, a fact which made him eligible for the plate. He entered and won it, the first occasion the consolation event was taken by the official favourite. The only other plate winner with a full championship already on his record was Arthur Gore in 1903.

Austin was seeded sixth and did better than the official reckoning in getting to the final. His immaculate but rather gentle strokes notably brought down Shields, who was the third seed, in the quarter-final. Perry was seeded fourth and fared less well than he should have done; he allowed the less dynamic but more accurate Australian, Crawford, who was seeded eighth, to bring him down in the quarter-final. By now the British men's game was well out of the slough of despond. In the doubles Perry and Hughes got to the final without losing a set. But French glories were revived here. Borotra, partnering Toto Brugnon, who won the title with Cochet in 1926 and 1928, also reached the last match unscathed. There, Perry and Hughes led two sets to one to no avail, for the Frenchmen took the next two sets 7–5 7–5.

Fred Perry and Pat Hughes (foreground)

Leather-jackets were a problem in 1932. To cherish the turf on the Centre Court the better, the Wightman Cup match was staged on Court One. The crowds for the Championships continued to increase. An attendance of 24 000 on the first Thursday made for what was then a record daily figure.

It was exceeded a year later when 30 000 was reached. For the third successive year the weather was idyllic—the phrase 'Wimbledon weather' came to mean a heat wave—and frequent patronage by King George V, as well as the almost constant attendance by Queen Mary, made nearly every day a distinguished social as well as sporting occasion.

The expectation of British success at Wimbledon in 1933 was not fulfilled. It came about elsewhere with Great Britain winning the Davis Cup. When the Championships started the British men were still three ties short of taking that trophy. The weight of expectation was expressed in the seeding. Uniquely three British men were seeded in the singles. Vines, the title holder, was first. The Australian Crawford was second, and Cochet was third, Perry was fourth, Austin was sixth and Harry Lee, a fine bustling player, had the eighth position.

This assessment proved over optimistic. Only Austin reached the last eight, where he lost to Jiro Satoh of Japan, whom he beat in the semi-final the year before. Satoh was a fine and popular player, gentle and skilled. He never returned to Wimbledon for the next year he disappeared overboard from the ship bringing the Japanese team to Europe.

Lee's quarter-final place was filled by his conqueror, the big-serving American Lester Stoefen. But the major British disappointment was the failure of Perry to get beyond the second round and the South African, Norman Farquharson. He was felt to have thrown away his chances. As it happened there were two British men in the last eight for apart from Austin the unseeded Pat Hughes beat the seeded American Cliff Sutter to get as far.

These happenings, however, were irrelevant to the destiny of the championship. Hughes lost to Crawford and so did Satoh. Cochet, fulfilling his seeding expectations at last, reached the semi-final where he lost to Vines.

The last was not quite the player he was the year before. The 25 year old Crawford came to the peak of his form to win a final that was agreed by all to have been the best ever seen. Equally it had no rival to its majestic quality and sustained uncertainty of outcome until the American Stan Smith and the Romanian Ilie Nastase met in the final of 1972.

Crawford gave the impression of having stepped out of the past. He used a square topped racket. He always wore a 'cricket' shirt, with long sleeves buttoned at the wrist. Sometimes he rolled up the sleeve on his right arm, betokening an extra effort. His playing strength was the quality of his ground strokes and his backhand was markedly sliced. He was a 'classic' player. His refreshment under the umpire's chair was hot tea, with milk and sugar.

Crawford had been mercilessly out-hit when he played his semi-final against Vines in 1932. In the memorable 1933 final the American pace-making was less devastating, the Australian defence more firm. Though he did not volley a lot Vines relied heavily on the power of his service. His ability to get his first delivery into court was the barometer of his progress.

Vines won the first set in the tenth game having at one time been two service breaks in front with a lead of 5–2. The second set extended to twenty games and its long course, in which both men were like two mighty wrestlers standing toe to toe, saw not a service break, and hardly a hint of one, until the last game. Then, notably, Vines did not get a first serve into court. By taking that set 11–9 Crawford saved what would almost have been certain defeat. He could hardly have presumed to come back from a deficit of two sets to love.

The Australian momentum was maintained. There was a touch of weariness about Vines's backhand. Compared with what had gone before the third set was one-sided and Crawford took it 6–2. Then he, too, had to pause to recharge his batteries. Vines won the fourth set by the same score and after nearly one hundred minutes the outcome was as uncertain as it had been at the start.

Crawford, as he had all through, had the advantage of serving first. At four games all in the fifth set the Australian, sensing the psychological moment for a change of tactics, followed his own serve to the net. It was rare to see him press like that. It took him to 5–4. Vines served to save the match but by this stage he had given of his all and had nothing left. Crawford pressed him still from the net and Vines lost his service to love. Thus passed the championship from Vines to Crawford and the standing ovation was for both victor and vanquished.

Borotra and Brugnon won the doubles for the second year in succession in 1933. It was, in fact, the last triumphant clarion note sounded by any of the 'musketeers' at Wimbledon where they had added richly to the scene in a decade of magnificent performance. Cochet, who turned professional, played his last Wimbledon in 1933. Borotra was destined to be an enthusiastic Wimbledon competitor for many years. His last appearance in the Championships was not until 1964 and there was the non-championship veterans' event to occupy him subsequently.

Having been without a men's singles champion since 1909 and without a women's singles champion since 1926, British lawn tennis was brought to its peak of patriotic fervour, never equalled since, by taking both events in 1934. Perry and Dorothy Round, the former just over 25 and the latter just short of it, became the singles champions.

It was also a notable year in a more humdrum aspect. In 1934 both the All England Club and the Lawn Tennis Association formalised their joint control of the Championships by signing an agreement which locked their interests together. Then, as now, the greater weight in the Championships Committee belonged to the All England Club, furnishing twelve out of the eighteen members as well as the chairman, and, by custom, the secretary. Financially the LTA has more interest for the surplus from the Championship meeting belongs to the Association. The British game would be hard pressed to function without it. Ownership of the land and buildings at Wimbledon is vested in the All England Ground Company, jointly owned by the Club and the LTA.

Another feature of the 1934 meeting threatened to be serious. Many players and spectators were laid low by a debilitating, feverish condition known as 'Wimbledon throat'. No real diagnosis of what it was seems to have been made. Its cause was attributed to the use of the emergency watering system because of the drought conditions prior to the start. The tank, situated at the top of the ivy-covered tower which forms such a landmark at the All England Club, draws its supply from the near-by lake in Wimbledon Park. The groundsman, Edwin Fuller, found that the use of this water not only brought all kinds of weeds into the turf but left a crystal like deposit which had to be swept away. It was assumed that some virus carried by the crystals caused the 'Wimbledon throat'. In all five events there were 63 withdrawals, most due to the strange sickness.

The most noted sufferer was the title holder, Crawford. When he played Stoefen in the quarter-final on the second Monday it was after spending the weekend in bed and in defiance of his doctor's orders. After about thirty minutes he appeared to be in such distress that the referee, Frank Burrow, was sent for to see if the match ought to be stopped. None the less Crawford survived and came through to the final.

The victory of Perry was not only hoped for, it was generally expected as well. His brilliance as a daring and opportunist match player had been the major contribution to the success of Great Britain in the Davis Cup in 1933. Later that year Perry won the American Championship at Forest Hills, the first British player to do so since Laurie Doherty in 1903. In January he won the Australian title. In the French Championships, however, Perry had lost in the quarter-final to Stefani. Austin had gone out in the same round to the Frenchman, Christian Boussus.

Perry and Austin had between them done so well for Great Britain in the Davis Cup that a singles final between them in 1934 would have surprised no one. Perry was all dash and fire, notable for his 'running forehand', the ball played dangerously early. Austin had a beauty and symmetry of ground stroke that delighted every purist but his overhead and service power were almost non-existent. Nor did the commentators of that time fail to stress a social contrast between the two top Englishmen. Austin, it was usually stressed, was the product of Repton and Cambridge. That sort of background was then regarded as normal in the British game. Perry, it was pointed out, was the son of a Labour Member of Parliament and born in Stockport!

There was, though, destined to be no all-British final because Austin, after coming through four rounds without yielding a set, lost in the quarter-finals to the American, Frank Shields. He threatened to win all the way, taking the first two sets, leading 3–1 in the third set and by 3–0 and 5–4 in the fifth. But in the semi-finals Shields suffered a like fate against Crawford, who beat him after losing the first and second sets.

As for Perry, he made determined and irresistible progress, though not without being checked. In the first round he dropped the third set to Raymond Tuckey, member of a noted British lawn tennis family, a regular army officer and destined to find fame as a doubles man with Hughes. The American, Norris Williams, 42 years old, was an easy second-round hurdle. In the third, Perry had to cope with a dangerous opponent, the Czech, Roderick Menzel, who won the first set to love and led two sets to one. The rugged Australian, Adrian Quist, did not get a set from Perry in the next round. The American, George Lott, gave him a difficult quarter-final. Perry won 6–4 2–6 7–5 10–8, having been lucky with a line decision not to trail 3–5 in the third set and saving the fourth from 2–5.

The ivy-covered water tower: one of the distinctive landmarks at Church Road

The Perry versus Sidney Wood semi-final echoed that of 1931 when Wood beat Perry at that stage and went on to take the title. Perry revealed what an admirable and determined match player he was. He led all through and won (with a net cord shot at match point) a long, dour struggle in the fifth set.

The final, in which Perry beat Crawford 6–3 6–0 7–5, was what became known as vintage Perry! The Australian began with a lead of 3–1. The year before his immaculate strokes had humbled the fiery Vines. On this occasion he himself was devastated by Perry's dash and verve. Perry spectacularly took the next twelve games in succession, to give him the second set to love (and for the total loss of eight points only) and a lead of 1–0 in the third set. In this spell Perry made scarcely an error and was irrepressible. Crawford came back to lead 5–4, with his own service to follow, in the third set but Perry recovered and the Australian eventually lost his title on a double fault, having been footfaulted on his first service. The incident stupefied the crowd into a dazed acceptance of Perry as the first British champion for a quarter of a century.

Perry's reign over the Championships and, indeed, over the Davis Cup as well, was jauntily and ably maintained in 1935 and 1936. A young American, Don Budge, made an impact in both years by reaching the singles semi-final. A German, Baron Gottfried von Cramm, made a bigger one by reaching the final.

He won the French title in 1934. In 1935 he lost it in the final to Perry. With that win Perry made himself the first player in the history of the game to have been champion of Australia, France, Wimbledon and the United States. But every time von Cramm played he added to his reputation as the world's most immaculate player. Every stroke was copy-book. 'Correct' in style, his court behaviour was even more so. The only line decisions ever queried by von Cramm were in favour of his opponent.

There was never a doubt in 1935 about the identity of the finalists. In the quarter and semi-finals Perry beat Menzel and then Crawford to arrive in the last match having been taken to four sets three times. The German, beating the Australian, Vivian McGrath (the first of the notable double-fisted players) and then Budge, reached there with the same tally. If there were an inevitability about the joint progress to the final there was equally an inevitability about the outcome. It was a paceful match in which Perry led all the way. Von Cramm tried in vain to get a dividend from the presumed weakness on Perry's backhand and was himself brought down by Perry's greater verve and daring.

A year later, 1936, the difference in the picture was in von Cramm having beaten Perry in the final of the French Championships not long before. Perry lost one set in reaching the Wimbledon final. That was to Budge. Von Cramm lost a set to the Spaniard, Enrique Maier, in the fourth round, none to Crawford in the quarters but another to Austin in the semi-final. As for the final it was the most remarkable of its kind ever staged. In the second game von Cramm pulled a muscle in his thigh. It was many games later before the injury was detected by some spectators. The German stoically disguised his infirmity and went through the motions as though nothing were amiss. The opening game went to deuce ten times and lasted eight minutes. That augured a Homeric clash. Instead of which the match as a whole occupied less than three-quarters of an hour and Perry won it 6–1 6–1 6–0, equalling Renshaw's 1881 win against Hartley as the briefest final.

This was the summit of British success. In 1934 there were Americans in command of the men's doubles, Lott and Stoefen. In 1935 there were Australians, Crawford and Quist. In 1936 Hughes and Tuckey won an all-British final against Charles Hare and Frank Wilde. The only title to go overseas that year was the women's singles, which belonged to Helen Jacobs. But by the end of the year Perry was a professional, joining Vines who had acquired that status three years before. The curtain came down on British men's success at Wimbledon.

It was also the last year of Frank Burrow as referee. Having reached the age of 70 he retired. For eighteen years, the longest stint by any referee, he had peered from behind his half spectacles and cigar and ruled the meeting with unquestioned and able authority. He was succeeded, in 1937, by his former assistant, Hamilton Price, who had as his assistant Duncan Macaulay, destined to control Wimbledon as secretary in the years after the war.

Having had a reverberating men's singles champion for three years in Perry, the Championships had an even more booming victor in 1937 and 1938 in Don Budge. He was invincible both years, not only in singles but in men's doubles (with the Hungarian born and Californian reared Gene Mako) and mixed (with Alice Marble) as well. The red-headed Budge set new standards for ground-stroke power. His major strength was his backhand, a stroke he rolled to impart tremendous weight of shot. It was an entirely elegant and effective weapon.

Budge yielded one set in winning the singles in 1937, this to his fellow American, Frank Parker, in the semi-final. The finalist against him was, remarkably, von Cramm, twice beaten in the last two finals by Perry and this time destined to be outgunned for the third year running without the consolation of a set. Budge and Mako did not take the doubles easily. In the semi-final they trailed two sets to love to von Cramm and Henner Henkel, the latter a player not far short of his partner's calibre who was fated to be killed in the German army at Stalingrad. Hughes and Tuckey carried their title defence as far as the final.

When Budge defended his three titles in 1938 he had, by winning the French Championship a few weeks before, carved himself a distinctive niche in the game. That success had made him the first-ever winner of the 'Grand Slam'. The habit has been to date Budge's 'Grand Slam' as 1938, for indeed he did that year win all the four major titles of Australia, France, Wimbledon and the United States. But his success is more properly dated 1937–8 for it was by taking the French title in June 1938 that this giant of a player became the current holder of all four titles at the same time two belonging to 1937. He sustained this status until he failed to defend his Australian title early in 1939.

In the Wimbledon singles in 1938 Budge set new pace-making records by winning without the loss of a set. He was thrice taken to 7–5 but he never lost more than eight games in any round. The fewest he conceded was in the final and this was against Austin.

If consistency of high effort were the sole criterion then Austin would rank among the finest players of all time. He was inevitably overshadowed by the striking exploits of Perry. Yet when he came through to the final in 1938 it was his second time as finalist, his fifth as semi-finalist and his ninth as a quarter-finalist since his first challenge in 1926. Not that it was a vintage last eight in 1938. Some spark had gone. Von Cramm was missing from the field entirely. He had fallen foul of the Nazis and had been imprisoned by the Gestapo. Henkel was a semi-finalist against Austin. The Yugoslav, Ferenc Puncec had the challenge against Budge at that stage.

Budge beat Austin 6–1 6–0 6–3. It was more of a contest than had been the Austin final, against Vines in 1932. Yet it was very one-sided none the less for Budge's heavy shots made those of Austin look more light weight than they really were. Budge won a total of 129 games in the singles. His opponents garnered only 48. In the doubles Budge and Mako lost one set in the final against the German Davis Cup pair, Henkel and G. von Metaxa, the latter formerly Austrian in his allegiance. This was the only set won against Budge in any of the three events, for he and Miss Marble were unscathed in the mixed. This mighty player was the first man to make himself triple Wimbledon champion. Uniquely he did it two years running.

The meeting of 1938 saw all five titles go to the United States. It was the same in 1939 when both Miss Marble and Bobby Riggs were triple champions. It was a successful meeting save that the shadow of obviously impending war hung over everything. In Riggs the meeting had perhaps its cheekiest and most confident winner. Other champions may have backed themselves to win but of a certainty Riggs was the first to try to back himself to win all three titles. In the event the bookmaker would quote him only for the singles.

Austin was the top seed. He made himself a quarter-finalist, this for the tenth time, but was whittled out by the American Elwood Cooke. Then, as he had been for some years, Austin was much occupied in the Campaign for Moral Rearmament. Cooke went on to beat Henkel to make for an all-American final against Riggs. The latter emulated another Californian, Vines, in winning Wimbledon at his first attempt.

Riggs was too obviously self-confident to be a popular champion as Budge had been. He was a splendid all-round player, though the field from which he won was short of the finest. In a dull final he recovered from a leeway of two sets to one. Cooke was his doubles partner.

Bobby Riggs, the confident champion of 1939

British players made something of a show on 8 July 1939. Hare and Wilde, as in 1936, were in the final of the men's doubles. Wilde was also a finalist in the mixed with Nina Brown, though unavailingly against Riggs and Miss Marble. It was not until 23 June 1946 that the Centre Court was again in use.

11 THE INCOMPARABLE SUZANNE (*Women* 1919-1926)

One of the most momentous happenings in the history of the Championships was the arrival in 1919 of Suzanne Lenglen. She was skilled as a player. She moved like a ballerina and her dresses were daringly short for those days. Her vivid, compelling and tempestuous Gallic temperament created an appeal that made the name of Suzanne a byword.

All this was immediately apparent in 1919. The precocious skill of this young French player was well known in 1914 and her failure to compete that year had been a matter of disappointment. The overwhelming genius of Suzanne, her awesome invincibility over the years, was as yet not known. This unique player arrived for her first Wimbledon challenge at the age of 20. She was accompanied by her father who had been a professional racing cyclist. Her prowess on the Riviera had been remarkable; she had won every event for which she entered without losing a set.

She had not, though, played on grass. She was expected to do well but the Wimbledon test in 1919 was to be against, as far as could be assessed, the finest player in the history of the game, Dorothea Lambert Chambers, seven times Wimbledon champion. It seems odd at this distance of time that there could be serious speculation about the merits of a 20-year-old player and one twice that age. But the powers of Mrs Lambert Chambers at the age of 40 should not be underestimated. When she was nearly 47 she won both a singles and a doubles in the Wightman Cup on the only occasion in the first 50 years that Britain won the trophy in the United States. Not that reference was made to the age of the defending champion in 1919, for that would have been considered ungallant.

Lenglen *père* shadowed his daughter through the early rounds of the women's singles like Svengali with Trilby. The extraordinary high talent of Suzanne was manifest from the start. In the first four rounds she lost a total of only five games and her victims included the 1912 champion, Ethel Larcombe, whom she beat 6–2 6–1. The Californian Elizabeth Ryan, her doubles partner, held her to 6–4 7–5 in the semi-final but she won the All Comers' Final against Phyllis Satterthwaite, a notoriously sticky performer, with ease and so qualified for the challenge round without having lost a set. This was the match that lifted the women's game into the front rank of spectator appeal, a position it never subsequently lost at Wimbledon. It was the triumph of a new generation. It was the psychological breakthrough for the most impressive woman player in the game's history.

The 44 games over which the combat lasted stood in the records as the most rigorous final of the event for more than 50 years. King George V, Queen Mary and their daughter Princess Mary watched it, as entranced as any of the 8000 spectators around the court. Suzanne won by 10–8 4–6 9–7 after twice being within a stroke of losing. She also had two set points against her in the first set.

One may wonder how different might have been the course of lawn-tennis history had this marginal issue turned the other way. Forty years old or no, Mrs Lambert Chambers would have stood as an eight-times singles champion and Suzanne would not have acquired invincibility. One need not be an expert psychologist to realise that the secret of Suzanne's incredible success as a player was her confidence. Whether she could have built a like confidence had she lost and not won at her first appearance at Wimbledon is a matter of speculation.

Be that as it may, she did win, albeit adventurously. She was the more aggressive player in that she volleyed more. None the less she suffered the first set-back in that when leading 5–3 in the first set she missed a set point and, after losing three games in a row, had to save two set balls against her at 5–6. She eventually won the set without falling behind again, taking the last point with a stop volley.

In the second set, a struggle faster and more rigorous than Wimbledon had seen between women, Suzanne, falling behind 1–4, began to show signs of physical distress. Her father fortified her with sugar soaked in brandy and with renewed verve she pulled up to four games all. But the old guard had its triumph after all, for Mrs Lambert Chambers secured the next two games for one set all.

In the last set the initial recovery was reversed. Suzanne went to 4–1 and it was the defender who hauled back. Not only that, she went ahead to 5–4, only to lose her service to love. Mrs Lambert Chambers again broke service to be 6–5 and on her own delivery led 40–15. The pre-war champion thus stood with a double chance to win for the eighth time. On the first match point, Suzanne, in mid court near the net, was lobbed and, in attempting a smash, barely caught the ball with her racket producing a winner that just fell over the net. It was a fluke from the wood! On the second match point Suzanne projected a winning backhand down the line that raised the chalk. Two match points for the defender had come and gone.

Suzanne won her serve to 15 to reach 7–6; Mrs Lambert Chambers squared with the next game but it was near the end and the French challenger finished with a love game against the service. All commentators agreed that it was the finest women's match seen at Wimbledon.

Thus began a career which is unrivalled in its record of invincibility. Wimbledon's fortunes were not made by the attraction of this *belle laide*, the irresistible player from Picardy, for it was obvious in 1914 and earlier that somewhere bigger than the Worple Road site needed to be found. Her popularity, however, made a move a matter of urgency. Whether they liked it or not Wimbledon's organisers were saddled with a major show-business enterprise, far removed from the gentle sporting occasion with which the tournament had started. Until Suzanne, the women at Wimbledon, though not denied the Centre Court, were tolerated in that arena as a matter of courtesy. With Suzanne it became imperative.

In 1920 and 1921 Suzanne defended her singles in challenge rounds at Worple Road. The crowds who came to watch had no expectation of seeing her crown seriously disputed; they came to see a queen going through the formalities of crowning herself again. Mrs Lambert Chambers was again her rival in 1920 and was in splendid form. She beat the best of the Americans, Molla Mallory, 6–0 6–3 and the ubiquitous Miss Ryan 6–2 6–1 in the final. But in the challenge round she could not raise the spark of the year before or approach the already matured expertise and majestic control of Suzanne. Suzanne lost just three games. The next year she lost only two, this time to Miss Ryan.

Spectators had more value for their money from Suzanne in the doubles. In the women's doubles she and Miss Ryan were dominant for five successive years. In the mixed it was possible to find Suzanne on the losing side. In 1919 she partnered her compatriot H. Laurentz and they lost in the quarter-final to Randolph Lycett and Miss Ryan. A year later she played with the Australian Gerald Patterson and became triple champion. In 1921 she entered again partnered by a Frenchman, André Gobert, but scratched after one round. They did not get on well together and Gobert had an injured ankle anyway. The last match played in the championships at Worple Road was on 3 July 1921. It was the final of the women's doubles in which Suzanne and Miss Ryan overwhelmed Mrs Beamish and Mrs Peacock 6–1 6–2. Appropriately perhaps, it fell to Suzanne to strike the last ball, a smash that allowed no return. It was six days short of 44 years since Spencer Gore or one of his pioneer associates had hit the first ball in a notable series of championship meetings and a pastime had grown into a thriving sport.

At the new venue for the Championships in 1922 at the Church Road ground, when for the first time all events had the defending champions 'playing through', Suzanne set a record of invincibility which surprised no one then but which has not since been equalled. It stands as a record for either sex. Suzanne not only won all three events, singles, doubles and mixed to become triple champion but she did so without yielding a set in any match.

Six rounds of singles, in that wet year, gave her that event by 12 sets to nil, 75 games to 20. Five rounds of women's doubles gave her that by 10 sets to nil, 61 games to 14. Six rounds of mixed were won by 12 sets to nil, 72 games to 25. Miss Ryan was her women's partner, the Australian Pat O'Hara Wood her companion in the mixed. Suzanne played just three advantage sets in 1922, two at 7–5 and one at 8–6. Her average concession of games per set was 1·7.

Her victims in the singles included Kitty McKane, the outstanding British player who later twice won the championship. She had the distinction of forcing Suzanne to a 7–5 set. Miss Ryan in the quarter-final did even better, stretching the champion to 8–6. The final was something of a needle affair, for this was against the American champion Molla Mallory. The previous year Suzanne had made her ill-fated journey to Forest Hills. The controversial drama of what befell her there is not part of Wimbledon's story but it provided the only occasion in Suzanne's post-war career when she was beaten—if, indeed, she can be said to have been beaten. In an unseeded draw she was pitchforked soon after her arrival into her opening match in the US Championships against, of all opponents, the best in America, the Norwegian-born Mrs Mallory. Suzanne was unwell, lost the first set 6–2 and soon afterwards staggered from the court in default. When they met again nine months later Suzanne needed to rebut the American charge that she was a 'quitter' and inferior to Mrs Mallory.

The Frenchwoman took uncomprising revenge after a match that was dramatic in its brevity and the Wagnerian quality of its setting. Because of rain it did not start until one minute past seven in the evening. At 7.26 Suzanne was the winner by 6–2 6–0 after ruthless exploitation of the most vigorous pace and control from the back of the court.

A year later, 1923, Suzanne went through the singles with never a set going beyond nine games. The most games she lost were those in the final; this was against Miss McKane and the score was 6–2 6–2! The women's doubles was similarly formal, Miss Ryan again being her partner, and if the two events be taken together the French triumph was taking 22 sets for the average loss of less than 1·3 games. But there was no triple championship that year. Partnered by the Belgian, J. Washer, she lost to Lycett and Miss Ryan in the semi-final of the mixed.

Her start in the 1924 Wimbledon Championships was meteoric enough to promise the most overwhelming win of all time. In the singles it was 6–0 6–0 in both the first and second rounds. Then it was 6–0 6–0 again, this remarkably because it was against Hazel Wightman, the former US champion. Suzanne could claim another unique record in this; she took half a dozen love sets in sequence. With no pressure she and Miss Ryan won two rounds of the women's doubles and with Jean Borotra three rounds of the mixed. But she had had an attack of jaundice in the spring and it was clear that her recovery was not complete. She had difficulty in winning her quarter-

Suzanne the acrobat

final against Miss Ryan. She survived merely by 6–2 6–8 6–4. The loss of the set was noteworthy. Certainly Miss Ryan had never played better and Miss Ryan, probably more than anyone, could play the Frenchwoman with a measure of confidence. Suzanne, having pushed herself to the limit to survive, retired sick from the meeting.

The gap thus opened brought a revival of British fame. Kitty McKane, the best of the British, had the walkover against Suzanne and met an American of 18 in the final. This was Helen Wills, later to be Helen Wills Moody and, quantitatively, the greatest of all Wimbledon singles champions. The previous autumn she won the US singles for the first time. Her progress to the final was, more or less, as overwhelming as Suzanne had achieved in the past. After five matches she was one step short of the title having dropped only eleven games in five contests.

One of the most famous women's matches of all time was in 1926 at Cannes when Suzanne Lenglen beat Helen Wills 6–3 8–6. It was the only clash between the two most formidable players in the history of the women's game. But for Suzanne's illness their meeting would have been two years earlier in the final at Wimbledon—or, at least—such is reasonable to assume. That it never came about was regrettable but

Suzanne the pace-maker

none the less Suzanne's absence brought a spectacular climax to the women's championships. It would have been an even more piquant contest at the time had spectators known that they were watching the only occasion Miss Wills was to lose in singles at Wimbledon. It was a staunch win for Kitty McKane and, uncharacteristically, the American let slip a winning lead. Miss McKane lost the first set 4–6, trailed 1–4 and was four times within a point of falling to 1–5 in the second, before former British glories were reasserted with a victory by 4–6 6–4 6–4. Wimbledon did not see the remarkable Miss Wills for another three years.

In 1925, however, Suzanne was seen with vengeance. As in 1922 she became triple champion, gaining the women's doubles for the sixth time with Miss Ryan and the mixed, this time with Borotra, for the third. But she was a shade less invincible than in 1922, for she lost a set in the semi-final of the mixed. None the less, her singles record was the most shattering.

She was unlucky in the draw in that nearly all the best players were in her half—Wimbledon was still a year short of having full merit seeding. In her first match Suzanne beat Miss Ryan, who was ranked fourth best in the world that year, by 6–2 6–0. In the next she beat Elsie Goldsack, one of the leading British women, 6–1 6–0. Then she beat Mrs Beamish, British Wightman Cup player, 6–0 6–0. Next, this being the semi-final, she met the title holder Kitty McKane. Suzanne won 6–0 6–0. The finalist was another British player, Joan Fry, from Staffordshire. That was an astonishing story in itself, for Miss Fry, competing for the first time at the age of 19, valiantly burst her way through to the last match despite a county selection committee that had omitted her earlier in the year. Miss Fry was beaten 6–2 6–0.

The record, then, for the impeccable Suzanne was five matches won, ten sets won, for the entire loss of five games. She conceded two games in two matches, one in another and that was all. Miss McKane, whom she whitewashed, was, that year, ranked third best player in the world.

This was Suzanne Lenglen's last championship, for events in 1926 were curious and dramatic. The singles she had taken six times in seven years, the doubles six times also, all with Miss Ryan. The mixed she had won three times, so all in all Suzanne Lenglen recorded her Wimbledon immortality with a total of fifteen championships. Her scores in the singles finals stress her breathtaking superiority:

1919 beat Mrs Lambert Chambers 10–8 4–6 9–7
after which no rival got near
1920 beat Mrs Lambert Chambers 6–3 6–0
1921 beat Miss Ryan 6–2 6–0
1922 beat Mrs Mallory 6–2 6–0
1923 beat Miss McKane 6–2 6–2
1925 beat Miss Fry 6–2 6–0

The events of 1926, which brought an end to the incredible amateur career of Suzanne Lenglen, should perhaps be put in focus by the happenings which preceded her ill-fated swan song. There was the backcloth of her one-sided victory of the year before. On the Riviera circuit the long-awaited clash between Suzanne and the new American star, Helen Wills, had at last come about when, at Cannes, the Frenchwoman won by 6–3 8–6. Then, in the French Championships held in those days at St Cloud, Miss Wills had withdrawn with appendicitis. Here Suzanne surpassed her 1925 Wimbledon effort. She took the singles for the total loss of only four games in five matches, Miss Fry having the distinction of winning three of them in the semi-final.

Thus when Suzanne began her Wimbledon challenge in 1926 it was to a background of utter invincibility and expectation of overwhelming success. She was more than a dynamic and irresistible player. She was, *par excellence*, a prima donna, her fame and prestige extending far beyond the sporting world.

This, though, was a year when the meeting was heightened by other out of the ordinary happenings. It was celebrated as Jubilee Year with the assemblage of as many old champions as could be mustered; the Royal patronage at the commemorative ceremonies on the Centre Court was the occasion of special interest and excitement. There was more stress on Wimbledon's status as an event than on individual personality. Suzanne Lenglen proved, on this occasion, to be an embarrassment that was echoed in accounts recorded by those who shared in them.

Suzanne's 'walk out' from the Championships that year had its roots in a conflict between two strong personalities, that of Suzanne herself, and Frank Burrow, the referee. Burrow, who was certainly an efficient referee, was equally certainly an authoritarian in his office. He was not the sort of referee any player could 'push around'. Equally Suzanne was hardly a player who could be 'pushed around'. Her status in the championships was such that it had become the custom for one of the executives to escort her each day to the referee's office to be told the time she would be required on the morrow. In 1926 after she had beaten the American Mary Browne in the opening round (by 6–2 6–3) on the first Tuesday, this was not done. She left without getting in touch with Burrow. He, in due course, made out his order of play, putting Suzanne to play her second round singles on the Centre Court at two o'clock with a doubles later.

Queen Mary was in the Royal Box, doubtless as avid to see the incomparable Suzanne in action as everyone else. There was no Suzanne! She arrived at the ground at 3.30. So far as the Wimbledon executive was concerned she was an absentee and liable to be scratched from the singles.

Suzanne herself had learned from her partner, Didi Vlasto, that morning, but only that morning, that she was wanted for a singles. In vain she tried to telephone Wimbledon to tell them she wished only to play the doubles. She settled in the end for ringing her compatriot Toto Brugnon and asked him to pass on the message. This he did in due course but it seems the message was not passed to Burrow. Suzanne, arriving in what she thought was good time for just one doubles match, found herself treated not with the usual courtesy but summoned before the committee and reprimanded for being late. This was not the sort of treatment a prima donna was accustomed to; she retreated to the dressing room in hysterics.

The singles had by then been abandoned as a prospect for that day. An attempt was made to stage the doubles and in the end Jean Borotra, acting as a go-between, was deputed to penetrate the women's dressing room to cajole Suzanne into playing. He did his best but reported that his compatriot was absolutely unfit to appear. She was, moreover, insistent that when she did resume in the tournament she would play the doubles before the singles on pain of withdrawing.

Normally a singles, of course, takes precedent over a doubles in the book of any player. In this case Suzanne had a point. Her singles, against Evelyn Dewhurst, was unlikely to be difficult, at least for a player of her skill. The doubles, in contrast, had prospect of being the key match in the whole event, for Suzanne and Mlle Vlasto were opposed to the redoubtable Miss Ryan, whose capacity Suzanne knew as well as anyone, and one of the strongest Americans, Mary Browne. This was the match that was in due course played on Thursday. In the meantime, the stormy scenes at Wimbledon had been reported far and wide and lost nothing in the telling. Suzanne had kept the Queen waiting. The Queen was offended—it seems in fact she was by no means that and had been very understanding—but overnight the hint of *lèse majesté* was enough to turn Wimbledon's favourite into something of an ogress.

The doubles was played on the Thursday on a wettish sort of day. It went ill for the French pair. After twice being at match point in the second set Suzanne and Mlle Vlasto were beaten 3–6 9–7 6–2. The singles against Miss Dewhurst which should have followed was delayed by rain and not staged until the Friday. Suzanne won it 6–2 6–2.

On the Saturday Suzanne, partnering Borotra, had an easy first round in the mixed. It was put on the Centre Court and there was no welcome for Suzanne. Rather there were signs of open hostility and Borotra, as adept as anyone in using the lawn tennis court as a theatre, clowned in an effort to win the crowd to better humour. That was the last match (won against H. I. P. Aitken and Miss B. C. Brown 6–3 6–0) the incomparable Frenchwoman played at Wimbledon. Over the week-end she scratched from the singles and the mixed on the plea of sickness. It was sad that so glorious a lawn tennis career had to end in such a sorry fashion. She turned professional soon after, playing against Mary Browne, who signed a contract at the same time, and met with success in what were essentially exhibition matches. Later she opened a lawn-tennis school in Paris. Her death, in July 1938 at the age of 39, from pernicious anaemia, was as untimely as her exit from Wimbledon.

The only defeats ever suffered by Suzanne at Wimbledon were in two mixed doubles, with Laurentz in 1919 and with Washer in 1923, and in one women's doubles with Mlle Vlasto in 1926. Her record in singles was: played 32, won 32. Reduced to sets it was: played 66, won 64. Reduced to games it was: played 507, won 405. Of those 66 sets she won 59 by a score of 6–2 or better, 29 of them in fact were by 6–0.

That there was conflict at Wimbledon between Suzanne and the executive was probable, that there was misunderstanding was certain. It was the clash of an institution, already rich in tradition, against a powerful personality. Inevitably the institution survived the fuss but not without scars. Wimbledon could never but regret Suzanne's last year.

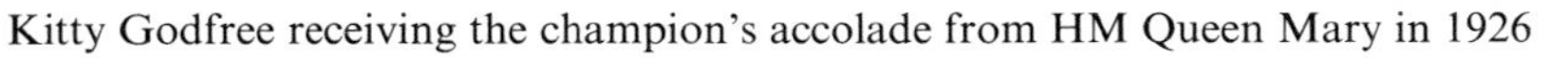

Kitty Godfree receiving the champion's accolade from HM Queen Mary in 1926

12
THE INVINCIBLE HELEN
(*Women* 1926-1939)

When Suzanne Lenglen walked out of Wimbledon in 1926 it left a vacancy that was filled by Kitty McKane—or, rather, by Kitty Godfree, whom she had by then become. For the second time in her distinguished career she wore the premier crown, this time after being opposed by a brilliant finalist. This was Lili de Alvarez, of mercurial skill and of warm personality, with a capacity to drive volley and to half volley not before seen from her sex. Not surprisingly she had a frail side to her brilliance, a liability to gross error. Three times this striking Spaniard poised herself on the brink of taking the Wimbledon singles but in each of successive years, 1926, 1927 and 1928, she lost in the final, to the grief of the crowds who adored her. She never came closer to the title than in 1926 when she had a point to lead 4–1 in the final set against Mrs Godfree, only to be worsted 6–2 4–6 6–3. In both her singles successes Mrs Godfree came back from behind, a testimony to her resolute match capacity. And in this year she pulled off another notable feat, for she and her husband, Leslie Godfree, a British Davis Cup player and noted for his doubles skill, won the mixed, a unique accomplishment for a married couple.

Helen Wills returned to Wimbledon in 1927, not having been there since her losing final in 1924. Her plan to be there in 1926 had been thwarted by appendicitis. In the first round she met Gwen Sterry, daughter of Charlotte Sterry, the champion of 1908. She won by 6–3 3–6 6–3 and the date was 21 June. The date is stressed because it was the last set lost by Helen Wills until 8 July 1933, six years later. This was not just the last set lost at Wimbledon but the last lost in a singles in any match anywhere, in the course of a period in which she won Wimbledon five times, the US title four times, the French title four times and played twelve singles in the Wightman Cup. When she did at last yield a set it was again at Wimbledon, in the 1933 final when she beat Dorothy Round 6–4 6–8 6–3.

That was one aspect of her invincibility. Her freedom from defeat in singles lasted longer still. This extended from August 1926, when she lost to Molla Mallory at the Westchester Club, Rye, New York, to her retirement, when 0–3 in the third set, in the US final on 25 August 1933, against Helen Jacobs. She retired sick on that occasion. Her first straightforward defeat was not until 14 June 1935 when she lost 6–0 6–4 to Kay Stammers on a wet court at Beckenham.

From 1927 the invincibility of Miss Wills in singles was absolute. With her it was as with Suzanne Lenglen. The question was not whether she would win, but how. In the third round in 1927 she beat Eileen Bennett, famed not only for her skill but also for her beauty, by 7–5 6–3. Not until 1933 was Miss Wills taken as far as advantage games in any set. She won 68 sets in sequence, at 6–4 or better; the strongest domination of its kind in the history of the game.

Her quality was, like that of Suzanne Lenglen's, superfine and was built on superb control of ground strokes. Extraordinarily, she was not very mobile. Indeed, for an athlete of her calibre, she was oddly immobile. But she hit hard and was free from error. She herself wrote that after losing the final in 1924 'it impressed upon me the necessity for control in concentration'. Certainly her concentration was her forte from then on and she gave the impression that a bomb exploding by the court side would not disturb her. She had the sobriquet 'Poker Face'; cool, detached, emotionless, no player deserved it more.

The women's singles from 1927 to 1930 was the first sequence of her success. In 1930 she had become Mrs Frederick S. Moody, following her marriage to a Californian stockbroker, a marriage that later ended, though not until after her lawn tennis career had finished. She missed a year and returned in 1932 when, with the total loss of thirteen games in six matches, she had her strongest success of all. In 1933 came the first hint of vulnerability, when she lost (albeit only after a controversial line decision) the middle set in the final against Miss Round. She returned in 1935 and won with difficulty, memorably being match point down in the final against Helen Jacobs. But she won none the less, that being for the seventh time. She came back, for the last time, in 1938 and again triumphed without losing a set and so gaining her eighth singles title when she was 32 years old.

Her ambition had been to beat the sevenfold success of Mrs Lambert Chambers. That record seemed impressive enough but one cannot in truth talk of the two achievements in the same breath. Three of Mrs Lambert Chambers's successes were obtained by winning just one match, the challenge round. Mrs Moody played through every time. She played 56 singles in the championships at Wimbledon and lost just one. She played 117 sets and won 111. She played 952 games and won 698.

One of the more touching incidents in the story of lawn tennis took place in 1935. On the morning of her final Mrs Moody was approached in her London hotel by an elderly lady with grey hair, grey eyes and the look of an out-of-doors *habituée*. She had come to wish her well in her coming match. She was Maud Watson, the pioneer women's champion of 1884.

The year when the redoubtable Miss Wills had her first singles success, 1927, was also a stimulating year for Britain in that Betty Nuthall made herself a quarter-finalist for the first time. She reached new dimensions as a popular British idol and was prodigiously good when young. She never showed her highest talents at Wimbledon and never at any time got beyond the last eight. Popular hopes ran high that year because, unseeded (this was the first fully seeded draw), she beat the American Molla Mallory in the second round by 2–6 6–2 6–0. Joan Fry, also unseeded, despite her prowess in reaching the final two years before, put her out in the quarter-final but was in turn beaten in the semi-final by Miss Wills.

The final, in which Miss Wills beat Senorita de Alvarez 6–2 6–4, was more exciting than the score indicates. Indeed, the Spaniard was always enthralling to watch and it was said that the rally which Miss Wills won to make the score four games all in the second set was the finest played between women at Wimbledon. About 40 breathtaking shots were exchanged, all of which drained the loser dry.

A year later, 1928, the match was repeated. Unlike her opponent, Lili de Alvarez struggled somewhat to survive to the final having been within two points of losing to Phyllis Covell in the second round. She gained one game less in the final than she had done a year earlier. She had, though, made herself a treasured memory among Wimbledon *habitués* for there was something of the divine spark about her majestic ease of shot. But she was not a rugged match winner and Lili de Alvarez flits across the pages of Wimbledon's history as three times a finalist and never a winner.

The losing finalist in 1929 was Helen Jacobs and her rivalry with Helen Wills was the major motif of the women's game for many years. She, like Miss Wills, came from Berkeley, California. The two Helens were arch rivals, Miss Jacobs, three years younger, being allowed only those prizes Miss Wills did not choose to take. It was Miss Jacobs's second visit to Wimbledon in 1929. She lost to the Australian Daphne Akhurst the year before and failed to justify her seeding at number eight. She was destined to have no like failure. Neither American looked like losing a set on the way to the final and once there, Miss Wills' victory was simple; at 6–1 6–2 it was, in fact, the most one sided of all her finals.

That year, 1929, was a landmark of sorts in lawn tennis fashion history. During the course of it, a South African, Billie Tapscott, was daring enough to play without stockings. The heavens did not fall. Nor was her temerity in any way punished and she reached the last eight. Also in the last eight was, astonishingly, May Sutton Bundy, winner of the championships 22 years earlier. Her most notable victim was Eileen Bennett, who ranked that year as seventh best player in the world.

For the first time ever no British woman was in the last four of the singles in 1930, the term British being used in the sense of belonging to the Commonwealth. That was the point made at the time when Mrs Moody, as she had now become, took her fourth

Helen Wills Moody

singles as a matter of course. It was so much a matter of course that the 6–3 6–2 by which she beat the resolute Frenchwoman, Mme Simone Mathieu, was her hardest match. Her compatriot, Bunny (Elizabeth) Ryan played her in the final and got one game less. There were many mishaps in the event that year. Phoebe Holcroft Watson, seeded number two and Britain's leading challenger, fell sick and had to scratch before the start; the ever popular Lili de Alvarez also had to pull out; the German Cilly Aussem hurt her ankle when four games all in the last set of her semi-final against Miss Ryan. The last was triple finalist and though denied the singles, this for the second time in the title match, she collected the other two championships, the women's doubles with Mrs Moody, the mixed with the Australian Jack Crawford. Miss Ryan had by now acquired sixteen Wimbledon titles.

Mrs Moody did not play in 1931 and there were hopes of a British victory. They rested mainly on Betty Nuthall, now 20 years old and very much the 'pin up' girl in popular esteem, and she was seeded second. The top seed was Cilly Aussem. The German had grace, charm but no great physical strength and, short of a British success, the eventual justification of her seeding was popular. Miss Nuthall lost to Miss Jacobs in the quarter-final and the title match was Fräulein Aussem against Fräulein Hilda Krahwinkel.

This all-German final in the women's singles stands as a Wimbledon oddity. Hilda Krahwinkel, who was then 23, was tall, long legged and could run interminably. No one could call her an exciting player but she was effective and her patient skill, with its numbing effect on both spectators and opponents, was part of the Wimbledon scene in the 1930s. As Fru Sperling —she married a Dane—she was a semi-finalist for the sixth time in 1939.

Cilly Aussem acquired her Wimbledon championship after a dreary final, dreary because both players had blistered feet. She had also won the French title that year and as something of a protégée of Big Bill Tilden she probably disappointed her mentor in not impinging more strongly on the pages of the game's history than she did. She was not robust enough to stand up to the hurly-burly of the competition over the years. Appendicitis prevented her defending her Wimbledon title in 1932 and her last effort there was in 1934 when she reached the last eight. She married an Italian, Count Della Corta Brae, and gave up lawn tennis before she was 30. The memory she left in the game was of fine and fragile porcelain.

The formalities of Mrs Moody's expertise were resumed in 1932 and it was, if measured by the number of games conceded, her most devastating year. Her total loss of thirteen games in the course of six rounds and her hardest match, the final against Helen Jacobs, was won by 6–3 6–1. Elizabeth Ryan won the mixed with the Spaniard, Enrique Maier, making seventeen championships in all. She would have had the women's doubles as well had not she and Helen Jacobs lost in the final to the French-Belgian couple Doris Metaxa and Josane Sigart.

The strength of the British women's game was displayed in 1933 when Dorothy Round, who had to learn to live with her popular description as 'the Worcestershire Sunday School teacher', reached the singles final. It was against Mrs Moody and the Californian had been less rigorously dominating than the year before, being almost hard pressed, by her standards, to win her semi-final against Fräulein Krahwinkel. Miss Round beat Miss Jacobs at the same stage to justify her status as the second seed. The final proved a patriotic occasion for although Miss Round did not win, she averted defeat in a manner which for long had seemed impossible against the all conquering Mrs Moody.

The American victory was measured 6–4 6–8 6–3. It was the first set lost by the Californian for six years and that was enough to make it a memorable occasion. It was not, though, an unalloyed British triumph for if Miss Round merited her success by the stalwart nature of her resistance the actual manner of it owed something to luck. Even so it was an exacting fight, the like of which Mrs Moody had not endured for years. The sentiments of the crowd were inflamed when Miss Round had a 40–15 chance to lead 5–4 in the first set. In the second her mixture of short and long drives continued to harass the champion and the British girl got in front 7–6. In the next game, Miss Round, serving, was 30–40, having been 15–40. On the next rally she overdrove the baseline. Or, at least, so she thought, together with Mrs Moody and the umpire, who called the score seven games all. The linesman, though, stuck to his decision of a line ball which everyone thought to be an error. The umpire acquiesced, as strictly he had to do, but the incident, coming at so vital a point, proved a terrible distraction. Miss Round got the next two points to win the set. The crowd applauded practically every shot she played in the last set but by then her concentration had been marred.

Afterwards Mrs Moody recorded that her feet became so blistered during the match that she was in bed for four days. As to the incident which brought her to the loss of a set after so long an immunity she maintained her astonishing sang-froid: 'Whatever our feelings on the court, there was hardly time to dwell on them, as the action of the match required all of our attention.'

British patriotism, having been thus stirred, was satisfied in rich measure in 1934. In the men's singles there was the victory of Fred Perry, the first home winner for 25 years. Dorothy Round matched it with the women's singles and if it were only eight years since Kitty Godfree's success in 1926 it was a quarter of a century since there had been the double triumph. Miss Round won in the absence of Mrs Moody and did so at the expense of the other notable Californian, Helen Jacobs, who was the number one seed. Miss Round had a mettlesome victory. She was taken the full distance in the fourth round by her British rival Phyllis King and by the resolute Simone Mathieu in the semi-final. She and Miss Jacobs were balanced for the title as far as three games all in the third set when Miss Round courageously plied attacking pressure by volleying. Miss Round also won the mixed with the Japanese Ryuki Miki.

The champion from Britain, Dorothy Round

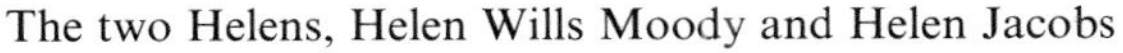

The two Helens, Helen Wills Moody and Helen Jacobs

The women's doubles fell to Mme Mathieu and Bunny (Elizabeth) Ryan, their second success in two years. This was Miss Ryan's last Wimbledon title and her nineteenth in all since she took her first, the women's doubles with Miss A. M. Morton in 1914. In the mixed she was paired with Maier, with whom she had won in 1932 but an attack of what was known as 'Wimbledon throat'—the unpleasant virus infection which took a big toll of players and spectators alike see p. 60—brought withdrawal. Miss Ryan was unlucky, then, to miss a twentieth Wimbledon title. Even so her Wimbledon career, which began in 1912, was unparalleled and her nineteen championships were gained from the outcome of 27 finals. She was 42 years old when taking her last Wimbledon title, having been 22 when she got her first. Her volleying prowess was the foundation of her unique success as a doubles player and she used it as the culminating stroke from a forehand chop. She turned professional towards the end of 1934, her last tournament success being to win the women's doubles in the Pacific South West Championships with Caroline Babcock against the British pair, Miss Nuthall and Freda James. On a conservative reckoning this was Miss Ryan's 662nd tournament win.

Miss Round could not, in 1935, carry her title defence beyond the singles quarter-final. The Australian Joan Hartigan reached the last four for the second year running when, despite the loss of the first set, she rigorously punished Miss Round's errors. But the major preoccupation of the event this year was the challenge of Mrs Moody, since the challenge was made in the context of more frailty than had ever been known. Normally Mrs Moody's 'run up' to Wimbledon had been as formal as her success when she got there. On this occasion in the final of the Kent Championships at Beckenham she lost to the British left hander Kay Stammers. The win was by 6–0 6–4 and it was Mrs Moody's first defeat since August 1926, save for her retirement to Helen Jacobs in the US final of 1933.

This novel aspect of Mrs Moody as less than an invincible player was made evident in the fourth round. Not without difficulty a little Czech girl, barely 18 years old with long flaxen hair, had crept so far. Her name was Slecna Çepkova and she was as talented as she was inexperienced. She played Mrs Moody on Court One and the American was, by her own former standards, incredibly loose and bad. Little Miss

Cepkova, with nothing to lose, played the sort of 'blinder' often seen in such circumstances and, hitting winners all round, roared happily along to lead 6–3 4–1. At that point she obviously had only to continue her uninhibited flair to win.

At the change over she looked at the scoreboard and, as she did so, it became clear that until then she had no idea what the situation was. She almost froze as she prepared to serve. From that stage, she, who had hardly hit a ball wrong, hardly hit a ball right. Mrs Moody won eleven out of the next thirteen games. Never in her career can the American have so nearly lost to a player so much below her standards. In the next round she beat Mme Mathieu in more forthright fashion and so too Miss Hartigan in the semi-final. But the final was one of Wimbledon's most dramatic affairs.

Helen Jacobs reached the last match with less perturbations than Mrs Moody. The all-Californian battle lasted 100 minutes. Both were in a familiar situation. For Mrs Moody it was her eighth singles final. Miss Jacobs had been there three times before and never with success. And on two of these occasions, 1929 and 1932, Mrs Moody had beaten her drastically. For ten years they had been keen rivals and on the only occasion Miss Jacobs looked like satisfying her ambition with a victory, the final of the US Championships in 1933, the other Helen had taken away the savour by retiring.

Partisanship among the crowd was divided. As the match progressed both sides had cause for feeling happy. Mrs Moody won the first three games of the match, but trailed 0–40 for a 3–4 deficit, having lost 11 points running, before she pulled the set round. Mrs Moody tried to volley more in the second set but was often passed. She lost the initiative and Miss Jacobs, always the more flexible set player, squared the match by taking the second set. In the third the momentum of Miss Jacobs's success carried her along, apparently irresistibly. She served the more strongly and volleyed effectively and her aggression took her to 5–2. She had match point in the next game on her own service and from near the net she needed only to put away the shortest of short lobs—Mrs Moody had been able merely to scrape the ball back—to take the championship. As Miss Jacobs shaped to smash, a gust of wind deflected the ball a trifle; she mistimed her stroke and put the ball into the net. She played the rest of the match in a kind of mild stupor and in the last game had to be reminded that it was her turn to serve. Mrs Moody won the game, her fifth in succession, to take the crown for the seventh time having been within one lucky (for her) shot of seeing it go elsewhere.

Dorothy Round was the top seed for 1936 but expectation of another British triumph in the absence of Mrs Moody was not fulfilled. Her downfall came curiously, in the quarter-final when she lost to Fru Sperling. This was on Court One and the manner of it a reflection of what now seems prudish overtones. Miss Round was in some distress when in the course of a match that was bound to be difficult anyway, she broke the strap of her 'bra'. It was not the sort of repair that could be done on court and somewhat embarrassed, she asked the umpire if she might leave the court, expecting feminine sympathy from her opponent. The umpire asked Fru Sperling if she objected. She did. Miss Round was not able to settle to her best effort and she was beaten 6–3 8–6. The upshot of all this was the rule which allows a player to leave court, with permission, for clothing to be adjusted. That, though, lay in the future and at the time the umpire lacked power to suspend the 'play shall be continuous' rule. But sympathy was universally with Miss Round and Fru Sperling, who could never have been called an inspired player, hardly rated high in Wimbledon's popularity polls from then on.

Fru Sperling went on to win one of her interminable base line battles against Mme Mathieu—years later Mme Mathieu confessed that she always knew how to beat Fru Sperling but she could rarely bear to inflict so tedious an undertaking on spectators—and so reached the final for the second time since 1931. This time Miss Jacobs and not another German was her opponent. Miss Jacobs was hard pressed to survive when she met Anita Lizana in the quarter-final. The latter, from Chile, rated as one of Wimbledon's most adored personalities; her drop shots were superb examples of natural talent.

The final was gruelling and Miss Jacobs was denied what promised an easier victory when she won the first set and led 3–1 in the second. Fru Sperling did not, in fact, get in front but kept pulling back and it was not until her third match ball that Miss Jacobs won by 7–5 in the third set to take, at last, the singles title that had eluded her in four previous finals.

Both the women's doubles and mixed doubles followed the same course as in 1935. Freda James and Kay Stammers again danced a happy and effective way through the women's while the mixed went once more to Miss Round in harness with Fred Perry, making it, for Miss Round, three in a row. This was Perry's last Wimbledon.

It was not for Miss Round. She was seeded only seventh in 1937. Kay Stammers was eighth and numbers one to six were from overseas. On that reckoning she should have lost to Miss Jacobs, the official favourite, in the quarter-final; instead of which Miss Round dispossessed the holder at that stage and went on to beat Mme Mathieu. Jadwiga Jedrzejowska of Poland qualified to meet her in the final, having beaten the talented, super sharp but still unfulfilled Alice Marble in the round before.

The course of the final was such that it seemed likely there would be a Polish champion. Miss Jedrzejowska, like Miss Round, was a trenchant driver. Miss Round, having taken the opening set 6–2, lost the second by the same score and then trailed 1–4 in the final set. Her recovery was a tribute not only to her ability to volley but to her stamina and staunch match temperament. This was Miss Round's third singles final and every one went the full distance.

In 1938 Mrs Moody came back. She was 32 years old. Her winning margin at her last attempt, in 1935, had been narrow. What more had she to gain? All this precise and perfect and ice-cool Californian had left was to win the singles championships more times than anyone else. Willie Renshaw was seven times men's singles champion, Mrs Lambert Chambers was seven times women's singles champion. With one more she would break the record.

And break the record she did. Her eighth success at Wimbledon was, in fact, less perilous than her seventh three years before. In her preparatory tournaments she lost to the British Mary Hardwick at Weybridge and to Fru Sperling at Queen's Club; once at Wimbledon she reassumed her former invincibility, even though it was expressed with much less to spare than in her halcyon years. She was not far from losing a set to the South African Bobbie Heine Miller in the fourth round; she beat Kay Stammers easily in the quarter-final but she was within a point of losing the first set to Fru Sperling in the semi-final, winning only by 12–10 6–4. In the other half of the draw events shaped unexpectedly. Helen Jacobs, who had not been fit, was not seeded. None the less, she brought down, all in two sets, Peggy Scriven, one of the staunchest British players, Miss Jedrzejowska, the finalist of the previous year, and then her compatriot Alice Marble. The final, though, was an anti-climax. It in no way repeated 1935. It was level as far as four games all, when Miss Jacobs strained a leg muscle and could only hobble ineffectively to the end. It could be said, then, that Mrs Moody had luck in thus setting a peak of Wimbledon achievement. But who better deserved it than this lawn tennis machine?

A year remained before the Second World War brought down the curtain and Miss Marble came into her own. Her first Wimbledon title was the mixed doubles with Don Budge in 1937. In 1938 she retained the mixed with Budge (losing no set and only 30 games in so doing) and won the women's doubles with Sarah Fabyan. In 1939 she became triple champion. The women's game moved a step forward with her prowess. She brought the serve-and-volley technique to a tempo approaching masculine standards. She was, incidentally, the first woman triple champion at Wimbledon since Mlle Lenglen in 1925. The mixed she won with Bobby Riggs, who was also a triple champion, and the women's doubles once more with the elfin and charming Mrs Fabyan. The singles she took without yielding a set. Her quarter-final was 6–1 6–4 against Miss Jedrzejowska, her semi-final 6–0 6–0 against Fru Sperling and the final 6–2 6–0 against the popular British idol Kay Stammers who, despite patriotic hopes, could not live against the sharp American expertise.

Among the last eight in 1939 was Miss Jacobs, beaten there by Miss Stammers. It was her eleventh appearance as a quarter-finalist and she had been eight times a semi-finalist, six times a finalist and once the winner. The French Mme Mathieu was there also. It was her tenth quarter-final match and six times she had gone one step further. Fru Sperling played her eighth quarter-final and fifth semi-final.

Dorothy Round, who had become Mrs Little, did not compete as title holder in 1938; she came back to the list in 1939 only to yield in the fourth round to Mrs Fabyan.

Whether Mrs Moody or Mlle Lenglen be held the greatest woman player between the wars is a matter of opinion. Mlle Lenglen was never beaten in a singles at Wimbledon and won six times. Mrs Moody was beaten once and won eight times. What is certain is that they were in the lead by far, and all rivals could only trail behind.

What Miss Marble might have achieved, had not the war interrupted international lawn tennis, is an interesting speculation. Her command of the serve-and-volley game in 1939 was such that many held her to be the greatest woman player of all time. She became a professional in 1941 and consequently took no part in the resumption of traditional lawn tennis events when they resumed after the war in 1946. She was, in any case, then 32 years old. It was her standard of aggressive expertise that inspired the American women's game.

In both 1938 and 1939 all five championships at Wimbledon were won by Americans. Such a dominance by players from one nation was unique, for in the days when British champions won as a matter of course there were not five championships to be contested. Even more remarkable about 1939 was a triple championship being won by both Bobbie Riggs and Miss Marble. Only four names graced the championships roll that year, Riggs, Miss Marble, Elwood Cooke and Sarah Fabyan. Never was so much won by so few!

13 USA VERSUS AUSTRALIA (1946-1955)

From the outbreak of war in 1939 the All England Club was on a survival basis for the next six years. Its secretary, Dudley Larcombe, retired because of ill health in October 1939. Nora Cleather ably served the executive committee that carried on the business of the Club for the whole of its care and maintenance period. The club had its share of German bombing and major damage was suffered in the first incident. This was a bomb that fell on the corner of the competitors' stand on the Centre Court on 11 October 1940. It was not possible to effect repairs until 1947 and the first post-war Championships in 1946 were staged with 1200 fewer seats than normal.

Duncan Macaulay was appointed club secretary in 1946. The Committee of Management of the Championships, under the chairmanship of Sir Louis Greig, had its first post-war meeting on 18 January 1946 when the decision was taken to revive the meeting the same year. It was a time of acute post-war shortages in every sphere. Captain A. K. Trower was appointed referee, Hamilton Price having died.

Despite difficulties the Championships of 1946 were successful in every way. There had, as usual, to be a ballot for tickets. The entry represented the best world strength. Nor was world form an unknown quantity. The Australian Championships had been staged early in the year and the American national meeting had never ceased at any time. The usual qualifying competition, however, was not held, the entire entry being by selection.

Dinny Pails, beaten in the final of the Australian Championships by John Bromwich, was seeded first. Nottingham born and 25 years old he seemed the best Australian challenger. Jack Kramer, Las Vegas born but reared in California, was the best of the Americans and seeded second. He was 24. The latter, it can be said with hindsight wisdom, was certainly the best player in the field. Mischance took a hand and robbed both Kramer and Pails of their chances.

In the case of Kramer it was a blistered playing hand. Having got through three rounds with the total loss of only five games he was impossibly handicapped when he met the Czech Jaroslav Drobny in the fourth round. Drobny had been a pre-war competitor and a deadly left-handed serve made him an intimidating opponent. He beat Kramer over five sets and 67 games, 32 of them in the second set. But Drobny, in due course, went down to an even more formidable server, the Australian Geoff Brown. It is doubtful if a player so small as Geoff Brown ever served so fast. He had an electrifyingly speedy swing and, at its best, an untakable cannon-ball of a delivery. He was double fisted on the forehand side, where he also had an overwhelming punch of shot.

The misfortune of Pails was to get lost on London's Underground when on his way to play his quarter-final. He arrived at the ground late and in a state of nervous apprehension because of it. The upshot was that he lost in four sets to the tall Frenchman, Yvon Petra, a shambling giant of a player without polish of game, one would have thought, to take a major championship. Petra went on to win a semi-final against the only American in the last four, Tom Brown. He did so when Brown lost confidence after taking the first two sets.

With the final between Geoff Brown and Petra, the title, it seemed, belonged more or less automatically to the former. There seemed no reason why he should not blast Petra off the court. As a pace-maker the Australian seemed to be without a peer. But, extraordinarily, he was advised, prior to the final, to slow the pace and not hit hard. This was like a fast bowler trying to turn himself into a spinner. The upshot was that he lost the first two sets before he realised his misjudgement. With difficulty he retrieved the third and fourth sets but psychologically he was not equipped for a long contest and he lost his opening service in the fifth set. Consequently Petra, cheerfully beaming at his own surprising success, emerged as the first post-war Wimbledon champion.

Kramer had the consolation of winning the doubles with Tom Brown. The Australians Geoff Brown and Pails were the losing finalists. One of the sights at the 1946 meeting was that of Geoff Brown, chronically untidy in appearance with shirt never at anchor with his shorts, meeting the challenge of being 0–40 on his service by delivering the next five balls as though they were bullets from a gun. But he hit too hard to have a long life as the game's most meteoric player.

Kramer, this time free from blisters, made 1947 entirely his year. He was seeded first and it proved almost a formality. He was a model of what a great lawn tennis player should be, inviting comparison with Don Budge. He met Geoff Brown in the quarter-final and lost only four games. He played Pails in the semi-final. Here he lost the second set but gave away only two games in the other three. The final was against his doubles partner of the year before, Tom Brown, who beat Petra in the quarter-final and Budge Patty (who had beaten Drobny and Bromwich) in the semi-final. The title match was no more than an exhibition canter for Kramer, the winner by 6–1 6–3 6–2 in 48 minutes.

Despite the loss of a set against Pails it was the most one-sided victory by a men's singles champion playing through. Kramer lost a total of only 37 games in his seven rounds. Even Budge, who won without yielding a set in 1938, gave away 48 games. To complete his invincibility Kramer, partnered by Bob Falkenburg, won the doubles. This was without the loss of a set in any round.

Kramer, having won his own US title for the second time in 1947, became a professional. Few critics who saw him would fail to rate him among the all time 'greats' of lawn tennis.

A piquant aspect of the 1947 meeting was the prominence achieved by Tony Mottram, who that year showed himself to be the best player in Great Britain, a position sustained for many seasons. Mottram, partnered by the Australian, Bill Sidwell, got to the final of the doubles, having had a spectacular semi-final win over Bromwich and Pails. The patriotic fervour of the crowds stressed how hungry the British were for a British success, even though it was clear that Mottram's flair consisted in backing up Sidwell's exploits, these being often near to the limit of what was humanly possible on court. Alas, the title was not within their capability.

So far as the men's singles was concerned 1948 was a year of constant surprises, not least of all in its ultimate winner, Bob Falkenburg, from California. Nothing quite like Falkenburg had been seen before. He was tall, slender and, sweating profusely, prone to ration his energies in a manner that met with criticism. His habit of 'resting' for whole games and sometimes sets was combined with snail-like slowness between each point and did not make for popularity. He was 23 years old.

Apart from Falkenburg's dramatically achieved success there was excitement throughout. The American, Frank Parker, was seeded first, mainly on his having been runner-up to Kramer in the 1947 US meeting. Notably he had won the French Championships, confirming his reputation as a hard-court exponent more than as a man for fast grass. Parker, whose racial origin was Polish, lost in the fourth round to the tall Swede Lennart Bergelin, a player of princely fluency. Bergelin's winning score was 5–7 7–5 9–7 0–6 10–8 after being 3–5 in the fifth set, at which stage an attack of cramp proved less disturbing to the sufferer, Bergelin, than it did to Parker.

British patriotism ran high in the event and centred on Mottram. Now firmly entrenched as Britain's number one he brought off an exciting third round win against the Italian, Giani Cucelli (who had beaten the seeded Drobny) by 6–8 6–3 10–12 9–7 6–2. He then beat the Belgian, Phillipe Washer to make himself a quarter-finalist. He got no further—and it was to be many years before another British man got as far—losing in four sets to the American, Gardnar Mulloy.

Falkenburg, with umpires frequently asking him to 'get on with it', made his way to the final by beating the Australian Frank Sedgman, then 20 years old, in the fourth round, Bergelin in the quarter-final and then Mulloy in the semi-final. Falkenburg was the number seven seed. The number two seed faced him in the final. This was the Australian, Bromwich. His quarter- and semi-final victories were against Budge Patty and the Hungarian, Joseph Asboth.

Bromwich was a much-loved player. Not only did he have a gentle personality but a persuasively gentle game. Craft and skill and guile were his all, never muscle and pace. His racket was light-weight, the grip small and could have been a girl's. He was double fisted on the forehand. His ability to tease pace-making opponents into defeat by the accuracy of his slow returns was entrancing to watch. Add all this to the fact that he was an Australian opposed to an American whose personality verged on the abrasive and there was a final in which spectators more clearly indicated, perhaps than any other, their preference as to who should win and who should lose.

Falkenburg, having won the first set 7–5, palpably threw the second at 0–6. The tactics were legitimate but they hardly endeared him to the crowd. He took the third set 6–2. Bromwich won the fourth 6–3. By then the effectiveness of Falkenburg's big serve had declined. And he was missing much with his forehand volley, a shot all his own, scoring seldom. He had the knack of slicing the volley almost parallel to the net. Bromwich controlled the fifth set decisively, so much so that he led 5–2, 40–15, on his own service. On the two match points Falkenburg played shots that were pure gambles, screaming backhand returns of service. Bromwich had his third match point at advantage and Falkenburg repeated his performance. The Australian 'died' as an effective player from that stage. Falkenburg devoured the remaining games. If Bromwich was heart-broken he shared the sentiment with nearly every spectator round the court.

It was a shame that so attractive a player as Bromwich, who was then 29, never had the accolade of a Wimbledon singles championship. There was some consolation for him in his taking the men's doubles with Sedgman. One might be tempted to class Falkenburg as the least popular of champions, save that when some years later he came to play in the

Davis Cup against Great Britain for Brazil—his residence there gave him qualification—his geniality and good sportsmanship were unquestioned.

The spectacular and controversial victory of Falkenburg was followed a year later by another spectacular champion in Ted Schroeder. Like his predecessor he was a Californian but he was very different. Rather stocky, he had a rolling gait which made him look as though he had just got off a horse. Except when he was actually playing he always seemed to have a pipe in his mouth, a corn cob as often as not. He was just short of 28 when he made his first and only challenge in the Championships. He had made himself famous by appearing, as it were, from nowhere to play with fine success for his country in the Davis Cup Challenge Round, having played little elsewhere.

The draw in 1949 was unusually interesting. Mulloy, doubtless with his tongue in cheek, made a fuss about it being 'fixed'. His criticism was taken in good humour, so much so that when the draw came to be made he was invited to pull the counters out of the bags himself. Americans had the top four seeding places, Schroeder, Ricardo Gonzales, Parker and Falkenburg followed by Bromwich, Drobny, the South African, Eric Sturgess and Sedgman. Mulloy himself had missed being seeded by a hair's breadth and was about the strongest man 'running wild'. The draw went on in accustomed form, Mulloy pulling out the names. It reached the point when it was complete except for the last counter, this to fill the only vacant place which was against Schroeder at the tail end of the draw. As was then obvious, Mulloy had no choice but to extract his own name. He had claimed the draw would be 'fixed' so that he met his big rival Schroeder in the first round. If so he had done the 'fixing' himself.

Accordingly the Championships started with an exciting opening-day clash, the top seed against one of his keenest rivals. It was, in fact, the second meeting between Schroeder and Mulloy in three days, for on the preceding Saturday they had met in the final of the London Championships at Queen's Club, with Schroeder winning a hard first set and an easy second. Opening on this high note and favoured by perfect weather throughout, the Championships had the biggest crowds to date. Mulloy won the first two sets but physical exhaustion took its toll and Schroeder yielded only one game in the third and fourth. In the fifth Schroeder nosed out from five games all. For the next three rounds he was able to win less precariously.

The crisis match for Schroeder was his quarter-final against Sedgman. Played on the Saturday on Court One, the Australian won the first two sets 6–3 8–6. Schroeder took the next two 6–3 6–2. It was a broiling hot day and as the fifth set progressed, Sedgman, as nimble as a cat, gave the impression of standing the physical strain the better. He led 3–0. Schroeder drew level but Sedgman maintained his odd game lead. At 5–4 Sedgman had the first of his two match points. Schroeder, serving, was footfaulted. In this moment of tension he was the coolest man on the ground. Quite unperturbed he followed his second serve to the net and projected a winning volley. Americans had long called him 'Lucky' Schroeder. He salvaged another match point against him at 5–6, this time with a fine backhand passing shot down the line. He took the set 9–7, leading for the first time in the match in the last five minutes.

The defending champion, Falkenburg, got no further than the last eight and Bromwich. The Australian had revenge of sorts for his defeat of the previous year by winning after yielding the first two sets. In turn, however, Bromwich could not cope with Drobny. The Czech—then still officially designated as such though within a few weeks of leaving his homeland for good—had an easy semi-final win. Schroeder got through the same stage with more hardship, trailing two sets to one against the fluent South African, Eric Sturgess. This was Schroeder's third five-set match. His fourth was the final against Drobny. It was a battle of keen serving. In this match, Schroeder though losing the opening set and though being within a point of trailing 0–2 in the fifth, was less precariously situated than he had been.

The second seed, Gonzales, got no further than an eager Geoff Brown in the fourth round. Yet the only visit of this outstanding player to Wimbledon as an amateur was not without success. He and Parker won the men's doubles, gaining an easy final against Mulloy and Schroeder after peril in the semi-final—a near 1–4 fifth-set deficit—against Patty and Sturgess.

Statistically Schroeder heads the table of singles champions most hardly pressed. He lost eight sets in all and 119 games. Even Henri Cochet, the outstanding tightrope walker, yielded only seven sets and 114 games during his extraordinary exploits of 1927. Schroeder exuded independence from every fibre of his being and he can, perhaps, be classed as the last of great amateurs. He was sorely missed when he never came back to Wimbledon.

By 1950 Gonzales and Parker had become professionals. Yet the strength of the men's challenge was more impressive than ever. Four notable Americans, Billy Talbert, Tony Trabert, Vic Seixas and Art Larsen, made their debuts and so did two outstanding Australians, Ken McGregor and Mervyn Rose. For the first time sixteen seeds were selected for the singles, the senior four being Sedgman, Talbert, Drobny and Sturgess. Drobny's national allegiance looked curious in the draw. He then had an Egyptian passport. Not until 1959 did 'Egypt' become 'GB'.

The winner was Patty, to the delight of those to whom beauty of style is important. This expatriate Californian—Paris was then his adopted home—had won the French Championships not long before and was the first man to bring off the double triumph since Don Budge in 1938. He had acquired the reputation of being a 'playboy' and accounted for his success by adopting a more athletic approach to training for the first time. He had fluent ease of stroke all round but none more so than with his forehand volley.

With so many seeded it was not surprising that all eight quarter-finalists were thus favoured. With numbers one to seven surviving it was almost copybook and Seixas, number twelve, who beat Bromwich at number eight, was the only junior survivor. Yet the quarter-finals progressed less smoothly than is usually the case at Wimbledon.

On a drizzly second Monday it for long looked as if there would be no play. The decision to stage two of the scheduled quarter-finals on the Centre and Number One Courts was taken late. In retrospect it was seen to be an obviously unwise decision.

Sedgman began against Larsen and Talbert began against Patty. After a spell both matches had to be called off. Some members of the crowd reacted in a way unusual at Wimbledon. It recalled the time in 1936 when Court One was covered in cushions hurled by spectators angered at having the inter-zone Davis Cup match between the United States and Germany interrupted. They gathered outside the main entrance to the club, chanting that their money be returned. It was not a pleasant half hour for Wimbledon's executive who eventually compromised by arranging priority for admission the next day. Whether the ill temper shown justified the colourful description of 'Wimbledon Riots' is, perhaps, a matter of semantics.

Sedgman, who was that year suffering from an injured wrist, eventually beat Larsen, a prince of touch players if ever there were one (and utterly oblivious to the normal demands of athletic training) after losing the first two sets and being within a point of trailing 3–5 in the fifth set. In the semi-final round he was similarly led two sets to love by Drobny.

Patty's progress to the final was more simple, four sets against Talbert and then four sets against Seixas. He never was taken to a fifth set for he won in four in the final against Sedgman. Patty gave the impression of being the most sophisticated champion of all time.

The doubles, won by Bromwich and Adrian Quist in an all-Australian final against Geoff Brown and Sidwell, had its most remarkable match to that time. McGregor and Sedgman had a notable third-round success by beating the second seeds, the Americans Mulloy and Talbert, 8–6 8–6 8–10 10–8. That was 64 games, a sizeable total. In the quarter-final they were beaten by Patty and Tony Trabert. The match, interrupted once by rain, lasted four hours and the score was 6–4 31–29 7–9 6–2. The 60-game set and the overall total of 94 games set a record.

Patty having been a surprising American singles winner in 1950 there was an even more surprising American champion in 1951, Richard Savitt. He was a solid ground-stroke player with a backhand of impressive accuracy and weight and unlike his four predecessors owing nothing to California. He came, in fact, from New Jersey. He also won the Australian singles in 1951 but despite that and despite his Wimbledon triumph he was asked to play in the Davis Cup only in easy ties against Japan and Canada. He was 24 when he joined the select band of men winning Wimbledon at their first attempt.

His triumph turned on a quarter-final success against his compatriot Larsen and a striking semi-final win against Flam, who put out the top seed, Sedgman, after losing the first two sets in the quarters. Flam led Savitt by 6–1 5–1 before Savitt got into the match. He eventually took the second set 15–13 and then lost only five games in the next two. In the final he faced the Australian, Ken McGregor, and became a fairly easy winner.

Savitt had his success to the background of Patty failing to carry his title defence beyond the second round. Ham Richardson, from Louisiana and a Rhodes Scholar, made a name for himself with a five-set win. In the next round British patriotism was richly fed by Mottram. On Court One he rallied from a leeway of two sets to one to beat the second seed, Drobny. This was perhaps the finest victory of his career. He was able to get no further for in the fourth round he could make no show at all against the fluency of the Swede, Bergelin, taking only three games.

Dick Savitt, winner at his first attempt to become the champion of 1951

Sedgman at last justified his great talent by winning in 1952, the first Australian singles champion since Jack Crawford in 1933. There were twelve seeds, with Sedgman at the top and a formal air about the outcome. The top eight seeds filled the quarter-final places and the numbers one and two (Drobny was the second seed) played the final. It was a notable year for newcomers. Two 17-year-olds from Australia, Lew Hoad and Ken Rosewall, made a mark both jointly and severally. They did so as a pair by reaching the doubles semi-final, notably winning a quarter-final against the number two seeds, Gardnar Mulloy and Savitt.

Hoad won three rounds in the singles before losing, and then only in four sets, to Drobny. Rosewall won a round before falling to Mulloy. Australian might belonged in its richest measure to Sedgman. Drobny, as the seedsmen forecast, made himself the finalist against him. Hoad proved his first difficult opponent. In the quarter-final McGregor came within two points of beating him in four sets. In the semi-final, Flam took Drobny the full distance also. In the final, played in a blustery wind, Sedgman controlled events once he found his overhead power. He lost the first set. He had lost but one other, to the Belgian, Phillipe Washer, in the third round.

Savitt's title defence died against Rose in the quarter-final, Rose, in turn, giving way to Sedgman. With McGregor Sedgman won the doubles for the second year running. With Doris Hart he took the mixed as well. Accordingly Sedgman made himself a triple champion. He stands as the last of three men to do so, Budge (1937 and 1938) and Riggs (1939). Among the all-time 'greats' this little, athletic Australian clearly has a place.

An absentee from the 1952 meeting was Queen Mary. She had been the meeting's most constant and avid spectator since 1919. She died early in 1953. Sir Louis Greig died a few days before. He was replaced as chairman by Bob Riseley, elder brother of Frank Riseley. Bob Riseley had done as much as anyone to keep the club alive amid the hardships and difficulties of the war. Another change was made in the administration of the Championships in 1951 when Colonel John Legg, following the death of Trower, became referee. His precise authority was reminiscent of that of Burrow in pre-war days, even though it was exercised less despotically.

Sedgman had become a professional and did not defend his title in 1953. The singles that year reverted to American domination with Vic Seixas, who, like Big Bill Tilden, came from Philadelphia, ruggedly and valiantly carrying himself through seven matches without defeat. He was hardly the prettiest player in the world, for his strokes smacked more of expediency than fluency and polish, but he gave the impression of being prepared to go on attacking for ever. He was seeded second. He beat Hoad in the quarter-final, narrowly by 9–7 in the fifth set, and Mervyn Rose in the semi-final, after trailing two sets to one and after a total of 72 games.

He had an unexpected finalist, the Dane, Kurt Nielsen. Here was another rugged player and only the second unseeded man to get this far. The key to his success was his quarter-final victory over the number one seed, Ken Rosewall. Nielsen, employing a chopped forehand down the middle of the court, found the knack of negativing the compelling game of Rosewall. He went on to beat Drobny but could not get a set in the last match against Seixas.

The eclipse of Drobny came after a match by which the 1953 meeting will be remembered. In the third round Drobny met Patty, a friend and rival of long standing, a constant touring companion. They usually had long even contests when they met. On this occasion they transcended everything.

They began, at about five o'clock, on the Centre Court. They were locked together, in keen combat, with service dominating everything, until between a quarter and twenty minutes past nine o'clock. Then, with the scoreboard twinkling in dusk that was almost night, and with the referee standing at the back of the court ready to call a halt, Drobny at last emerged the winner of a Herculean duel. His winning score was

Frank Sedgman (*left*) at last justifies his talent by beating Jaroslav Drobny 4–6 6–2 6–3 6–2 in the final of 1952

8–6 16–18 3–6 8–6 12–10, a total of 93 games, the most played in a singles at Wimbledon to that time. Patty almost won in the fourth set when he had three match points. He had another three in the fifth. Drobny survived all six. The Management Committee gave both players inscribed gold cigarette cases to commemorate one of the outstanding occasions of Wimbledon.

Both men were so exhausted that the wonder was that Drobny, who suffered a strained leg muscle, was able to continue. He limped through two more rounds, against the Australian, Rex Hartwig and the Swede, Sven Davidson before yielding to Nielsen.

As for the doubles, that gave Hoad and Rosewall their first Wimbledon title. Drobny and Patty were one of the seeded pairs but, not surprisingly, they gave a walkover.

Emotionally 1954 was the most satisfying year for most spectators for a long time. As a refugee from Czechoslovakia, Drobny, who had a warm personality in any case, had gained wide sympathy. His left-handed skill on hard courts was often awesome. His punishing service, following a shoulder injury, was perhaps less effective than it had been but his backhand, the left hander's traditional weakness, had developed a surprising amount of bite. Yet if he were much liked he was hardly expected to win. His being seeded eleventh out of twelve seemed reasonable.

In the event, Drobny, still a hero at Wimbledon by virtue of his exploit in 1953 against Patty, was a rapturously popular champion. He emerged from an American–Australian field which looked strong enough to swamp anyone. The top eight seeded men were divided fifty–fifty between Americans and Australians, with Tony Trabert number one and Lew Hoad number two. Only the number six, the American, Larsen, failed to reach the quarter-final and his place was taken by Drobny.

At that stage Drobny achieved his key win. He beat Hoad, who was spectacular but erratic. In the semi-final Drobny met his old rival, Patty, their fourth clash at Wimbledon. It produced Drobny's third win. The drama of the previous year was not repeated, though it was close enough, Patty failing to clinch a 5–3 lead for two sets all. The other semi-final saw Rosewall recover from a leeway of two sets to one to beat Trabert. Accordingly Rosewall, then 19 years old and already with a backhand that was superlative and with a reaction on the volley that sometimes seemed superhuman, reached his first Wimbledon singles final. Drobny, 32 years old, was in the final for the third time.

When Mahony beat Baddeley in the title match of 1896 he did so after playing 57 games. Crawford, beating Vines in 1933, won after 56 games. The Drobny versus Rosewall final of 1954 set a record of 58 games, though extending over four sets only. Drobny measured his superiority 13–11 4–6 6–2 9–7 and no better final had been seen since Crawford and Vines 21 years before. Perhaps the first set was the crux. In this, Rosewall, who had trailed 3–5, had a set point at 10–9 against the service. An ace by Drobny gave him no chance. The match lasted 2 hours 35 minutes and Drobny's success was at his eleventh attempt, his first Wimbledon challenge being at the age of 16 in

The Duchess of Kent, with the victorious Jaroslav Drobny (*centre*) and Ken Rosewall after they had set the all-time record of a 58-game final

1938. At that time he was equally promising as an ice hockey player. The only left-handed champion to precede him was Norman Brookes.

The warmth of Drobny's reception as champion could not have been greater had he been a genial Englishman. In a sense he was, for he had married an Englishwoman and lived in Sussex. At that time, though, his official designation as 'GB' belonged to the future and his official nomination in the draw was as from Egypt. He is unique in the Wimbledon records in possessing four different national descriptions, Czechoslovakia in 1938 and 1946–9, Egypt 1950–9 and Great Britain from 1960. In 1939 he had the brief-lived description 'BM', standing for Bohemia Moravia and indicating the checkered history of his native land.

Tony Trabert, who took the singles in 1955, was from Cincinnati, Ohio, and 24 years old when he came to the culminating point of his career. He won the US title in 1953 and the French in 1954. He was a very solid player, with a heavy backhand. At the start of 1955 Rosewall beat him in the semi-final of the Australian Championship. That stopped Trabert from achieving the 'Grand Slam', for this likeable, sporting player went on to win in France and take the Wimbledon and US titles as well.

His success at Wimbledon was overwhelming. For the first time since Don Budge in 1938 he won every one of the seven rounds of the singles without losing a set. At the end of 1955 he became a professional and somehow was never regarded as among the first flight of champions. Possibly this was because events that year at Wimbledon failed to be as spectacular as expected.

Trabert was seeded one. Second was Ken Rosewall. The strength of the field was emphasised by Drobny, the defending holder, being rated no better than sixth. Seixas, the 1953 champion, was graded third and Patty, the 1950 winner, seventh. Another brilliant young Australian, Lew Hoad—and it was an open question at that time whether he or Rosewall were the most outstanding—held status as the fourth seed.

Seixas got no further than the second round, beaten by the little-known American, Gil Shea. Trabert suffered no pressure until he met Drobny in the quarter-final but the Czech had lost his brilliance of the year before. In the same round, Patty was at his most suave and brilliant in beating Hoad. That made for a semi-final between Trabert and Patty which was settled in effect on the outcome of the opening set. Rosewall should on expectation have been the finalist against Trabert, instead of which it was again Nielsen. As in 1953 this stalwart Dane reached the last match without being seeded and for much the same reason, his ability to beat Rosewall. This time it was in the semi-final, when Nielsen again went on attacking the Australian down the middle of the court to take an industrious and manful victory in four sets, the first, taken by Nielsen, going to twenty games.

Trabert had much the same sort of final win against Nielsen as had Seixas two years before. He was the better-class player and while he applied his talents he was secure. With this rather humdrum climax the over-all domination of Trabert was rather obscured. He had won 21 sets and lost none. He won 131 games, lost 60. Budge, in winning 129 games had lost only 48.

Hoad and Rex Hartwig won the doubles in 1955 to provide the sixth successive Australian victory in that event and the seventh in the post-war decade. The seventy per cent success by Australia in the doubles was equalled by a seventy per cent success by the Americans in the singles.

Outside American and Australian ranks there was small share of the Wimbledon titles for men in the ten years from 1946. Of the 21 inscribed on the list of champions, singles, men's doubles and mixed, only Yvon Petra of France, the singles champion of 1946, Jaroslav Drobny, nominally of Egypt, the singles winner of 1953, and the South African, Eric Sturgess, the mixed champion in 1949 and 1950, were not from Australia or the US.

Vic Seixas from Philadelphia, the 1953 champion

14
THE TWILIGHT OF SHAMATEURISM (1956-1967)

A great and formidable Australian player, Lew Hoad, won the singles at his fifth attempt in 1956 to establish himself as one of the more memorable champions. While his steely wrist wreaked havoc among his opponents, a loss in the first round that year passed almost unnoticed. An Australian novice of 17, Rod Laver, red haired, left handed and with unobtrusive personality, made his brief appearance. He was beaten by the giant Italian, Orlando Sirola, a clumsy player more noted as a doubles man with his compatriot Nicola Pietrangeli than as a singles exponent. Laver was eliminated 7–5 6–4 6–2. He raised a bigger ripple in the waters of the junior game, reaching the final of the invitation boys' singles. He was beaten easily, 6–1 6–1, by the more robust American Ron Holmburg. Thus while one famous Australian, Hoad, came to a crescendo of form, another, destined to be even more famous, met with his Wimbledon baptism.

It would have been difficult at the start of the meeting in 1956 to be certain who had made the more striking impression in the game, the burly Hoad, with his dynamic power, or the slighter Ken Rosewall, with his superb ground strokes and incredibly quick volleying reactions that needed, one would have thought, only a strong service to make the finest player of all time. The expectation was that these two Australians, who had more or less grown up together, who had but 21 days' difference in their ages (Rosewall was the elder and each was 21 years old when they played at Wimbledon in 1956), would dominate. They did. Seeded first and second they reached the singles final. Top seeded together they won the doubles.

Rosewall lost only one set in getting to the semi-final. At that stage he met the champion of three years before, Vic Seixas. It was a dogged contest and one of its most burning moments was when the American, who, more rugged than polished and a player who maintained his attacking pressure inexorably, led 5–2 in the fifth set. A ball on the sideline that gave Seixas this lead was close enough to look like a wrong decision in the eyes of many. Rosewall thought so and for a spell his normal cool manners deserted him. He circled on the court like an angry bear, saying nothing. His response was to win the next five games and so make himself a finalist for the second time.

Hoad's progress to the last match was never entirely smooth but he was never taken to a fifth set. He dropped the first to his compatriot Mal Anderson and won the fourth only by 13–11. That was in the quarter-final. In the semi-final the American Ham Richardson, who had beaten him at Bournemouth earlier in the season, won the opening set also.

Whether Hoad or Rosewall would be the champion was uncertain until the last ten minutes of a splendid final. Hoad, projecting many more winners but also many more losers, narrowly emerged in front two sets to one, taking the third set from five games all. Rosewall led 4–1 in the fourth set when Hoad found a spell of his most compelling genius. He flogged the ball almost contemptuously and hit a constant series of winners that gave him five games in a row and the championship.

As rivals they made a fine singles climax to Wimbledon. As allies they won the doubles for the second time. The only set they lost was to Bob Howe and Art Larsen in the semi-final. In the final they met the unseeded Nicola Pietrangeli and Orlando Sirola who, normally used to enriching their talents with a Latin sense of humour, were constrained rather by the weight of the occasion.

This was the seventh successive year that the men's

doubles was won by an Australian pair. It was also Rosewall's last appearance at Wimbledon—his last, that is, as an 'amateur'. He signed a professional contract later that year. This was after winning the US Championship by beating Hoad in the final; but for that Hoad would have taken the 'Grand Slam' in 1956.

Prior to the championships in 1957 expensive structural changes were made round the Centre Court. When the stands were built the stanchions supporting the roof were taken for granted, since no other method of construction was possible. Full remedial action was possible only by complete rebuilding, impracticable since no one would undertake to do so in less than a year. A compromise was made by the insertion of supporting cantilevers and the removal of most, though not all, of the pillars that obstructed the spectators' view.

The meeting was graced in 1957 by a visit, on the last Saturday, by Queen Elizabeth II. Her presence inspired an odd happening in the middle of the men's doubles final, when a woman, displaying a banner protesting against the iniquities of bankers, jumped from her seat and ran across towards the Royal Box. The happening, which hardly seemed to threaten harm since the demonstrator looked as if a knitting needle would be her most dangerous weapon, inspired the referee, Colonel Legg, to display his authority in its most icy and efficient manner. He escorted the woman from the court and the police could only follow in his wake.

If Lew Hoad were generally favoured to keep his title—and his status as the top seed was unquestioned—he came to Wimbledon after a display of uneven form. Yet he lost a set only in the quarter-final, this to his fellow Australian Mervyn Rose. In the semi-final he beat the Swede, Sven Davidson. In the other half, Ashley Cooper, seeded second, survived a longer semi-final against Neale Fraser. For the first time three out of the last four survivors were Australian. If Cooper were heartened by reaching the final at this third challenge he can hardly have been stimulated by his fate when he got there.

Hoad won the final 6–2 6–1 6–2 in 57 minutes. It was a display of genius and it is to be doubted if such dynamic shot making was sustained with such accuracy before. If Cooper felt he had played badly he had no chance to do anything else. Hoad was 'superhuman'. It never began to be a contested match.

Hoad having taken the singles for the second successive year, the first man to do so in post-war years, the men's doubles provided excitement that was off-beat and entrancing. Gardnar Mulloy and Budge Patty were an unseeded pair. An aura of controversy always seemed to attach to Mulloy. It had been markedly so the year before when his partner was another American, Bud Robineau, whose ambition to play at Wimbledon clearly surpassed his talents. The pairing of Mulloy and Patty was unexceptionable but with Mulloy aged 43 and Patty not all that young at 33 no one regarded them as possible winners. Perhaps they were fortunate that the only seeds they met prior to the final were Mal Anderson and Cooper very much out of form. They beat them 6–3 6–3 6–0.

The British Roger Becker and Howe put out the second seeds, Ham Richardson and Seixas, in the quarter-final and yielded in the next round to Mulloy and Patty. By this stage they found more inspiration with every game. In the final Mulloy and Patty opposed the top seeds, Hoad and Neale Fraser. Possibly there was a diminution of Hoad's powers following upon his singles victory the day before. At any rate Mulloy and Patty hardly put a foot wrong in a final that had genial overtones. The Queen was in the Royal Box. The woman with the grievance and banner was, until ejected, on the court. Mulloy and Patty, with 76 years between them and with Mulloy, the oldest player to stand so near a title, revelling in every moment, won the match 8–10 6–4 6–4 6–4. Seven years of Australian domination was ended by an American partnership that had shown no cause to be taken seriously before.

This was the last match played by Hoad as an 'amateur'. At the Lawn Tennis Association Ball on the closing Saturday he made reference in his champion's speech to coming back the next year. Yet within 24 hours he had, in America, signed a professional contract. Over two years he was guaranteed £44 600. The sum then set a new record.

Without Hoad and without Rosewall the Championships in 1958 undoubtedly lost some of their glamour, though the continuing heavy over-subscription for tickets stressed that the meeting itself was certainly as attractive as individual personalities. British patriotism was this year brought to a rare peak in the men's singles when Bobby Wilson reached the last eight for the first time. This gifted touch player, then 22 years old, always thrived on the fast turf of Wimbledon, compensating for disappointing efforts elsewhere.

Prior to 1939 British participation in the men's quarter-finals was taken for granted. Indeed, apart from 1927 and 1938 no championship went by without at least this hope of a British semi-finalist. Since 1946 only Tony Mottram, in 1948, had penetrated these preserves. Wilson did so at the expense of the fifth seeded player Luis Ayala from Chile, who had lost in the third round to the Italian, Nicola Pietrangeli. Wilson was able to master Pietrangeli in three sets, though the first of them lasted twenty games. In his quarter-final Wilson met the number one seed, the rugged Cooper, not one bit the worse for having been so ruthlessly taken to pieces in the 1957 final by Hoad. Wilson, who lost the first two sets, came near to winning in a fifth set when he was within a stroke of breaking Cooper's serve to lead 6–5. The backhand passing shot across the court by which the Australian saved himself was a winner by only a fraction at best.

As the year before, the semi-finals were three parts Australian and the final all Australian. Cooper went on to the final by beating the left hander Mervyn Rose. Another Australian left hander, Neale Fraser, reached the last four by beating the Swede, Sven Davidson, 8–6 in the fifth set. The survivors would almost certainly have been all Australian had not the number two seed, the Queenslander, Mal Anderson, then the current holder of the US title, injured himself in his quarter-final against Kurt Nielsen. There was a mammoth third set between Fraser and Nielsen, which the Dane won by 19–17, the most ruggedly fought of four rugged sets. Cooper's second final was entirely more successful than his first. He was not the most polished of Australian players but, like the American Seixas, he seemed prepared to ply his service–volley–net pressure, come rain, come shine. He lost the first set to Fraser, then won the next two and eventually the third after 24 games. Drobny had played as long a set, 13–11, against Rosewall four years before.

For the second year running the men's doubles champions were unseeded. Mulloy and Patty got no further in defence of their title than the third round.

The top seeds were Cooper and Fraser. They lost in the final, surprisingly in any case but astonishingly in three sets, to the Swedes, Davidson and Ulf Schmidt. Thus for the second year there was something of a *tour de force* from nowhere and Swedish names were inscribed on the honours board for the first time.

The rate of loss to the professional ranks increased. In 1958, Cooper, Anderson and Rose ceased to be amateurs. In 1959 there was no champion to defend the men's singles title and it had been the same in 1958, 1956 and 1953 as well as 1948. But in 1959 another Wimbledon figure was tragically missing from the scene.

Dr Colin Gregory, Wimbledon's chairman, died suddenly early in the year, aged only 55. He took over from Bob Riseley in 1957 and the brevity of his tenure of office was distressing to many people. Gregory became a lawn tennis hero in 1952 when, despite his 48 years, he took the place of the injured Geoff Paish in the doubles in the Davis Cup tie against Yugoslavia in Belgrade and helped to secure a British win. Gregory's successor as chairman, Herman David, was also a former British Davis Cup player. He was destined to steer the affairs of the Championships through stormy waters.

As the previous year the second week of the men's singles in 1959 had strong patriotic overtones. Wilson was seeded, the first British man to be so regarded since 1939, and he was assessed as high as number four. In the event he did not justify the rating but he got to the quarter-finals for the second year. In the fourth round he was involved in an exciting third set that went to 17–15 against the tall Frenchman, Jean Noel Grinda. In the quarter-finals the mercurial talents of the Queenslander, Roy Emerson, ended Wilson's hopes. Emerson's mobility in the execution of a serve and volley game was presaged as a 14-year-old schoolboy able to run 100 yards in 10·6 seconds.

The last four were Barry Mackay, Laver, Emerson and Alex Olmedo. The last was the top seed and was the eighth American since 1946 to take the title. The description American is reasonable enough, for the dark Olmedo's lawn tennis belonged to California, where he learned the game. By birth and race he was Peruvian. He was a fast, compelling player and there was, perhaps, a touch of the proud authority of the Incas about his demeanour on court. Olmedo beat Emerson quite easily in the semi-final and did not have much more difficulty in winning against Laver.

The career of Laver then lay before him. His major fame at Wimbledon in 1959 was in getting as far as the final as an unseeded player. There was a curious run of matches in the first and second round—at least they can be seen as curious with hindsight knowledge. Nielsen, seeded seventh but noted for having twice been in the final unseeded, 1953 and 1955, beat Martin Mulligan, who got to the final unseeded in 1962. Mulligan, solidly then Australian and with no notion of becoming Italian, was in turn beaten by Laver, whose unseeded status was at that early stage unquestioned.

Laver's semi-final win against Mackay was the major battle of the meeting. It endured for three and three-quarter hours. The tall Mackay, with a big and spidery volleying reach, was notorious for his double faulting. It was, though, deceptive to assume that his opponents benefited much. More often than not a double fault was a preparation for one or more aces. In the preceding quarter-final Mackay had taken five sets and 52 games to beat Fraser. Laver beat Mackay after 87 games: 11–13 11–9 10–8 7–9 6–3.

While the singles belonged to America, thanks to the keen eye of a Peruvian, the men's doubles reverted to a familiar pattern. The Australians who won it were Emerson in harness with Fraser. The last match provided the second losing final for Laver. His partner was the more burly Bob Mark and of these two young Australians it was not then entirely clear who looked the more promising. Mark subsequently settled in South Africa and his lawn tennis career never rose to the heights reached by Laver. But then, whose did?

It was noteworthy that 1959 widened the international field. For the second year Communist China sent challengers and, dressed in identical raincoats and identical suits, they looked on the scene with identical lack of emotion. Two were in the singles. C. Chu lost in the first round to J. C. Molinari of France. F. Mei beat the Brazilian, Ron Barnes, 3–6 9–11 11–9 6–1 6–1 before losing easily to the Dane, Torben Ulrich. Since they met Laver and Mark in the first round of the men's doubles it was not surprising they did not get far in that event. One would have thought it not unpromising but the challenge from Communist China was not carried further.

In contrast the first challenge from the USSR heralded a subsequent familiar picture with Russian players always well to the fore. The Soviet pioneers were Andreyev Potanin, Toomas Lejus and Serge Likhachev (together with Anna Dmitrieva among the women). Success in singles eluded them, though Lejus won the junior event.

This was Laver's third year at Wimbledon and he was a triple finalist. Beaten in the men's events he had his success in the mixed in partnership with the American, Darlene Hard. The top seeded pair were Billy Knight and the trim Mexican, Yola Ramirez, the former one of the most stalwart of the British men, albeit with a left-handed game suited better to hard courts than to grass.

Olmedo aspired without success to double his Wimbledon singles with the American title. He lost in the final at Forest Hills to Fraser. He turned professional none the less. Wimbledon champions in

The champion *in excelsis* (1961, 1962, 1968, 1969)—Rod Laver

defence of their title were becoming thin on the ground.

Even so the Championships continued to prove resilient to the drain of talent. As the nineteen fifties turned into the nineteen sixties the clear sparkle of the success of the meeting continued unabated. The year 1960 was notable on two counts: for the arrival on finals day of Prince Philip and Princess Anne by helicopter, which even the inventive Henry Jones of immortal memory of the 1870s would hardly have envisaged, and for a men's singles final between two left handers, and Australian left handers at that, for the first time.

The meeting was staged in the expectation it would be the last restricted to 'amateurs'. In the event, the move to change the rules, despite strong support, failed by a narrow margin at the meeting of the International Lawn Tennis Federation the following week in Paris.

The left-handed finalists were Fraser and Laver,

the former aged 26 and from Victoria, competing for the seventh time, the latter, from Queensland and 21 years old, challenging for the fourth time. For each it was their second final, Fraser losing to Cooper in 1958 and Laver to Olmedo in 1959. At that stage of his career, Fraser, well liked for his outstanding sportsmanship, had developed a deadly 'googly' service that, breaking the wrong way and coming from a left hander in any case, was something of a terror to all who had to play it.

No American got as far as the semi-final. Barry Mackay, the number two seed, was put out by Nicola Pietrangeli in the quarters, the loss of an opening set of 30 games foreshadowing this result. The other American in the last eight was Earl Buchholz, a 19-year-old from St Louis. He found unique distinction in 1958 by winning the boys' events in Australia, France, Wimbledon and America, a junior 'Grand Slam'. Buchholz, unwittingly and to his disappointment, was the catalyst which enabled Fraser to bring about one of the more dramatic recoveries achieved *en route* to a championship.

In an exciting hurly-burly of a match, dominated by surging services and skilled and daring volleying, Buchholz built a lead of two sets to one, 6–4 3–6 6–4. In the fourth set the young American kept hoisting himself towards a victory. At the same time cramp increasingly assailed him in his legs. A psychologist could no doubt talk at length about the cause. Six times during the course of a long and wavering set Buchholz came within one point of winning. Once, with a virtually open court before him, he netted a smash when there hardly seemed room between himself and the net into which to mishit the ball. The score was fifteen games all when Buchholz, collapsing with cramp for the second time, was ruled *hors de combat* by the umpire.

In the semi-final Fraser easily beat the Indian, Ramanathan Krishnan, a burly man with a beautiful touch. Laver was more onerously pressed at the same stage by Pietrangeli who led two sets to love but who was eventually ousted after a total of 55 games. The final, won by Fraser after 47 games and the loss of the second set, was the longest of all the six in which Laver took part. It was one of the better matches at that stage, where so often the protagonists are too nervous to give of their best. Fraser had the air of a sixth former refusing to be intimidated by a rival from the fifth who, none the less, was always on the verge of upsetting his senior status.

The doubles was vastly stimulating. Old values were thrown away. In the first place a British pair made striking progress in an event in which home players had taken but small share for many years. Wilson and Mike Davies had a perilous escape in the second round when they survived match points against the Germans, Wilhelm Bungert and D. Ecklebe, winning 6–4 6–4 6–8 4–6 8–6. They went on to eliminate the top seeds, Emerson and Fraser, in the quarter-final and then survived to the final.

While patriotic fervour sparkled over their progress, events as unpredictable took place in the other half. Another unseeded pair was invincible there, Rafael Osuna and Dennis Ralston. Osuna was a

Above: Rafael Osuna, Mexico's dynamic champion and, *below*, Dennis Ralston, his doubles partner from California who became the youngest male champion

Mexican of 21 with abnormal speed of foot and quick turning ability on the volley. Ralston, from California, was a rugged, young 17 year old. His form not recognised he was originally put in the qualifying competition for the Championships. Only his success in the Manchester tournament brought about a hurried recognition of his quality. Osuna and Ralston proved invulnerable. They beat the third seeds, Pietrangeli and Sirola in the second round; the second seeds, Laver and Mark, in the semi-final. This last success was after something of a contest! The score was 4–6 10–8 15–13 4–6 11–9. They were hardened to long matches. In the opening round they beat the British, Humphrey Truman and Gerald Oakley, only by 6–3 6–4 9–11 5–7 16–14. The final was simpler. Osuna and Ralston, the latter making himself the youngest man to take a Wimbledon championship, beat Wilson and Davies in three sets.

Apart from the glory in the women's singles, with its all-British final, Angela Mortimer against Christine Truman, the men's singles in 1961 brought the finest home success since before the war. To have two players in the last eight and one in the last four is not the ultimate of sporting achievement. But the sweet waters of even moderate success had been doled out so sparsely to Great Britain that the occasion was one for rejoicing. Wilson and Mike Sangster were the players who were hailed as heroes. Wilson had a spectacular fourth round win by beating the title holder Fraser. The Australian was not at his fittest, though fit enough to win the doubles with Emerson. Wilson yielded in the quarter-final to the exuberant pressures of McKinley. Sangster, a hard, fast server, was at that time somewhere near the peak of a game that, based on the overwhelming power of his delivery, gave him a psychological edge over many rivals. Without having to meet a seed he boomed his way into the semi-final. He, like Wilson, went down to McKinley.

This, though, was Laver's championship. Apart from the Australian singles, which he took in 1960, it was the first of his major triumphs. Yet it was touch and go whether this outstanding player, perhaps the finest of all time—views will differ over that but no one would dismiss the claim out of hand—would win the singles in 1961. In the second round he was perilously situated against the Frenchman, Pierre Darmon. He survived a point to trail 4–5 in the fifth set before pulling through. In the next round also he was taken the full distance by the German, Wilhelm Bungert. Having done as much his difficulties were over. He did not afterwards lose a set. He rattled through the final against McKinley in less than an hour.

The 75th meeting was staged in 1961 and the occasion was celebrated by gathering together as many champions as possible. The oldest guest at the celebratory lunch was Charlotte Sterry, not far short of her 91st birthday. She flew, unaccompanied and unconcerned, from Scotland for the occasion. It is said that one former champion, eyeing another across the tables, hurried across to remind him of what happened when last they were together. 'Do you realise', she is alleged precipitously to have cried, 'that if you hadn't missed that smash we would have won!' The occasion referred to was some 50 years before.

The following year, 1962, the expert Laver took Wimbledon as he took all the other important meetings of the world, those of Australia, Italy, France, Germany and America, to record the most impressive success in the game. His progress in France had been dangerous, for he was match point down against Mulligan, but there was no like risk at Wimbledon. He failed to be a three-set winner only in the quarter-final. That was against the Spaniard, Manuel Santana. Laver lost the first set 14–16 and was hard pressed to take the second 9–7. He then beat Fraser and, in the final, Mulligan. It was nothing like their match in Paris. Mulligan, unseeded, was fortunate to have the second seed, Emerson, concede to him because of a toe injury. Mulligan can hardly have enjoyed the final for Laver, watched by the Queen and Princess Margaret, allowed him only five games. This was Laver's last Wimbledon appearance until the game became open. Later that year he signed a £50 000 professional contract.

To the background of Laver's resounding success the men's singles shaped to different patterns from normal. There was no American in the last eight, this for the first time since 1922. Six Australians got as far and the last four were exclusively Australian. They were Laver, Neale Fraser, Mulligan and, also unseeded, John Fraser. The last was a brother of Neale and, a doctor by profession, a claimant to no more than a good club standard. His modesty belied his talents for if he were a lucky semi-finalist—the Indian, Krishnan, retired to him with an injured ankle in the third round to open the door—he was able enough to take advantage of his fortune. With two brothers so prominent Wimbledon again echoed to the memory of the Renshaws and the Dohertys.

Bob Hewitt and Fred Stolle won the doubles to make the men's titles an Australian copyright for the second year. In the final they beat the Yugoslavs, Boro Jovanovic and Nikki Pilic, who beat two seeded pairs, the Americans, McKinley and Ralston and the Australians, Emerson and Fraser, to reach that stage. There was an overtone of irony in this, for earlier that year Yugoslavia had been excluded from the Davis Cup under the rule which at that time excluded 'weak' nations in turn!

Administratively 1963 was a notable year. Colonel Duncan Macaulay retired from the secretaryship after a signally creative period in office since the end of the war. He was succeeded by his assistant, Major David Mills. The referee, Colonel John Legg, also stepped down. His place was taken by his son-in-law, Michael Gibson.

If the term eccentric could be applied to a tournament the Championships in 1963 merited that description. The new administrators did not have an easy time. In the first place it was a very wet two weeks. That would have passed with no more than normal problems had it not rained its hardest on the second Saturday. The meeting did not have its finals day until the third Monday and the new men's champion, who had, following the normal custom, been found on the second Friday, had no women's singles champion with whom to open the LTA Ball.

The men's singles champion, who accordingly danced with his wife, was the American, Chuck McKinley. In the absence of Laver he had the reward for his capacity to cover the ground between the base-line and forecourt with acrobatic skill and speed. He was seeded fourth. He never played another seed. Extraordinarily that year no seed ever did meet another. The seeding was, in any case, the most controversial that could be remembered.

The eighth seed, the Briton, Sangster, lost in the first round to the German, Bungert. The sixth seed, Darmon, lost in round two to the Australian, Bob Howe. So did the third seed, Australian, Ken Fletcher, who lost to his compatriot Stolle. Round three left the seeds secure but the fourth round saw the number seven, the Swede, Jan Erik Lundquist, brought down by the German, Christian Kuhnke and the fifth, Mulligan, beaten by Wilson. Accordingly only three seeds were in the last eight, Emerson, who was rated first, Santana, the second choice and McKinley. Emerson was beaten 8–6 3–6 6–3 4–6 6–3 in the quarters by a brilliant Bungert. Unless McKinley and Santana met in the final no seed would meet another. In due course Santana was beaten in the semi-final by Stolle. McKinley won against Bungert and, despite a longish first set, volleyed too ably for Stolle in the final.

McKinley emulated the American singles winner of eight years before, Tony Trabert, in taking his title without losing a set in any round. The only other champion to do so (since the abolition of the challenge round in 1922) was Don Budge in 1938. The ability to go through the event thus unscathed appears peculiarly American. Yet while Budge measured his success 129 games to 48, and Trabert by 131 games to 60, McKinley's figures were 140 games to 82.

Wilson lost to McKinley in the quarter-final. It was the fourth appearance of this finely moulded British player in the last eight.

For the fourth time in seven years the men's doubles champions were unseeded. For Osuna it was his second triumph, this time with a fellow Mexican as partner, Antonio Palafox. With Ralston in 1960 he lost six sets. With Palafox he lost eight. Their easiest victory, curiously, was in the final against the Frenchmen, Jean Claud Barclay and Darmon, also unseeded.

Australian dominance was reassumed in 1964 with vengeance. Indeed, had not the Brazilian, Maria Bueno, taken the women's singles, all five events would have belonged to Australia. Emerson got the first of his two championships. Stolle was again the losing finalist. The men's doubles final was also exclusively Australian with Hewitt and Stolle winning against Emerson and Fletcher. For that matter the mixed was another Australian preserve, Stolle and Lesley Turner beating Fletcher and Margaret Smith.

The mercurial Emerson, who in his career won every important singles championship except that of Italy, had been a keen contender at Wimbledon since being a semi-finalist in 1959. (Queensland had only one more distinguished lawn tennis son, Laver.) In 1964 he was 27. He was seeded first and he never looked like impairing that forecast. The tall Pilic ran him fairly hard in the second round. There was a second set of twenty games and Emerson lost the third. There was a close second set in the semi-final against Bungert. But having won it after 28 exciting games the match was virtually finished. It was different from the year before when Bungert put out Emerson in a *tour de force* that perhaps indicated the high-water mark of that German's genius for taking an early ball. Stolle, surprisingly, was the finalist against Emerson, having beaten the holder McKinley in a long and rigorous semi-final. The runner-up did not give in easily. Emerson needed all his speed, all his fitness to make his net play effective against the tall Stolle, whose level of performance never fell below first class.

The spectre of international politics, from which Wimbledon, as Wimbledon, had been free over the years, raised itself. This year the Soviet player, Alex Metreveli, unable to resist the pressure from home, withdrew to the South African, Abe Segal, in the third round. There were also scratchings in the women's and mixed doubles that were obviously politically motivated. No one blamed the individual players and whatever the feelings aroused by apartheid policies, lawn tennis players were notoriously a-political. The Management Committee issued dire warnings that future entry would be imperilled by such 'political' withdrawals and were able to quench the threatened fire. The administrators of the Davis Cup proved less successful.

If not a carbon copy the Championships of 1965 were much the same as those of the year before. The dominance of Australian men was maintained unchecked. The singles final repeated itself, Emerson against Stolle, the outcome this time being simpler for Emerson than in 1964. History of 30 years before was recalled, for just as Gottfried von Cramm was the losing singles finalist in 1935, 1936 and 1937, Stolle suffered the same sublime failure in 1963, 1964 and 1965. The men's doubles was entirely Australian, John Newcombe and Tony Roche putting themselves among the champions for the first time when they beat Fletcher and Hewitt.

A tall American from Pasadena, California, Stan Smith, challenged for the first time. Having won a round he was beaten by the dazzling volleying of Osuna. Smith was 18 years old. A year later another newcomer appeared. He was from Romania and five months younger than Smith. This was Ilie Nastase. Their skill and personality was later to make a big impression on the Championships.

Nothing seemed more probable in 1966 than Emerson, who was so lithe and skilled and fit, would set new standards and take the singles for the third time. He was seeded first as a matter of course. A fellow Australian, the left handed Tony Roche was seeded second. Stolle, hopeful at least of a fourth successive final, was third and the fourth was the Spaniard, Manuel Santana. He was French champion in 1961 and 1964. His status at Wimbledon was due to his prowess the previous autumn at Forest Hills when he won the US singles.

Fred Stolle, three times a finalist, never a winner

Roy Emerson, the supreme athlete

Emerson's defence was broken by an accident that would hardly have occurred had he not been so fleet of foot. Playing the Australian left hander Owen Davidson in the quarter-final he was over-zealous in chasing a short ball and injured himself against the umpire's chair. Davidson was then able to beat him and Emerson had to pull out of the doubles thus denying himself consolation there.

The throne, vacant for the first time for two years, was filled by Santana and there could have been no more popular occupant. This cheery Spaniard, the essence of good sportsmanship and the epitome of happiness on court, was a touch player with magic shots on a hard court. He should not have flourished on fast turf. Yet he had at Forest Hills and he did at Wimbledon. His forte had been in pulling a lost match round from nowhere, never quite finding his genius of shot—and when he did he was unplayable—until *in extremis*. He was close run none the less. In the quarter-final Fletcher threatened to win as far as five all in the fifth set. Davidson did the same in the semi-final.

The finalist against Santana was the Californian, Dennis Ralston, now six years beyond his precocious doubles title. Like another American of some years before, Barry Mackay, Ralston disturbed his supporters by an abnormal quota of double faults. He got to the last match after a major semi-final effort against the South African, Cliff Drysdale, possibly the smoothest exponent of double-fisted backhands. Ralston powered his way through from a leeway of two sets to one. If Ralston had achieved a reputation for being rather a tetchy player nothing could have been more infectiously good natured than the final. Ralston had the muscle; Santana had the touch. The Spaniard won a good and courteous final, with the really close issue the 11–9 second set, to bring the uproarious applause of the crowd. The solicitude with which Santana commiserated with Ralston for losing was surpassed only by the warmth with which Ralston congratulated him for winning.

The doubles final was again all Australian. For Great Britain, Mark Cox and Alan Mills stirred hopes as semi-finalists but that was mainly because of Emerson falling *hors de combat*. Newcombe was again the winner but as an unseeded contender. With Roche not fit he paired with Fletcher. They brought off a forthright victory after unexpected difficulty in the first round when they trailed two sets to love to Clay Iles and Stanley Matthews. There was another first round match of some moment. Pilic and the American, Gene Scott, played long and hard before beating the Texan, Cliff Richey, and the Dane, Torben Ulrich. The score, 19–21 12–10 6–4 4–6 9–7, comprised 98 games and set a new high for the greatest number played in the championships.

The 81st Championship meeting staged in 1967 was the last restricted to 'amateurs'. The events which led to the change the following year still lay in the future when the meeting opened. It did so with its most striking upset since Henri Cochet lost in the first round to Nigel Sharpe in 1931. But in that year Cochet was not actually the top seed nor the title holder. Santana, top seed and title holder, did not survive his curtain raising contest on the Centre Court. He was beaten, not one-sidedly but none the less quite surely, by the American, Charles Pasarell. The score was 10–8 6–3 2–6 8–6. Santana beamed sportingly. He had set a record in maintaining his tenure as champion for less than two hours after the start of the new meeting.

The top half of the singles draw had a very empty look for not one of the four seeds there reached the quarter-final. Roche, the fourth favourite, was beaten in the second round after a tremendous match against Richey. The Texan won 3–6 3–6 19–17 14–12 6–3. In the third round the Australian Bill Bowrey, the eighth seed, lost to Wilson. In the fourth, Drysdale, the fifth seed, yielded to the Yorkshireman, Roger Taylor. Wilson failed to go further. He lost to Bungert. Taylor came through against the Australian Ray Ruffels, who had beaten Richey, and became the second Briton to be a semi-finalist since before the war. But Taylor had Bungert standing between him and a place in the final and the impressive fluency of the German proved better than the rugged left-handed skill of Taylor.

The bottom half also saw seeding casualties. Emerson, seeded second and favourite with the defeat of Santana, failed unexpectedly to Pilic in the fourth round.

The Dane, Jan Leschly, who was seeded seventh, had not survived the second round and Pilic faced a quarter-final against the Australian, John Cooper. He was the younger brother of Ashley Cooper, the champion nearly ten years before. Pilic entered the semi-final at Cooper's expense. That, then, made for three non-seeds in the last four, Bungert, Taylor and Pilic, the last two left handers.

The third seed, John Newcombe, and the sixth seed, Ken Fletcher, survived to the last eight to stress that somewhere down the line results must follow form. Their quarter-final was the only meeting of seeded players and Newcombe won more easily against his fellow Australian than he did in earlier rounds against the Americans, Stan Smith and Clark Graebner, each an apostle, like himself, of the relentless forcing game. Newcombe having beaten Pilic in four sets routed Bungert for the loss of only five games in the final. Bungert had by then clearly had enough. Wearily he offered only nominal opposition. Yet though the winner of the last amateur Wimbledon had had one of its most one-sided final victories, there was no doubt about his power and quality as champion.

Newcombe, for all his forthright power, won the singles only. He and Roche surprisingly lost in the quarter-final of the doubles to the British pair, Peter Curtis and Graham Stilwell. They fell in the next round to Emerson and Fletcher, though with excitement a-plenty before they yielded—6–4 8–6 4–6 5–7 9–7 was the score—but the title went to South Africa. Hewitt and Frew McMillan went through the whole meeting without losing a set. Hewitt's South African affiliation at that time had the ring of novelty about it. Having been Australian he adopted it when he married a girl from South Africa and settled there.

Wimbledon's last 'amateur' set a new attendance record. The three hundred thousand mark was passed for the first time. The total for the twelve days was 301 896. The surplus from the meeting that year, accruing to the Lawn Tennis Association for the benefit of the British game at large, was £54 863.

This was a strangely non-American year among the men. In the singles the USA was represented neither among the eight seeds nor among those who got to the last eight; the semi-finals in the doubles were similarly lacking.

In the first ten years from 1946 seven men's singles championships belonged to America. In the last ten years to 1967 seven belonged to Australia.

15 THE OPEN WIMBLEDON (1968-1976)

There was an air of exhilaration about the start of the Championships in 1968. The events which led to the change to open lawn tennis are recounted on pages 218–20 and with them Wimbledon was not, technically at any rate, a participant. It had been expected that Wimbledon would be open to professionals and amateurs in 1960. That had not come about. When the change came in 1968 it was not that the meeting had become open to two classes of players, rather that all distinction had ceased to exist.

By later standards the prize money offered was modest. The total was £26 150. For the men's singles champion it was £2000 but for the women's a mere £750. But everybody got something. The first round men's singles loser was offered £50, the women's half that, £25. Later that year the US Open meeting at Forest Hills offered a good deal more than that. There the money came from sponsorship. At Wimbledon it came out of the normal revenues from the gate.

The thrill of an Open Wimbledon in 1968 did not come from the fact that the players were to be rewarded by direct payment. It came from renewed eligibility of many distinguished competitors who, having

switched from their technical amateur status to one of direct professionalism, had been unable to compete. The amount of prize money was almost an irrelevance.

The men's singles entry emphasised how many notable players had been kept away from the meeting. There was Ricardo Gonzales, manifestly one of the most powerful exponents in the world, a giant of a player in every way. His last appearance in the Championships was 1949. There was Ken Rosewall with his classic perfection of shot, not seen in the Championships since 1956. The unique power of Lew Hoad had its last championship challenge in 1957. The genius of Rod Laver belonged, in championship terms, to 1962. Sixteen seeds were selected as a matter of course. There was a request by the 'contract professionals' (some players were under contract to promoters and this phrase was used to distinguish them from the one-time 'amateurs') that they should be seeded apart from the rest of the field. This was refused and a straight seeding on merit undertaken. The actual list produced was a little controversial.

Laver was seeded top and Rosewall second. The Spaniard, Andres Gimeno, was third and this proved an overestimate of his skill. John Newcombe, who took the title in an amateur championship and defended it in an open, was seeded fourth. There were six men in the field who had worn the mantle as singles champion, not only Newcombe and Laver, but Roy Emerson, seeded fifth, Manuel Santana, seeded sixth, Hoad seeded seventh and Alex Olmedo, not seeded at all.

At this stage the professionals of long standing were still meeting difficulties in adapting to the rough and tumble and more varied standards of the tournaments to which they had been denied entry. That had been shown at the first of the open meetings, the British Hard Court Championships at Bournemouth. It was reflected in some degree at the first Open Wimbledon. No one would have denigrated the skill and awesome power of Gonzales, for example, even if he were 40 years old. Seeded eighth he got no further than the third round and the Soviet player, Alex Metreveli,

A giant among giants, Ricardo Gonzales

a winner in four sets. Hoad, another mighty player, lost at the same stage. Bob Hewitt, able to hit the ball with genius even though with sometimes a less than calm temperament, eliminated him. Hoad, bothered by a weakness in the back, was unable to shine as once he had.

It proved different with his original stable companion, Rosewall. Yet at the 1968 meeting this memorable performer, who not only won the first open event at Bournemouth but the first French Open as well (some fifteen years after his first success in Paris), did not justify his second seeding. Tony Roche, deploying his left-handed arts with verve and bite, beat Rosewall in three sets in the fourth round.

Newcombe also lost in the fourth round. Arthur Ashe, then competing as an amateur because of his army service, was responsible. Emerson went out in that round also. Having beaten Olmedo he yielded to the Dutchman, Tom Okker. Perhaps Emerson had lost some of his speed that day. Certainly Okker looked faster. The only former champion to reach the last eight was Laver.

So far as this player was concerned he might have said, 'As I was saying when I was interrupted . . .' and gone on from there. Having been unbeaten in the Championship singles in 1961 and 1962 he picked up six years later precisely where he left off. As in the past he paced his effort with consummate skill. He took four sets to win his first match, which was against the American, Gene Scott. His draw was not easy. In the second round he met another American, Stan Smith, whom he beat in three sets. There was a third American, Marty Riessen, who extended Laver to four sets. The British Mark Cox, whose left-handed hitting had done damage amongst the 'pros' at Bournemouth, also won a set in round four.

Laver faced a fourth American opponent, Dennis Ralston, who had beaten Metreveli, in the quarter-finals. It was his hardest contest. Laver needed five sets in that round. Then he moved into top gear to beat Ashe, the fifth American to oppose him. In the meantime Roche beat Buchholz in the quarters and the unseeded Clark Graebner, a fine, rugged serve-and-volley man, in the semi-final. Laver reached his most commanding form in the final. He was entirely authoritative against Roche. For the first time for many years the Wimbledon Championship had put all the world's finest players against one another. It was clear that a great player had won a great meeting and Laver was the man.

Some resoundingly good pairs contested the doubles. Emerson and Laver were officially reckoned the best. They were not good enough to get through a semi-final against Newcombe and Roche, whose seeding was fourth. Hewitt and McMillan, defending the title, were seeded only sixth. They, too, fell in the semi-final, to the second seeds, Rosewall and Stolle. Newcombe and Roche won the title, as they had done three years before. In the final they beat Rosewall and Stolle 3–6 8–6 5–7 14–12 6–3 and its total of 70 games was the highest at that stage.

The weather at first did not welcome an Open Wimbledon. For five days it was miserably damp. A 'go slow' on the railways was another hardship spectators had to undergo. The total attendance was 276 710, a shortfall on the year before but no bad figure none the less. With £26 000 in prize money to pay out, the profits for the Lawn Tennis Association fell correspondingly. It was £35 960 for 1968.

A year later, 1969, the aspect of Wimbledon as an open meeting was a novelty no longer. The excitements of that year owed nothing to the piquancy of a heightened atmosphere, only to their own intrinsic heat. The most outstanding aspect of it was the renewed success of Laver.

Four Wimbledon singles championships after playing through was a feat never before accomplished. Laver led the field like a thoroughbred. Yet the opposition was high, probably as high as it could be and this neat and expert Queenslander was often stretched, though never, as it turned out, to the limit. He was, and this surprisingly, in apparent danger in the second round. Here, against the Indian, Premjit Lall, he dropped the first two sets and then three games in the third. Laver won the last two sets to love to stress his mastery but it was abnormal progress for a champion whose last defeat in the Championships belonged to the final of 1960! He was also taken the full distance when he met Smith for the second time in two years, on this occasion in the fourth round. But the big American was always fighting from behind. Laver then beat Drysdale and Ashe and, in the final, Newcombe. The master was masterly.

There were other memorable happenings. Roche, who later lost a long semi-final to Newcombe, had a tremendous quarter-final against Graebner, winning 4–6 4–6 6–3 6–4 11–9 after an exchange of the most searing services. This year Graebner was seeded

Tony Roche, five times men's doubles champion

number seven in a field of sixteen. Smith, the number sixteen seed, had a striking first round match when he beat the Australian, Allan Stone only by 20–22 6–4 9–7 4–6 6–3. That, because of its 87 games, would have been remembered had it not been for another of the first-round clashes. No one, having seen it, could forget the match in which Gonzales, huge, hot blooded as one would expect a man of Mexican origin to be, and acknowledged by all to have been the greatest power player of the 1950s, survived, perilously and dramatically, against another American, Charles Pasarell.

The bare bones of it was that Gonzales beat Pasarell, born in Puerto Rico 25 years before, by 22–24 1–6 16–14 6–3 11–9. The total of 112 games had never been exceeded in any event at Wimbledon (and with the tie break operating probably never will be). The duration of the match was 5 hours 12 minutes. Virtually every moment of it was absorbing. It began on the evening of Tuesday, 24 June around half past six. It was getting on for nine before even the first set, let alone the match, was finished. The long service and volley interchange recalled the Herculean struggle between Jaroslav Drobny and Budge Patty sixteen years before.

Having lost the set Gonzales did not like the situation at all. Light was fading and he asked for a postponement. From behind the stop netting, the referee, Michael Gibson, indicated it should go on. Gonzales did not hide his anger. He slashed at many a ball in pique and the upshot was an easy set for Pasarell. Then a halt was called with the younger man leading two sets to nil. On resumption at two o'clock the next day most expected nothing but a formal finish. Gonzales was, after all, 41 years old. His reaction provided this great player with perhaps his finest hour. It was as if, having been denied the prestige rewards of championships which must surely have fallen to him, had the political history of the game been different, he was determined to reveal all his majestic quality in a belated hour at Wimbledon.

Gonzales made the long, hard road back. He won the third set 16–14. When he did that it was obvious that lawn tennis history was being made. That was 83 games and the match was not yet over. The fourth set was simple, 6–3 to Gonzales. Pasarell then surged forward towards victory once again. In the twenty games of the fifth set Pasarell was seven times within a stroke of winning. On two occasions Gonzales, serving, had 0–40 against himself and defeat. At last he won, this in the 112th game and 312th minute of the match.

Whatever else he did Gonzales had done enough in the Championships to be remembered for ever. He won another two rounds and lost to Ashe. He got one round further than Rosewall, who fell to the American, Bob Lutz.

Again the doubles was distinguished and exciting. There was a quarter-final in which Hewitt and McMillan beat Lutz and Smith after a fifth set of 38 games. The South Africans lost in the semi-final to the title holders, Newcombe and Roche. The other semi-final had Emerson and Laver yielding to Tom Okker and Marty Riessen but the latter pair, for all their electric skill, could not deter the sweeping power of Newcombe and Roche from another triumph.

The prize money had grown to a total of £33 370, the attendance to 298 811 (despite a wash-out on the opening day) and the LTA netted a record £93 684. This was following a special broadcasting fee that was paid. Otherwise it would rank as a record, though profits accruing to the LTA looked much less healthy after tax had been paid.

A break with precedence was made in the timetable in 1969. Since 1933 it was the custom to stage the men's singles final on the second Friday, the women's singles the next day. A reversion was made to earlier practice and the schedule planned for the women's singles and the men's doubles finals on the Friday with the other finals making the climax on Saturday.

The last eight of the men's singles in 1970 contained five Australians, a measure of rich talent, but it did not contain the most illustrious Australian of all—Laver was absent. A magnificent reign came to an end. He lost on Saturday, 27 June. The last occasion anyone had seen this masterly left hander beaten in a singles on the court at Wimbledon was Friday, 1 July ten years earlier, when he lost in the final to Neale Fraser.

Wimbledon spectators would have been sad for the downfall of so superb a player had not the victor stirred their emotions more. Another left hander, from Yorkshire, beat Laver. Roger Taylor bludgeoned a skilful win which none expected—the number sixteen seed was better than the number one. Laver was, that afternoon, an *artiste manqué*. At the age of 31 (and having won 31 Wimbledon championship singles in glorious succession) he revealed the normal failings of a lawn tennis player.

Taylor, then 28 years old, manfully carried his triumph further. By beating Graebner, when a second set of 20 games and a third of 22 emphasised the muscle power of their services, Taylor made himself a semi-finalist for the second time. No other British man had done as much since 1938. Two of the major quarter-finals in 1970 though, were entirely Australian. Newcombe battled for more than three hours before beating Emerson and when he did, by 6–1 5–7 3–6 6–2 11–9, it was after saving break points against his service in the 3rd, 5th, 9th and 11th games in the fifth set. Rosewall, demonstrating masterly precision, beat Roche in four sets.

Taylor could not deny Rosewall a place in the final. He had not the subtlety of stroke to do so and Rosewall won in four sets. And the Spaniard, Andres Gimeno, who beat Arthur Ashe earlier in the event, did not have the power to hold Newcombe in check in the other semi-final. The final was between Newcombe, the champion of 1967 and runner-up of 1969, and Rosewall. It was also Rosewall's third final. A difference was that his last adventures there were in 1956 and 1954. Who would have reckoned, seeing Rosewall lose to Hoad in 1956, that they could be watching the same player in the title match fourteen years later?

Newcombe, younger by 10 years, won in five sets after 163 exciting minutes. He lost the first set 5–7 after having a point for it at 5–4. He established what seemed complete mastery but, having won the second set 6–3 and the third 6–2 and led 2–0 in the fourth, he fell into a kind of trance. He came to and his weight of shot reasserted itself in the fifth set. It was the first five-set final for 21 years.

This was Newcombe's year. Having got the singles for the second time he won the doubles for the fifth, for the third year in succession and the fourth in all with Roche. Rosewall and Stolle were the losing finalists. For Newcombe and Roche the key match was the semi-final against Hewitt and McMillan from whom they wrested a narrow victory by 7–5 8–6 5–7 5–7 6–4.

Changes were made in 1971. The number of seeds for the men's singles reverted to its old figure of eight, having been sixteen for three previous years. The tie break was introduced for the first time. This followed its use in the United States the year before, experimental systems having been sanctioned by the ILTF. There were many who did not favour the tie break and a great many more who strongly opposed the American 'sudden-death' method. This was played over the best of nine points and, if the players were level at four points each, the next rally constituted a set point (or match point) for both at the same time. It had the merit of being exciting. The Wimbledon Management Committee compromised with the innovation. Instead of a 'sudden-death' nine-point tie break, one of twelve points was adopted in which it was necessary to have a lead of at least two points. If the values of lawn tennis were abbreviated by the use of the tie break the British system at least had the merit of maintaining the traditional principle of a winner being at least two units ahead of the loser. A conservative approach was further maintained by not bringing in the tie break until eight games all and never in the deciding set of a match. It was this system which became, with minor amendments, the official ILTF method in due course.

Although Newcombe was the defending holder he was seeded second. Laver, despite his defeat the year before, did not lose his status as the official favourite. Rosewall was the third seed. He was the reigning champion of the United States. Smith, the best of the Americans and a player of might and muscle, was seeded fourth. The only one of these senior men who did not reach the semi-finals was Laver. Having beaten strong players in Graebner and Okker he was put out in the quarter-final by Tom Gorman, a cheery, able and vigorous man from Seattle. Like Taylor the year before, Gorman played above himself to win and he did so in three sets. Laver's genius was not displayed. Gorman accordingly became an unseeded semi-finalist but his effort against Laver was such that an old back injury flared up again. He had small hope of containing Smith and was not able to do so. But Smith's success in the semi-final was not as one-sided as that of Newcombe over Rosewall.

The evergreen Rosewall burned himself out in the ground before. The outstanding contest in the singles was his quarter-final win against the Texan, Cliff Richey, with Rosewall coming from behind to survive 6–8 5–7 6–4 9–7 7–5. Both men played superb lawn tennis. The upshot was that Rosewall had nothing left to offer when he met Newcombe in the semi-final. The five-set final of the year before was replaced by a tame affair. As for the final, Newcombe and Smith made for a clash of heavyweights. It went the full distance and Newcombe showed he had the margin of flexibility and staying power in recovering from a two sets to one deficit.

This was Newcombe's third singles title. Surprisingly he did not then get his sixth doubles championship. He and Roche, having been champions for three years in a row, a feat not achieved since the abolition of the challenge round, were beaten in the first round by Drysdale and Pilic. This major upset presaged a host of others. Hewitt and McMillan disappeared in the first round also. The other two seeded players, Rosewall and Stolle, the Romanians, Ilie Nastase and Ion Tiriac, did not get beyond the quarters. All four semi-finals pairs were unseeded. In the final Emerson and Laver beat Ashe and Ralston.

After four years as an open tournament a name other than that of an Australian had yet to be added to Wimbledon's honours board in the men's events. It was Laver's first success in the doubles field. It was his 100th winning match during the Wimbledon fortnight.

The murk of politics clouded the meeting of 1972. Reflecting the unease in the administration of the game, with commercial interests at odds with the amateur control of the traditional events, the Wimbledon Championships were staged at a time when professionals under contract were barred from ILTF tournaments. Wimbledon was destined to meet bigger problems later. On this occasion 'contract' professionals were ineligible. The irony of it was that peace between the ILTF and World Championship Tennis, the body involved, was obviously just around the corner. One did not need to be a Nostradamus to see that by late August Forest Hills would be free and unfettered for all. None the less the Championships in 1972 had to deny entry to some of the best men players, even the champion Newcombe, who was personally keen on defending his title. Laver, Rosewall and Ashe were missing also.

That it was a diminished field cannot be gainsaid. How ironic was it then that the final of the men's singles produced the best since the classic between Jack Crawford and Ellsworth Vines in 1933! Stan Smith and Ilie Nastase in 1972 replaced that encounter as the yardstick by which 'great' Wimbledon finals could be measured. To make it more memorable it was played on a Sunday. This followed a completely wet final Saturday and, no charge being made for admission, many spectators had their treat for free!

The opening day had the excitement of a seeding upset but over all the accuracy of the forecast could hardly have been bettered. There was only one event where the numbers one and two seeds did not meet in the final, the women's doubles, and there it was the first and third! The initial upset was achieved by an American newcomer, Jim Connors, aged 19. He had appeared in the draw in 1971 but had not turned up. He wielded his double-fisted backhand with exuberant and uninhibited pressure to beat Hewitt, the seventh favourite. It was no fluke. He won three more rounds and yielded only in the quarter-final to Nastas was a distinguished debut. Another first appeara was in the junior event. This was won, resoundin well for one so young, by the Swede, Bjorn Borg, just 16.

The only Australian to have a place in the singles last eight was the big-serving Colin Dibley. He did not survive further and the semi-finals, Smith versus the Czech, Jan Kodes, the Spaniard, Manuel Orantes versus Nastase, contained three continental European players for the first time since 1928. All the quarter-finals were decided in three sets and the precedent for that was also pre-war; one could not deny a measure of humdrum quality. Smith needed four sets to win his semi-final against Kodes. Nastase beat Orantes more quickly. All in all when rain filled the scene on the final Saturday, the men's singles looked like finishing as an event of no more than ordinary dimensions.

The final left burning memories of a splendid match. It had tremendous quality from the first shot and uncertain issue until the last ball was struck. Smith, trenchant, forceful and relentless as the tide, produced one of his finest displays, perhaps the finest of his career. Nastase, less relentless but with more sensitive touch, played within the confines of his Latin temperament, rising to greater heights, falling to lower depths. For four sets he nervily switched from racket to racket. Only for the fifth set did he find one that had tension to suit him. Smith lost the opening set, staunchly took the next two. But he lost the fourth. It was anybody's match at two sets all. It was still anybody's match at four games all. Then came the match's most dramatic moment. Smith, serving, was 0–30 and, being forced to stretch wide for a forehand volley, might easily have been 0–40. The ball hit the wood of his racket and rebounded across the net as a perfect stop volley. With that lucky shot Smith was saved from probable defeat and three games later he was champion.

Australia, having had small share of the singles, was also kept out of the doubles. Hewitt and McMillan got the second of their championships five years after their first and their victims in the final were American, Smith and Erik van Dillen. For Hewitt it was his fourth title, having won twice with Stolle; then he wore his native Australian cap, not his adopted South African.

If politics muddied the waters in 1972 they befouled them entirely in 1973. It was the most troubled year experienced at Wimbledon, when every top-class man player in the world, with a handful of notable exceptions, boycotted the meeting. As it happened the tournament emerged none the worse from a chastening experience and the attendance, passing 300 000, was the second highest of all time. The normal run up to the meeting was traumatic.

Overleaf:
The Romanian Ilie Nastase seen here at full stretch

The Association of Tennis Professionals, ATP for short, was formed only the previous September. Jack Kramer was its executive director, the South African player, Cliff Drysdale, its president. Most of the world's leading men players were members.

The dispute with ATP followed the suspension, by the Yugoslav Federation, of Nikki Pilic for failing to play for Yugoslavia in a Davis Cup tie. The suspension albeit reduced from nine months to one month, was upheld on appeal by the ILTF and meant that the entry of Pilic for the Championships could not be accepted—unless the Management Committee ignored the ruling of the world's governing body. ATP claimed that the suspension was unjust.

Pilic appealed to the British High Court against the validity of his suspension. His action failed. None the less ATP, holding the view that if Pilic could not play, none would, called on its members to withdraw their entries. In the meantime preparations for the draw had gone on in the usual way. The seeding list was issued. For the singles it had sixteen selections. The draw itself, timed as usual for the Wednesday preceding the start of the meeting, was postponed. When it took place 79 ATP members had withdrawn. The seeding, reduced to eight, was recast and the qualifying competition at Roehampton halted. It was obvious that with so many gaps to fill it was pointless playing it further.

What was the saddest Wimbledon draw of all time was conducted two days late on the Friday. Of the original sixteen seeds only three remained. They were Nastase, who had been number two, Kodes, who had been fifteen and Taylor, who had been sixteen. In the revised list they filled the top three places. The other five spots were taken, in merit order, by the Soviet player, Alex Metreveli, by Jim Connors, by the young Bjorn Borg, by Owen Davidson and the German, Jurgen Fassbender. They had had unexpected promotion. So had a host of aspiring challengers, including many who had already been beaten in the qualifying rounds.

Before the draw took place the chairman of the Championships, Herman David, commented on the unique nature of the occasion. He deplored the dispute. 'But', he added, 'there will be no recriminations.' Nor were there.

Notably three members did not fall in with the instructions of ATP to withdraw. One was Nastase, who claimed that his Romanian association had instructed him to play. Taylor, torn between loyalty to his own championship and other interests, chose to be patriotic. The Australian, Ray Keldie also did not fall into line with ATP. All three were subsequently fined by ATP for competing. Kodes and all other competitors were not then ATP members.

So far as the dispute between ATP and the traditional ruling authorities in lawn tennis was a struggle for a share in control of the game, the victory, if one can call it that, lay with ATP; Wimbledon was not in direct dispute with them.

Certainly the many ATP members who regretted that they made their stand against Wimbledon rather than some other championship were sincere; all the world knew that the springs of open lawn tennis, from which they had had such enormous benefits, were fed copiously by Herman David from an early date. Even at the height of the controversy the amount of bitterness was not great. There was, though, no public sympathy for the players who withdrew. The ATP leader, Jack Kramer, did not take up his normal occupation as one of the leading BBC TV commentators for the fortnight.

Taylor's action as a 'blackleg' turned him almost into a national hero. And the fact that Wimbledon had been 'blacked' to use a union term, by most of the great men players of the world brought a widespread sympathy. The public, rather than staying away, reacted, it seemed, by coming in greater numbers. The attendance figure for the first Friday was 32 445, the highest for many years. And what should have been, in the men's events, a poor championship was, in fact, a good one.

It produced in Kodes a champion worthy of his predecessors. It produced a new teenage idol in the youthful Borg. Indeed, in this sense, 1973 was, perhaps, a turning-point. Nastase had for some time represented a changed aspect of the Championships as a spectacle. Increasingly, young spectators gave vent to the sort of enthusiasm common to the world of 'pop' music. The advent of Borg provided an acceleration of this frenzied expression of popularity. It became a matter of routine for the police to escort both Nastase and Borg to their courts.

Borg made a striking debut in the Championships. He could have been 27, not 17. He opened with a fascinating Centre Court duel with the Indian, Premjit Lall. The climax of it was a tie break in the third set which Borg eventually won by 20 points to 18. Nastase disappointed his followers. He should have been in a class of his own. He assuredly was not when he met Sandy Mayer, from New York, on the first Saturday. Out of touch, Nastase pulled himself together sufficiently to save a threatened defeat in three sets but could not avert his loss in four. Mayer was joined by the Indian, Vijay Amritraj as an unseeded quarter-finalist but only Mayer went further to the last four. There Metreveli, who had beaten Connors with difficulty, brought him down and became a finalist.

Borg met his end in a long, struggling quarter-final against Taylor. The Yorkshire left hander, who trailed two sets to one, won the fifth set at 7–5 after leading 5–2. At the same stage Kodes had much the same kind of match against Amritraj. The semi-final in which Kodes beat Taylor 7–5 in the fifth set was the most dramatic of the meeting, though in pure lawn tennis terms the finest was probably in the third round when Fassbender beat Keldie by 15–13 in the deciding set.

Taylor was in the last four for the third time. Even in a year of diminished values the possibility of a British finalist lost nothing of its appeal. If many suspected that Kodes was a rank or two higher in the class structure of the game it would have seemed unpatriotic to most spectators to think in terms other than Taylor winning. He nearly did. A splendid match had its excitements heightened by the miserable weather. Kodes lost the first set 8–9 after having three

Above: Roger Taylor, a semi-finalist in 1973, preparing to serve

chances to win it. It was very close. So was the second set which the Czech won 9–7. The third, won by Taylor at 7–5, was an uphill struggle in which his frequent double faults marked the extent to which he strove to keep the pressure up behind his service. Kodes came back with the fourth set at 6–4. The fifth set continued in fading light. Taylor was ahead 5–4 when a drizzle brought a halt. The interruption was fatal to Taylor. His momentum checked, he lost the next three games on resuming and Kodes was through to the final.

There have been worse finals than that between Kodes and Metreveli and there have been better. Kodes, more experienced in the rigours of leading tournaments—he was champion of France in 1970, 1971 and runner-up at Forest Hills in 1971 as well—took the occasion more calmly. Metreveli was obviously nervous; he muffed a point he had for the second set 5–4. Kodes played competently to win. This was not a vintage Wimbledon year with its entry so depreciated. None the less Kodes by no means reduced the status of Wimbledon singles champions.

Nor did the winners of the doubles. Nastase paired with Connors to take the title, the latter thus winning at his first attempt. The losing finalists were Australian, John Cooper paired with one who was certainly no stranger to the courts, Neale Fraser, 39 years old and looking younger.

For the second year the meeting overran its timetable and ended on Sunday. This time only the mixed doubles was involved, Davidson and Billie Jean King, winning first the semi-final and then the final on that day.

Despite the boycott the attendance figures were the second highest at 300 172. One cannot say that

Below: The Egyptian, El Shafei, after his third round victory over the up and coming Borg in 1974

sponsorship came into the meeting but there was a change. The provision of cars for the transport of players ceased to be the financial responsibility of the management. British Leyland took over that service. It meant the loss of the dignity of big limousines and dark-uniformed chauffeurs. The gain was bright feminine charm and more colour all round perhaps more in keeping with Nastase and Borg and the teenage idolatry they attracted.

A year later all was peace and the course of the Championships went on from where it had been in 1971. Alas, the meeting in 1974 continued under a new guiding hand. Herman David died on 25 February that year, having served the club, the Championships and lawn tennis as a whole with notable distinction as chairman for fifteen years. His place was taken by Air Chief Marshal Sir Brian Burnett.

A rather abrasive and brash young American, Connors, took the singles. He was 21 years old and since his triumph was paralleled by another young American, Chris Evert, who was 19, winning the women's singles it was hard to escape the impression that a new generation had taken over. At the time they were engaged to be married and the romance added piquancy to the meeting. But if the bold hitting of Connors made him look like one of the most forthright champions of all time—his recipe was to hit for winners whatever the situation, and, left handed and double fisted on the backhand, he was extraordinarily skilful in so doing—the exploits of Rosewall, approaching his 40th birthday, stirred spectators, young and old, almost to nostalgic ecstasy.

It was a vibrant Championship throughout. Borg disappointed his clamorous supporters. After taking the French Championships, a most notable triumph for one barely 18 years old, he failed to justify his fifth seeding when he tamely yielded in the third round to the Egyptian, Ismail El Shafei. Nor did Nastase live up to his talents. Seeded second, this vital and controversial Romanian was hammered to defeat by the American, Dick Stockton in the fourth round. Stockton went on to beat Metreveli and so became an unseeded semi-finalist, losing to Connors.

Kodes defended his title manfully. A freshness had gone from his game but clearly he was determined to prove himself something more than a player who had picked up a championship in a cheap year. In the second round he was taken to a fifth set of ten games by the Swede, Lief Johansson. In the third round the Australian, Dick Crealy, stretched him to a fifth set of twelve games. In the fourth the American, Gorman, not only led him two sets to nil but had four match balls during the course of a sixteen-game fourth set. When Kodes met Connors in the quarter-final another five setter took place before the old champion yielded to the young man on his way to becoming the new.

It was not Connors's hardest match. That took place in the second round against the Australian, Phil Dent. Connors was behind 5–6, 0–30, in the fifth set before he won. Another two points and there would have been a different champion.

Would it have been Rosewall? If sentiment had ruled in 1974 he would have been. His heroics began in the fourth round when, to the surprise of some, he beat the American, Roscoe Tanner (from the splendidly named Tennessee community of Lookout Mountain). Tanner had beaten Ashe in the round before. Rosewall then played Newcombe in the quarter-final and the big Newcombe, three times a recent champion (1967, 1970 and 1971) and victor, moreover, against Rosewall in the final of 1970 and in the semi-final of 1971, appeared prospectively to have a formality ahead of him. On a windy day and in a lunch-time match it turned out differently. It was a lunch-time match because rain in the early days of the meeting had disrupted the timetable. To make up leeway most of the second week's play began at noon instead of the normal two o'clock. Rosewall won an easy first set. Newcombe took the second set just as simply; events reversed themselves unpredictably as Rosewall took the third set to love for the loss of only twelve points. A keenly fought fourth set had Rosewall playing with precision and he had the only service break in the twelfth game to gain his victory.

This unexpected turn was followed by one that was even more astonishing. The mighty American, Smith, was as the seeding forecast, the semi-finalist against Rosewall. Smith was the dominant player for the greater part of the time. He led 8–6 6–4 5–3. He served for the match one game later. One point was all he won. With the tie break at eight games all, Smith, ahead six points to five, stood within a stroke of winning. Rosewall had the service and made no mistake. Smith's big strokes ebbed in power. Rosewall's precision grew more sharp. Rosewall won the third set 9–8 and took the next two 6–1 6–3.

This made him singles finalist for the fourth time in his career. It rather strained the imagination to realise that when Rosewall played his first final in 1954 his opponent was not two years old, that when Rosewall played first at Wimbledon in 1952 Connors was not born! The final was realistic. To use racing parlance, Rosewall 'did not show'. It was all too evident that a man of nearly 40 had exhausted himself in surviving two demanding rounds. It was all too evident that Connors was bold, skilled and irresistible. He hit joyous and punishing winners right, left and centre and Rosewall was overwhelmed.

Not that Connors was allowed to go through the meeting unscathed. He and Nastase took their men's doubles defence as far as the semi-final but no further. There, the long-standing partnership of Australian talent and fortitude awaited them. Newcombe and Roche beat them from a deficit of two sets to love and went on to win the final against the Americans, Lutz and Smith. It was their fifth Championship together.

Nothing vital changed in the Championships in 1975 but there were differences. A bookmaker's tent made its appearance in the north-east corner of the ground. It did good business. Not all welcomed it. ATP was a body that frowned at the innovation and forbade its members to take part in its activities. The Commercial Union Assurance Company, the sponsor of the Grand Prix of which the Wimbledon meeting was a part, were allowed to erect hospitality tents on the hard courts.

What would the worthy Henry Jones have said? One suspects that Dr Jones, who, despite his fertile and creative imagination, can hardly have envisaged what Wimbledon was to become, would have welcomed the modernity.

Few men can have started their title defence so strongly favourite as Connors. He was young and skilled and supremely confident. His progress through round after round merely strengthened the expectation of his success. The climax was a semi-final against Tanner, winner of a five-setter quarter-final against the Argentinian, Guillermo Vilas, established by this time as one of the master players of the world. Connors hit the ball so hard and with such control against Tanner that it seemed he was taking the game to new dimensions. He arrived in the final without losing a set.

The rest of the event was played in the shadow of Connors. Rosewall was seeded second. This paid tribute to his performance of the previous year. It could not realistically be hoped that he would do as well. He did not fall far short of it. He lost in the fourth round to his fellow Australian, Tony Roche. This left hander, bothered on and off throughout his career with physical problems, promised a revival of old glories.

The glamour players, if they can be called that, had varying fates. Nastase, tempestuously brooding, got no further than the second round and the American, Sherwood Stewart, who came from Goose Creek, Texas. Borg, seeded third, came within sight of justifying his high status. He lost to Ashe in the quarter-final.

Ashe, seeded number six, had disappointed his supporters at Wimbledon more often than not. His best in previous years was to be semi-finalist in 1968 and 1969. He was almost 32 years old. He had his best career performance at Wimbledon when, having beaten Borg, he proceeded to eliminate Roche, after a five setter to reach the final. Connors was by that time playing so well that it seemed that Ashe was doing no more than making himself a sacrifice. The only discussion before the final was on how Connors would win, not whether he would.

In fact the bookmakers in the tent presumably made a killing. Connors, having for eleven days looked as if he could demolish a mountain single handed, found himself taut with normal, human nerves when he faced the task of taking the singles for the second year. Ashe, in contrast, played perhaps not the best match of his life but certainly his most astute. Reasoning that pace-making would just feed the fires of Connors's power engine he soft pedalled on his own natural game. He exploited widely angled shots to render the opposition more impotent. With difficulty Connors won the third set, having taken only two games in the first two. In the end he was well beaten, utterly unexpectedly, and Ashe, the winner of the first US Open in 1968, won his first Wimbledon title seven years later.

James Scott Connors, the aggressive singles champion of 1974

Above: Stan Smith and Ilie Nastase in the memorable final of 1972

Right: Ken Rosewall, again a finalist in 1974—and for the fourth time in a long career

Below: Success for John Newcombe, making him in 1971, singles champion for the third time

Above: Arthur Ashe in action on the Centre Court, he went on (*right*) to win the singles title in 1975 and so become the first Black American male champion

Below: Roscoe Tanner: reputedly with one of the most powerful services to have been seen at Wimbledon

It was the first all-American singles final since 1947. Ashe was not the first black American on the Wimbledon honours board. As a woman champion, Althea Gibson had that distinction nearly twenty years before.

If Ashe had a surprising victory it was because Connors could not fulfil expectations. In the men's doubles, normal tenets of form entirely faded. Out of eight seeded pairs only one, Hewitt and McMillan, reached the quarter-finals and they got no further. They were beaten by Colin Dowdeswell of Rhodesia and Allan Stone of Australia, who went on to reach the final. The last were a scratch pair and had never met each other until Dowdeswell, hearing that Stone had lost his partner, Ray Ruffels, because of injury, suggested he might enjoy a game or two together.

The champions were two New Yorkers, Vitas Gerulaitis and Sandy Mayer. If their victory surprised everybody it probably surprised themselves. It was not obvious why form was so upside down.

Missing from the field were Newcombe and Roche, for Newcombe had an injury and was not a contender in the singles. Neither the top seeds, Brian Gottfried and Paul Ramirez, an American-Mexican partnership that triumphed in the World Championship Tennis finals and elsewhere, nor the second, Connors and Nastase, the champions two years earlier, got beyond round two. It seemed as if a malaise came over pairs of proven ability.

The attendance figures set new records. On the first Wednesday 37 018 spectators were in the ground. On the first Friday it was even higher, no less than 37 290. The total for the two weeks was 338 591.

Had it not been for the interruption of the two World Wars 1976 would have been the 100th staging of the Championships. It was in fact the 90th and probably the hottest and driest of all time. There was a new referee, Fred Hoyles, a Lincolnshire farmer, and he watched the sun beat down mercilessly day after day with scarcely ever a cloud seen in the sky.

This tropical meeting brought the youngest winner of the men's singles for 45 years. The Swede Bjorn Borg became the champion at the age of 20 years 27 days. There were just two players on the honours board who were younger. The American Sidney Wood was 19 years 8 months 3 days old when he won on a walkover in 1931. The British Wilfred Baddeley was 19 years 5 months 23 days old when he won in 1891.

Borg's precocious victory was one of maturity compared with what he had done elsewhere. When he won the French Championship for the first time in 1974 he was only just 18 years old. The surprise was that his normally heavily top-spun forehand and his double-fisted backhand, strokes perfected on slow courts, adapted so well to the demands of grass that was never drier or faster. Despite bother with a strained stomach muscle that necessitated pain-killing injections Borg played dynamic and irresistible lawn tennis from first to last. He lost a set in no round.

The Mexican Raul Ramirez in action

A reflective Bjorn Borg was champion at the age of 20

Since the abolition of the challenge round such unscathed champions have been rare among the men. The American Chuck McKinley did not lose a set in 1963, nor did Tony Trabert, American also, in 1955. Don Budge conceded no set in 1938. Borg was the fourth of the line.

Ashe made a frail defence of his title and got no further than the fourth round and another American Vitas Gerulaitis. Connors, seeded second, began as the overwhelmingly popular favourite. A quarter-final against the scorching services of Roscoe Tanner brought his downfall.

There was no Australian in the last eight and apart from the freak year of 1973 this was the first time since 1939 that this was so. While Borg dominated one half of the draw the other was equally dominated by the Romanian Ilie Nastase. Never, it seemed, had this fine genius of a touch player taken a tournament so seriously. But having reached the final without losing a set he quite failed in the last match to reveal his finest talents. His previous final, in 1972 against Stan Smith, provided a breathtaking climax. His final against Borg was anything but that. Borg was brilliant and the Romanian opposition quailed before him. A man of muscle, a man of iron, that was Borg in 1976 and he never put a foot wrong from start to finish.

Having got everything wrong the previous year the seedsmen for the men's doubles were able to claim accuracy in their selection of the American-Mexican partnership of Brian Gottfried and Paul Ramirez as the best pair. The event was chock-a-block with seeding claimants but even so it was surprising that out of eight selections so notable a pairing as John Newcombe and Tony Roche were omitted. This pair had no less than five prior championships to confirm their quality.

The fact of their omission from the seeding was highlighted by the draw. They clashed with the top seeds Gottfried and Ramirez in the opening round and the match they played could reasonably have been the final. Newcombe and Roche won the first two sets (9–7 9–8) but their inability to clinch the next—they lost it at 9–7—proved fatal. Their energies drained too fast. The admirable combination of pace and subtlety which had served Gottfried and Ramirez well in events elsewhere in the world had its triumph, albeit narrowly.

The new doubles champions were not taken to five sets again until the final, where they were challenged by the unseeded partnership of two younger Australians, Ross Case and Geoff Masters.

The turf this year was under the care of a new head groundsman, Jack Yardley. He succeeded Bob Twynan whose services to the club had extended to more than 50 years.

Right: Bjorn Borg, the 1976 champion, receives the cup from the President after a dynamic match and precocious victory (*facing page*)

Below: Raul Ramirez won the doubles in 1976 with his American partner, Brian Gottfried

16
AMERICAN AMAZONS (*Women* 1946-1958)

When in 1946 British lawn tennis began anew after its six years hiatus the first event to be staged at the All England Club, apart from an Allied services event in 1945, was the Wightman Cup contest. For the women this provided an obvious pointer to what form in the Championship might be like. There was a change in that it was staged not on the Centre Court but on Court One. This remained the setting for the Wightman Cup in Britain until the move to North Wales in 1974.

Inevitably the Americans were favourites, if only because the US game had continued throughout the war. Yet there was much British optimism that the home side would acquit itself well. As the British game resumed in 1946 it became evident that the two outstanding British women were Kay Menzies, as Kay Stammers had become, and Jean Bostock. Kay Stammers had been the losing finalist to Alice Marble at the last pre-war Wimbledon. Jean Bostock, as Jean Nicoll, had been conspicuous as a junior, winning all three events in the last pre-war Junior Championships at Wimbledon in 1938. Arguably she was the best young player Britain had had. Her natural genius was in happy evidence when she won the British Hard Court Championship at Bournemouth in 1946, beating Kay Menzies in the final.

Four Americans made their debut on the turf at Wimbledon when Pauline Betz, Margaret Osborne, Louise Brough and Doris Hart played against Great Britain for the Wightman Cup on 14 and 15 June. The British began hopefully. It was soon evident that they would be lucky to salvage anything. They suffered the most widespread defeat inflicted on the British in the history of the competition. They were routed 7–0. The Americans did not concede a set in any rubber. Only one set went to advantage games, the third-place singles in which Louise Brough beat Joan Curry 8–6 6–3.

The United States put forward many strong sides in the immediate post-war years but none so strong as this. Miss Betz was 26, Miss Osborne 28, Miss Brough 23 and Miss Hart 19. All became Wimbledon champions. Miss Brough was to take the Wimbledon singles three times running and four times in all. She was only the third-place singles player! Miss Hart, a majestically fine performer, was the tail ender of the side and played only in the second doubles combination with Miss Betz. There was no player in this quartette of Americans who would not be listed by anyone putting forward candidates for a ranking list of all-time greats. Miss Betz, as it happened, featured in the game only that year since early in 1947 she was declared professional by the USLTA for having discussed a professional contract. But between them the four Americans won no less than 111 of the world's four major titles in the course of impressive careers.

When the Championships began in 1946 it was obvious, after the lesson of the Wightman Cup, that American women would dominate. The degree with which they did so was emphatic. The British resistance extended as far as the last eight of the singles, no further. Mrs Menzies, seeded fourth, yielded at that stage to Dodo Bundy, cherubic, charming and skilled. Her mother, May Sutton, had first won the title 41 years before. Mrs Bostock yielded in the same round to Miss Brough. There was a clear-cut semifinal win for Miss Betz against Miss Bundy, a much less certain struggle before Miss Brough beat Miss Osborne, their serve and volleying tactics against each other a revelation of the heights to which American women raised the attacking game.

Miss Betz lost six games in the final against Miss Brough. Appropriately this climax was her closest match. She stood markedly above the rest of the field, even her best American rivals. She had everything as a player, superb consistency and such a standard of bread and butter strokes that it was rare for her to be so pressed as to have to call on the more sensational. She was beautifully mobile and had a cool match temperament well above the normal.

This was her first and only Wimbledon. As a professional, a status forced on her willy-nilly by her association, she had scope for what was virtually only exhibition play. Lawn tennis was the poorer for it.

The depth and quality of American resources in the women's game was a revelation in 1946. Miss Hart did not get beyond the last eight of the singles. There she ran into Miss Brough, who beat her in three sets. Also among the challengers was Pat Todd, a tall, fluent and commanding American whose only major singles championship was to be the French in 1947. Had she been ordained by fate to flourish amid less exalted company she would certainly have won others.

Every event at Wimbledon in 1946 in which women were involved produced an American champion. Miss Brough and Miss Osborne won the doubles from an all-American final against Miss Betz and Miss Hart. The mixed went to Miss Brough in partnership with her compatriot Tom Brown. Thus was set the post-war pattern. American women came first and all others followed. It was to be thirteen years before any but an American won the singles, ten years before the doubles went elsewhere. It was eleven years before a non-American came in as singles finalist. Out of 44 semi-final places in the singles 1946 to 1955 there was only one who was not American.

This immediate post-war decade was the more impressive in its American invincibility because it was not a question of dominance by one but by several players. If one failed there were many ready to take her place!

There was not, at this time, any sign that Brazil might be building a threat to American power and only the mildest of hints that Australia might intrude on the scene. In 1947 one of the quarter-finalists in the women's singles was Nancye Bolton. Her easy fluency of stroke and piercing quality of shot had been noted before the war when she was Nancye Wynne. But she fell to Miss Brough at Wimbledon in 1947 and her majesty of game always surpassed her capacity as a match player.

The semi-final intruder in 1947 in the singles was from South Africa, Sheila Summers. She had played pre-war as Sheila Piercey. She upset form, though only to the extent of the number seven seed proving better than the number four, by winning in the quarters against Mrs Todd. She was then unable to put any check on Miss Osborne's progress to the final. Nor, in the final, did Miss Hart look like stopping Miss Osborne taking her first and only Wimbledon singles title. Like Miss Betz the year before Miss Osborne lost no set in any round. Miss Brough, beaten by Miss Hart in the semi-final, had compensation by taking the mixed for the second year, this time with the Australian John Bromwich.

The betting was that she would take the women's doubles as well and it was a miracle she did not. If anything seemed a virtual certainty in 1947 it was that Miss Brough and Miss Osborne would retain their title. At that time they had taken the US Championship together for five successive years and looked invincible. Miss Hart and Mrs Todd reached the final against them. The 1946 champions looked more unbeatable than ever when, despite the loss of the first set, they dominated the third to lead 5–3 40–0. Somewhere during the course of the next three points it seemed that the players' control of events was taken away. The crowd took over. A fine half-volley lob by Mrs Todd on the first match point was the catalyst by which the players were reduced to puppets controlled by the mass will power of those who watched them.

Amid a crescendo of enthusiasm both Mrs Todd and Miss Hart became increasingly inspired. Equally Miss Osborne and Miss Brough had their rigour sapped. It was an occasion of extraordinary atmosphere and, merely because they were the under-dogs Mrs Todd and Miss Hart (and 14 000 odd spectators) won the set 7–5. For the second year all the women's events went to America; rather it was the fourth, for the two years 1939 and 1938 had been the same.

In 1948 Miss Osborne came back as Mrs W. du Pont, her husband an American millionaire from Delaware. Miss Brough was still Miss Brough and as such, though already with three Wimbledon titles behind her, she began to write her name large in the record books. Of nine principal championship finals, 1948, 1949 and 1950, Miss Brough was to play in all of them. She won eight.

Miss Hart, a finalist for the second year running, reached the last match against her, having dispossessed the champion Mrs du Pont in the semi-final. It was a good, gruelling final, as was Miss Brough's semi-final against Mrs Todd. None of the top Americans yielded easily one to the other and Miss Brough had only two opponents that year who were not compatriots. Jean Bostock was again a quarter-finalist for Britain, this for the last time. She never fulfilled her original high talent and her death some years later, albeit well before her time, was a sad episode in the story of the British game.

While the redoubtable Miss Brough was in the course of taking her first singles title a second round match in the event was played without great stir at the time. Mlle A. Weiwers beat Mrs O. Anderson. She took a long time to do so. In the next round she was easily beaten, winning only one game, by Sheila Summers. Mlle Weiwers was from Luxembourg. Mrs Anderson was formerly the British Wightman Cup player Rita Jarvis, then married to an American. Later she married Jaroslav Drobny.

The remarkable thing about this match was the score. Mlle Weiwers won 8–10 14–12 6–4. This total of 54 games set a record for the event.

The women's doubles final that year was the same as the year before but its breathtaking climax was not repeated. Miss Brough and Mrs du Pont got their revenge against Miss Hart and Mrs Todd. Miss Brough took the mixed again with Bromwich. This was the first of her triple championships.

For the men 1949 was an outstanding year. For the women it was, in some degree, routine. Miss Brough kept her singles title. But for the first time since 1932 as many as four British women reached the last eight. They were Molly Blair, Jean Walker-Smith, Peggy Dawson-Scott and Betty Hilton. Four Anglo-American quarter-finals, however, resulted in four American victories. In the final Miss Brough was engaged by Mrs du Pont and she played a long match that, despite its interesting score, never quite came to life. She won 10–8 1–6 10–8. In the first set she led 4–0, trailed 4–5 and saved four set points against her. In the decider she was within two points of defeat at 5–6 before she survived. The women's doubles was not entirely a foregone conclusion; Miss Brough and Miss du Pont, tired after their singles, won rather an untidy all-American final against Gussy Moran and Pat Todd. Miss Brough was denied a second triple championship in the final of the mixed doubles. In a spectacular final, a fitting climax to a notable meeting the mixed went to the South Africans Eric Sturgess and Sheila Summers when they beat Bromwich and Miss Brough 9–7 9–11 7–5, its total of 48 games the most ever played for the title.

Where the women's event was not routine in 1949 was in the person of Gussy Moran. She was then the seventh-ranking player in the United States, 25 years old, from Santa Monica, California. She had an engaging personality, a trim, captivating figure and was a good player, albeit by no means a great one, by any standard.

Just prior to the Championships that year, at the International Club garden party at Hurlingham, her costume, designed by Teddy Tinling, caught the attention of photographers, the popular press and the world at large. Her 'lace panties' became famous overnight. A good deal of attention at Wimbledon that year was devoted to them, though it was something of an anti-climax when Miss Moran, having won two rounds in the women's singles, yielded to Gem Hoahing. But by her reaching the final of the doubles the photographers were given plenty to occupy them.

The story of Miss Moran belongs more to that of lawn tennis at large than to Wimbledon in particular and, in her case, perhaps to social history as a whole. Lawn tennis was a woman's game from its inception. It was sometimes a matter for debate what the women wore. The South African Billie Tapscott had in 1929 created something of a fuss by discarding stockings. The onset of shorts for women in the 1930s shocked the traditionalists. Hitherto no one had openly shown what women wore underneath. After 1949 and Gussy Moran and her lace panties it became not only possible to do so but almost impossible not to do so. But it would be idle to pretend that at the time this move towards more liberal thinking, or whatever be the word, was officially welcomed. Certainly dress designer Teddy Tinling and the Wimbledon chairman, Sir Louis Greig, saw things differently and Tinling, who had long filled a useful role in the organisation of the meeting as an assistant in the referee's office, ceased after 1949 to do so.

The British resurgence of 1949 was not maintained one year later. Only one British woman reached the last eight of the singles, the energetic and always forceful Betty Harrison, as Betty Hilton had become, doing so for the second time as the sole home representative. The rest of the field was American. Miss Brough, beating first Shirley Fry, then Doris Hart and then Margaret du Pont, won the singles for the third year running. She was the first to do so since Helen Wills in 1929.

With seven Americans out of the eight singles quarter-finalists 1950 was the peak of US domination. The doubles final was all American, Miss Brough and Mrs du Pont winning against Miss Fry and Miss Hart. Miss Brough had a new partner in the mixed. It was the South African, Sturgess, and they won. Thus was Miss Brough triple champion for the second year out of three and winner of eleven Wimbledon Championships in five years.

In 1951 American domination diminished in that two British players, Kay Tuckey and Jean Walker-

'Gorgeous Gussie.' Gussie Moran in 1949

Smith penetrated the fastness of an otherwise all-American preserve of the singles last eight. But the American onslaught had changed its pattern. Miss Brough, her high skill blunted and prone to double fault because of her inability to throw up the ball accurately, was beaten in the semi-final by Miss Fry. Mrs du Pont was eliminated one round earlier, by Beverley Baker in the quarter-final. The latter, with a captivating yet athletic figure and an appealing personality, was ambidextrous and penetratingly skilful with it. Miss Hart beat her in the semi-final, however, quite easily and went on to have a one-sided win against Miss Fry.

Accordingly Miss Hart won the singles title for the first and only time without having lost a set in seven matches. There was a majestic quality about her play, a grace and power which made her best rallies seem works of art. From Florida, she had taken up the game at the age of 6 as a remedial exercise for a leg infirmity which threatened to make her a cripple.

The displacement of Miss Brough and Mrs du Pont by Miss Hart and Miss Fry extended to every event. The singles finalists won the doubles final against them and did so, moreover, in two sets, though the second, 13–11, was the longest played at that time. Miss Hart won the mixed with the Australian Frank Sedgman. In one brilliant fortnight Miss Hart had made herself triple champion and the only set she lost in any event was in the mixed. Thus did the fourth member of the 1946 US Wightman Cup side, which had been Wimbledon's introduction to the awesome heights to which the American game had risen, join her colleagues in being stamped with the hallmark of a champion outstanding among champions.

American standards had never been higher. It was to rise yet further for in 1952 Maureen Connolly, from San Diego, California, and 17 years old, made her meteoric debut. She came not as an unknown youngster but as American champion, she won that title in the autumn of 1951, while still 16, already with the cool efficiency that marked her entire career.

She was seeded second and Miss Hart, the defending champion, number one. As it happened Miss Hart did not carry her title defence very far, for she lost a long duel in the quarter-final to her compatriot Pat Todd. In turn Mrs Todd yielded to Miss Brough and the former champion became the finalist. There were two Britons in the last eight, Jean Rinkel-Quertier and Jean Walker-Smith, and the Australian Thelma Long. But the whole *raison d'être* of the women's singles that year seemed to be, and in fact turned out to be, the prodigious Miss Connolly. Prodigious and precociously skilled she certainly was. She had arrived at Wimbledon via Surbiton and Manchester and the Wightman Cup, unbeaten; she remained unbeaten and she was, indeed, never beaten (in singles, that is) in Britain at any time.

The pressures under which she played were enormous. There was the basic pressure of being expected to win. There was a blaze of publicity because Miss Connolly, for reasons of her skill, her charm and achievement, was 'news' in everything she did. And her guidance went sour at this her first Wimbledon challenge. Her mentor and coach was the Californian teacher Eleanor Tennant, who had produced Alice Marble. She had, one could say, an unusually possessive personality.

On the Saturday prior to the start of Wimbledon Miss Connolly withdrew from the mixed final at Queen's Club because of a shoulder strain. On the Monday Miss Tennant announced she had advised her pupil to scratch, lest she do herself permanent harm. None the less, Miss Connolly played the next day and won easily against Mrs C. G. Moeller of Yorkshire.

Miss Connolly's *savoir faire* was as remarkable as her playing skill. Afterwards she called a press conference and announced 'I don't regard Miss Tennant's advice as sensible. My shoulder had only the slightest strain and I'm perfectly fit to play. I intend to go on doing so. Miss Tennant is no longer my coach.'

The break was complete and final. One can hardly visualise a more calamitous start to a Wimbledon challenge than such a quarrel between coach and pupil. Miss Connolly was only 17 years old.

Miss Connolly then beat Angela Mortimer. Her next match, for a place in the last eight, was against Susan Partridge, who had played number three for Britain in the Wightman Cup. It was a very tough match and Miss Connolly barely managed to win 6–3 5–7 7–5. She then had a limited range of shot. Her strength was her driving skill, tremendous on the forehand but overwhelmingly so, such was its pace and control, from the backhand. Her service had little bite. Her volleying ability hardly existed. Theorists had reasoned that the best way to play her was down the middle of the court, giving no angles and no great pace.

That she was vulnerable to such tactics was evident. It was another thing to put theory into practice and succeed. The Connolly winners outnumbered the Connolly mistakes that were induced. The pressure exerted by Miss Patridge was, as it transpired, the nadir of her fortunes. In the next round Mrs Long, who needed tactical lessons from no one, won the first set but was subsequently allowed only two more games. Miss Fry was beaten 6–4 6–3 in the semi-final and in the final Miss Brough yielded 7–5 6–3 after having a point to take the first set.

Like Miss Betz six years before Miss Connolly had taken the title at her first attempt. Unlike Miss Betz she was to come back and her authority at Wimbledon was, in singles, never questioned. Yet her doubles skill fell well short of her singles supremacy, mainly because of her relative gawkiness on the volley and overhead. Miss Connolly partnered Miss Brough and Miss Brough had to do most of the effective work. They were beaten in the final by Miss Fry and Miss Hart. The latter also won the mixed for the second year with Sedgman.

The pattern in 1953 was almost the same. The difference was that Miss Connolly had in no way to prove herself. By now she was playing like an efficient machine, though still essentially a baseliner and short of being an all-round player. Her concentration, on the court, was entire. When she won a point she gave a little nod of the head as she turned to resume her position at the back. It was a little gesture that tended

The invincible Maureen Connolly, champion 1952, 1953 and 1954, with the women's singles trophy

to make spectators assume she was contemptuous of the opposition. She was less popular than was warranted, for few players so charming and generous hearted had appeared on the green swards of Wimbledon.

She took the singles in 1953 without losing a set. She met Miss Hart in the final and Miss Hart was the only player able to be reasonably hopeful of playing Miss Connolly on something approaching level terms (two out of the four defeats suffered by Miss Connolly in the first-class game were against Miss Hart). It was a contest of classic standards and Miss Connolly won it 8–6 7–5.

The mixed went to Miss Hart for the third successive year but not with Sedgman. This time a fellow American Vic Seixas was her partner and for the first time since 1938 the title was taken without the champions yielding a set. Miss Hart won the doubles with Miss Fry, this for the third successive year, and the winners here also did not lose a set. It was in fact the most sweeping victory of all time in the event.

Miss Hart and Miss Fry began with a bye and then had a walkover; they beat Mrs P. F. Glover (who had been Nancy Lyle) and Mrs H. Weiss from the Argentine 6–0 6–0. In the quarters they defeated the South Africans Miss D. Kilian and Miss L. van der Westhusen 6–2 6–2. The semi-final against the British pair Helen Fletcher and Jean Rinkel-Quertier was taken 6–0 6–0. The final was against Miss Connolly and Julie Sampson, the latter an American accompanying her partner partly as player and partly as a chaperone. Miss Hart and Miss Fry won 6–0 6–0, this being only the second time in Wimbledon's history that a championship turned on such a devastating score. The first was 42 years earlier in 1911 when Mrs Lambert Chambers whitewashed Dora Boothby in the singles. It is an ironic footnote to the story of Wimbledon that Miss Connolly, arguably the third finest woman player of all time (assuming Suzanne Lenglen and Helen Wills Moody to rate higher) should be on the losing side in the most abject of defeats.

The third year of Miss Connolly's conquests, 1954, brought her, marginally, her easiest triumph. There were two Britons in the last eight, Miss Mortimer and Helen Fletcher. In the all-American semi-finals Miss Brough beat Miss Hart and Miss Connolly beat Betty Pratt, the former Miss Rosenquest. Miss Connolly won 6–2 7–5 against Miss Brough having been 2–5 in the second set; the whole event was accounted a trifle dull because of the inevitability of the eventual winner. Miss Connolly, without losing a set, won 73 games and lost but 19.

The pendulum in the women's doubles swung back. The three-year tenure of Miss Hart and Miss Fry was broken and the lease taken up again by Miss Brough and Mrs du Pont who beat them in the final. The winning score was 4–6 9–7 6–3 and the defenders had two match points at 5–3 in the second set. It avenged events of 1947 when in the final Miss Brough and Mrs du Pont were denied match points by Miss Hart in partnership with Mrs Todd. Miss Hart let a title slip but she and Seixas were again invincible in the mixed.

Miss Connolly, never having lost in singles, did not come back to Wimbledon as a competitor. The 1954 meeting was her last major championship—and she had lost in none of the big four—for in July she broke her leg while riding in California. She did not play lawn tennis again except to coach. She was still short of 21 when she retired, having won Wimbledon and the US title three years running; with the French and Australian titles she achieved the Grand Slam, not then won by a woman, in 1953. She had a happy marriage with a fellow American, Norman Brinker. Tragically she died of cancer in June 1969.

In 1955 Miss Brough was 32. The throne was vacant. Miss Hart was made the top seed but she did not get beyond the semi-final and the ambidextrous court craft of Beverley Fleitz, as the elfin-like Miss Baker had become. The only British player in the last eight was Angela Buxton. Susie Kormoczi, a much-liked player from Hungary, and the Australian Barbara Penrose were the other two non-Americans. Among the quarter-final winners was the strong and vigorous Darlene Hard but Miss Brough beat her in the semi-final. In the final Miss Brough beat Mrs Fleitz 7–5 8–6 after a contest of quality and tension, for with Mrs Fleitz in the lead 5–4 in both sets it was desperately close throughout.

This was Miss Brough's fourth singles and her thirteenth and last championship title. Her last final, her twentieth, was the mixed with the Argentinian Enrique Morea. They lost to Seixas and Miss Hart. It was the fifth successive year as mixed champion for Miss Hart, the last three with Seixas. That too was Miss Hart's last Wimbledon title and her tenth. It was almost the end of the Wimbledon saga of the four American Wightman Cup players of 1946. After ten years their joint tally of Wimbledon titles was Miss Betz 1, Miss Brough 13, Miss Hart 10 and Mrs du Pont 6, totalling 30 between them. How it was pushed up to 31 belongs to the story of Wimbledon in 1962.

There was a straw in the wind indicating that this decade of American dominance might be threatened. There were unexpected happenings in the women's doubles in 1955. They began with the defeat in the opening round of the top seeds, Miss Hart and Barbara Davidson (who had been Miss Scofield). To everybody's astonishment, including those who beat them, they were put out by two English girls, Jennifer Middleton and Doreen Spiers. It left the way clear for Miss Mortimer and her hard-volleying partner, Anne Shilcock, to go through without undue difficulty to the final. On the seeding the Americans Miss Hard and Mrs Fleitz should have opposed them, instead of which it was another British pair, Shirley Bloomer and Pat Ward. This, the first all-British Wimbledon final in any event since 1936, was taken by Miss Mortimer and Miss Shilcock; they were the first British champions since Dorothy Round won the singles in 1937.

Shirley Fry, a formidable American but hardly so formidable as her immediate predecessors, won the singles in 1956. It was rather a bizarre event. Four Britons were in the last eight and three of them, Angela Mortimer, Pat Ward and Angela Buxton were all in the top half of the draw. The American there was Beverley Fleitz. She should have played Miss Buxton in the quarter-final but she did not after Colin Gregory had found himself doubling up his roles as tournament chairman and family doctor. He made a simple diagnosis of pregnancy and Miss Buxton had a free passage into the semi-final. There she met Miss Ward, who had beaten Miss Mortimer, and won confidently to take her place in the final.

Miss Buxton was an object lesson of the value of hard work and patient application. Intelligence and effort rather than natural genius had taken her to the top of the British game. Miss Fry emerged as the finalist after beating a noted American newcomer, the black Althea Gibson, in the quarters, and then Miss Brough in the semi-final. The title match was by no means a stimulating contest and Miss Fry won easily. As for Miss Buxton she had consolation in taking the women's doubles with Miss Gibson. Miss Fry partnered Seixas when the men's singles champion of 1953 took the mixed for the fourth year running.

The ranging Miss Gibson, with long limbs, wide reach and intimidating overhead skill, had the first of two triumphs in 1957. She was then 29 years old, a late developer in a lawn tennis sense. She and the sturdy Darlene Hard dominated the women's events entirely, for Miss Hard was the losing finalist to Miss Gibson in the singles, her partner in taking the women's doubles and, with the Australian Mervyn Rose, the victor against Neale Fraser and Miss Gibson in the final of the mixed. Miss Brough was still in the lists and, indeed, the second seed but she yielded to Miss Hard in the quarters. There were two British seeds that year, Shirley Bloomer at number three and Miss Mortimer at number seven and neither made the grade.

Miss Bloomer did not do so because she lost to a 16-year-old British novice from Loughton, Christine Truman. At this, her first challenge, Miss Truman won a happy Centre Court duel against the American Betty Pratt in the quarter-final to follow up her success against Miss Bloomer and thus challenged Miss Gibson in the semi-final. The engaging Miss Truman, with whom the Wimbledon spectators were entirely in love, was thoroughly routed but she was a beloved British player from that time.

This was Miss Brough's last year; she had competed eleven out of a dozen years. It was the only occasion she did not get beyond the quarter-final stage in the singles. Was there ever such a trenchant player?

As for Miss Gibson the overtones of her success were heard beyond the confines of the sport. She was the first negro to stand so high in the game. A year later she was back to defend both her singles and doubles titles. She had small trouble in doing so. Notably she had a Brazilian partner in the doubles, Maria Bueno, who made her first Wimbledon appearance in 1958 with a reputation established as victor in the Italian Championships in Rome.

There was nothing stereotyped about the meeting in 1958. Miss Gibson was seeded first as a matter of course as the defending holder but the second seed was the 17-year-old Miss Truman. Since she had beaten Miss Gibson not long before, thus contributing to the first British Wightman Cup victory since 1930, it was justified. For Miss Truman, though, the burden of expectation proved too great and she fell to the little American Mimi Arnold, one of the visiting Wightman Cup side, in the fourth round.

The newcomer Miss Bueno, then 18 but the regal quality of her imperious strokes already in evidence, was seeded fourth. On a damp, cheerless day she just fell short of taking her semi-final place when she yielded to the British Ann Haydon, just one year her senior.

With Miss Haydon as one British semi-finalist (and she was routed there by Miss Gibson) there was a second when Miss Mortimer, unseeded, came through. Her quarter-final opposition came from another non-seed, Mrs du Pont, now aged 40 but unable to keep away from a battleground she had enjoyed so much. Miss Mortimer, beating the Hungarian Susie Kormoczi for the loss of one game only, reached the final.

There she played a strong first set but could not, despite the firmness of her backhand, thwart from the baseline the big guns that Miss Gibson fired from the net. The doubles final was all American except for Miss Bueno, the losing finalists being none other than Mrs du Pont in partnership with Margaret Varner, the latter notable for having acquired international honours in lawn tennis, badminton and squash rackets. For the first time the mixed championship was taken by two Australians, Bob Howe and Lorraine Coghlan. They beat Kurt Nielsen and Miss Gibson in the final and among the victims of that pair was Miss Truman in harness with an Australian newcomer, Rod Laver.

In the thirteen years since the war the women's singles had been won by an American every time. The US was a long way short of yielding pride of place as leaders of the women's game but their Amazonian grip at Wimbledon had come to an end.

17 WIDER HORIZONS (*Women* 1959-1976)

An optimistic spirit in the British women's game, engendered among other things by Britain possessing the Wightman Cup, was reflected in the singles seeding in 1959. Christine Truman was made number one and Angela Mortimer number two. It was unique for the seeding committee to be so hopefully patriotic. For all that Britain got less near a title than the year before.

Miss Truman lost in the fourth round to the Mexican Yola Ramirez, a good all-round aggressive player, a splendid volleyer, albeit a trifle lightweight in shot. Miss Mortimer progressed one round further but lost in the quarter-final to the South African Sandra Reynolds, a player of Dresden china beauty, a frail physique but with a typically Western grip South African forehand that could knock the stuffing out of the opposition. No British player got beyond the last eight. Ann Haydon, the third of the British seeds and number eight in status, almost did so but she lost 7–5 in the third set to Darlene Hard. A semi-final win over Miss Reynolds took Miss Hard to the last match. Her opponent was Maria Bueno.

The Brazilian played better as the tournament progressed. She lost the first set in the second round against the German Margot Dittmeyer and also in the third against Mimi Arnold. For Miss Bueno the margin between being very good, when her timing was perfect, and rather bad, when her timing was imperfect, was narrow. Mundane shots did not exist for her. It was either caviare or starvation. But from the fourth round Miss Bueno did not lose a set, bringing down the New Zealander Ruia Morrison, the German Edda Buding, the American Sally Moore and then the player with whom she was most closely associated, Miss Hard.

Majestically outplayed by Miss Bueno in the singles final, Miss Hard consoled herself by winning the other two title matches in which she was involved. The women's doubles was in partnership with Jean Arth, a school-teacher from Minnesota who quickly made an impact on the game and just as quickly left it. The losing finalists were Miss Truman and Beverley Fleitz. In the mixed Miss Hard won with Rod Laver. It was his first Wimbledon championship.

There was in 1960 no American in the last four of the women's singles. One had to go back to 1925 to

Maria Bueno, the graceful champion from Brazil

find a parallel. Miss Hard was the only American seed. She was number two but she lost in the quarter-final when Miss Reynolds avenged her defeat of the previous year. There were two British semi-finalists but neither got further. Miss Haydon, who had already beaten one South African, Renée Schuurman, failed against her partner Miss Reynolds. Miss Truman clashed with Miss Bueno and won the middle set. She had small share in the sets on either side of it. In the final the resistance of Miss Reynolds was confined to the first set.

Miss Hard won the doubles with Miss Bueno, her third success in the event with her third different partner. She won the mixed also for she and Laver kept their title. The last match, in which Miss Bueno came within three match points of being triple champion, was among Wimbledon's more freakish happenings. This was not because Miss Bueno and her Australian partner Bob Howe were so close to winning. (They led 5–2 in the third set and had three match points at 5–4.) Nor was it because it was the second longest final of the mixed ever staged. (The winning score was 13–11 3–6 8–6, a total of 47 games, one short of the 48 played when Eric Sturgess and Sheila Summers won in 1949.) It was because after Howe and Miss Bueno reached 5–2 in the final set Miss Hard suddenly vanished from the court. About five minutes later, perhaps less, she reappeared. The puzzled spectators had to draw their own conclusions. The reason was an embarrassingly feminine one.

The odds in 1961 against the graceful and peerless Miss Bueno taking the singles for the third year running cannot have been long but it happened that she fell ill with jaundice during the French Championships and did not defend. Nor was Miss Hard in the lists. The top seed was Miss Reynolds, the second Margaret Smith, making her first overseas tour. The latter, already twice champion of Australia, had yet, save for the Italian mixed doubles with Roy Emerson, to win a major title abroad. The only American seed was Karen Hantze at number eight. There were three British. Ann Haydon, number three, fell to Miss Schuurman in the fourth round. Miss Truman was number six and Miss Mortimer number seven.

Miss Truman clashed with Miss Smith in the quarter-final, which is what the seeding ordained. It was one of those Wimbledon occasions when half England seemed to be holding its breath. Miss Truman, pounding away with her trenchant forehand, lost the first set, squared at a set all, and then trailed 1–4. After the Australian had had two match points, and lost both with bad volleys, Miss Truman triumphed 3–6 6–3 9–7. She then avenged Miss Haydon's loss with a semi-final win against Miss Schuurman to take herself within one match of the major lawn tennis honour.

In the meantime, Miss Mortimer, 29 years old, had come through a little less resoundingly, for her skill was always relatively unobtrusive. She justified her seeding when she beat the American Justina Bricka, she improved on it when she entered the last four at the expense of Vera Sukova from Czechoslovakia. She won her semi-final, like Miss Truman, against South African opposition, beating Miss Reynolds in two sets, the first going to twenty games. The final, then, was the British Miss Mortimer against the British Miss Truman. A home winner—the first since Dorothy Round in 1937—was a certainty for the first time since 1914.

It would be unjust to say the crowd was partisan. There was no doubt, however, about the favourite, for Miss Truman was adored. In the event she began by taking the first set at 6–4. Miss Mortimer, a baseliner defending shrewdly against an aggressor, had the worst of it, though by no very great margin. There was a rain delay of some 40 minutes. Then Miss Truman's pressure, her weighty forehand, her net excursions, again had their effect. She was within a point of leading 5–3 when, turning to cope with a lob, she fell awkwardly. She was clearly rather shaken. Miss Mortimer did not hesitate to drop shot in the next rally. Miss Truman never recovered her former impetus. She struggled from behind to level the third set five games all but Miss Mortimer measured her victory by 4–6 6–4 7–5.

The simple assessment was that Miss Truman had been robbed of victory by falling when she did. That could well have been the case. But it was not entirely certain, not only because nothing is certain in lawn tennis but because there had been previous meetings when Miss Truman had been unable to sustain equally commanding leads against Miss Mortimer. Miss Mortimer was born in Plymouth. The women's singles champion of 54 years before, May Sutton, was born there also.

Miss Smith, a first-time challenger, had been ushered on to the Wimbledon stage with something of a fanfare. A 17-year-old Californian made her debut also. She was Billie Jean Moffitt and she lost in the first round to the Mexican Yola Ramirez. In the doubles Miss Moffitt and Miss Hantze made their mark. They won the title unseeded, beating three seeded pairs (Miss Reynolds and Miss Schuurman, Sally Moore and Lesley Turner, Jan Lehane and Miss Smith) without losing a set. They were the only Americans on the championship roll that year. The mixed doubles was won by Fred Stolle and Miss Turner for Australia.

The seeding committee was able to do little right in 1962, the year the women's singles was won by the bottom in the list of favourites, Karen Susman (the Miss Hantze of the year before) against a finalist, the Czech Vera Sukova, who was not seeded at all. The top seed was Miss Smith, competing as current champion not only of Australia but of Italy and France. She did not survive her first match. She lost to the firmer nerves of Miss Moffitt. She was beaten 1–6 6–3 7–5, having been fine steel in the opening games but flaccid string thereafter. In due course Miss Moffitt was put out in the quarter-final by Miss Haydon who in turn yielded to Mrs Susman.

Miss Mortimer, the defending champion, was seeded no higher than six. The assessment was realistic and Miss Mortimer fell short of that when she went out in the fourth round to Mrs Sukova, a player more steady than herself on the day. Miss Hard was back in the fray and seeded second. She lost also to the Czech, one round later in the quarters. Miss Bueno

Vera Sukuova with the 1962 champion, Karen Susman

was also back and seeded third. She progressed as far as the last four and she too went down to Mrs Sukova. This Czech had a spell of unexpected glory. She was efficient but short of glamorous. Because of this very fact she endeared herself all round, far more than Mrs Susman, whose habit of walking tortoise like between rallies aroused impatience.

The progress of Mrs Sukova was arrested in the last match. She had wretched luck in falling and hurting her ankle prior to the final and this happening did not make for a very good match. Mrs Susman had a straightforward and uneventful win to take the title back to America after it had been elsewhere for three years. Mrs Susman, it was noteworthy, had been taught and trained from an early age by Eleanor Tennant who proclaimed her as a future champion when as young as 11. She was the third Wimbledon champion to emerge from that stable, the others being Maureen Connolly and Alice Marble.

There was no change in the doubles. Having won the year before as outsiders, Miss Moffitt and Mrs Susman found it more difficult to win as second favourites; a hectic final against the South Africans Miss Schuurman and Mrs Price (*née* Sandra Reynolds) was secured only by 7–5 in the third set. The mixed had noteworthy winners with the American Dennis Ralston and Miss Haydon losing in an exciting final by 13–11 in the final set. Their conquerors were Fraser in partnership with none other than Margaret du Pont, the singles champion of 15 years before. She was 44 years old. She had played in the singles and lost to Miss Truman.

Australia had its first men's singles champion in 1907, Norman Brookes. It was not until 1963 that the women's singles went the same way when Margaret Smith, who had by then already taken the American and French titles, the Italian twice and the Australian four times, succeeded at her third attempt. It was no more than expected for the Australian challenge was now formidably strong in depth. Mrs Susman did not defend. Miss Smith was seeded top, her compatriot Lesley Turner second and a third Australian, the double-handed Jan Lehane, was fifth. Britain's Ann Jones, Miss Haydon's new identity, was third. The only American seed was Darlene Hard at fourth.

As it transpired, American strength was underestimated. Miss Smith, Miss Hard and Mrs Jones all made their proper places in the last four. The Californian Miss Moffitt, with insistent and dynamic aggressive skills, beat Miss Turner, Miss Bueno and then Mrs Jones to arrive unseeded in the final. There she challenged Miss Smith whose only concession of a set was in the quarters to Miss Schuurman. One of the losers to Mrs Jones, in the second round, was a bright and ambitious British youngster, Virginia Wade, competing for the first time.

Right: Billie Jean Moffitt from California had already been Wimbledon Champion three times before going on as Mrs Larry King for a further sixteen titles

Below: Christine Truman, later Mrs Janes, always popular at Wimbledon, never won a title. She played in the All British final in 1961 losing to Angela Mortimer

Ann Jones was twice champion in 1969, winning both the singles and mixed doubles titles that year

Margaret Court, Australia's finest woman player

A final between Miss Smith and Miss Moffitt had piquant overtones. It repeated in the last round what had taken place in the first the year before. Then Miss Smith, the top seed, had lost to Miss Moffitt with a nervy dissipation of her talents. Now she controlled her tension better—her confidence built up by two subsequent meetings in the US which she had won—and came through 6–3 6–4 after leading 4–0 in the second set.

She had two more finals to play that day and Miss Smith was on the Centre Court for getting on for six hours. The women's doubles eluded her, going to Miss Bueno and Miss Hard 8–6 9–7 after an exacting struggle against Miss Smith and Robyn Ebbern. In the mixed she had an Australian partner also, Ken Fletcher and they won the final, 11–9 6–4, against Bob Hewitt, then playing under his native Australian allegiance, and Miss Hard. This mixed success dovetailed into an achievement of more than usual note; it gave Fletcher and Miss Smith their third leg on the Grand Slam which they went on to complete in America.

This year the LTA Ball at Grosvenor House Hotel, Park Lane, held on the Saturday evening to celebrate the end of the Championships, took place with the two singles champions unable to make the traditional start to the dancing. At that stage only the men's singles champion was known, the final having been played as usual on the Friday. All other finals, including the women's singles, were postponed until the Monday because of rain. At that time the notion of playing on Sunday was considered unacceptable.

By 1964 the basic pattern of the women's game at the top level had developed into a rivalry between the supreme athlete Miss Smith and the supreme artist Miss Bueno with Miss Moffitt intervening. Miss Moffitt was more of an artist and less of an athlete than Miss Smith but less of an artist and more of an athlete than Miss Bueno. Miss Smith was seeded first, Miss Bueno second and Miss Moffitt third. Since at that time the seeding positions were fixed, that involved a semi-final clash between Miss Smith and Miss Moffitt and the Australian won by precisely the same score by which she had gained the title match twelve months earlier.

Miss Turner, seeded fourth—making a perfect forecast by the seeding committee at the stage of the last four—lost in a three-set semi-final to Miss Bueno. The final accordingly brought the ultimate rivalry in the women's game to its peak in its finest setting. It was, in fact, the twelfth meeting between Miss Smith and Miss Bueno. Miss Smith had won seven times, Miss Bueno three, with their last clash, at Beckenham, two weeks before the start of Wimbledon, unfinished because of rain.

The Australian hardly made an auspicious start. She began by double faulting three times. This nervy start she recouped, though a lot of mistakes were made by both as they moved to one set all. Miss Bueno looked as if she would yield when in the final set Miss Smith was 3–2 with her service to follow; the outcome was a Brazilian triumph, Miss Bueno taking the last four games of the match. It was her third singles championship, a fitting success for one whose grace and beauty of play gave perhaps more satisfaction to more spectators than any other post-war player.

Miss Smith was again a triple finalist, but the only title she won was that in which she failed in 1963, the women's doubles. With Miss Turner she dominated the event and their final victory over Miss Moffitt and Mrs Susman was easy. In the mixed she and Fletcher, who were again threatening to achieve the Grand Slam, lost to Stolle and Miss Turner. The only non-Australian winner this year was Miss Bueno.

One of the great spectaculars in 1965 was the warmly appreciated progress of the British favourite Christine Truman. She was not seeded but stirred patriotic enthusiasm when she beat the American Carole Graebner, the number six seed, in the second round after a tremendous struggle. She went from strength to strength and beat the Texan Nancy Richey, seeded fourth, to enter the semi-final. There she was worsted with athletic emphasis by Miss Smith. This was the Australian's year in singles *par excellence*, her nerves under control, her all-round skill and strength of game never better.

It was like the previous year except for the intrusion of Miss Truman. The other semi-finalists were Miss Bueno and Miss Moffitt and in this match the Brazilian lost a set for the first time at Wimbledon. For the second year Miss Smith and Miss Bueno contended for the world's major crown. They had met five times in the intervening twelve months and the Australian won every time. The final in some degree reflected that fact. Miss Smith won 6–4 7–5 to take her second singles title having lost no set and with the easiest over-all victory since Maureen Connolly in 1954.

Miss Smith again with Fletcher also won the mixed. She could have had the mixed Grand Slam for the second time had it not been that the event in Australia was left unfinished in the final. But Miss Smith was not this year a triple finalist. To the delight of the French, Françoise Durr and Janine Lieffrig—each rather ungainly in style and certainly more at home on hard courts—beat Miss Smith and Miss Turner in the third round. The French went on to reach the final where they were well beaten by Miss Bueno with Miss Moffitt.

A year later the Californian assumed a new identity at Wimbledon as Mrs Larry King. It signalled a start of a new personal domination. The tripartite rivalry was still Miss Smith, Miss Bueno and the erstwhile Miss Moffitt and in 1966 these three players, as they had been for the two previous years, were again semi-finalists, this time with Mrs Jones intervening. Such was the seeding anticipation.

The expectation of a Smith versus Bueno final for the third successive year was not fulfilled. Miss Bueno came through, though with the utmost difficulty for Mrs Jones, having won a second set of twenty games, yielded only by 7–5 in the third. Miss Smith did not. Mrs King beat Miss Smith in two nine-game sets, only her third success in twelve meetings. The final fluctuated as Miss Bueno tried in vain to make her strokes as penetrating as they were fluent. Mrs King won the match 6–1 in the third set. She was only the second American to take the singles since 1958.

In the doubles Mrs King played with Rosemary Casals. Unseeded they were beaten by the Australian partnership of Miss Smith with Judy Tegart who went on to reach the final. The title went to Miss Bueno with Miss Richey and it was a better final than many. As for the mixed, Fletcher and Miss Smith kept to familiar courses, taking it for the third time in four years and this time with Ralston and Mrs King as the losers.

Miss Smith became Mrs Barry Court in the course of 1967. She played neither at Wimbledon nor elsewhere. The old tripartite rivalry was finished for when she came back to the game in 1968, Miss Bueno, beset with injury, was not the force she was. Mrs King and Miss Bueno were the leading challengers in 1967 but Miss Bueno did not survive a fourth-round encounter against Miss Casals, whose minute physique housed a battery of energy.

Mrs Jones, who had first reached the semi-final in 1958, did so for the fifth time. At last she got one stage further. Her quarter-final opponent, the American Mary Ann Eisel, she found difficult and she survived only by 7–5 in the third set. In the semi-final she came through only by the same onerous margin against Miss Casals. As for Mrs King, seeded number one, nothing deterred the champion. She arrived in the last match without losing a set and did not lose one when there, for she vanquished Mrs Jones 6–3 6–4, comfortably to keep her title.

It was very much Mrs King's year. She and Miss Casals took the doubles, Miss Bueno and Miss Richey yielding their title in a lively final. Mrs King took the mixed as well, this with the Australian, Owen Davidson; with that the Californian was triple champion, the first woman as such since Doris Hart in 1951. Mrs King now had seven Wimbledon titles.

For 1968, the year when lawn tennis became open, there was no change for the women's events. Mrs King, having won the singles twice as a technical amateur, came back to defend it as a technical professional. She clashed with Mrs Jones in the semi-final and her familiar technique against the British left hander, a serve to a defensive backhand to open up a simple volley, worked with difficulty. She lost the opening set and survived the second only by 7–5 before taking the decider.

The seeding forecast a final against Mrs Court who was weary of retirement and anxious to reap the rewards of her skill. She was a casualty in the quarters, losing to Miss Tegart. Miss Bueno fell at the same stage, yielding to Miss Richey. It was left to the sturdy Miss Tegart to survive to the final. In extending Mrs King to two advantage sets she did better than many expected. It left Mrs King the champion for the third successive year. She kept her doubles title with Miss Casals but the mixed was denied her. She and Davidson lost in the semi-final to Fletcher and Mrs Court who won the final against opposition that was entirely unexpected. This was the Soviet pair Alex Metreveli—as a Georgian he disliked the description Russian—and Olga Morozova.

It happened that year that Miss Wade was to write her name large as the first winner of the women's singles of the US Open at Forest Hills. Events at Wimbledon hardly presaged such a triumph for,

Doubles champions. *Above*: Nancy Richey from Texas, 1969. *Below*: The Australian, Judy Dalton (*née* Tegart), 1969

Right: Since her first appearance in 1963, Virginia Wade has been a favourite of the Wimbledon crowds but a title has always eluded her

Below: Margaret Court from Australia has won ten Wimbledon championships and more international championships than any other player, having won the 'Grand Slam' in 1963 and 1970

seeded fifth, she disappointed sadly by losing in the opening round to the Swedish Christina Sandberg. Her compensation was to win the consolation plate.

Two British women were seeded for the singles in 1969, Miss Wade and Mrs Jones. Understandably, Miss Wade had priority as champion of America. She was three and Mrs Jones number four. Mrs Court was one and Mrs King number two, the relative status reflecting the outcome of the final of the Australian Championship at the start of the year. Miss Wade suffered one of those let-downs which were disappointing to her admirers. Leading Pat Walkden of South Africa by 5–4, 40–0, her game crumpled to nervy inepititude and she painfully won only one more game in the match.

In contrast Mrs Jones found her greatest inspiration that year. When she arrived in the semi-final, having had a difficult set against the American, Peggy Michel and then brought down the Texan, Nancy Richey with some *élan*, she had fulfilled expectations. Her performance against Mrs Court was something of a revelation, for having lost a tough opening set in the 22nd game, she threw caution to the winds and attacked with such zestful flair that she outgunned her opponent. In the final she faced Mrs King, champion for the three preceding years. Once again Mrs Jones lost the opening set and then cast away her normal attributes as a defensive player. Inevitably British spectators were blatantly on her side. Mrs King's ability to resist seemed to vanish and Mrs Jones was a first-time Wimbledon champion at 30.

Her success, eight years after the only other British post-war success in singles, that of Miss Mortimer in 1961, came after many years of effort, after being once (1967) a finalist, seven times a semi-finalist and nine times a quarter-finalist. Having got one Wimbledon title for Britain she shared another, taking the mixed with Stolle. Her first challenge was in 1956. She made this, her most successful year, her last.

The seeding forecast in 1970 was a final with Mrs Court against Mrs King and such turned out to be the case. The singles, as far as the final, was not a particularly exciting event. Helga Niessen, the top player of Germany and noted for her studied rather than inspired approach, contrived to win the first set from Mrs Court in the quarter-final; she exhausted herself so utterly in the process that she won no more games. The French Françoise Durr, her backhand violating every theory in the coaching manuals, reached the last four, though unseeded. Miss Wade, who should have been there, vanished in the fourth round, having had a match when almost every shot she projected had an uncertain destination. Mrs King lost one set on the way to the final to the tall Australian, Karen Krantzcke.

The final was memorable, perhaps the best ever played so far as the quality of shot making and the tempo of the rallies was concerned. Mrs Court took the title for the third time when she won 14–12 11–9 after a battle of 2 hours 27 minutes in which the margin between her and Mrs King was never more than one game. Its 46 games, every one of which was marked by searing attack, superb defence and often by splendid counter attack by one player or the other, was the highest ever in the final, two more than that between Suzanne Lenglen and Dorothea Lambert Chambers in 1919. Mrs King led 3–2 in the first set with her service to follow. She was in the same position of command at 5–4 7–6 and 8–7. In the second set she was similarly 1–0 with her service to come but did not get in front again. Mrs Court had a match point at 7–6. She had four more at 10–9 before at last she won. At no time did the standard fall below that of superfine and, in victory or defeat, it could be held the finest hour for either player.

Mrs King partnered Miss Casals for their third doubles victory in harness, the sixth for Mrs King. As in 1968, the Soviet pair, Metreveli and Miss Morozova, were in the final of the mixed. It was won by an unseeded partnership, the Romanian Ilie Nastase with Miss Casals. As the meeting ended Mrs King had 10 championships behind her, 3 singles, 6 doubles and 1 mixed. Mrs Court had 9, 3 singles, 2 doubles and 4 mixed.

The Australian might have added three more in 1971. In fact she added none, suffering the intimidating experience of reaching the final of all three events and being beaten in every one. Doris Hart had a like misfortune in 1948. Mrs King, on the other hand, pushed up her championship total to twelve by taking both doubles, the women's with her familiar colleague Miss Casals and the mixed with an equally steady supporter, Owen Davidson. The outcome of the women's singles was one of the most popular of all time.

Evonne Goolagong, an Australian with aboriginal ancestry, had competed at Wimbledon only once before, in the previous year when, already a wide favourite with the public, she had, because of that, been put early on the Centre Court. This was a rigorous baptism and she lost to the steady American, Peaches Bartkowicz. The entrancing Miss Goolagong captivated spectators not only because of her seemingly natural flair for the game and command of outrageously daring shots but because, in what had become a rigorously professional world, she actually seemed to enjoy playing. In 1971 she was just short of her 20th birthday and had proved her mettle not long before by winning the French Championships. There seemed no reason why Miss Goolagong could not win anything—save only for her habit of losing concentration and indulging in dreamy spells which came to be described as 'walkabouts'.

There were British disappointments this year when Miss Wade, seeded five, lost to the Australian Judy Dalton (previously she had been Miss Tegart). The only British last-eight survivor was the Scot, Winnie Shaw and she lost to Mrs Court at that stage. In the other half Miss Goolagong went happily from strength to strength. In the course of getting to the last four she yielded a set only to her fellow Australian, Lesley Hunt. In the semi-final she beat the number two seed, Mrs King, in two straightforward sets. In the final she was even more forthright and yielded only five games to Mrs Court.

The two finalists were on the same side of the net in the doubles where Mrs King, again with Miss Casals, had revenge of a sort for her singles defeat.

Mrs Court had no consolation at all. The mixed final, which brought Mrs Court with her American partner, Marty Riessen, again in opposition to Mrs King, was notable for its hectic and long drawn-out finish. Davidson and Mrs King won by 15–13 in the third set, this being the longest set played at that stage of the event.

America avenged Australian audacity in 1972. This was the year that Chris Evert made her debut. The reputation of this cool youngster from Florida, who was then but 17, had preceded her. She had revived women's lawn tennis values that had almost been forgotten, strength and steadiness from the back of the court. Her backhand was double fisted. She was seeded fourth and she justified the grading precisely. Miss Goolagong, seeded one, put her out in the semi-final.

The Australian had survived as far after an uneasy adventure against the Russian, Olga Morozova, in the fourth round, winning narrowly by 9–7 in the third set. Miss Evert rather than Miss Goolagong threatened to be the finalist. The Australian trailed 4–6, 0–3, before she was stirred by the threat of defeat to play more in accord with her talents. Exploiting Miss Evert's vulnerability to a short ball against the backhand she pulled the match round, winning from level pegging at four all in the final set by taking eight out of the last nine points.

Mrs King arrived in the final having lost a set only to Miss Wade in the quarter-final. The high competence of her professional skill was in evidence all the way. Miss Goolagong never looked like winning more than the three games she got in each set of the final. This was Mrs King's fourth singles success. In doubles an old partnership had split. Mrs King paired with the Dutch Betty Stove to win. It gave her her fourteenth title in all. Mrs Court was not in the lists, preoccupied with the arrival of her first baby.

The meeting of 1973 brought more attention to the women's events than ever before. The political upsets which diminished the men's field had no repercussions among the women who were there in full strength. The accuracy of the seeding was uncanny. All eight selections reached the quarter-final. The top four went through to the semi-final, by which time it was clear cut Australian–American rivalry, Mrs Court against Miss Evert, Miss Goolagong against Mrs King. Miss Evert, losing a one-sided middle set by the same 6–1 margin with which she won the other two, was too steady for the former champion. Mrs King was too solidly aggressive for Miss Goolagong in a long semi-final in which the ambitions of the players fell short of their powers of execution. An all-American final was certainly nothing new. It was though, the first since 1957.

Miss Evert, then 18 years old and already a losing finalist in Rome and Paris, allowed the awe of the occasion to handicap her over much. Mrs King was allowed to take the first eight games of the final for the loss of only ten points. The title was won for the fifth time by Mrs King in only 53 minutes. She thus built a record for post-war years, surpassing Miss Brough's 1955 achievement when she won for the fourth time.

Evonne Goolagong, later Mrs Roger Cawley

There was no stopping Mrs King anywhere. Back with Miss Casals in the doubles they lost a set only in the final against Françoise Durr and Miss Stove. That made her ninth win, the fifth with the same partner. With the mixed she had her second triple championship, her partner again being Davidson with whom she had won twice before. The tally of Mrs King's championships moved ahead to seventeen. This was arrived at on the Sunday because rain caused the mixed doubles to finish one day late.

The picture of events in 1974 was in different colours. Mrs King and Miss Evert were cast by the seeding committee to repeat their performance of the year before. It did not work out like that. The forecast was close to being upset early on. Miss Evert's first match was against the Australian, Lesley Hunt and did not begin until 5.30 on a skiddy Centre Court after a day of rain. After 50 minutes Miss Evert was thankful to struggle through the opening set 8–6. In almost the same time she was forced to yield 5–7 in the second, for Miss Hunt, a player who invariably did well against crack opponents, had inspiration and endless attacking energy. In the third set Miss Evert lost a lead of 5–3 and trailed 5–6. Later she was also behind at 8–9. At nine games all, with the light nearly spent and the match having lasted 2 hours 40 minutes, the issue was postponed overnight. On resumption Miss Hunt could not pick up where she had left off and Miss Evert won two quick games on the morrow to come through. It turned out to be her most dire peril.

Mrs King, out of form, failed in the quarter-final to Mrs Morozova (strictly speaking she was Mrs Rubinoff but adhered to the Russian custom of keeping her single name). The Russian was as fervent a net player as Mrs King. On the day she played that game

Above: Billie Jean King won her nineteenth Wimbledon championship in 1975. She announced her intention to retire from the singles that year after winning a total of 173 matches out of 195 played

Below: Evonne Cawley (*née* Goolagong), became singles champion in 1971, the year after her first appearance at Wimbledon

Chris Evert, from Florida, made her Wimbledon debut in 1972, becoming a semi-finalist that year, a finalist in 1973 and singles champion in 1974 and 1976

vastly better. On the same day Miss Goolagong was also beaten. She yielded to her compatriot Kerry Melville. Here again the winner was aided by deficiencies on the other side. British hopes ran high when Miss Wade arrived as a semi-finalist for the first time in her career but she could not sustain what looked a winning lead against Mrs Morozova in the second set after taking a first that was one-sided.

Miss Evert was irresistible after her damp initiation. She triumphed over Miss Melville in the semi-final and then in the final over Mrs Morozova, the first Russian to get so near the singles title, to put a seal on what was already a notable career at the age of 19. Her progress was in perfect sequence, semi-finalist in 1972, finalist in 1973, winner in 1974.

It was nearly but not quite a blank year for Mrs King. She and Miss Casals lost their doubles title, falling to the Australians, Helen Gourlay and Karen Krantzcke in the quarter-final. The winners in turn lost the final to another unseeded pair, Miss Goolagong with the American, Peggy Michel. The consolation for Mrs King was in the mixed, where she and Davidson, beating surprise British finalists, Mark Farrell and Lesley Charles, won for the fourth time. This was the eighteenth notch in Mrs King's championship tally.

The meeting in 1975 had not progressed very far when Mrs King announced that in singles she was playing her last championship. It proved a happy augury and her singles career ended on a happy note. With Mrs Court back in the field renewal of old rivalries could be expected. The Australian was now the mother of two children. Miss Goolagong was there also having become but a few days earlier, Mrs Roger Cawley and thus become entitled to a United Kingdom passport.

British hopes that Miss Wade would do better than the year before were disappointed. After surviving match points against the American, Janet Newberry in the third round, she played confidently to beat Miss Casals only to lose a fine battle against Mrs Cawley in the quarter-final. Mrs Court came through the same stage against the 18-year-old Martina Navratilova, a notable exponent of the attacking game but unable to sustain her second-seeding status against one as experienced as the Australian. Miss Evert and Mrs King came through the other half, with Mrs King avenging her previous year's loss against Mrs Morozova.

Mrs Cawley was the more impressive semi-final winner when she beat Mrs Court. Mrs King lost the first set to Miss Evert before beating the defending champion. The final was unfortunately a travesty of what that match ought to be. Mrs Cawley could find neither touch nor control. She was utterly routed and won only one game. This gave the singles title to Mrs King for the sixth time. Only Suzanne Lenglen (6 wins), Blanche Hillyard (6), Dorothea Lambert Chambers (7) and Helen Wills Moody (8) had done as well or better. It was Mrs King's nineteenth Wimbledon title. Another Californian, Elizabeth Ryan, achieved as many in 1934. No one else had done so. Miss Ryan never won the singles. Mrs King's record speaks for itself.

The women's doubles had unseeded winners, Ann Kiyomura and Kazuko Sawamatsu, each Japanese by race but Miss Kiyomura an American and only Miss Sawamatsu native born and Japanese speaking. The mixed went in more orthodox fashion to Riessen with Mrs Court. This was Mrs Court's tenth Wimbledon championship and, incredibly, her 91st major crown.

In 1976 the women's singles provided for the first time the perfect event so far as the seeding was concerned. In the first instance all the eight seeds survived to the quarter-finals. Then the numbers one, two, three and four choices became the semi-finalists. Numbers one and two reached the final. Number one became the champion. It was a perfect forecast, perhaps a little dull.

Miss Evert, now 21, became singles champion for the second time. Old, keen and effective rivals, who might have been presumed to run her hard early on, failed to do so. The Australian Lesley Hunt, the Dutch Betty Stove and the Russian Olga Morozova, were among her victims as she took up her place in the last four for the total loss of only ten games. The Czech Martina Navratilova extended her to the full distance in the semi-final. In the final she faced the Australian Evonne Cawley, who had been the more brilliant in their Virginia Slims Final clash in Los Angeles earlier in the season. Mrs Cawley, though vastly more effective than in her sad final the previous year against Mrs King, extended Miss Evert to a hard, good final. Yet she never quite looked like taking control of it.

There were two British players in the last eight to stir patriotic feelings, Virginia Wade and the Devonian, Sue Barker. The latter faded in the end after threatening Miss Navratilova. Miss Wade went through to the semi-final where she failed to do herself justice against Mrs Cawley.

Mrs King, though retired from singles, gave herself two chances to add to her nineteen Wimbledon championships. In the mixed doubles, where she partnered the American Sandy Mayer, she did not get far. In the women's doubles she resumed her pairing with the Dutch Betty Stove, with whom she won in 1972. Mrs King's twentieth Wimbledon title loomed near, but not near enough. In the final she and Miss Stove were beaten 7–5 in the third set by Miss Evert in harness with Miss Navratilova.

As for the mixed doubles, which provided a stirring climax to the meeting with the new champions coming back from match point, that was taken by Tony Roche and Françoise Durr. The former got an Australian on the roll of champions for 1976. The latter at last got her name on the roll of champions after many near misses, having been losing finalist in the women's doubles in 1965, 1968, 1970, 1972, 1973 and 1975.

Miss Durr became the 186th player to have her name inscribed among Wimbledon champions since 1877. Of the 364 championship events played the United States claims 126 and a half. Great Britain, with most success before 1914, claims 118, and Australia 64.

After one hundred years the Wimbledon Championships, albeit in a manner that Henry Jones can never have dreamed of, flourished as never before.

RESULTS

THE CHAMPIONSHIP ROLL

MEN'S SINGLES

1877	Spencer W. Gore
1878	P. F. Hadow
1879	Rev J. T. Hartley
1880	Rev J. T. Hartley
1881	W. Renshaw
1882	W. Renshaw
1883	W. Renshaw
1884	W. Renshaw
1885	W. Renshaw
1886	W. Renshaw
1887	H. F. Lawford
1888	E. Renshaw
1889	W. Renshaw
1890	W. J. Hamilton
1891	W. Baddeley
1892	W. Baddeley
1893	J. Pim
1894	J. Pim
1895	W. Baddeley
1896	H. S. Mahony
1897	R. F. Doherty
1898	R. F. Doherty
1899	R. F. Doherty
1900	R. F. Doherty
1901	A. W. Gore
1902	H. L. Doherty
1903	H. L. Doherty
1904	H. L. Doherty
1905	H. L. Doherty
1906	H. L. Doherty
1907	N. E. Brookes
1908	A. W. Gore
1909	A. W. Gore
1910	A. F. Wilding
1911	A. F. Wilding
1912	A. F. Wilding
1913	A. F. Wilding
1914	N. E. Brookes
1915–18	not held
1919	G. L. Patterson
1920	W. T. Tilden
1921	W. T. Tilden
1922	G. L. Patterson
1923	W. M. Johnston
1924	J. Borotra
1925	J. R. Lacoste
1926	J. Borotra
1927	H. J. Cochet
1928	J. R. Lacoste
1929	H. J. Cochet
1930	W. T. Tilden
1931	S. B. Wood
1932	H. E. Vines
1933	J. H. Crawford
1934	F. J. Perry
1935	F. J. Perry
1936	F. J. Perry
1937	J. D. Budge
1938	J. D. Budge
1939	R. L. Riggs
1940–5	not held
1946	Y. Petra
1947	J. A. Kramer
1948	R. Falkenburg
1949	F. R. Schroeder
1950	J. E. Patty
1951	R. Savitt
1952	F. A. Sedgman
1953	E. V. Seixas
1954	J. Drobny
1955	M. A. Trabert
1956	L. A. Hoad
1957	L. A. Hoad
1958	A. J. Cooper
1959	A. Olmedo
1960	N. A. Fraser
1961	R. G. Laver
1962	R. G. Laver
1963	C. R. McKinley
1964	R. S. Emerson
1965	R. S. Emerson
1966	M. Santana
1967	J. D. Newcombe
1968	R. G. Laver
1969	R. G. Laver
1970	J. D. Newcombe
1971	J. D. Newcombe
1972	S. R. Smith
1973	J. Kodes
1974	J. S. Connors
1975	A. R. Ashe
1976	B. Borg

WOMEN'S SINGLES

1884	Miss M. E. E. Watson
1885	Miss M. E. E. Watson
1886	Miss B. Bingley
1887	Miss C. Dod
1888	Miss C. Dod
1889	Mrs G. W. Hillyard
1890	Miss H. B. G. Rice
1891	Miss C. Dod
1892	Miss C. Dod
1893	Miss C. Dod
1894	Mrs G. W. Hillyard
1895	Miss C. Cooper
1896	Miss C. Cooper
1897	Mrs G. W. Hillyard
1898	Miss C. Cooper
1899	Mrs G. W. Hillyard
1900	Mrs G. W. Hillyard
1901	Mrs A. Sterry
1902	Miss M. E. Robb
1903	Miss D. K. Douglass
1904	Miss D. K. Douglass
1905	Miss M. G. Sutton
1906	Miss D. K. Douglass
1907	Miss M. G. Sutton
1908	Mrs A. Sterry
1909	Miss D. P. Boothby
1910	Mrs R. Lambert Chambers
1911	Mrs R. Lambert Chambers
1912	Mrs D. R. Larcombe
1913	Mrs R. Lambert Chambers
1914	Mrs R. Lambert Chambers
1915–18	not held
1919	Mlle S. Lenglen
1920	Mlle S. Lenglen
1921	Mlle S. Lenglen
1922	Mlle S. Lenglen
1923	Mlle S. Lenglen
1924	Miss K. McKane
1925	Mlle S. Lenglen
1926	Mrs L. A. Godfree
1927	Miss H. Wills
1928	Miss H. Wills
1929	Miss H. Wills
1930	Mrs F. S. Moody
1931	Frl C. Aussem
1932	Mrs F. S. Moody
1933	Mrs F. S. Moody
1934	Miss D. E. Round
1935	Mrs F. S. Moody
1936	Miss H. H. Jacobs
1937	Miss D. E. Round
1938	Mrs F. S. Moody
1939	Miss A. Marble
1940–5	not held
1946	Miss P. M. Betz
1947	Miss M. E. Osborne
1948	Miss A. L. Brough
1949	Miss A. L. Brough
1950	Miss A. L. Brough
1951	Miss D. J. Hart
1952	Miss M. C. Connolly
1953	Miss M. C. Connolly
1954	Miss M. C. Connolly
1955	Miss A. L. Brough
1956	Miss S. J. Fry
1957	Miss A. Gibson
1958	Miss A. Gibson
1959	Miss M. E. Bueno
1960	Miss M. E. Bueno
1961	Miss A. Mortimer
1962	Mrs J. R. Susman
1963	Miss M. Smith
1964	Miss M. E. Bueno
1965	Miss M. Smith
1966	Mrs L. W. King
1967	Mrs L. W. King
1968	Mrs L. W. King
1969	Mrs P. F. Jones
1970	Mrs B. M. Court
1971	Miss E. F. Goolagong
1972	Mrs L. W. King
1973	Mrs L. W. King
1974	Miss C. M. Evert
1975	Mrs L. W. King
1976	Miss C. M. Evert

MEN'S DOUBLES

1884 E. Renshaw and W. Renshaw
1885 E. Renshaw and W. Renshaw
1886 E. Renshaw and W. Renshaw
1887 P. Bowes-Lyon and H. W. W. Wilberforce
1888 E. Renshaw and W. Renshaw
1889 E. Renshaw and W. Renshaw
1890 J. Pim and F. O. Stoker
1891 H. Baddeley and W. Baddeley
1892 H. S. Barlow and E. W. Lewis
1893 J. Pim and F. O. Stoker
1894 H. Baddeley and W. Baddeley
1895 H. Baddeley and W. Baddeley
1896 H. Baddeley and W. Baddeley
1897 H. L. Doherty and R. F. Doherty
1898 H. L. Doherty and R. F. Doherty
1899 H. L. Doherty and R. F. Doherty
1900 H. L. Doherty and R. F. Doherty
1901 H. L. Doherty and R. F. Doherty
1902 F. L. Riseley and S. H. Smith
1903 H. L. Doherty and R. F. Doherty
1904 H. L. Doherty and R. F. Doherty
1905 H. L. Doherty and R. F. Doherty
1906 F. L. Riseley and S. H. Smith
1907 N. E. Brookes and A. F. Wilding
1908 M. J. G. Ritchie and A. F. Wilding
1909 H. Roper Barrett and A. W. Gore
1910 M. J. G. Ritchie and A. F. Wilding
1911 M. Decugis and A. H. Gobert
1912 H. Roper Barrett and C. P. Dixon
1913 H. Roper Barrett and C. P. Dixon
1914 N. E. Brookes and A. F. Wilding
1915–18 not held
1919 P. O'Hara-Wood and R. V. Thomas
1920 C. S. Garland and R. N. Williams
1921 R. Lycett and M. Woosnam
1922 R. Lycett and J. O. Anderson
1923 R. Lycett and L. A. Godfree
1924 F. T. Hunter and V. Richards
1925 J. Borotra and J. R. Lacoste
1926 J. Brugnon and H. J. Cochet
1927 F. T. Hunter and W. T. Tilden
1928 J. Brugnon and H. J. Cochet
1929 W. L. Allison and J. Van Ryn
1930 W. L. Allison and J. Van Ryn
1931 G. M. Lott and J. Van Ryn
1932 J. Borotra and J. Brugnon
1933 J. Borotra and J. Brugnon
1934 G. M. Lott and L. R. Stoefen
1935 J. H. Crawford and A. K. Quist
1936 G. P. Hughes and C. R. D. Tuckey
1937 J. D. Budge and C. G. Mako
1938 J. D. Budge and C. G. Mako
1939 E. T. Cooke and R. L. Riggs
1940–5 not held
1946 T. P. Brown and J. A. Kramer
1947 R. Falkenburg and J. A. Kramer
1948 J. E. Bromwich and F. A. Sedgman
1949 R. A. Gonzales and F. A. Parker
1950 J. E. Bromwich and A. K. Quist
1951 K. McGregor and F. A. Sedgman
1952 K. McGregor and F. A. Sedgman
1953 L. A. Hoad and K. R. Rosewall
1954 R. N. Hartwig and M. G. Rose
1955 R. N. Hartwig and L. A. Hoad
1956 L. A. Hoad and K. R. Rosewall
1957 G. Mulloy and J. E. Patty
1958 S. Davidson and U. Schmidt
1959 R. S. Emerson and N. A. Fraser
1960 R. H. Osuna and R. D. Ralston
1961 R. S. Emerson and N. A. Fraser
1962 R. A. J. Hewitt and F. S. Stolle
1963 R. H. Osuna and A. Palafox
1964 R. A. J. Hewitt and F. S. Stolle
1965 J. D. Newcombe and A. D. Roche
1966 K. N. Fletcher and J. D. Newcombe
1967 R. A. J. Hewitt and F. D. McMillan
1968 J. D. Newcombe and A. D. Roche
1969 J. D. Newcombe and A. D. Roche
1970 J. D. Newcombe and A. D. Roche
1971 R. S. Emerson and R. G. Laver
1972 R. A. J. Hewitt and F. D. McMillan
1973 J. S. Connors and I. Nastase
1974 J. D. Newcombe and A. D. Roche
1975 V. Gerulaitis and A. Mayer
1976 B. E. Gottfried and R. Ramirez

WOMEN'S DOUBLES

Non-Championship Event

1899 Mrs G. W. Hillyard and Miss B. Steedman
1900 Mrs W. H. Pickering and Miss M. E. Robb
1901 Mrs G. W. Hillyard and Mrs A. Sterry
1902 Miss A. M. Morton and Mrs A. Sterry
1903 Miss D. K. Douglass and Mrs W. H. Pickering
1904 Miss W. A. Longhurst and Miss E. W. Thomson
1905 Miss W. A. Longhurst and Miss E. W. Thomson
1906 Mrs G. W. Hillyard and Miss M. G. Sutton
1907 Mrs R. Lambert Chambers and Miss C. M. Wilson
1908–12 not held

Full Championship Event

1913 Miss D. P. Boothby and Mrs R. J. McNair
1914 Miss A. M. Morton and Miss E. Ryan
1915–18 not held
1919 Mlle S. Lenglen and Miss E. Ryan
1920 Mlle S. Lenglen and Miss E. Ryan
1921 Mlle S. Lenglen and Miss E. Ryan
1922 Mlle S. Lenglen and Miss E. Ryan
1923 Mlle S. Lenglen and Miss E. Ryan
1924 Mrs G. Wightman and Miss H. N. Wills
1925 Mlle S. Lenglen and Miss E. Ryan
1926 Miss M. K. Browne and Miss E. Ryan
1927 Miss E. Ryan and Miss H. N. Wills
1928 Mrs P. H. Watson and Miss P. Saunders
1929 Mrs P. H. Watson and Mrs L. R. C. Michel
1930 Mrs F. S. Moody and Miss E. Ryan
1931 Mrs D. C. Shepherd-Barron and Miss P. E. Mudford
1932 Mlle D. Metaxa and Mlle J. Sigart
1933 Mme R. Mathieu and Miss E. Ryan
1934 Mme R. Mathieu and Miss E. Ryan
1935 Miss F. James and Miss K. E. Stammers
1936 Miss F. James and Miss K. E. Stammers
1937 Mme R. Mathieu and Miss A. M. Yorke
1938 Mrs M. Fabyan and Miss A. Marble
1939 Mrs M. Fabyan and Miss A. Marble
1940–5 not held
1946 Miss A. L. Brough and Miss M. E. Osborne
1947 Miss D. J. Hart and Mrs P. C. Todd
1948 Miss A. L. Brough and Mrs W. D. du Pont
1949 Miss A. L. Brough and Mrs W. D. du Pont
1950 Miss A. L. Brough and Mrs W. D. du Pont
1951 Miss S. J. Fry and Miss D. J. Hart
1952 Miss S. J. Fry and Miss D. J. Hart
1953 Miss S. J. Fry and Miss D. J. Hart
1954 Miss A. L. Brough and Mrs W. D. du Pont
1955 Miss A. Mortimer and Miss J. A. Shilcock
1956 Miss A. Buxton and Miss A. Gibson
1957 Miss A. Gibson and Miss D. R. Hard
1958 Miss M. E. Bueno and Miss A. Gibson
1959 Miss J. Arth and Miss D. R. Hard

1960 Miss M. E. Bueno and Miss D. R. Hard
1961 Miss K. Hantze and Miss B. J. Moffitt
1962 Miss B. J. Moffitt and Mrs J. R. Susman
1963 Miss M. E. Bueno and Miss D. R. Hard
1964 Miss M. Smith and Miss L. R. Turner
1965 Miss M. E. Bueno and Miss B. J. Moffitt
1966 Miss M. E. Bueno and Miss N. Richey
1967 Miss R. Casals and Mrs L. W. King
1968 Miss R. Casals and Mrs L. W. King
1969 Mrs B. M. Court and Miss J. A. M. Tegart
1970 Miss R. Casals and Mrs L. W. King
1971 Miss R. Casals and Mrs L. W. King
1972 Mrs L. W. King and Miss B. F. Stove
1973 Miss R. Casals and Mrs L. W. King
1974 Miss E. F. Goolagong and Miss M. Michel
1975 Miss A. K. Kiyomura and Miss K. Sawamatsu
1976 Miss C. M. Evert and Miss M. Navratilova

MIXED DOUBLES

Non-Championship Event

1900 H. A. Nisbet and Mrs W. H. Pickering
1901 H. L. Doherty and Mrs A. Sterry
1902 H. L. Doherty and Mrs A. Sterry
1903 S. H. Smith and Miss E. W. Thomson
1904 S. H. Smith and Miss E. W. Thomson
1905 A. W. Gore and Miss C. M. Wilson
1906 A. F. Wilding and Miss D. K. Douglass
1907 B. C. Wright and Miss M. G. Sutton
1908 A. F. Wilding and Mrs R. Lambert Chambers
1909 H. Roper Barrett and Miss A. M. Morton
1910 S. N. Doust and Mrs R. Lambert Chambers
1911 T. M. Mavrogordato and Mrs E. G. Parton
1912 J. C. Parke and Mrs D. R. Larcombe

Full Championship Event

1913 H. Crisp and Mrs C. O. Tuckey
1914 J. C. Parke and Mrs D. R. Larcombe
1915–18 not held
1919 R. Lycett and Miss E. Ryan
1920 G. L. Patterson and Mlle S. Lenglen
1921 R. Lycett and Miss E. Ryan
1922 P. O'Hara-Wood and Mlle S. Lenglen
1923 R. Lycett and Miss E. Ryan
1924 J. B. Gilbert and Miss K. McKane
1925 J. Borotra and Mlle S. Lenglen
1926 L. A. Godfree and Mrs L. A. Godfree
1927 F. T. Hunter and Miss E. Ryan
1928 P. D. B. Spence and Miss E. Ryan
1929 F. T. Hunter and Miss H. Wills
1930 J. H. Crawford and Miss E. Ryan
1931 G. M. Lott and Mrs L. A. Harper
1932 E. Maier and Miss E. Ryan
1933 G. von Cramm and Frl H. Krahwinkel
1934 R. Miki and Miss D. E. Round
1935 F. J. Perry and Miss D. E. Round
1936 F. J. Perry and Miss D. E. Round
1937 J. D. Budge and Miss A. Marble
1938 J. D. Budge and Miss A. Marble
1939 R. L. Riggs and Miss A. Marble
1940–5 not held
1946 T. P. Brown and Miss A. L. Brough
1947 J. E. Bromwich and Miss A. L. Brough
1948 J. E. Bromwich and Miss A. L. Brough
1949 E. W. Sturgess and Mrs S. P. Summers
1950 E. W. Sturgess and Miss A. L. Brough
1951 F. A. Sedgman and Miss D. J. Hart
1952 F. A. Sedgman and Miss D. J. Hart
1953 E. V. Seixas and Miss D. J. Hart
1954 E. V. Seixas and Miss D. J. Hart
1955 E. V. Seixas and Miss D. J. Hart
1956 E. V. Seixas and Miss S. J. Fry
1957 M. G. Rose and Miss D. R. Hard
1958 R. N. Howe and Miss L. Coghlan
1959 R. G. Laver and Miss D. R. Hard
1960 R. G. Laver and Miss D. R. Hard
1961 F. S. Stolle and Miss L. R. Turner
1962 N. A. Fraser and Mrs W. D. du Pont
1963 K. N. Fletcher and Miss M. Smith
1964 F. S. Stolle and Miss L. R. Turner
1965 K. N. Fletcher and Miss M. Smith
1966 K. N. Fletcher and Miss M. Smith
1967 O. K. Davidson and Mrs L. W. King
1968 K. N. Fletcher and Mrs B. M. Court
1969 F. S. Stolle and Mrs P. F. Jones
1970 I. Nastase and Miss R. Casals
1971 O. K. Davidson and Mrs L. W. King
1972 I. Nastase and Miss R. Casals
1973 O. K. Davidson and Mrs L. W. King
1974 O. K. Davidson and Mrs L. W. King
1975 M. C. Riessen and Mrs B. M. Court
1976 A. D. Roche and Miss F. Durr

THE CHAMPIONSHIPS

The following is the record of the results in the Lawn Tennis Championships from the first meeting in 1877 to date.

In singles they are recorded from the stage of the last eight onwards, in doubles from the last four. Because of their special interest the full results in the inaugural men's singles of 1877 and the inaugural women's singles of 1884 have been recorded.

In the case of both men's and women's singles, the champion was the winner of the challenge round and his or her name appears in bold type. The challenge round was abolished after 1921.

Unless otherwise indicated the nationality of players is British or, prior to 1921, Irish.

Abbreviations

ARG	Argentina	G	Germany	NZ	New Zealand
AU	Austria	GRE	Greece	POL	Poland
AUS	Australia	HK	Hong Kong	RHOD	Rhodesia
B	Belgium	HU	Hungary	ROM	Romania
BERM	Bermuda	IN	India	SA	South Africa
BRA	Brazil	INDO	Indonesia	SP	Spain
CAN	Canada	IRE	Ireland	SWE	Sweden
COL	Columbia	IT	Italy	SWI	Switzerland
CZ	Czechoslovakia	J	Japan	US	United States of America
DEN	Denmark	LUX	Luxembourg	USSR	Union of Soviet Socialist Republics
EG	Egypt	MEX	Mexico	VEN	Venezuela
F	France	NOR	Norway	YU	Yugoslavia
FIN	Finland	NTH	Netherlands		

MEN'S SINGLES

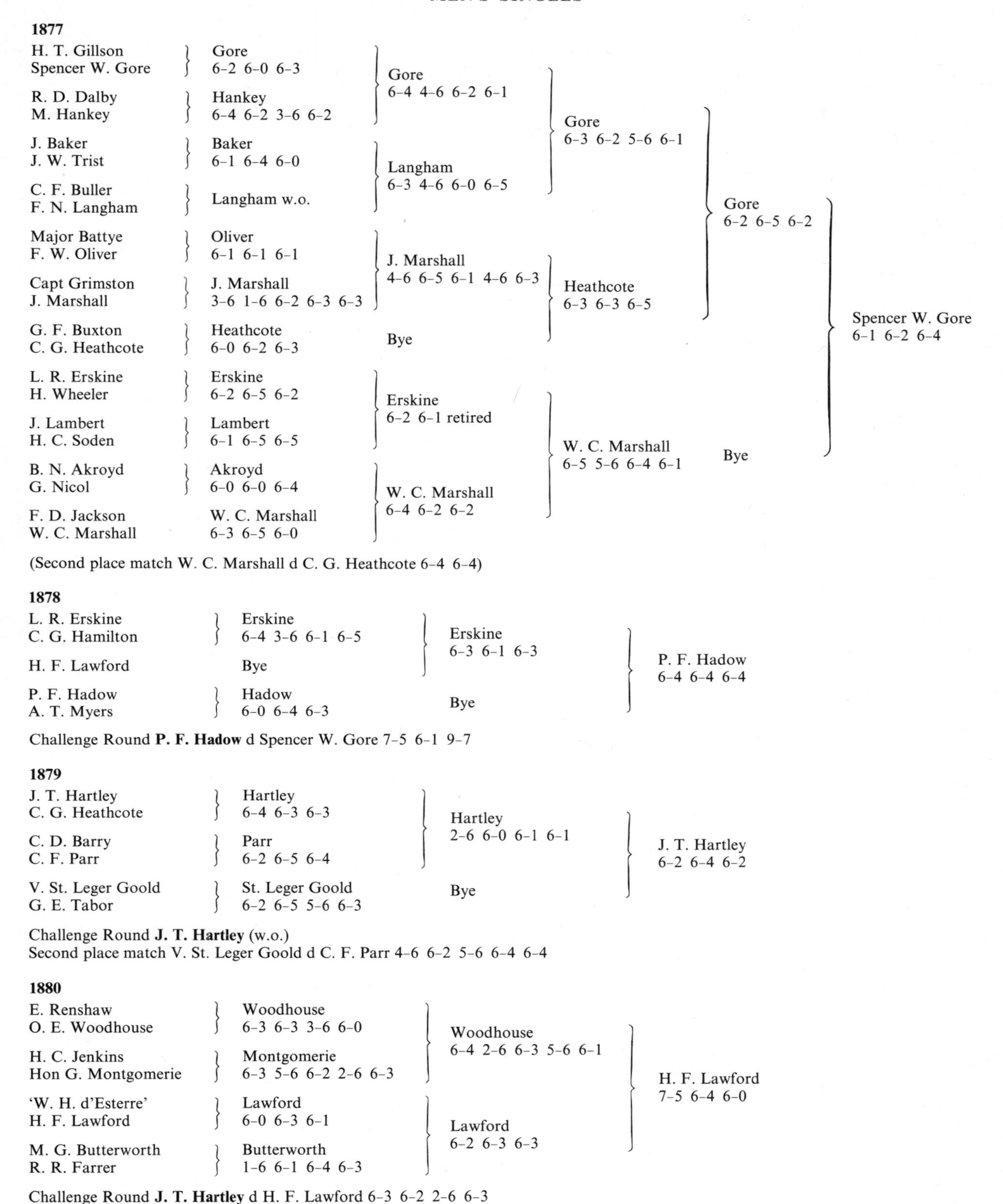

1877

Players	First Round	Second Round	Third Round	Semi-final	Final
H. T. Gillson / Spencer W. Gore	Gore 6–2 6–0 6–3	Gore 6–4 4–6 6–2 6–1	Gore 6–3 6–2 5–6 6–1	Gore 6–2 6–5 6–2	Spencer W. Gore 6–1 6–2 6–4
R. D. Dalby / M. Hankey	Hankey 6–4 6–2 3–6 6–2				
J. Baker / J. W. Trist	Baker 6–1 6–4 6–0	Langham 6–3 4–6 6–0 6–5			
C. F. Buller / F. N. Langham	Langham w.o.				
Major Battye / F. W. Oliver	Oliver 6–1 6–1 6–1	J. Marshall 4–6 6–5 6–1 4–6 6–3	Heathcote 6–3 6–3 6–5		
Capt Grimston / J. Marshall	J. Marshall 3–6 1–6 6–2 6–3 6–3				
G. F. Buxton / C. G. Heathcote	Heathcote 6–0 6–2 6–3	Bye			
L. R. Erskine / H. Wheeler	Erskine 6–2 6–5 6–2	Erskine 6–2 6–1 retired	W. C. Marshall 6–5 5–6 6–4 6–1	Bye	
J. Lambert / H. C. Soden	Lambert 6–1 6–5 6–5				
B. N. Akroyd / G. Nicol	Akroyd 6–0 6–0 6–4	W. C. Marshall 6–4 6–2 6–2			
F. D. Jackson / W. C. Marshall	W. C. Marshall 6–3 6–5 6–0				

(Second place match W. C. Marshall d C. G. Heathcote 6–4 6–4)

1878

Players	First Round	Second Round	Final
L. R. Erskine / C. G. Hamilton	Erskine 6–4 3–6 6–1 6–5	Erskine 6–3 6–1 6–3	P. F. Hadow 6–4 6–4 6–4
H. F. Lawford	Bye		
P. F. Hadow / A. T. Myers	Hadow 6–0 6–4 6–3	Bye	

Challenge Round **P. F. Hadow** d Spencer W. Gore 7–5 6–1 9–7

1879

Players	First Round	Second Round	Final
J. T. Hartley / C. G. Heathcote	Hartley 6–4 6–3 6–3	Hartley 2–6 6–0 6–1 6–1	J. T. Hartley 6–2 6–4 6–2
C. D. Barry / C. F. Parr	Parr 6–2 6–5 6–4		
V. St. Leger Goold / G. E. Tabor	St. Leger Goold 6–2 6–5 5–6 6–3	Bye	

Challenge Round **J. T. Hartley** (w.o.)
Second place match V. St. Leger Goold d C. F. Parr 4–6 6–2 5–6 6–4 6–4

1880

Players	First Round	Second Round	Final
E. Renshaw / O. E. Woodhouse	Woodhouse 6–3 6–3 3–6 6–0	Woodhouse 6–4 2–6 6–3 5–6 6–1	H. F. Lawford 7–5 6–4 6–0
H. C. Jenkins / Hon G. Montgomerie	Montgomerie 6–3 5–6 6–2 2–6 6–3		
'W. H. d'Esterre' / H. F. Lawford	Lawford 6–0 6–3 6–1	Lawford 6–2 6–3 6–3	
M. G. Butterworth / R. R. Farrer	Butterworth 1–6 6–1 6–4 6–3		

Challenge Round **J. T. Hartley** d H. F. Lawford 6–3 6–2 2–6 6–3

1881

First Round		Second Round	Final
W. Renshaw O. E. Woodhouse	Renshaw 4–6 6–4 6–0 6–3	Renshaw 1–6 6–3 6–2 5–6 6–3	W. Renshaw 6–4 6–2 6–3
G. M. Hill H. F. Lawford	Lawford 6–1 6–1 6–0		
W. H. Darby R. T. Richardson	Richardson 6–0 6–4 6–1	Bye	

Challenge Round **W. Renshaw** d J. T. Hartley 6–0 6–1 6–1
Second place match R. T. Richardson d H. F. Lawford 6–3 4–6 6–1 3–6 7–5

1882

First Round		Second Round	Final
H. Berkley E. Renshaw	Renshaw 6–5 6–1 6–4	Renshaw 6–4 4–6 6–2 3–6 6–0	E. Renshaw 7–5 6–3 2–6 6–3
H. F. Lawford H. W. W. Wilberforce	Lawford 6–2 6–5 6–5		
R. T. Richardson C. E. Woodhouse	Richardson 6–1 6–0 6–2	Richardson 6–1 6–2 6–1	
F. Benson	Bye		

Challenge Round **W. Renshaw** d E. Renshaw 6–1 2–6 4–6 6–2 6–2

1883

First Round		Second Round	Final
D. Stewart H. W. W. Wilberforce	Stewart 6–5 3–6 5–6 6–5 6–4	Stewart 6–0 6–1 6–3	E. Renshaw 0–6 6–3 6–0 6–2
M. Constable W. C. Taylor	Taylor 6–3 6–5 5–6 4–6 6–3		
C. W. Grinstead E. Renshaw	Renshaw 6–4 6–3 6–3	Bye	

Challenge Round **W. Renshaw** d E. Renshaw 2–6 6–3 6–3 4–6 6–3

1884

First Round		Second Round	Final
W. Milne E. Renshaw	Renshaw 6–3 6–3 7–5	Grinstead 2–6 6–4 6–2 6–3	H. F. Lawford 7–5 2–6 6–2 9–7
E. de S. H. Browne C. W. Grinstead	Grinstead 5–7 4–6 7–5 6–4 6–1		
H. Chipp W. C. Taylor	Chipp 10–8 6–1 6–4	Lawford 7–5 6–4 6–4	
H. F. Lawford	Bye		

Challenge Round **W. Renshaw** d H. F. Lawford 6–0 6–4 9–7

(After 1884 the method of making the draw was amended so as to eliminate all byes except in the first round.)

1885

First Round		Second Round	Final
H. Chipp E. Renshaw	Renshaw 6–4 6–4 7–5	Renshaw 6–4 8–6 2–6 5–7 6–4	H. F. Lawford 5–7 6–1 0–6 6–2 6–4
E. de S. H. Browne M. G. Macnamara	de S. H. Browne 6–1 7–5 6–2		
J. Dwight (US) A. J. Stanley	Dwight 6–3 6–3 6–4	Lawford 6–2 6–2 6–3	
H. F. Lawford P. Bowes-Lyon	Lawford 6–3 7–5 6–3		

Challenge Round **W. Renshaw** d H. F. Lawford 7–5 6–2 4–6 7–5

1886

First Round		Second Round	Final
W. J. Hamilton H. F. Lawford	Lawford 8–6 6–1 8–6	Lawford 6–3 6–2 6–0	H. F. Lawford 6–2 6–3 2–6 4–6 6–4
T. R. Garvey W. C. Taylor	Garvey 8–6 6–4 2–6 6–3		
E. W. Lewis E. Renshaw	Lewis 4–6 5–7 6–4 6–1 6–0	Lewis 3–6 6–2 1–6 6–1 6–3	
C. H. A. Ross H. W. W. Wilberforce	Wilberforce 3–6 2–6 6–4 6–2 6–4		

Challenge Round **W. Renshaw** d H. F. Lawford 6–0 5–7 6–3 6–4

1887

H. Grove P. B. Lyon	Grove 6–3 6–2 10–8	Lawford 4–6 6–3 7–5 7–5	H. F. Lawford 1–6 6–3 3–6 6–4 6–4
H. F. Lawford O. Milne	Lawford 7–5 6–0 6–3		
E. W. Lewis E. Renshaw	Renshaw 7–5 6–2 6–4	Renshaw w.o.	
W. Milne E. Lacy Sweet	Lacy Sweet 6–2 6–2 4–6 6–1		

Challenge Round **H. F. Lawford** (w.o.)

1888

E. Renshaw H. W. W. Wilberforce	Renshaw 4–6 6–3 7–5 4–6 6–0	Renshaw 7–5 7–5 5–7 6–3	E. Renshaw 7–9 6–1 8–6 6–4
W. J. Hamilton W. Renshaw	Hamilton 5–7 7–5 6–4 6–2		
E. W. Lewis H. S. Scrivener	Lewis 7–5 6–3 6–1	Lewis 9–7 6–4 6–4	
F. L. Rawson W. C. Taylor	Taylor 6–4 6–0 4–6 4–6 6–1		

Challenge Round **E. Renshaw** d. H. F. Lawford 6–3 7–5 6–0

1889

W. J. Hamilton E. W. Lewis	Hamilton 4–6 7–5 6–3 5–7 6–4	Barlow 3–6 6–3 2–6 6–3 6–3	W. Renshaw 3–6 5–7 8–6 10–8 8–6
H. S. Barlow G. W. Hillyard	Barlow 7–5 6–2 6–4		
M. F. Goodbody W. Renshaw	Renshaw 7–5 6–4 6–4	Renshaw 7–5 5–7 6–3 6–2	
H. F. Lawford A. G. Ziffo	Lawford 6–3 6–2 6–1		

Challenge Round **W. Renshaw** d E. Renshaw 6–4 6–1 3–6 6–0

1890

J. Pim H. S. Scrivener	Pim 6–3 12–10 6–0	Hamilton 0–6 6–4 6–4 6–2	W. J. Hamilton 2–6 6–4 6–4 4–6 7–5
W. Baddeley W. J. Hamilton	Hamilton 6–3 6–0 6–1		
E. W. Lewis D. Miller (US)	Lewis 6–3 6–1 6–1	Barlow 7–5 6–4 4–6 7–5	
H. S. Barlow D. G. Chaytor	Barlow 8–10 6–4 2–6 6–1 6–1		

Challenge Round **W. J. Hamilton** d W. Renshaw 6–8 6–2 3–6 6–1 6–1

1891

H. Grove E. Renshaw	Renshaw 6–3 7–5 6–2	Baddeley 6–0 6–1 6–1	W. Baddeley 6–4 1–6 7–5 6–0
E. J. Avory W. Baddeley	Baddeley 6–0 6–1 4–6 6–2		
H. A. B. Chapman H. S. Mahony	Mahony 6–2 6–0 6–1	Pim 6–4 6–0 6–2	
H. S. Barlow J. Pim	Pim 5–7 0–6 6–2 6–3 7–5		

Challenge Round **W. Baddeley** (w.o.)

1892

W. V. Eaves	Lewis 7–5 6–2 6–2	Lewis 2–6 6–3 6–1 6–2	J. Pim 2–6 5–7 9–7 6–3 6–2
E. W. Lewis			
H. A. B. Chapman	Chapman 6–4 6–0 6–1		
R. A. Gamble			
A. W. Gore	Mahony 4–6 6–2 6–3 6–4	Pim 6–1 12–10 2–6 6–2	
H. S. Mahony			
H. S. Barlow	Pim 3–6 9–7 6–3 7–5		
J. Pim			

Challenge Round **W. Baddeley** d J. Pim 4–6 6–3 6–3 6–2

1893

H. S. Barlow	Barlow 7–9 6–2 10–8 6–8 6–1	Pim 9–7 6–2 6–3	J. Pim 9–7 6–3 6–0
A. W. Hallward			
M. F. Goodbody	Pim 8–6 3–6 6–3 6–1		
J. Pim			
W. V. Eaves	Mahony 10–8 11–9 6–0	Mahony 3–6 6–3 6–3 6–1	
H. S. Mahony			
M. Durlacher	Archdale Palmer 6–3 6–4 7–5		
Archdale Palmer			

Challenge Round **J. Pim** d W. Baddeley 3–6 6–1 6–3 6–2

1894

W. Baddeley	W. Baddeley 6–2 6–1 6–3	W. Baddeley w.o.	W. Baddeley 6–0 6–1 6–0
J. F. Talmage			
T. Chaytor	Chaytor 1–6 6–1 6–8 8–6 6–4		
E. G. Meers			
E. W. Lewis	Lewis 6–2 6–3 6–2	Lewis 2–6 7–5 6–3 1–6 7–5	
G. M. Simond			
H. Baddeley	H. Baddeley 0–6 6–3 4–6 6–1 6–1		
H. S. Barlow			

Challenge Round **J. Pim** d W. Baddeley 10–8 6–2 8–6

1895

W. Baddeley	W. Baddeley 6–1 6–4 8–6	W. Baddeley w.o.	W. Baddeley 4–6 2–6 8–6 6–2 6–3
H. S. Barlow			
H. Baddeley	H. Baddeley 6–4 6–2 6–4		
R. F. Doherty			
J. M. Flavelle	Meers 6–1 6–2 6–1	Eaves 6–3 7–9 9–11 6–4 6–1	
E. G. Meers			
W. V. Eaves	Eaves 6–4 6–2 7–5		
G. M. Simond			

Challenge Round **W. Baddeley** (w.o.)

1896

H. S. Mahony	Mahony 7–5 5–7 7–5 6–3	Mahony 6–4 2–6 8–6 4–6 6–3	H. S. Mahony 6–2 6–2 11–9
F. L. Riseley			
H. A. Nisbet	Nisbet 2–6 6–4 6–4 1–6 6–3		
G. M. Simond			
C. H. L. Cazalet	Eaves 7–5 6–3 6–0	Eaves 6–4 6–3 6–4	
W. V. Eaves			
H. Baddeley	Baddeley 3–6 3–6 6–4 6–4 6–3		
W. A. Larned (US)			

Challenge Round **H. S. Mahony** d W. Baddeley 6–2 6–8 5–7 8–6 6–3

1897

G. W. Hillyard S. H. Smith	Smith 3-6 6-4 6-2 6-4	Eaves 6-2 5-7 1-6 6-2 6-1	R. F. Doherty 6-3 7-5 2-0 retired
W. V. Eaves G. Greville	Eaves 6-1 6-2 8-10 6-0		
W. Baddeley H. L. Doherty	Baddeley 6-4 6-2 6-2	Doherty 6-3 6-0 6-3	
R. F. Doherty F. L. Riseley	Doherty w.o.		

Challenge Round **R. F. Doherty** d H. S. Mahony 6-4 6-4 6-3

1898

C. Hobart (US) M. J. G. Ritchie	Hobart 6-2 3-6 6-3 6-2	Doherty 6-1 6-4 6-3	H. L. Doherty 6-1 6-2 4-6 2-6 14-12
H. L. Doherty J. M. Flavelle	Doherty 6-2 6-3 3-6 6-0		
A. W. Gore S. H. Smith	Gore 4-6 6-0 4-6 6-3 7-5	Mahony 6-2 3-6 4-6 6-2 6-4	
H. S. Mahony G. M. Simond	Mahony 6-2 6-4 6-4		

Challenge Round **R. F. Doherty** d H. L. Doherty 6-3 6-3 2-6 5-7 6-1

1899

A. W. Gore P. G. Pearson	Gore 6-3 6-2 9-7	Gore 6-3 4-6 3-6 7-5 6-1	A. W. Gore 3-6 6-2 6-1 6-4
G. Greville H. S. Mahony	Mahony 6-3 9-7 2-6 10-8		
H. A. Nisbet S. H. Smith	Smith 6-3 7-5 6-4	Smith 2-6 11-9 4-6 8-6 8-6	
H. Roper Barrett C. Hobart (US)	Barrett 8-6 7-5 6-4		

Challenge Round **R. F. Doherty** d A. W. Gore 1-6 4-6 6-2 6-3 6-3

1900

A. W. Gore F. J. Plaskitt	Gore 6-3 6-2 6-0	Gore 4-6 8-6 8-6 6-1	S. H. Smith 6-4 4-6 6-2 6-1
H. L. Doherty R. J. McNair	Doherty 6-1 6-2 6-4		
H. Roper Barrett S. H. Smith	Smith 6-1 4-6 7-5 6-2	Smith 6-0 6-1 6-1	
H. A. Nisbet F. W. Payn	Nisbet 6-2 6-8 6-4 3-6 6-2		

Challenge Round **R. F. Doherty** d S. H. Smith 6-8 6-3 6-1 6-2

1901

H. S. Mahony R. J. McNair	Mahony 6-4 6-3 3-6 6-3	Dixon 6-3 6-4 11-9	A. W. Gore 6-4 6-0 6-3
C. P. Dixon G. M. Simond	Dixon 6-4 7-5 1-6 6-3		
H. Roper Barrett S. H. Smith	Barrett 7-5 6-4 8-6	Gore 8-6 6-1 7-5	
A. W. Gore G. W. Hillyard	Gore 6-1 2-6 4-6 8-6 6-2		

Challenge Round **A. W. Gore** d R. F. Doherty 4-6 7-5 6-4 6-4

1902

A. E. Crawley M. J. G. Ritchie	Ritchie 6–2 6–1 2–6 6–3	Ritchie 6–4 4–6 6–4 6–4	H. L. Doherty 8–6 6–3 7–5
H. Roper Barrett S. H. Smith	Smith 6–3 6–4 6–3		
H. L. Doherty G. Greville	Doherty 6–1 1–6 6–3 7–5	Doherty 4–6 4–6 8–6 2–0 retired	
H. S. Mahony F. W. Payn	Mahony 6–2 6–2 6–4		

Challenge Round **H. L. Doherty** d A. W. Gore 6–4 6–3 3–6 6–0

1903

G. W. Hillyard F. L. Riseley	Riseley 6–1 6–4 6–4	Riseley 7–5 6–3 7–9 1–6 9–7	F. L. Riseley 1–6 6–3 8–6 13–11
H. Pollard S. H. Smith	Smith 6–2 6–3 6–1		
G. A. Caridia E. S. Salmon	Caridia 6–3 6–4 6–2	Ritchie 6–1 6–0 4–6 6–1	
M. J. G. Ritchie E. C. Wills	Ritchie 6–1 6–2 6–2		

Challenge Round **H. L. Doherty** d F. L. Riseley 7–5 6–3 6–0

1904

A. W. Gore F. L. Riseley	Riseley 3–6 6–1 3–6 6–4 6–3	Riseley 7–5 5–7 8–6 5–7 retired	F. L. Riseley 6–0 6–1 6–2
G. A. Caridia S. H. Smith	Smith 7–5 8–6 6–3		
W. Lemaire (B) M. J. G. Ritchie	Ritchie 6–1 8–6 6–4	Ritchie 6–3 6–1 6–1	
P. de Borman (B) R. J. McNair	de Borman 6–0 6–4 6–4		

Challenge Round **H. L. Doherty** d F. L. Riseley 6–1 7–5 8–6

1905

A. W. Gore A. F. Wilding (NZ)	Gore 8–6 6–2 6–2	Brookes 6–3 9–7 6–2	N. E. Brookes (AUS) 1–6 6–4 6–1 1–6 7–5
N. E. Brookes (AUS) F. L. Riseley	Brookes 6–3 6–2 6–4		
W. A. Larned (US) S. H. Smith	Smith 6–2 6–4 6–4	Smith 6–0 3–6 6–4 4–6 6–1	
A. K. Cronin M. J. G. Ritchie	Ritchie 6–0 6–2 6–0		

Challenge Round **H. L. Doherty** d N. E. Brookes (AUS) 8–6 6–2 6–4

1906

M. J. G. Ritchie A. F. Wilding (NZ)	Wilding 6–4 6–1 4–6 3–6 6–2	Gore 9–7 6–1 8–6	F. L. Riseley 6–3 6–3 6–4
A. E. Crawley A. W. Gore	Gore 6–0 6–1 8–6		
R. D. Little (US) F. L. Riseley	Riseley 6–3 6–1 6–4	Riseley 8–6 2–6 6–2 6–4	
C. H. L. Cazalet S. H. Smith	Smith 6–2 4–6 7–5 retired		

Challenge Round **H. L. Doherty** d F. L. Riseley 6–4 4–6 6–2 6–3

1907

Players	Quarter-final	Semi-final	Final
A. W. Gore A. R. Sawyer	Gore 6–0 6–3 6–0	Gore 9–7 7–5 6–2	N. E. Brookes (AUS) 6–4 6–2 6–2
W. V. Eaves L. H. Escombe	Eaves 6–0 4–6 6–3 1–6 6–3		
S. H. Adams N. E. Brookes (AUS)	Brookes 6–1 6–3 6–3	Brookes 6–0 6–1 6–4	
O. Kreuzer (G) M. J. G. Ritchie	Ritchie 6–4 6–1 6–2		

Challenge Round **N. E. Brookes (AUS)** (w.o.)

1908

Players	Quarter-final	Semi-final	Final
W. Lemaire (B) R. B. Powell (CAN)	Powell 6–4 8–6 6–4	Gore 10–8 6–4 6–2	A. W. Gore 6–3 6–2 4–6 3–6 6–4
C. P. Dixon A. W. Gore	Gore 10–8 6–3 3–6 6–0		
W. C. Crawley M. J. G. Ritchie	Ritchie 6–1 6–3 6–2	Barrett 6–3 6–1 3–6 6–1	
H. Roper Barrett A. F. Wilding (NZ)	Barrett 2–6 6–4 6–4 6–0		

Challenge Round **A. W. Gore** (w.o.)

1909

Players	Quarter-final	Semi-final	Final
G. A. Caridia T. M. Mavrogordato	Mavrogordato 6–1 9–7 2–6 4–6 6–4	Ritchie 3–6 6–3 6–3 6–2	M. J. G. Ritchie 6–2 6–3 4–6 6–4
C. P. Dixon M. J. G. Ritchie	Ritchie 8–10 6–1 6–1 6–4		
H. Roper Barrett L. H. Escombe	Barrett 4–6 7–5 11–9 retired	Barrett 6–4 6–2 6–8 7–5	
F. G. Lowe F. W. Rahe (G)	Rahe 12–10 6–0 6–4		

Challenge Round **A. W. Gore** d M. J. G. Ritchie 6–8 1–6 6–2 6–2 6–2

1910

Players	Quarter-final	Semi-final	Final
A. E. Beamish J. C. Parke	Parke 8–6 5–7 6–4 6–3	Wilding 7–5 6–1 6–2	A. F. Wilding (NZ) 4–6 4–6 6–3 6–2 6–3
O. Froitzheim (G) A. F. Wilding (NZ)	Wilding 6–1 6–1 6–2		
S. N. Doust (AUS) A. H. Lowe	Lowe 6–3 6–3 2–6 6–4	Wright 6–3 3–6 6–4 6–4	
R. B. Powell (CAN) B. C. Wright (US)	Wright 6–3 6–1 6–1		

Challenge Round **A. F. Wilding (NZ)** d A. W. Gore 6–4 7–5 4–6 6–2

1911

Players	Quarter-final	Semi-final	Final
M. Decugis (F) R. W. Heath (AUS)	Decugis 10–8 6–4 7–5	Dixon 6–2 5–7 6–2 6–3	H. Roper Barrett 5–7 4–6 6–4 6–3 6–1
C. P. Dixon G. A. Thomas	Dixon 6–4 5–7 8–6 6–3		
H. Roper Barrett A. E. Beamish	Barrett 6–1 1–6 6–4 6–3	Barrett 6–2 6–3 6–2	
F. G. Lowe F. W. Rahe (G)	Lowe 5–7 6–3 6–2 9–7		

Challenge Round **A. F. Wilding (NZ)** d H. Roper Barrett 6–4 4–6 2–6 6–2 retired

1912

A. H. Gobert (F)	Gobert		
F. W. Rahe (G)	6–1 6–2 7–5	Gobert	
H. Roper Barrett	Decugis	6–3 6–3 1–6 4–6 6–4	
M. Decugis (F)	6–3 7–5 4–6 6–4		A. W. Gore
A. E. Beamish	Beamish		9–7 6–2 7–5 6–1
J. E. H. Zimmermann	6–4 6–3 6–1	Gore	
A. W. Gore	Gore	6–2 0–6 11–9 6–4	
R. B. Powell (CAN)	6–3 6–2 4–6 6–2		

Challenge Round **A. F. Wilding (NZ)** d A. W. Gore 6–4 6–4 4–6 6–4

1913

W. A. Ingram	McLoughlin		
M. E. McLoughlin (US)	6–1 6–2 6–4	McLoughlin	
J. C. Parke	Parke	6–4 7–5 6–4	
R. D. Watson	6–4 6–1 6–4		M. E. McLoughlin (US)
K. Powell	Kreuzer		6–3 6–4 7–5
O. Kreuzer (G)	6–4 6–1 5–7 6–0	Doust	
H. Crisp	Doust	6–3 6–2 6–3	
S. N. Doust (AUS)	7–5 6–3 3–6 11–9		

Challenge Round **A. F. Wilding (NZ)** d M. E. McLoughlin (US) 8–6 6–3 10–8

1914

O. Froitzheim (G)	Froitzheim		
J. C. Parke	5–7 6–2 9–7 6–2	Froitzheim	
A. Germot (F)	Mavrogordato	6–3 6–2 7–5	
T. M. Mavrogordato	6–3 2–6 6–4 6–1		N. E. Brookes (AUS)
A. E. Beamish	Beamish		6–2 6–1 5–7 4–6 8–6
P. M. Davson	6–4 6–2 6–1	Brookes	
N. E. Brookes (AUS)	Brookes	6–0 6–3 6–2	
A. W. Gore	7–5 6–1 6–2		

Challenge Round **N. E. Brookes (AUS)** d A. F. Wilding (NZ) 6–4 6–4 7–5

1915–18 not held

1919

C. P. Dixon	Ritchie		
M. J. G. Ritchie	4–6 6–4 6–3 6–3	Patterson	
A. H. Gobert (F)	Patterson	6–1 7–5 1–6 6–3	
G. L. Patterson (AUS)	10–8 6–3 6–2		G. L. Patterson (AUS)
A. R. F. Kingscote	Kingscote		6–2 6–1 6–3
P. O'Hara Wood (AUS)	6–4 3–6 6–3 1–6 6–4	Kingscote	
C. S. Garland (US)	Garland	6–1 6–4 2–6 5–7 6–4	
R. V. Thomas (AUS)	6–4 6–0 6–1		

Challenge Round **G. L. Patterson (AUS)** d N. E. Brookes (AUS) 6–3 7–5 6–2

1920

T. M. Mavrogordato	Mavrogordato		
R. N. Williams (US)	6–3 4–6 9–7 7–5	Shimidzu	
Z. Shimidzu (J)	Shimidzu	3–6 6–4 6–0 6–2	
N. Willford	6–0 6–1 6–2		W. T. Tilden (US)
R. Lycett	Tilden		6–4 6–4 13–11
W. T. Tilden (US)	7–5 4–6 6–4 7–5	Tilden	
C. R. Blackbeard (SA)	Garland	6–4 8–6 6–2	
C. S. Garland (US)	4–6 6–1 6–3 6–1		

Challenge Round **W. T. Tilden (US)** d G. L. Patterson (AUS) 2–6 6–3 6–2 6–4

1921

R. Lycett Z. Shimidzu (J)	Shimidzu 6–3 9–11 3–6 6–2 10–8	Alonso 3–6 7–5 3–6 6–4 8–6	B. I. C. Norton (SA) 5–7 4–6 7–5 6–3 6–3
M. Alonso (SP) A. R. F. Kingscote	Alonso 6–1 6–3 2–6 6–2		
Hon C. Campbell F. T. Hunter (US)	Hunter 6–2 7–5 3–6 6–4	Norton 6–0 6–3 5–7 5–7 6–2	
H. G. Mayes (CAN) B. I. C. Norton (SA)	Norton 4–6 6–2 6–2 6–2		

Challenge Round **W. T. Tilden (US)** d B. I. C. Norton (SA) 4–6 2–6 6–1 6–0 7–5

(Challenge Round abolished)

1922

P. M. Davson R. Lycett	Lycett 2–6 6–1 6–4 8–6	Lycett 8–6 9–7 6–3	G. L. Patterson (AUS) 6–3 6–4 6–2
J. B. Gilbert T. M. Mavrogordato	Gilbert 6–4 3–6 6–3 3–6 6–2		
J. O. Anderson (AUS) P. O'Hara Wood (AUS)	Anderson 6–3 6–3 2–6 2–6 6–4	Patterson 6–1 3–6 7–9 6–1 6–3	
Hon C. Campbell G. L. Patterson (AUS)	Patterson 7–9 6–3 6–2 6–1		

1923

Hon C. Campbell W. M. Johnston (US)	Johnston 6–1 5–7 6–2 6–2	Johnston 6–4 6–2 6–4	W. M. Johnston (US) 6–0 6–3 6–1
B. I. C. Norton (SA) M. Woosnam	Norton 7–5 6–3 6–4		
D. M. Evans F. G. Lowe	Lowe 6–2 8–6 7–5	Hunter 6–3 7–5 6–4	
Conte de Gomar (SP) F. T. Hunter (US)	Hunter 3–6 4–6 6–1 6–3 6–2		

1924

J. R. Lacoste (F) J. Washer (B)	Lacoste 6–1 5–7 6–4 6–2	Lacoste 6–1 3–6 6–2 6–3	J. Borotra (F) 6–1 3–6 6–1 3–6 6–4
A. R. F. Kingscote R. N. Williams (US)	Williams 5–7 6–4 6–3 6–4		
J. Borotra (F) V. Richards (US)	Borotra 6–4 4–6 6–0 6–3	Borotra 6–2 6–4 7–5	
L. Raymond (SA) W. M. Washburn (US)	Raymond 6–0 7–5 17–15		

1925

H. Cochet (F) J. Hennessey (US)	Cochet 7–9 4–6 6–1 6–3 6–0	Borotra 5–7 8–6 6–4 6–1	J. R. Lacoste (F) 6–3 6–3 4–6 8–6
H. S. L. Barclay J. Borotra (F)	Borotra 6–3 5–7 6–3 6–3		
J. O. Anderson (AUS) H. C. Fisher	Anderson 6–1 6–1 6–4	Lacoste 6–4 7–5 6–1	
J. R. Lacoste (F) S. M. Jacob (IN)	Lacoste 6–3 6–8 6–0 6–4		

1926

J. Brugnon (F) C. H. Kingsley	Brugnon 6–2 4–6 6–2 4–6 6–4	Kinsey 6–4 4–6 6–3 3–6 9–7	J. Borotra (F) 8–6 6–1 6–3
Howard Kinsey (US) P. D. B. Spence (SA)	Kinsey 6–3 6–3 3–6 6–3		
H. Cochet (F) J. C. Gregory	Cochet 3–6 6–4 6–2 4–6 6–3	Borotra 2–6 7–5 2–6 6–3 7–5	
J. Borotra (F) J. Kozeluh (CZ)	Borotra 6–4 4–6 9–7 6–1		

1927

Players	Quarter-final	Semi-final	Final
J. Brugnon (F) W. T. Tilden (US)	Tilden 6–3 6–1 3–6 7–5	Cochet 2–6 4–6 7–5 6–4 6–3	H. Cochet (F) 4–6 4–6 6–3 6–4 7–5
H. Cochet (F) F. T. Hunter (US)	Cochet 3–6 3–6 6–2 6–2 6–3		
J. Kozeluh (CZ) J. R. Lacoste (F)	Lacoste 6–4 6–3 6–4	Borotra 6–4 6–3 1–6 1–6 6–2	
J. Borotra (F) H. Timmer (NTH)	Borotra 6–1 3–6 6–3 6–0		

1928

Players	Quarter-final	Semi-final	Final
H. Cochet (F) J. Hennessey (US)	Cochet 6–4 6–1 5–7 6–3	Cochet 11–9 3–6 6–2 6–3	J. R. Lacoste (F) 6–1 4–6 6–4 6–2
C. Boussus (F) J. Brugnon (F)	Boussus 12–10 10–8 6–2		
J. R. Lacoste (F) H. L. de Morpurgo (IT)	Lacoste 6–2 6–3 6–4	Lacoste 2–6 6–4 2–6 6–4 6–3	
J. Borotra (F) W. T. Tilden (US)	Tilden 8–6 3–6 6–3 6–2		

1929

Players	Quarter-final	Semi-final	Final
H. Cochet (F) H. Timmer (NTH)	Cochet 6–4 7–5 6–2	Cochet 6–4 6–1 7–5	H. Cochet (F) 6–4 6–3 6–4
P. Landry (F) W. T. Tilden (US)	Tilden 6–4 2–6 6–3 7–5		
J. Borotra (F) G. M. Lott (US)	Borotra 6–3 6–3 6–4	Borotra 6–1 10–8 5–7 6–1	
H. W. Austin B. von Kehrling (HU)	Austin 6–2 8–6 6–3		

1930

Players	Quarter-final	Semi-final	Final
W. L. Allison (US) H. Cochet (F)	Allison 6–4 6–4 6–3	Allison 6–3 4–6 8–6 3–6 7–5	W. T. Tilden (US) 6–3 9–7 6–4
J. H. Doeg (US) G. S. Mangin (US)	Doeg 6–3 1–6 6–3 6–4		
J. C. Gregory W. T. Tilden (US)	Tilden 6–1 6–2 6–3	Tilden 0–6 6–4 4–6 6–0 7–5	
J. Borotra (F) G. M. Lott (US)	Borotra 2–6 6–3 6–3 6–4		

1931

Players	Quarter-final	Semi-final	Final
G. P. Hughes S. B. Wood (US)	Wood 4–6 6–4 6–3 6–1	Wood 4–6 6–2 6–4 6–2	S. B. Wood (US) w.o.
F. J. Perry J. W. Van Ryn (US)	Perry 6–4 8–6 7–5		
J. Borotra (F) J. Satoh (J)	Borotra 6–2 6–3 4–6 6–4	Shields 7–5 3–6 6–4 6–4	
H. W. Austin F. X. Shields (US)	Shields 6–3 2–6 5–7 7–5 6–1		

1932

Players	Quarter-final	Semi-final	Final
E. Maier (SP) H. E. Vines (US)	Vines 6–2 6–3 6–2	Vines 6–2 6–1 6–3	H. E. Vines (US) 6–4 6–2 6–0
J. H. Crawford (AUS) F. J. Perry	Crawford 7–5 8–6 2–6 8–6		
H. W. Austin F. X. Shields (US)	Austin 6–1 9–7 5–7 6–1	Austin 7–5 6–2 6–1	
J. Satoh (J) S. B. Wood (US)	Satoh 7–5 7–5 2–6 6–4		

1933

R. Menzel (CZ)	Vines 6–2 6–4 3–6 6–3	Vines 6–2 8–6 3–6 6–1	J. H. Crawford (AUS) 4–6 11–9 6–2 2–6 6–4
H. E. Vines (US)			
H. Cochet (F)	Cochet 3–6 6–4 6–3 6–1		
L. R. Stoefen (US)			
H. W. Austin	Satoh 7–5 6–3 2–6 2–6 6–2	Crawford 6–3 6–4 2–6 6–4	
J. Satoh (J)			
J. H. Crawford (AUS)	Crawford 6–3 6–4 2–6 6–4		
G. P. Hughes			

1934

J. H. Crawford (AUS)	Crawford 7–5 2–6 7–5 6–0	Crawford 2–6 4–6 6–4 6–3 6–4	F. J. Perry 6–3 6–0 7–5
L. R. Stoefen (US)			
H. W. Austin	Shields 4–6 2–6 7–5 6–3 7–5		
F. X. Shields (US)			
G. M. Lott	Perry 6–4 2–6 7–5 10–8	Perry 6–3 3–6 7–5 5–7 6–3	
F. J. Perry			
V. G. Kirby (SA)	Wood 6–1 6–4 3–6 6–0		
S. B. Wood (US)			

1935

R. Menzel (CZ)	Perry 9–7 6–1 6–1	Perry 6–2 3–6 6–4 6–4	F. J. Perry 6–2 6–4 6–4
F. J. Perry			
J. H. Crawford (AUS)	Crawford 6–4 6–3 6–8 5–7 6–1		
S. B. Wood (US)			
H. W. Austin	Budge 3–6 10–8 6–4 7–5	von Cramm 4–6 6–4 6–3 6–2	
J. D. Budge (US)			
V. B. McGrath (AUS)	von Cramm 6–4 6–2 4–6 6–1		
G. von Cramm (G)			

1936

B. M. Grant (US)	Perry 6–4 6–3 6–1	Perry 5–7 6–4 6–3 6–4	F. J. Perry 6–1 6–1 6–0
F. J. Perry			
J. D. Budge (US)	Budge 6–2 6–4 6–4		
A. K. Quist (AUS)			
W. L. Allison (US)	Austin 6–1 6–4 7–5	von Cramm 8–6 6–3 2–6 6–3	
H. W. Austin			
J. H. Crawford (AUS)	von Cramm 6–1 7–5 6–4		
G. von Cramm (G)			

1937

J. H. Crawford (AUS)	von Cramm 6–3 8–6 3–6 2–6 6–2	von Cramm 8–6 6–3 12–14 6–1	J. D. Budge (US) 6–3 6–4 6–2
G. von Cramm (G)			
H. W. Austin	Austin 6–1 7–5 6–4		
B. M. Grant (US)			
H. Henkel (G)	Parker 6–3 7–5 4–6 4–6 6–2	Budge 2–6 6–4 6–4 6–1	
F. A. Parker (US)			
J. D. Budge (US)	Budge 6–3 6–1 6–4		
V. B. McGrath (AUS)			

1938

H. W. Austin	Austin 6–2 6–1 6–2	Austin 6–2 6–4 6–0	J. D. Budge (US) 6–1 6–0 6–3
M. Ellmer (SWI)			
L. Hecht (CZ)	Henkel 7–5 6–1 6–2		
H. Henkel (G)			
D. MacPhail	Puncec 6–2 6–1 6–1	Budge 6–2 6–1 6–4	
F. Puncec (YU)			
J. D. Budge (US)	Budge 6–3 6–0 7–5		
F. Cejnar (CZ)			

1939

H. W. Austin E. T. Cooke (US)	Cooke 6–3 6–0 6–1	Cooke 6–3 4–6 6–4 6–4	R. L. Riggs (US) 2–6 8–6 3–6 6–3 6–2
H. Henkel (G) F. Kukuljevic (YU)	Henkel 6–1 6–3 6–2		
F. Puncec (YU) E. Smith (US)	Puncec 6–0 6–2 6–2	Riggs 6–2 6–3 6–4	
Ghaus Mohammed (IN) R. L. Riggs (US)	Riggs 6–2 6–2 6–2		

1940–5 not held

1946

D. Pails (AUS) Y. Petra (F)	Petra 7–5 7–5 6–8 6–4	Petra 4–6 4–6 6–3 7–5 8–6	Y. Petra (F) 6–2 6–4 7–9 5–7 6–4
T. P. Brown (US) F. Puncec (YU)	Brown 6–2 8–6 6–4		
L. Bergelin (SWE) G. E. Brown (AUS)	Brown 13–11 11–9 6–4	Brown 6–4 7–5 6–2	
J. Drobny (CZ) P. Pellizza (F)	Drobny 6–4 6–4 6–4		

1947

J. Drobny (CZ) J. E. Patty (US)	Patty 3–6 6–4 7–9 6–2 6–3	Brown 6–3 6–3 6–3	J. A. Kramer (US) 6–1 6–3 6–2
T. P. Brown (US) Y. Petra (F)	Brown 7–5 6–2 6–4		
R. Falkenburg (US) D. Pails (AUS)	Pails 4–6 4–6 6–3 6–0 6–2	Kramer 6–1 3–6 6–1 6–0	
G. E. Brown (AUS) J. A. Kramer (US)	Kramer 6–0 6–1 6–3		

1948

J. E. Bromwich (AUS) J. E. Patty (US)	Bromwich 6–4 7–5 6–1	Bromwich 6–3 14–12 6–2	R. Falkenburg (US) 7–5 0–6 6–2 3–6 7–5
J. Asboth (HU) T. P. Brown (US)	Asboth 4–6 6–3 4–6 6–1 6–1		
A. J. Mottram G. Mulloy (US)	Mulloy 6–2 1–6 7–5 6–1	Falkenburg 6–4 6–4 8–6	
L. Bergelin (SWE) R. Falkenburg (US)	Falkenburg 6–4 6–2 3–6 6–4		

1949

G. E. Brown (AUS) J. Drobny (CZ)	Drobny 2–6 7–5 1–6 6–2 6–4	Drobny 6–1 6–3 6–2	F. R. Schroeder (US) 3–6 6–0 6–3 4–6 6–4
J. E. Bromwich (AUS) R. Falkenburg (US)	Bromwich 3–6 9–11 6–0 6–0 6–4		
F. A. Parker (US) E. W. Sturgess (SA)	Sturgess 3–6 6–4 3–6 6–1 6–3	Schroeder 3–6 7–5 5–7 6–1 6–2	
F. R. Schroeder (US) F. A. Sedgman (AUS)	Schroeder 3–6 6–8 6–3 6–2 9–7		

1950

A. Larsen (US) F. A. Sedgman (AUS)	Sedgman 8–10 5–7 7–5 6–3 7–5	Sedgman 3–6 3–6 6–3 7–5 6–2	J. E. Patty (US) 6–1 8–10 6–2 6–3
J. Drobny (EG)* G. Mulloy (US)	Drobny 6–3 6–4 6–4		
E. V. Seixas (US) E. W. Sturgess (SA)	Seixas 9–7 6–8 3–6 6–2 7–5	Patty 6–3 5–7 6–2 7–5	
J. E. Patty (US) W. F. Talbert (US)	Patty 3–6 6–4 6–2 6–3		

* Drobny, hitherto with Czech affiliation, this year adopted Egyptian nationality. From 1960 his affiliation became British.

1951

Players			
H. Flam (US)	Flam	Savitt	R. Savitt (US)
F. A. Sedgman (AUS)	2-6 1-6 6-3 6-4 7-5	1-6 15-13 6-3 6-2	6-4 6-4 6-4
A. Larsen (US)	Savitt		
R. Savitt (US)	6-1 6-4 6-4		
E. W. Sturgess (SA)	Sturgess	McGregor	
A. Vieira (BRA)	6-2 6-0 6-3	6-4 3-6 6-3 7-5	
L. Bergelin (SWE)	McGregor		
K. McGregor (AUS)	6-0 4-6 5-7 6-2 6-4		

1952

Players			
F. A. Sedgman (AUS)	Sedgman	Sedgman	F. A. Sedgman (AUS)
E. W. Sturgess (SA)	7-5 6-1 6-0	6-4 6-4 7-5	4-6 6-2 6-3 6-2
M. G. Rose (AUS)	Rose		
R. Savitt (US)	6-4 3-6 6-4 4-6 6-2		
H. Flam (US)	Flam	Drobny	
E. V. Seixas (US)	6-4 3-6 6-3 7-5	6-2 6-4 0-6 8-10 6-4	
J. Drobny (EG)	Drobny		
K. McGregor (AUS)	6-0 3-6 2-6 7-5 7-5		

1953

Players			
L. A. Hoad (AUS)	Seixas	Seixas	E. V. Seixas (US)
E. V. Seixas (US)	5-7 6-4 6-3 1-6 9-7	6-4 10-12 9-11 6-4 6-3	9-7 6-3 6-4
A. Larsen (US)	Rose		
M. G. Rose (AUS)	6-3 6-3 16-14		
S. Davidson (SWE)	Drobny	Nielsen	
J. Drobny (EG)	7-5 6-4 6-0	6-4 6-3 6-2	
K. Nielsen (DEN)	Nielsen		
K. R. Rosewall (AUS)	7-5 4-6 6-8 6-0 6-2		

1954

Players			
J. Drobny (EG)	Drobny	Drobny	J. Drobny (EG)
L. A. Hoad (AUS)	6-4 6-3 6-3	6-2 6-4 4-6 9-7	13-11 4-6 6-2 9-7
J. E. Patty (US)	Patty		
E. V. Seixas (US)	7-5 4-6 6-3 6-2		
R. N. Hartwig (AUS)	Rosewall	Rosewall	
K. R. Rosewall (AUS)	6-3 3-6 3-6 6-3 6-1	3-6 6-3 4-6 6-1 6-1	
M. G. Rose (AUS)	Trabert		
M. A. Trabert (US)	6-2 6-2 7-5		

1955

Players			
S. Davidson (SWE)	Rosewall	Nielsen	M. A. Trabert (US)
K. R. Rosewall (AUS)	6-4 6-1 6-2	11-9 6-2 2-6 6-4	6-3 7-5 6-1
K. Nielsen (DEN)	Nielsen		
N. Pietrangeli (IT)	1-6 6-3 5-7 6-2 7-5		
L. A. Hoad (AUS)	Patty	Trabert	
J. E. Patty (US)	6-4 6-4 6-4	8-6 6-2 6-2	
J. Drobny (EG)	Trabert		
M. A. Trabert (US)	8-6 6-1 6-4		

1956

Players			
M. J. Anderson (AUS)	Hoad	Hoad	L. A. Hoad (AUS)
L. A. Hoad (AUS)	4-6 6-1 6-1 13-11	3-6 6-4 6-2 6-4	6-2 4-6 7-5 6-4
N. A. Fraser (AUS)	Richardson		
H. Richardson (US)	6-3 9-11 7-5 6-4		
J. A. Morris (US)	Seixas	Rosewall	
E. V. Seixas (US)	13-11 6-0 6-3	6-3 3-6 6-8 6-3 7-5	
K. R. Rosewall (AUS)	Rosewall		
U. Schmidt (SWE)	6-1 6-3 6-2		

1957

Players	Quarter-final	Semi-final	Final
A. J. Cooper (AUS) H. Flam (US)	Cooper 6–3 7–5 6–1	Cooper 1–6 14–12 6–3 8–6	L. A. Hoad (AUS) 6–2 6–1 6–2
N. A. Fraser (AUS) U. Schmidt (SWE)	Fraser 1–6 6–4 6–8 6–4 6–4		
S. Davidson (SWE) E. V. Seixas (US)	Davidson 5–7 6–4 6–4 6–4	Hoad 6–4 6–4 7–5	
L. A. Hoad (AUS) M. G. Rose (AUS)	Hoad 6–4 4–6 10–8 6–3		

1958

Players	Quarter-final	Semi-final	Final
M. J. Anderson (AUS) K. Nielsen (DEN)	Nielsen 6–2 6–3 retired	Fraser 6–4 6–4 17–19 6–4	A. J. Cooper (AUS) 3–6 6–3 6–4 13–11
S. Davidson (SWE) N. A. Fraser (AUS)	Fraser 6–4 6–8 6–2 3–6 8–6		
B. MacKay (US) M. G. Rose (AUS)	Rose 6–2 6–4 6–4	Cooper 7–9 6–2 6–2 6–3	
A. J. Cooper (AUS) R. K. Wilson	Cooper 6–4 6–2 3–6 4–6 7–5		

1959

Players	Quarter-final	Semi-final	Final
N. A. Fraser (AUS) B. MacKay (US)	MacKay 5–7 10–8 0–6 6–3 6–1	Laver 11–13 11–9 10–8 7–9 6–3	A. Olmedo (US) 6–4 6–3 6–4
R. G. Laver (AUS) J. C. Molinari (F)	Laver 6–3 6–3 6–0		
R. S. Emerson (AUS) R. K. Wilson	Emerson 6–3 6–4 6–2	Olmedo 6–4 6–0 6–4	
L. Ayala (Chile) A. Olmedo (US)	Olmedo 7–5 3–6 6–3 6–3		

1960

Players	Quarter-final	Semi-final	Final
B. MacKay (US) N. Pietrangeli (IT)	Pietrangeli 16–14 6–2 3–6 6–4	Laver 4–6 6–3 8–10 6–2 6–4	N. A. Fraser (AUS) 6–4 3–6 9–7 7–5
R. S. Emerson (AUS) R. G. Laver (AUS)	Laver 6–4 5–7 6–4 6–4		
L. Ayala (Chile) R. Krishnan (IN)	Krishnan 7–5 10–8 6–2	Fraser 6–3 6–2 6–2	
E. Buchholz (US) N. A. Fraser (AUS)	Fraser 4–6 6–3 4–6 15–15 retired		

1961

Players	Quarter-final	Semi-final	Final
L. Ayala (Chile) R. G. Laver (AUS)	Laver 6–1 6–3 6–2	Laver 6–2 8–6 6–2	R. G. Laver (AUS) 6–3 6–1 6–4
R. S. Emerson (AUS) R. Krishnan (IN)	Krishnan 6–1 6–4 6–4		
I. Pimentel (VEN) M. J. Sangster	Sangster 6–2 6–2 6–4	McKinley 6–4 6–4 8–6	
C. R. McKinley (US) R. K. Wilson	McKinley 6–4 6–4 4–6 6–4		

1962

Players	Quarter-final	Semi-final	Final
R. G. Laver (AUS) M. Santana (SP)	Laver 14–16 9–7 6–2 6–2	Laver 10–8 6–1 7–5	R. G. Laver (AUS) 6–2 6–2 6–1
N. A. Fraser (AUS) R. H. Osuna (MEX)	N. A. Fraser 6–3 6–1 4–6 4–6 6–2		
K. N. Fletcher (AUS) J. G. Fraser (AUS)	J. G. Fraser 1–6 7–9 6–4 6–1 6–2	Mulligan 6–3 6–2 6–2	
R. A. J. Hewitt (AUS) M. F. Mulligan (AUS)	Mulligan 6–8 6–4 6–3 6–4		

1963

Players			
W. P. Bungert (G) R. S. Emerson (AUS)	Bungert 8–6 3–6 6–3 4–6 6–3	McKinley 6–2 6–4 8–6	C. R. McKinley (US) 9–7 6–1 6–4
C. R. McKinley (US) R. K. Wilson	McKinley 8–6 6–4 6–2		
F. A. Froehling (US) F. S. Stolle (AUS)	Stolle 9–7 7–5 6–4	Stolle 8–6 6–1 7–5	
C. Kuhnke (G) M. Santana (SP)	Santana 6–3 6–4 6–4		

1964

Players			
R. S. Emerson (AUS) R. A. J. Hewitt (AUS)	Emerson 6–1 6–4 6–4	Emerson 6–3 15–13 6–0	R. S. Emerson (AUS) 6–4 12–10 4–6 6–3
W. P. Bungert (G) R. H. Osuna (MEX)	Bungert 6–4 6–2 6–3		
C. Kuhnke (G) F. S. Stolle (AUS)	Stolle 6–3 7–5 6–3	Stolle 4–6 10–8 9–7 6–4	
C. R. McKinley (US) A. Segal (SA)	McKinley 6–3 6–3 4–6 6–4		

1965

Players			
K. E. Diepraam (SA) R. S. Emerson (AUS)	Emerson 4–6 6–3 6–1 6–1	Emerson 6–1 6–2 7–9 6–1	R. S. Emerson (AUS) 6–2 6–4 6–4
R. D. Ralston (US) M. C. Riessen (US)	Ralston 3–6 2–6 6–4 6–2 6–2		
E. C. Drysdale (SA) A. E. Fox (US)	Drysdale 4–6 6–2 7–5 7–5	Stolle 6–3 6–4 7–5	
R. H. Osuna (MEX) F. S. Stolle (AUS)	Stolle 11–13 6–3 6–1 6–2		

1966

Players			
O. K. Davidson (AUS) R. S. Emerson (AUS)	Davidson 1–6 6–3 6–4 6–4	Santana 6–2 4–6 9–7 3–6 7–5	M. Santana (SP) 6–4 11–9 6–4
K. N. Fletcher (AUS) M. Santana (SP)	Santana 6–2 3–6 8–6 4–6 7–5		
R. A. J. Hewitt (AUS) R. D. Ralston (US)	Ralston 7–5 6–2 11–9	Ralston 6–8 8–6 3–6 7–5 6–3	
E. C. Drysdale (SA) A. D. Roche (AUS)	Drysdale 9–7 6–2 6–2		

1967

Players			
W. P. Bungert (G) T. Koch (BRA)	Bungert 6–4 4–6 4–6 6–1 6–3	Bungert 6–4 6–8 2–6 6–4 6–4	J. D. Newcombe (AUS) 6–3 6–1 6–1
R. O. Ruffels (AUS) R. Taylor	Taylor 6–4 8–6 6–4		
K. N. Fletcher (AUS) J. D. Newcombe (AUS)	Newcombe 6–4 6–2 6–4	Newcombe 9–7 4–6 6–3 6–4	
J. R. Cooper (AUS) N. Pilic (YU)	Pilic 14–12 8–10 6–4 6–2		

1968

Players			
R. G. Laver (AUS) R. D. Ralston (US)	Laver 4–6 6–3 6–1 4–6 6–2	Laver 7–5 6–2 6–4	R. G. Laver (AUS) 6–3 6–4 6–2
A. R. Ashe (US) T. S. Okker (NTH)	Ashe 7–9 9–7 9–7 6–2		
C. E. Graebner (US) R. J. Moore (SA)	Graebner 6–2 6–0 9–7	Roche 9–7 8–10 6–4 8–6	
E. Buchholz (US) A. D. Roche (AUS)	Roche 3–6 7–5 6–4 6–4		

1969

E. C. Drysdale (SA)	Laver		
R. G. Laver (AUS)	6-4 6-2 6-3	Laver	
A. R. Ashe (US)	Ashe	2-6 6-2 9-7 6-0	
R. C. Lutz (US)	6-4 6-2 4-6 7-5		R. G. Laver (AUS)
J. D. Newcombe (AUS)	Newcombe		6-4 5-7 6-4 6-4
T. S. Okker (NTH)	8-6 3-6 6-1 7-5	Newcombe	
C. E. Graebner (US)	Roche	3-6 6-1 14-12 6-4	
A. D. Roche (AUS)	4-6 4-6 6-3 6-4 11-9		

1970

C. E. Graebner (US)	Taylor		
R. Taylor	6-3 11-9 12-10	Rosewall	
A. D. Roche (AUS)	Rosewall	6-3 4-6 6-3 6-3	
K. R. Rosewall (AUS)	10-8 6-1 4-6 6-2		J. D. Newcombe (AUS)
R. J. Carmichael (AUS)	Gimeno		5-7 6-3 6-2 3-6 6-1
A. Gimeno (SP)	6-1 6-2 6-4	Newcombe	
R. S. Emerson (AUS)	Newcombe	6-3 8-6 6-0	
J. D. Newcombe (AUS)	6-1 5-7 3-6 6-2 11-9		

1971

T. W. Gorman (US)	Gorman		
R. G. Laver (AUS)	9-7 8-6 6-3	Smith	
O. Parun (NZ)	Smith	6-3 8-6 6-2	
S. R. Smith (US)	8-6 6-3 6-4		J. D. Newcombe (AUS)
G. C. Richey (US)	Rosewall		6-3 5-7 2-6 6-4 6-4
K. R. Rosewall (AUS)	6-8 5-7 6-4 9-7 7-5	Newcombe	
C. S. Dibley (AUS)	Newcombe	6-1 6-1 6-3	
J. D. Newcombe (AUS)	6-1 6-2 6-3		

1972

A. Metreveli (USSR)	Smith		
S. R. Smith (US)	6-2 8-6 6-2	Smith	
J. Kodes (CZ)	Kodes	3-6 6-4 6-1 7-5	
O. Parun (NZ)	6-2 6-3 6-4		S. R. Smith (US)
C. S. Dibley (AUS)	Orantes		4-6 6-3 6-3 4-6 7-5
M. Orantes (SP)	6-2 6-0 6-2	Nastase	
J. S. Connors (US)	Nastase	6-3 6-4 6-4	
I. Nastase (ROM)	6-4 6-4 6-1		

1973

J. Fassbender (G)	Mayer		
A. Mayer (US)	3-6 4-6 6-3 6-4 6-4	Metreveli	
J. S. Connors (US)	Metreveli	6-3 3-6 6-3 6-4	
A. Metreveli (USSR)	8-6 6-2 5-7 6-4		J. Kodes (CZ)
B. Borg (SWE)	Taylor		6-1 9-8* 6-3
R. Taylor	6-1 6-8 3-6 6-3 7-5	Kodes	
V. Amritraj (IN)	Kodes	8-9* 9-7 5-7 6-4 7-5	
J. Kodes (CZ)	6-4 3-6 4-6 6-3 7-5		

* Tie break

1974

J. D. Newcombe (AUS)	Rosewall		
K. R. Rosewall (AUS)	6-1 1-6 6-0 7-5	Rosewall	
I. El Shafei (EG)	Smith	6-8 4-6 9-8 6-1 6-3	
S. R. Smith (US)	9-8 7-5 6-8 7-5		J. S. Connors (US)
J. S. Connors (US)	Connors		6-1 6-1 6-4
J. Kodes (CZ)	3-6 6-3 6-3 6-8 6-3	Connors	
A. Metreveli (USSR)	Stockton	4-6 6-2 6-3 6-4	
R. L. Stockton (US)	6-4 7-5 6-1		

1975

J. S. Connors (US) R. Ramirez (MEX)	Connors 6–4 8–6 6–2	Connors 6–4 6–1 6–4	A. R. Ashe (US) 6–1 6–1 5–7 6–4
L. R. Tanner (US) G. Vilas (ARG)	Tanner 6–4 5–7 6–8 6–2 6–2		
A. R. Ashe (US) B. Borg (SWE)	Ashe 2–6 6–4 8–6 6–1	Ashe 5–7 6–4 7–5 8–9 6–4	
T. S. Okker (NTH) A. D. Roche (AUS)	Roche 2–6 9–8 2–6 6–4 6–2		

1976

V. Gerulaitis (US) R. Ramirez (MEX)	Ramirez 4–6 6–4 6–2 6–4	Nastase 6–2 9–7 6–3	B. Borg (SWE) 6–4 6–2 9–7
I. Nastase (ROM) C. M. Pasarell (US)	Nastase 6–4 6–2 6–3		
B. Borg (SWE) G. Vilas (ARG)	Borg 6–3 6–0 6–2	Borg 6–4 9–8 6–4	
J. S. Connors (US) L. R. Tanner (US)	Tanner 6–4 6–2 8–6		

WOMEN'S SINGLES

1884

First Round		Second Round	Semi-final	Final
Mrs A. Tyrwhitt Drake Miss M. Watson	Miss M. Watson 6–0 6–2	Miss M. Watson 7–5 6–0	Miss M. Watson 3–6 6–4 6–2	Miss M. Watson 6–8 6–3 6–3
Mrs C. Wallis Miss B. E. Williams	Miss Williams 6–2 6–1			
Miss B. Bingley Mrs C. J. Cole	Miss Bingley 6–3 6–3	Miss Bingley 6–0 6–8 6–3		
Miss E. Bushell Miss F. M. Winckworth	Miss Winckworth 6–0 6–1			
Miss C. Bushell Mrs G. J. Cooper	Mrs Cooper w.o.	Miss L. Watson 7–5 5–7 6–3	Miss L. Watson 6–4 6–1	
Miss L. Watson	Bye			
Miss M. Leslie Miss B. Wallis	Miss Leslie 6–2 6–1	Bye		

1885

First Round		Semi-final	Final
Miss B. Bingley Mrs Dransfield	Miss Bingley w.o.	Miss Bingley 6–1 6–2	Miss M. Watson 6–1 7–5
Miss E. Gurney Miss J. Meikle	Miss Gurney 7–5 6–4		
Miss Bryan Miss E. F. Hudson	Miss Hudson 6–3 6–0	Miss Watson 6–0 6–1	
Miss B. Langrishe Miss M. Watson	Miss Watson 6–0 6–2		

Challenge Round instituted

1886

First Round		Semi-final	Final
Miss J. Mackenzie Miss M. Shackle	Miss Shackle 6–3 6–4	Miss Tabor 6–4 7–5	Miss B. Bingley 6–2 6–0
Miss F. M. Pearson Miss A. Tabor	Miss Tabor 6–1 6–2		
Miss B. Bingley Miss J. Shackle	Miss Bingley 6–2 6–1	Miss Bingley 6–3 8–6	
Miss A. M. Chambers Miss L. Watson	Miss Watson 6–3 6–3		

Challenge Round **Miss B. Bingley** d Miss M. Watson 6–3 6–3

1887

First Round		Semi-final	Final
Miss C. Dod	Bye	Miss Dod 6–1 6–1	Miss C. Dod 6–2 6–3
Miss B. James Miss M. Shackle	Miss James 8–6 6–2		
Mrs C. J. Cole Miss J. Shackle	Bye Bye	Mrs Cole 6–4 6–1	

Challenge Round **Miss C. Dod** d Miss B. Bingley 6–2 6–0

1888

First Round		Semi-final	Final
Miss Howes	Bye	Miss Howes 6–4 6–2	Mrs G. W. Hillyard 6–1 6–2
Miss D. Patterson Miss Williams	Miss Patterson 6–0 6–3		
Miss Canning Mrs G. W. Hillyard	Mrs Hillyard 6–2 6–2	Mrs Hillyard w.o.	
Miss Phillimore	Bye		

Challenge Round **Miss C. Dod** d Mrs G. W. Hillyard 6–3 6–3

1889

Players	First Round	Second Round	Final
Miss H. B. G. Rice	Bye	Miss H. B. G. Rice 6–2 6–0	Mrs G. W. Hillyard 4–6 8–6 6–4
Miss M. Jacks Miss M. Steedman	Miss Jacks 6–4 6–2		
Mrs G. W. Hillyard Miss A. E. Rice	Mrs Hillyard 6–3 6–0	Mrs. Hillyard 8–6 6–1	
Miss B. Steedman	Bye		

Challenge Round **Mrs G. W. Hillyard** (w.o.)

1890

Players	First Round	Final
Mrs C. J. Cole Miss M. Jacks	Miss Jacks 6–4 7–5	Miss H. B. G. Rice 6–4 6–1
Miss H. B. G. Rice Miss M. Steedman	Miss Rice 7–5 6–2	

Challenge Round **Miss H. B. G. Rice** (w.o.)

1891

Players	First Round	Second Round	Final
Miss C. Dod Mrs Parsons	Miss Dod 6–0 6–0	Miss Dod 6–3 6–1	Miss C. Dod 6–2 6–1
Miss H. Jackson Miss M. Steedman	Miss Steedman 6–2 6–2		
Miss M. Jacks Miss M. Langrishe	Miss Langrishe 11–9 6–3	Mrs Hillyard 6–4 6–1	
Mrs G. W. Hillyard Miss P. Legh	Mrs Hillyard 6–3 6–2		

Challenge Round **Miss C. Dod** (w.o.)

1892

Players	First Round	Second Round	Final
Miss Barefoot Miss M. Steedman	Miss Steedman 6–0 6–1	Miss Shackle 6–4 6–3	Mrs G. W. Hillyard 6–1 6–4
Miss H. Jackson Miss M. Shackle	Miss Shackle 6–3 6–4		
Mrs Draffen Mrs G. W. Hillyard	Mrs Hillyard 6–2 6–2	Mrs Hillyard 1–6 6–3 9–7	
Miss L. Martin	Bye		

Challenge Round **Miss C. Dod** d Mrs G. W. Hillyard 6–1 6–1

1893

Players	First Round	Second Round	Final
Miss L. Austin Miss S. Robins	Miss Austin 6–2 6–1	Miss Shackle 6–0 6–2	Mrs G. W. Hillyard 6–3 6–2
Miss P. Legh Miss M. Shackle	Miss Shackle 10–8 6–1		
Miss C. Cooper Mrs Horncastle	Miss Cooper 6–4 6–1	Mrs Hillyard 6–3 6–1	
Mrs G. W. Hillyard	Bye		

Challenge Round **Miss C. Dod** d Mrs G. W. Hillyard 6–8 6–1 6–4

1894

Players	First Round	Second Round	Final
Miss Chatterton Clarke Mrs G. W. Hillyard	Mrs Hillyard 6–1 6–0	Mrs Hillyard 6–1 6–1	Mrs G. W. Hillyard 6–1 6–1
Miss Bryan Mrs Draffen	Miss Bryan 6–3 7–5		
Miss L. Austin Miss C. Cooper	Miss Austin 6–1 3–6 6–3	Miss Austin 6–1 6–1	
Mrs Edwardes Miss S. Robins	Miss Robins 6–2 6–1		

Challenge Round **Mrs G. W. Hillyard** (w.o.)

1895

Players	First round	Second round	Final
Mrs W. H. Pickering Miss M. Shackle	Mrs Pickering 3–6 6–3 6–3	Miss Jackson 6–4 3–6 8–6	Miss C. Cooper 7–5 8–6
Miss Bernard Miss H. Jackson	Miss Jackson 6–0 6–2		
Miss C. Cooper Miss L. Patterson	Miss Cooper 6–3 9–11 6–2	Miss Cooper 6–2 6–8 6–1	
Mrs Draffen Mrs Horncastle	Mrs Draffen 6–2 6–0		

Challenge Round **Miss C. Cooper** (w.o.)

1896

Players	First round	Second round	Final
Miss L. Austin Miss L. Patterson	Miss Austin 6–4 6–1	Miss Austin w.o.	Mrs W. H. Pickering 4–6 6–3 6–3
Mrs Horncastle	Bye		
Miss 'Hungerford' Mrs W. H. Pickering	Mrs Pickering 6–1 6–0	Mrs Pickering 6–3 7–5	
Mrs Draffen	Bye		

Challenge Round **Miss C. Cooper** d Mrs W. H. Pickering 6–2 6–3

1897

Players	First round	Second round	Final
Mrs Horncastle Miss E. M. Thynne	Mrs Horncastle 12–10 6–4	Mrs Hillyard w.o.	Mrs G. W. Hillyard 6–2 7–5
Miss L. Austin Mrs G. W. Hillyard	Mrs Hillyard 6–0 6–1		
Miss E. J. Bromfield Miss R. Dyas	Miss Dyas 6–0 6–3	Mrs Pickering 6–4 4–6 6–1	
Mrs W. H. Pickering	Bye		

Challenge Round **Mrs G. W. Hillyard** d Miss C. Cooper 5–7 7–5 6–2

1898

Players	First round	Second round	Final
Miss P. Legh Miss C. Morgan	Miss Legh 6–0 6–1	Miss Martin w.o.	Miss C. Cooper 6–4 6–4
Miss L. Martin Miss E. R. Morgan	Miss Martin 6–2 6–0		
Miss L. Austin Miss R. Dyas	Miss Austin 4–6 6–3 6–4	Miss Cooper 6–4 6–1	
Miss C. Cooper Miss B. Steedman	Miss Cooper 4–6 6–3 6–4		

Challenge Round **Miss C. Cooper** (w.o.)

1899

Players	First round	Second round	Final
Mrs N. Durlacher Miss M. E. Robb	Mrs Durlacher 6–1 5–7 6–3	Mrs Durlacher 6–4 6–2	Mrs G. W. Hillyard 7–5 6–8 6–1
Mrs Kirby Miss B. Steedman	Miss Steedman 4–6 6–2 6–2		
Miss L. Austin Mrs G. W. Hillyard	Mrs Hillyard 8–6 6–4	Mrs Hillyard 6–3 3–6 6–2	
Miss E. J. Bromfield Miss B. Tulloch	Miss Tulloch 3–6 6–2 6–1		

Challenge Round **Mrs G. W. Hillyard** d Miss C. Cooper 6–2 6–3

1900

Players	First round	Second round	Final
Miss C. Cooper Miss M. E. Robb	Miss Cooper 6–3 9–7	Miss Cooper 6–1 6–2	Miss C. Cooper 8–6 5–7 6–1
Mrs G. Greville Miss B. Tulloch	Mrs Greville 7–5 6–0		
Mrs G. E. Evered Miss M. Jones (US)	Mrs Evered 7–5 6–2	Miss Martin 6–0 6–2	
Miss D. K. Douglass Miss L. Martin	Miss Martin 6–4 6–3		

Challenge Round **Mrs G. W. Hillyard** d Miss C. Cooper 4–6 6–4 6–4

1901

Mrs G. Greville	Miss Martin		
Miss L. Martin	4-6 6-3 6-4	Miss Martin	
Miss A. M. Morton	Miss Morton	7-5 6-2	
Mrs W. H. Pickering	6-3 7-5		Mrs A. Sterry
Miss M. E. Robb	Mrs Sterry		6-3 6-4
Mrs A. Sterry	6-0 6-0	Mrs Sterry	
Miss Adams	Miss Adams	6-1 6-1	
Miss Hughes D'Eath	6-1 6-0		

Challenge Round **Mrs A. Sterry** d Mrs G. W. Hillyard 6-2 6-2

1902

Miss H. Lane	Miss Robb		
Miss M. E. Robb	6-1 7-5	Miss Robb	
Miss D. K. Douglass	Miss Douglass	6-4 2-6 9-7	
Mrs N. Durlacher	6-2 10-8		Miss M. E. Robb
Miss W. A. Longhurst	Miss Morton		6-2 6-4
Miss A. M. Morton	6-3 6-4	Miss Morton	
Mrs G. Greville	Mrs Greville	7-5 6-4	
Miss B. Steedman	6-1 3-6 6-2		

Challenge Round **Miss M. E. Robb** d Mrs A. Sterry 7-5 6-1
(Replay after abandoning at 4-6 13-11.)

1903

Miss T. Lowther	Miss Lowther		
Miss A. M. Morton	6-1 6-0	Miss Douglass	
Miss D. K. Douglass	Miss Douglass	6-4 6-2	
Mrs G. M. Houselander	6-2 6-0		Miss D. K. Douglass
Miss E. W. Thomson	Miss Thomson		4-6 6-4 6-2
Miss C. M. Wilson	6-4 8-6	Miss Thomson	
Miss E. J. Bromfield	Miss Greene	6-3 6-1	
Miss A. N. G. Greene	6-0 4-6 6-3		

Challenge Round **Miss D. K. Douglass** (w.o.)

1904

Mrs G. Greville	Mrs Sterry		
Mrs A. Sterry	8-6 9-7	Mrs Sterry	
Miss A. N. G. Greene	Miss Greene	6-2 6-1	
Mrs R. J. Winch	6-4 6-4		Mrs A. Sterry
Miss W. A. Longhurst	Miss Morton		6-3 6-3
Miss A. M. Morton	6-1 6-4	Miss Morton	
Miss E. L. Bosworth	Miss Wilson	3-6 6-4 8-6	
Miss C. M. Wilson	6-3 6-4		

Challenge Round **Miss D. K. Douglass** d Mrs A. Sterry 6-0 6-3

1905

Miss H. I. Harper	Miss Morton		
Miss A. M. Morton	6-2 6-4	Miss Sutton	
Miss M. Sutton (US)	Miss Sutton	6-4 6-0	
Miss E. W. Thomson	8-6 6-1		Miss M. Sutton (US)
Miss D. P. Boothby	Mrs Hillyard		6-3 8-6
Mrs G. W. Hillyard	6-3 6-2	Miss Wilson	
Miss B. M. Holder	Miss Wilson	7-5 9-11 6-2	
Miss C. M. Wilson	6-2 6-0		

Challenge Round **Miss M. Sutton (US)** d Miss D. K. Douglass 6-3 6-4

1906

Miss D. K. Douglass	Miss Douglass		
Miss W. A. Longhurst	6-4 6-3	Miss Douglass	
Mrs G. W. Hillyard	Miss Tulloch	6-2 6-2	
Miss B. Tulloch	6-3 6-1		Miss D. K. Douglass
Miss V. M. Pinckney	Mrs Sterry		6-2 6-2
Mrs A. Sterry	6-4 6-2		
Miss G. S. Eastlake Smith	Miss Lowther	Mrs Sterry	
Miss T. Lowther	6-3 6-3	4-6 8-6 6-4	

Challenge Round **Miss D. K. Douglass** d Miss M. Sutton (US) 6-3 9-7

1907

Miss C. Meyer	Miss Sutton		
Miss M. Sutton (US)	6-0 6-3	Miss Sutton	
Miss E. L. Bosworth	Miss Bosworth	6-2 6-2	
Miss M. E. Brown	6-1 6-2		Miss M. Sutton (US)
Miss A. N. G. Greene	Miss Wilson		6-4 6-2
Miss C. M. Wilson	6-2 9-7		
Mrs G. W. Hillyard	Mrs Hillyard	Miss Wilson	
Miss E. G. Johnson	6-2 6-3	6-3 6-2	

Challenge Round **Miss M. Sutton (US)** d Mrs R. Lambert Chambers (*née* Douglass) 6-1 6-4

1908

Miss D. P. Boothby	Miss Boothby		
Miss V. M. Pinckney	6-1 6-4	Mrs Sterry	
Mrs R. Lambert Chambers	Mrs Sterry	6-2 6-4	
Mrs A. Sterry	6-3 7-5		Mrs A. Sterry
Miss A. M. Morton	Miss Morton		6-4 6-4
Miss B. Tulloch	7-5 6-1	Miss Morton	
Mrs G. Lamplough	Mrs Lamplough	6-3 6-4	
Mrs C. O. Tuckey	6-3 6-1		

Challenge Round **Mrs A. Sterry** (w.o.)

1909

Mrs H. Edgington	Mrs Edgington		
Mrs O'Neill	7-5 6-4	Miss Morton	
Miss E. G. Johnson	Miss Morton	6-0 6-2	
Miss A. M. Morton	6-0 6-3		Miss D. P. Boothby
Miss H. M. Garfit	Miss Garfit		6-4 4-6 8-6
Mrs E. G. Parton	6-3 6-4	Miss Boothby	
Miss H. Aitchison	Miss Boothby	6-2 6-1	
Miss D. P. Boothby	6-4 3-0 retired		

Challenge Round **Miss D. P. Boothby** (w.o.)

1910

Miss S. Castenschiold (DEN)	Mrs Lamplough		
Mrs G. Lamplough	7-9 6-4 6-3	Miss Johnson	
Miss E. G. Johnson	Miss Johnson	1-6 6-0 6-3	
Mrs E. G. Parton	7-5 6-4		Mrs R. Lambert Chambers
Miss H. Aitchison	Mrs Lambert Chambers		6-4 6-2
Mrs R. Lambert Chambers	6-2 6-1	Mrs Lambert Chambers	
Mrs H. Edgington	Mrs McNair	6-1 6-0	
Mrs R. J. McNair	2-6 6-3 6-3		

Challenge Round **Mrs R. Lambert Chambers** d Miss D. P. Boothby 6-2 6-2

1911

Miss M. Coles Mrs G. Hannam	Mrs Hannam 6–4 4–6 7–5	Mrs Hannam 6–3 6–8 7–5	Miss D. P. Boothby 6–2 7–5
Miss H. Aitchison Mrs A. E. Hazel	Miss Aitchison 6–0 6–3		
Miss D. P. Boothby Mrs H. Edgington	Miss Boothby 6–2 6–4	Miss Boothby 6–3 6–4	
Miss E. D. Holman Mrs E. G. Parton	Mrs Parton 6–0 8–6		

Challenge Round **Mrs R. Lambert Chambers** d Miss D. P. Boothby 6–0 6–0

1912

Miss W. Longhurst Mrs A. Sterry	Mrs Sterry 6–1 6–3	Mrs Sterry 6–3 4–6 7–5	Mrs D. R. Larcombe 6–3 6–1
Miss E. D. Holman Miss A. M. Morton	Miss Holman 7–5 6–2		
Mrs D. R. Larcombe Mrs R. J. McNair	Mrs Larcombe 6–2 5–7 6–0	Mrs Larcombe 6–1 6–0	
Mrs G. W. Hillyard Miss E. Ryan (US)	Mrs Hillyard 3–6 8–6 6–3		

Challenge Round **Mrs D. R. Larcombe** (w.o.)

1913

Mrs R. J. McNair Mrs A. Sterry	Mrs McNair 0–6 6–4 9–7	Mrs McNair 2–6 6–2 7–5	Mrs R. Lambert Chambers 6–0 6–4
Miss E. D. Holman Mrs P. Satterthwaite	Miss Holman 6–4 6–1		
Miss M. Coles Mrs R. Lambert Chambers	Mrs Lambert Chambers 6–1 6–0	Mrs Lambert Chambers 6–2 6–3	
Miss H. Aitchison Mrs O'Neill	Miss Aitchison 6–2 6–0		

Challenge Round **Mrs R. Lambert Chambers** (w.o.)

1914

Mrs Craddock Mrs H. Edgington	Mrs Edgington 6–1 6–3	Mrs Larcombe 6–4 6–3	Mrs D. R. Larcombe 6–3 6–2
Mrs D. R. Larcombe Mrs C. O. Tuckey	Mrs Larcombe w.o.		
Miss H. Aitchison Miss B. Leader	Miss Aitchison 6–2 6–0	Miss Ryan 6–4 6–3	
Mrs Crundall Punnett Miss E. Ryan (US)	Miss Ryan 6–0 6–3		

Challenge Round **Mrs R. Lambert Chambers** d Mrs D. R. Larcombe 7–5 6–4

1915–18 not held

1919

Mrs A. E. Beamish Mrs H. Edgington	Mrs Beamish 6–8 6–3 6–2	Mrs Satterthwaite 6–4 10–8	Mlle S. Lenglen (F) 6–1 6–1
Mrs P. Satterthwaite Mrs Winch	Mrs Satterthwaite 6–3 6–4		
Mlle S. Lenglen (F) Miss K. McKane	Mlle Lenglen 6–0 6–1	Mlle Lenglen 6–4 7–5	
Mrs E. G. Parton Miss E. Ryan (US)	Miss Ryan 6–2 6–3		

Challenge Round **Mlle S. Lenglen (F)** d Mrs R. Lambert Chambers 10–8 4–6 9–7

1920

Players	Second round	Semi-final	Final
Miss V. M. Pinckney	Miss Ryan w.o.	Miss Ryan 6–4 6–3	Mrs R. Lambert Chambers 6–2 6–1
Miss E. Ryan (US)			
Mrs E. G. Parton	Mrs Parton 6–4 6–4		
Mrs P. Satterthwaite			
Mrs J. L. Leisk	Mrs Mallory 6–3 6–1	Mrs Lambert Chambers 6–0 6–3	
Mrs F. I. Mallory (US)			
Mrs R. Lambert Chambers	Mrs Lambert Chambers 3–6 6–0 6–2		
Mrs R. J. McNair			

Challenge Round **Mlle S. Lenglen (F)** d Mrs R. Lambert Chambers 6–3 6–0

1921

Players	Second round	Semi-final	Final
Mrs R. C. Clayton	Mrs Clayton 6–3 6–2	Mrs Satterthwaite 8–6 6–2	Miss E. Ryan (US) 6–1 6–0
Miss D. C. Shepherd			
Miss P. L. Howkins	Mrs Satterthwaite 6–1 6–8 6–1		
Mrs P. Satterthwaite			
Mrs R. J. McNair	Mrs Peacock 7–5 2–6 6–4	Miss Ryan 8–6 6–4	
Mrs G. Peacock (SA)			
Mrs F. I. Mallory (US)	Miss Ryan 0–6 6–4 6–4		
Miss E. Ryan (US)			

Challenge Round **Mlle S. Lenglen (F)** d Miss E. Ryan (US) 6–2 6–0

Challenge Round abolished

1922

Players	Quarter-final	Semi-final	Final
Mlle S. Lenglen (F)	Mlle Lenglen 6–1 8–6	Mlle Lenglen 6–4 6–1	Mlle S. Lenglen (F) 6–2 6–0
Miss E. Ryan (US)			
Miss P. H. Dransfield	Mrs Peacock 6–2 6–2		
Mrs G. Peacock (SA)			
Mrs A. E. Beamish	Mrs Beamish 8–6 6–1	Mrs Mallory 6–2 6–2	
Mrs Elliott			
Mrs H. Edgington	Mrs Mallory 6–2 6–4		
Mrs F. I. Mallory (US)			

1923

Players	Quarter-final	Semi-final	Final
Mrs A. E. Hazel	Mlle Lenglen 6–2 6–1	Mlle Lenglen 6–0 6–0	Mlle S. Lenglen (F) 6–2 6–2
Mlle S. Lenglen (F)			
Mrs A. E. Beamish	Mrs Beamish 4–6 7–5 6–4		
Mrs F. I. Mallory (US)			
Miss E. Goss (US)	Miss McKane 6–2 6–2	Miss McKane 1–6 6–2 6–4	
Miss K. McKane			
Miss E. F. Rose	Miss Ryan 6–0 6–0		
Miss E. Ryan (US)			

1924

Players	Quarter-final	Semi-final	Final
Mrs D. C. Shepherd-Barron	Mrs Satterthwaite 6–4 10–8	Miss Wills 6–2 6–1	Miss K. McKane 4–6 6–4 6–4
Mrs P. Satterthwaite			
Mrs J. L. Colegate	Miss Wills 6–1 6–0		
Miss H. N. Wills (US)			
Mrs J. B. Jessup (US)	Miss McKane 6–1 6–3	Miss McKane w.o.	
Miss K. McKane			
Mlle S. Lenglen (F)	Mlle Lenglen 6–2 6–8 6–4		
Miss E. Ryan (US)			

1925

Players	Quarter-final	Semi-final	Final
Miss E. Boyd (AUS)	Miss McKane 6–1 6–1	Mlle Lenglen 6–0 6–0	Mlle S. Lenglen (F) 6–2 6–0
Miss K. McKane			
Mrs A. E. Beamish	Mlle Lenglen 6–0 6–0		
Mlle S. Lenglen (F)			
Miss D. Akhurst (AUS)	Miss Fry 2–6 6–4 6–3	Miss Fry 6–2 4–6 6–3	
Miss J. Fry			
Mme M. Billout (F)	Mme Billout 6–3 6–3		
Mrs C. G. McIlquham			

1926

Sta E. de Alvarez (SP)	Sta de Alvarez 6–2 6–2	Sta de Alvarez 6–2 6–2	Mrs L. A. Godfree 6–2 4–6 6–3
Miss C. Beckingham			
Mlle K. Bouman (NTH)	Mrs Mallory 3–6 7–5 6–3		
Mrs F. I. Mallory (US)			
Mlle H. Contostavlos (F)	Mlle Vlasto 6–3 6–3	Mrs Godfree 6–4 6–0	
Mlle D. Vlasto (F)			
Mrs L. A. Godfree	Mrs Godfree 6–2 6–0		
Miss C. Tyrrell			

1927

Mrs L. A. Godfree	Miss Ryan 3–6 6–4 6–4	Sta de Alvarez 2–6 6–0 6–4	Miss H. N. Wills (US) 6–2 6–4
Miss E. Ryan (US)			
Sta E. de Alvarez (SP)	Sta de Alvarez 6–3 3–6 8–6		
Mrs P. H. Watson			
Mrs G. Peacock (SA)	Miss Wills 6–3 6–1	Miss Wills 6–3 6–1	
Miss H. N. Wills (US)			
Miss J. Fry	Miss Fry 1–6 6–3 6–4		
Miss B. Nuthall			

1928

Mrs P. H. Watson	Miss Wills 6–3 6–0	Miss Wills 6–1 6–1	Miss H. N. Wills (US) 6–2 6–3
Miss H. N. Wills (US)			
Mme H. Nicolopoulo (F)	Miss Ryan 6–1 4–6 6–2		
Miss E. Ryan (US)			
Sta E. de Alvarez (SP)	Sta de Alvarez 7–5 6–2	Sta de Alvarez 6–2 6–0	
Frl C. Aussem (G)			
Miss D. Akhurst (AUS)	Miss Akhurst 2–6 6–3 6–2		
Miss E. Bennett			

1929

Miss E. L. Heine (SA)	Miss Wills 6–2 6–4	Miss Wills 6–2 6–0	Miss H. N. Wills (US) 6–1 6–2
Miss H. N. Wills (US)			
Miss E. A. Goldsack	Miss Goldsack 6–3 6–3		
Miss R. Tapscott (SA)			
Miss H. H. Jacobs (US)	Miss Jacobs 6–1 6–0	Miss Jacobs 6–2 6–2	
Mrs C. G. McIlquham			
Mrs T. C. Bundy (US)	Miss Ridley 6–3 6–2		
Miss J. C. Ridley			

1930

Mrs F. S. Moody (US)	Mrs Moody 6–1 6–2	Mrs Moody 6–3 6–2	Mrs F. S. Moody (US) 6–2 6–2
Miss P. E. Mudford			
Mme R. Mathieu (F)	Mme Mathieu 6–2 6–1		
Miss J. C. Ridley			
Miss B. Nuthall	Miss Ryan 6–2 2–6 6–0	Miss Ryan 6–3 0–6 4–4 retired	
Miss E. Ryan (US)			
Frl C. Aussem (G)	Frl Aussem 6–2 6–1		
Miss H. H. Jacobs (US)			

1931

Frl C. Aussem (G)	Frl Aussem 2–6 6–2 6–1	Frl Aussem 6–0 2–6 6–3	Frl C. Aussem (G) 6–2 7–5
Mlle L. Payot (SWI)			
Mme R. Mathieu (F)	Mme Mathieu 1–6 6–2 7–5		
Miss M. C. Scriven			
Miss H. H. Jacobs (US)	Miss Jacobs 6–2 6–3	Frl Krahwinkel 10–8 0–6 6–4	
Miss B. Nuthall			
Frl H. Krahwinkel (G)	Frl Krahwinkel 7–5 6–3		
Miss D. E. Round			

1932

Mrs F. S. Moody (US)	Mrs Moody		
Miss D. E. Round	6–0 6–1	Mrs. Moody	
		6–2 6–0	
Miss M. Heeley	Miss Heeley		Mrs F. S. Moody (US)
Mrs F. Whittingstall	3–6 6–4 6–0		6–3 6–1
Miss H. H. Jacobs (US)	Miss Jacobs		
Frl H. Krahwinkel (G)	6–2 6–4	Miss Jacobs	
Mme R. Mathieu (F)	Mme Mathieu	7–5 6–1	
Miss B. Nuthall	6–0 6–3		

1933

Sgna L. Valerio (IT)	Miss Round		
Miss D. E. Round	6–3 6–2	Miss Round	
		4–6 6–4 6–2	
Miss H. H. Jacobs (US)	Miss Jacobs		
Mme R. Mathieu (F)	6–1 1–6 6–2		Mrs F. S. Moody (US)
			6–4 6–8 6–3
Frl H. Krahwinkel (G)	Frl Krahwinkel		
Miss M. C. Scriven	6–4 3–6 6–1	Mrs Moody	
Mrs F. S. Moody (US)	Mrs Moody	6–4 6–3	
Mlle L. Payot (SWI)	6–4 6–1		

1934

Mlle L. Payot (SWI)	Miss Round		
Miss D. E. Round	6–4 6–2	Miss Round	
		6–4 5–7 6–2	
Mme R. Mathieu (F)	Mme Mathieu		
Miss S. Palfrey (US)	6–3 6–8 6–2		Miss D. E. Round
			6–2 5–7 6–3
Frl C. Aussem (G)	Miss Jacobs		
Miss H. H. Jacobs (US)	6–0 6–2	Miss Jacobs	
Miss J. Hartigan (AUS)	Miss Hartigan	6–2 6–2	
Miss M. C. Scriven	3–6 6–3 6–1		

1935

Miss J. Hartigan (AUS)	Miss Hartigan		
Miss D. E. Round	4–6 6–4 6–3	Mrs Moody	
		6–3 6–3	
Mme R. Mathieu (F)	Mrs Moody		
Mrs F. S. Moody (US)	6–3 6–0		Mrs F. S. Moody (US)
			6–3 3–6 7–5
Miss H. H. Jacobs (US)	Miss Jacobs		
Mlle J. Jedrzejowska (POL)	6–1 9–7	Miss Jacobs	
Fru S. Sperling (DEN)	Fru Sperling	6–3 6–0	
Miss K. E. Stammers	7–5 7–5		

1936

Miss H. H. Jacobs (US)	Miss Jacobs		
Sta A. Lizana (Chile)	6–2 1–6 6–4	Miss Jacobs	
		6–4 6–2	
Mlle J. Jedrzejowska (POL)	Mlle Jedrzejowska		
Miss K. E. Stammers	6–2 6–3		Miss H. H. Jacobs (US)
			6–2 4–6 7–5
Frl M. Horn (G)	Mme Mathieu		
Mme R. Mathieu (F)	7–5 6–3	Fru Sperling	
Miss D. E. Round	Fru Sperling	6–3 6–2	
Fru S. Sperling (DEN)	6–3 8–6		

1937

Miss A. Marble (US)	Miss Marble		
Fru S. Sperling (DEN)	7–5 2–6 6–3	Mlle Jedrzejowska	
		8–6 6–2	
Mlle J. Jedrzejowska (POL)	Mlle Jedrzejowska		
Miss M. C. Scriven	6–1 6–2		Miss D. E. Round
			6–2 2–6 7–5
Sta A. Lizana (Chile)	Mme Mathieu		
Mme R. Mathieu (F)	6–3 6–3	Miss Round	
Miss H. H. Jacobs (US)	Miss Round	6–4 6–0	
Miss D. E. Round	6–4 6–2		

1938

Mme R. Mathieu (F) Miss A. Marble (US)	Miss Marble 6–2 6–3	Miss Jacobs 6–4 6–4	Mrs F. S. Moody (US) 6–4 6–0
Miss H. H. Jacobs (US) Mlle J. Jedrzejowska (POL)	Miss Jacobs 6–2 6–3		
Mrs M. Fabyan (US) Fru S. Sperling (DEN)	Fru Sperling 4–6 6–4 6–4	Mrs Moody 12–10 6–4	
Mrs F. S. Moody (US) Miss K. E. Stammers	Mrs Moody 6–2 6–1		

1939

Miss H. H. Jacobs (US) Miss K. E. Stammers	Miss Stammers 6–2 6–2	Miss Stammers 7–5 2–6 6–3	Miss A. Marble (US) 6–2 6–0
Mrs M. Fabyan (US) Mme R. Mathieu (F)	Mrs Fabyan 6–4 6–2		
Miss R. M. Hardwick Fru S. Sperling (DEN)	Fru Sperling 6–4 6–0	Miss Marble 6–0 6–0	
Mlle J. Jedrzejowska (POL) Miss A. Marble (US)	Miss Marble 6–1 6–4		

1940–5 not held

1946

Miss P. M. Betz (US) Miss P. J. Curry	Miss Betz 6–0 6–3	Miss Betz 6–2 6–3	Miss P. M. Betz (US) 6–2 6–4
Miss D. Bundy (US) Mrs M. Menzies	Miss Bundy 4–6 6–1 6–3		
Mrs E. W. A. Bostock Miss A. L. Brough (US)	Miss Brough 6–1 6–2	Miss Brough 8–6 7–5	
Miss D. J. Hart (US) Miss M. E. Osborne (US)	Miss Osborne 5–7 6–4 6–4		

1947

Mrs N. W. Bolton (AUS) Miss A. L. Brough (US)	Miss Brough 6–2 6–3	Miss Hart 2–6 8–6 6–4	Miss M. E. Osborne (US) 6–2 6–4
Mrs E. W. A. Bostock Miss D. J. Hart (US)	Miss Hart 4–6 6–1 6–2		
Mrs S. P. Summers (SA) Mrs P. C. Todd (US)	Mrs Summers 7–5 6–4	Miss Osborne 6–1 6–2	
Mrs M. Menzies Miss M. E. Osborne (US)	Miss Osborne 6–2 6–4		

1948

Mrs E. W. A. Bostock Mrs W. D. du Pont (US)	Mrs du Pont 7–5 6–3	Miss Hart 6–4 2–6 6–3	Miss A. L. Brough (US) 6–3 8–6
Miss D. J. Hart (US) Mme N. Landry (F)	Miss Hart 6–0 6–2		
Miss J. Quertier Mrs P. C. Todd (US)	Mrs Todd 6–2 6–4	Miss Brough 6–3 7–5	
Miss A. L. Brough (US) Miss S. J. Fry (US)	Miss Brough 3–1 retired		

1949

Mrs N. W. Blair Miss A. L. Brough (US)	Miss Brough 6–2 6–3	Miss Brough 6–3 6–0	Miss A. L. Brough (US) 10–8 1–6 10–8
Mrs P. C. Todd (US) Mrs J. J. Walker-Smith	Mrs Todd 3–6 6–4 6–3		
Mrs E. W. Dawson-Scott Mrs H. P. Rihbany (US)	Mrs Rihbany 7–5 7–5	Mrs du Pont 6–2 6–2	
Mrs W. D. du Pont (US) Mrs B. E. Hilton	Mrs du Pont 6–1 6–3		

1950

Players	Quarter-finals	Semi-finals	Final
Miss A. L. Brough (US) Miss S. J. Fry (US)	Miss Brough 2–6 6–3 6–0	Miss Brough 6–4 6–3	Miss A. L. Brough (US) 6–1 3–6 6–1
Miss D. J. Hart (US) Miss B. Scofield (US)	Miss Hart 6–1 6–1		
Mrs C. Harrison Mrs P. C. Todd (US)	Mrs Todd 6–2 6–2	Mrs du Pont 8–6 4–6 8–6	
Mrs W. D. du Pont (US) Miss G. Moran (US)	Mrs du Pont 6–4 6–4		

1951

Players	Quarter-finals	Semi-finals	Final
Miss B. Baker (US) Mrs W. D. du Pont (US)	Miss Baker 6–1 4–6 6–3	Miss Hart 6–3 6–1	Miss D. J. Hart (US) 6–1 6–0
Miss N. Chaffee (US) Miss D. J. Hart (US)	Miss Hart 6–3 6–3		
Miss S. J. Fry (US) Mrs J. J. Walker-Smith	Miss Fry 8–6 6–4	Miss Fry 6–4 6–2	
Miss A. L. Brough (US) Miss K. L. A. Tuckey	Miss Brough 5–7 6–1 6–3		

1952

Players	Quarter-finals	Semi-finals	Final
Miss M. Connolly (US) Mrs T. D. Long (AUS)	Miss Connolly 5–7 6–2 6–0	Miss Connolly 6–4 6–3	Miss M. Connolly (US) 7–5 6–3
Miss S. J. Fry (US) Mrs J. J. Walker-Smith	Miss Fry 6–3 6–3		
Miss A. L. Brough (US) Mrs J. Rinkel-Quertier	Miss Brough 6–1 9–7	Miss Brough 6–3 3–6 6–1	
Miss D. J. Hart (US) Mrs P. C. Todd (US)	Mrs Todd 6–8 7–5 6–4		

1953

Players	Quarter-finals	Semi-finals	Final
Miss D. J. Hart (US) Mrs Z. Kormoczi (HU)	Miss Hart 7–5 7–5	Miss Hart 6–2 6–2	Miss M. Connolly (US) 8–6 7–5
Mrs D. P. Knode (US) Mrs A. Mortimer	Mrs Knode 6–4 6–3		
Miss S. J. Fry (US) Miss J. Sampson (US)	Miss Fry 6–4 6–2	Miss Connolly 6–1 6–1	
Miss M. Connolly (US) Frau E. Vollmer (G)	Miss Connolly 6–3 6–0		

1954

Players	Quarter-finals	Semi-finals	Final
Miss H. M. Fletcher Miss D. J. Hart (US)	Miss Hart 6–1 6–3	Miss Brough 2–6 6–3 6–3	Miss M. Connolly (US) 6–2 7–5
Miss A. L. Brough (US) Miss A. Mortimer	Miss Brough 6–1 6–3		
Miss S. J. Fry (US) Mrs E. C. S. Pratt (US)	Mrs Pratt 6–4 9–11 6–3	Miss Connolly 6–1 6–1	
Miss M. Connolly (US) Mrs W. D. du Pont (US)	Miss Connolly 6–1 6–1		

1955

Players	Quarter-finals	Semi-finals	Final
Miss D. J. Hart (US) Mrs D. P. Knode (US)	Miss Hart 6–4 6–3	Mrs Fleitz 6–3 6–0	Miss A. L. Brough (US) 7–5 8–6
Miss A. Buxton Mrs J. Fleitz (US)	Miss Fleitz 6–2 6–2		
Miss D. R. Hard (US) Mrs Z. Kormoczi (HU)	Miss Hard 6–2 6–3	Miss Brough 6–3 8–6	
Miss A. L. Brough (US) Miss B. Penrose (AUS)	Miss Brough 6–2 6–0		

1956

Miss A. Buxton	Miss Buxton w.o.	Miss Buxton 6–1 6–4	Miss S. J. Fry (US) 6–3 6–1
Mrs J. Fleitz (US)			
Miss A. Mortimer	Miss Ward 6–3 6–0		
Miss P. E. Ward			
Miss S. J. Fry (US)	Miss Fry 4–6 6–3 6–4	Miss Fry 6–4 4–6 6–3	
Miss A. Gibson (US)			
Miss S. J. Bloomer	Miss Brough 5–7 6–1 6–3		
Miss A. L. Brough (US)			

1957

Miss A. L. Brough (US)	Miss Hard 6–2 6–2	Miss Hard 6–2 6–3	Miss A. Gibson (US) 6–3 6–2
Miss D. R. Hard (US)			
Mrs D. P. Knode (US)	Mrs Knode 6–4 6–0		
Miss R. M. Reyes (MEX)			
Mrs E. C. S. Pratt (US)	Miss Truman 9–7 5–7 6–4	Miss Gibson 6–1 6–1	
Miss C. C. Truman			
Miss A. Gibson (US)	Miss Gibson 6–3 6–4		
Miss S. Reynolds (SA)			

1958

Miss M. Arnold (US)	Mrs Kormoczi 6–1 5–7 8–6	Miss Mortimer 6–0 6–1	Miss A. Gibson (US) 8–6 6–2
Mrs Z. Kormoczi (HU)			
Mrs W. du Pont (US)	Miss Mortimer 4–6 6–3 10–8		
Miss A. Mortimer			
Miss M. E. Bueno (BRA)	Miss Haydon 6–3 7–5	Miss Gibson 6–2 6–0	
Miss A. S. Haydon			
Miss S. J. Bloomer	Miss Gibson 6–3 6–8 6–2		
Miss A. Gibson (US)			

1959

Miss A. Mortimer	Miss Reynolds 7–5 8–6	Miss Hard 6–4 6–4	Miss M. E. Bueno (BRA) 6–4 6–3
Miss S. Reynolds (SA)			
Miss D. R. Hard (US)	Miss Hard 1–6 6–4 7–5		
Miss A. S. Haydon			
Frl E. Buding (G)	Miss Bueno 6–3 6–3	Miss Bueno 6–2 6–4	
Miss M. E. Bueno (BRA)			
Miss S. M. Moore (US)	Miss Moore 6–3 6–2		
Miss Y. Ramirez (MEX)			

1960

Miss M. E. Bueno (BRA)	Miss Bueno 6–1 6–1	Miss Bueno 6–0 5–7 6–1	Miss M. E. Bueno (BRA) 8–6 6–0
Miss A. Mortimer			
Miss K. Hantze (US)	Miss Truman 4–6 6–4 6–4		
Miss C. C. Truman			
Miss A. S. Haydon	Miss Haydon 7–5 1–6 6–2	Miss Reynolds 6–3 2–6 6–4	
Miss R. Schuurman (SA)			
Miss D. R. Hard (US)	Miss Reynolds 6–1 2–6 6–1		
Miss S. Reynolds (SA)			

1961

Miss M. Smith (AUS)	Miss Truman 3–6 6–3 9–7	Miss Truman 6–4 6–4	Miss A. Mortimer 4–6 6–4 7–5
Miss C. C. Truman			
Miss K. Hantze (US)	Miss Schuurman 6–4 2–6 7–5		
Miss R. Schuurman (SA)			
Miss A. Mortimer	Miss Mortimer 6–3 6–4	Miss Mortimer 11–9 6–3	
Mrs V. Sukova (CZ)			
Miss Y. Ramirez (MEX)	Miss Reynolds 4–6 6–3 6–0		
Miss S. Reynolds (SA)			

1962

Miss A. S. Haydon	Miss Haydon		
Miss B. J. Moffitt (US)	6–3 6–1	Mrs Susman	
Miss R. Schuurman (SA)	Mrs Susman	8–6 6–1	
Mrs J. R. Susman (US)	6–4 6–4		Mrs J. R. Susman (US)
Miss M. E. Bueno (BRA)	Miss Bueno		6–4 6–4
Miss L. R. Turner (AUS)	2–6 6–4 6–2	Mrs Sukova	
Miss D. R. Hard (US)	Mrs Sukova	6–4 6–3	
Mrs V. Sukova (CZ)	6–4 6–3		

1963

Miss R. Schuurman (SA)	Miss Smith		
Miss M. Smith (AUS)	3–6 6–0 6–1	Miss Smith	
Miss D. R. Hard (US)	Miss Hard	6–3 6–3	
Miss J. P. Lehane (AUS)	6–1 1–2 retired		Miss M. Smith (AUS)
Mrs H. G. Fales (US)	Mrs Jones		6–3 6–4
Mrs P. F. Jones	6–4 6–1	Miss Moffitt	
Miss M. E. Bueno (BRA)	Miss Moffitt	6–4 6–4	
Miss B. J. Moffitt (US)	6–2 7–5		

1964

Miss N. Baylon (ARG)	Miss Smith		
Miss M. Smith (AUS)	6–0 2–0 retired	Miss Smith	
Mrs P. F. Jones	Miss Moffitt	6–3 6–4	
Miss B. J. Moffitt (US)	6–3 6–3		Miss M. E. Bueno (BRA)
Miss N. Richey (US)	Miss Turner		6–4 7–9 6–3
Miss L. R. Turner (AUS)	6–3 6–4	Miss Bueno	
Miss M. E. Bueno (BRA)	Miss Bueno	3–6 6–4 6–4	
Miss R. A. Ebbern (AUS)	6–4 6–1		

1965

Miss J. T. Albert (US)	Miss Bueno		
Miss M. E. Bueno (BRA)	6–2 6–2	Miss Bueno	
Miss B. J. Moffitt (US)	Miss Moffitt	6–4 5–7 6–3	
Miss L. R. Turner (AUS)	6–2 6–1		Miss M. Smith (AUS)
Miss N. Richey (US)	Miss Truman		6–4 7–5
Miss C. C. Truman	6–4 1–6 7–5	Miss Smith	
Miss J. Bricka (US)	Miss Smith	6–4 6–0	
Miss M. Smith (AUS)	6–3 6–0		

1966

Miss T. Groenman (NTH)	Miss Smith		
Miss M. Smith (AUS)	6–0 6–4	Mrs King	
Mrs L. W. King (US)	Mrs King	6–3 6–3	
Miss A. M. van Zyl (SA)	1–6 6–2 6–4		Mrs L. W. King (US)
Mrs P. F. Jones	Mrs Jones		6–3 3–6 6–1
Miss N. Richey (US)	4–6 6–1 6–1	Miss Bueno	
Miss M. E. Bueno (BRA)	Miss Bueno	6–3 9–11 7–5	
Mlle F. Durr (F)	6–4 6–3		

1967

Mrs L. W. King (US)	Mrs King		
Miss S. V. Wade	7–5 6–2	Mrs King	
Miss K. M. Harter (US)	Miss Harter	6–0 6–3	
Miss L. R. Turner (AUS)	7–5 1–6 6–2		Mrs L. W. King (US)
Miss M. A. Eisel (US)	Mrs Jones		6–3 6–4
Mrs P. F. Jones	6–2 4–6 7–5	Mrs Jones	
Miss R. Casals (US)	Miss Casals	2–6 6–3 7–5	
Miss J. A. M. Tegart (AUS)	7–5 6–4		

1968

Mrs W. W. Bowrey (AUS)	Mrs King		
Mrs L. W. King (US)	6–3 6–4	Mrs King	
Mlle F. Durr (F)	Mrs Jones	4–6 7–5 6–2	
Mrs P. F. Jones	6–2 6–2		Mrs L. W. King (US)
Miss M. E. Bueno (BRA)	Miss Richey		9–7 7–5
Miss N. Richey (US)	6–4 6–2	Miss Tegart	
Mrs B. M. Court (AUS)	Miss Tegart	6–3 6–1	
Miss J. A. M. Tegart (AUS)	4–6 8–6 6–1		

1969

Mrs B. M. Court (AUS)	Mrs Court		
Miss J. M. Heldman (US)	4–6 6–3 6–3	Mrs Jones	
Mrs P. F. Jones	Mrs Jones	10–12 6–3 6–2	
Miss N. Richey (US)	6–2 7–5		Mrs P. F. Jones
Mrs W. W. Bowrey (AUS)	Miss Casals		3–6 6–3 6–2
Miss R. Casals (US)	3–6 9–7 7–5	Mrs King	
Mrs L. W. King (US)	Mrs King	6–1 6–0	
Miss J. A. M. Tegart (AUS)	4–6 7–5 8–6		

1970

Mrs B. M. Court (AUS)	Mrs Court		
Frl H. Niessen (G)	6–8 6–0 6–0	Mrs Court	
Miss R. Casals (US)	Miss Casals	6–4 6–1	
Miss W. M. Shaw	6–2 6–0		Mrs B. M. Court (AUS)
Mlle F. Durr (F)	Mlle Durr		14–12 11–9
Miss C. A. Martinez (US)	6–0 6–4	Mrs King	
Mrs L. W. King (US)	Mrs King	6–3 7–5	
Miss K. M. Krantzcke (AUS)	3–6 6–3 6–2		

1971

Mrs B. M. Court (AUS)	Mrs Court		
Miss W. M. Shaw	6–2 6–1	Mrs Court	
Mrs D. E. Dalton (AUS)	Mrs Dalton	4–6 6–1 6–0	
Miss K. A. Melville (AUS)	6–2 3–6 6–3		Miss E. F. Goolagong (AUS)
Miss E. F. Goolagong (AUS)	Miss Goolagong		6–4 6–1
Mrs K. S. Gunter (US)	6–3 6–2	Miss Goolagong	
Mlle F. Durr (F)	Mrs King	6–4 6–4	
Mrs L. W. King (US)	2–6 6–2 6–2		

1972

Mlle F. Durr (F)	Miss Goolagong		
Miss E. F. Goolagong (AUS)	8–6 7–5	Miss Goolagong	
Miss C. M. Evert (US)	Miss Evert	4–6 6–3 6–4	
Miss P. S. A. Hogan (US)	6–2 4–6 6–1		Mrs L. W. King (US)
Miss R. Casals (US)	Miss Casals		6–3 6–3
Mrs K. S. Gunter (US)	3–6 6–4 6–0	Mrs King	
Mrs L. W. King (US)	Mrs King	6–2 6–4	
Miss S. V. Wade	6–1 3–6 6–3		

1973

Mrs B. M. Court (AUS)	Mrs Court		
Mrs O. Morozova (USSR)	4–6 6–4 6–1	Miss Evert	
Miss R. Casals (US)	Miss Evert	6–1 1–6 6–1	
Miss C. M. Evert (US)	6–2 4–6 6–2		Mrs L. W. King (US)
Miss E. F. Goolagong (AUS)	Miss Goolagong		6–0 7–5
Miss S. V. Wade	6–3 6–3	Mrs King	
Mrs L. W. King (US)	Mrs King	6–3 5–7 6–3	
Miss K. A. Melville (AUS)	9–8* 8–6		

* Tie break

1974

Mrs L. W. King (US)	Mrs Morozova		
Mrs O. Morozova (USSR)	7–5 6–2	Mrs Morozova	
Miss L. Boshoff (SA)	Miss Wade	1–6 7–5 6–4	
Miss S. V. Wade	6–3 6–2		Miss C. M. Evert (US)
Miss E. F. Goolagong (AUS)	Miss Melville		6–0 6–4
Miss K. A. Melville (AUS)	9–7 1–6 6–2	Miss Evert	
Miss C. M. Evert (US)	Miss Evert	6–2 6–3	
Frau H. Masthoff (G)	6–4 6–2		

1975

Miss C. M. Evert (US)	Miss Evert		
Miss B. F. Stove (NTH)	5–7 7–5 6–0	Mrs King	
Mrs L. W. King (US)	Mrs King	2–6 6–2 6–3	
Mrs O. Morozova (USSR)	6–3 6–3		Mrs L. W. King (US)
Mrs R. Cawley (AUS)	Mrs Cawley		6–0 6–1
Miss S. V. Wade	5–7 6–3 9–7	Mrs Cawley	
Mrs. B. M. Court (AUS)	Mrs Court	6–4 6–4	
Miss M. Navratilova (CZ)	6–3 6–4		

1976

Miss C. M. Evert (US)	Miss Evert		
Mrs O. Morozova (USSR)	6–3 6–0	Miss Evert	
Miss S. Barker	Miss Navratilova	6–3 4–6 6–4	
Miss M. Navratilova (CZ)	6–3 3–6 7–5		Miss C. M. Evert (US)
Mrs G. E. Reid (AUS)	Miss Wade		6–3 4–6 8–6
Miss S. V. Wade	6–4 6–2	Mrs Cawley	
Miss R. Casals (US)	Mrs Cawley	6–1 6–2	
Mrs R. Cawley (AUS)	7–5 6–3		

MEN'S DOUBLES

Played for the first five years at Oxford (see p. 21)

1879 L. R. Erskine & H. F. Lawford d F. Durant & G. E. Tabor

1880 W. Renshaw & E. Renshaw d C. J. Cole & O. E. Woodhouse

1881 W. Renshaw & E. Renshaw d W. J. Down & H. Vaughan

1882 J. T. Hartley & R. T. Richardson d J. G. Horn & C. B. Russell

1883 C. W. Grinstead & C. E. Welldon d R. T. Milford & C. B. Russell

Played at Wimbledon

1884

J. Dwight (US) & R. D. Sears (US) E. Renshaw & W. Renshaw	Renshaw & Renshaw 6–0 6–1 6–2	E. Renshaw & W. Renshaw 6–3 6–1 1–6 6–4
E. W. Lewis & E. L. Williams	Bye	

1885

C. E. Farrer & A. J. Stanley C. H. A. Ross & W. C. Taylor	Farrer & Stanley 6–3 8–6 6–2	E. Renshaw & W. Renshaw 6–3 6–3 10–8
J. Dwight (US) & E. W. Lewis E. Renshaw & W. Renshaw	Renshaw & Renshaw 4–6 6–1 6–4 6–4	

Challenge Round introduced

1886

H. Chipp & E. G. Meers C. E. Farrer & A. J. Stanley	Farrer & Stanley 6–4 6–1 10–8	C. E. Farrer & A. J. Stanley 7–5 6–3 6–1
P. Bowes-Lyon & H. W. W. Wilberforce W. Milne & C. H. A. Ross	Bowes-Lyon & Wilberforce 7–9 4–6 8–6 6–1 6–1	

Challenge Round **E. Renshaw & W. Renshaw** d C. E. Farrer & A. J. Stanley 6–3 6–3 4–6 7–5

1887

H. S. Barlow & A. P. Gaskell E. Barratt-Smith & J. H. Crispe	Barratt-Smith & Crispe 6–1 6–2	P. Bowes-Lyon & H. W. W. Wilberforce 7–5 6–3 6–2
N. M. Farrer & S. Winkworth P. Bowes-Lyon & H. W. W. Wilberforce	Bowes-Lyon & Wilberforce 6–4 6–3	

Challenge Round **P. Bowes-Lyon & H. W. W. Wilberforce** (w.o.)

1888

G. E. Brown & P. B. Brown E. Renshaw & W. Renshaw	Renshaw & Renshaw 6–4 8–6 6–2	E. Renshaw & W. Renshaw 6–3 6–2 6–2
H. Chipp & C. E. Farrer E. G. Meers & A. G. Ziffo	Meers & Ziffo 6–2 7–5 retired	

Challenge Round **E. Renshaw & W. Renshaw** d P. B. Lyon & H. W. W. Wilberforce 2–6 1–6 6–3 6–4 6–3

1889

A. W. Gore & G. R. Mewburn R. K. Micklethwait & W. Watkins	Gore & Mewburn w.o.	G. W. Hillyard & E. W. Lewis 6–2 6–1 6–3
H. Baddeley & W. Baddeley G. W. Hillyard & E. W. Lewis	Hillyard & Lewis 9–7 6–3 3–6 4–6 6–1	

Challenge Round **E. Renshaw & W. Renshaw** d G. W. Hillyard & E. W. Lewis 6–4 6–4 3–6 0–6 6–1

1890

G. E. Brown & P. B. Brown G. W. Hillyard & E. W. Lewis	Hillyard & Lewis 6–2 6–4 8–6	J. Pim & F. O. Stoker 6–0 7–5 6–4
H. Baddeley & W. Baddeley J. Pim & F. O. Stoker	Pim & Stoker 6–1 7–5 5–7 6–1	

Challenge Round **J. Pim & F. O. Stoker** (w.o.)

1891

H. Baddeley & W. Baddeley H. S. Mahony & G. R. Mewburn	Baddeley & Baddeley 13–11 4–6 8–6 7–5	H. Baddeley & W. Baddeley 4–6 6–4 7–5 0–6 6–2
H. S. Barlow & E. Renshaw W. Milne & A. J. Stanley	Barlow & Renshaw 7–5 6–1 7–9 6–0	

Challenge Round **H. Baddeley & W. Baddeley** d J. Pim & F. O. Stoker 6–1 6–3 1–6 6–2

1892

H. S. Barlow & E. W. Lewis O. S. Campbell (US) & G. W. Hillyard	Barlow & Lewis 6–3 6–4 6–2	H. S. Barlow & E. W. Lewis 8–10 6–3 5–7 11–9 6–1
A. W. Gore & A. Palmer H. S. Mahony & J. Pim	Mahony & Pim w.o.	

Challenge Round **H. S. Barlow & E. W. Lewis** d H. Baddeley & W. Baddeley 4–6 6–2 8–6 6–4

1893

A. W. Gore & A. Palmer J. Pim & F. O. Stoker	Pim & Stoker 6–2 5–7 6–1 6–4	J. Pim & F. O. Stoker 6–2 4–6 6–3 5–7 6–2
H. Baddeley & W. Baddeley M. F. Goodbody & H. S. Scrivener	Baddeley & Baddeley 6–1 6–4 6–3	

Challenge Round **J. Pim & F. O. Stoker** d H. S. Barlow & E. W. Lewis 4–6 6–3 6–1 2–6 6–0

1894

H. Baddeley & W. Baddeley C. H. L. Cazalet & G. W. Hillyard	Baddeley & Baddeley 6–4 6–2 6–4	H. Baddeley & W. Baddeley 5–7 7–5 4–6 6–3 8–6
F. S. Barlow & C. H. Martin C. O. S. Hatton & L. L. R. Hausburg	Barlow & Martin 6–0 5–7 12–10 3–6 6–4	

Challenge Round **H. Baddeley & W. Baddeley** (w.o.)

1895

H. S. Barlow & C. H. Martin W. V. Eaves & E. W. Lewis	Eaves & Lewis 5–7 4–6 6–0 6–4 6–4	W. V. Eaves & E. W. Lewis 6–4 6–4 6–3
W. G. Bailey & C. F. Simond C. H. L. Cazalet & G. R. Mewburn	Bailey & Simond w.o.	

Challenge Round **H. Baddeley & W. Baddeley** d W. V. Eaves & E. W. Lewis 8–6 5–7 6–4 6–3

1896

R. F. Doherty & H. A. Nisbet W. V. Eaves & E. W. Lewis	Doherty & Nisbet 6–3 8–6 6–4	R. F. Doherty & H. A. Nisbet 3–6 7–5 6–4 6–1
C. G. Allen & E. R. Allen H. L. Doherty & R. B. Scott	Allen & Allen 3–6 6–1 6–1 6–2	

Challenge Round **H. Baddeley & W. Baddeley** d R. F. Doherty & H. A. Nisbet 1–6 3–6 6–4 6–2 6–1

1897

H. L. Doherty & R. F. Doherty G. W. Hillyard & H. S. Mahony	Doherty & Doherty 6–3 6–4 4–6 6–4	H. L. Doherty & R. F. Doherty 6–2 7–5 2–6 6–2
C. H. L. Cazalet & S. H. Smith G. E. Evered & R. Sheldon	Cazalet & Smith 6–1 6–1 6–2	

Challenge Round **H. Baddeley & W. Baddeley** d H. L. Doherty & R. F. Doherty 6–4 4–6 8–6 6–4

1898

G. A. Caridia & G. M. Simond C. Hobart (US) & H. A. Nisbet	Hobart & Nisbet 6–0 10–8 6–4	C. Hobart (US) & H. A. Nisbet 2–6 6–2 6–2 6–3
A. W. Gore & G. R. Mewburn G. W. Hillyard & S. H. Smith	Hillyard & Smith 6–4 5–7 6–3 7–5	

Challenge Round **H. L. Doherty & R. F. Doherty** d C. Hobart (US) & H. A. Nisbet 6–4 6–4 6–2

1899

G. A. Caridia & G. M. Simond C. Hobart (US) & H. A. Nisbet	Hobart & Nisbet 3–6 4–6 6–1 6–4 6–2	C. Hobart (US) & H. A. Nisbet 6–4 6–1 8–6
C. P. Dixon & M. J. G. Ritchie A. W. Gore & H. Roper Barrett	Gore & Roper Barrett 3–6 6–4 6–4 6–1	

Challenge Round **H. L. Doherty & R. F. Doherty** d C. Hobart (US) & H. A. Nisbet 7–5 6–0 6–2

1900

A. W. Gore & G. M. Simond F. L. Riseley & S. H. Smith	Riseley & Smith 6–3 7–5 6–1	H. A. Nisbet & H. Roper Barrett 6–2 2–6 6–8 8–6 6–2
C. H. L. Cazalet & G. W. Hillyard H. A. Nisbet & H. Roper Barrett	Nisbet & Roper Barrett 6–3 7–5 10–8	

Challenge Round **H. L. Doherty & R. F. Doherty** d H. A. Nisbet & H. Roper Barrett 9–7 7–5 4–6 3–6 6–3

1901

Pairs	Semi-final	Final
C. H. L. Cazalet & S. H. Smith H. Roper Barrett & G. M. Simond	Roper Barrett & Simond 6–2 6–3 2–6 6–1	Dwight F. Davis (US) & Holcombe Ward (US) 7–5 6–4 6–4
H. W. Davies & R. A. Gamble Dwight F. Davis (US) & Holcombe Ward (US)	Davis & Ward 6–3 6–3 6–3	

Challenge Round **H. L. Doherty & R. F. Doherty** d Dwight F. Davis (US) & Holcombe Ward (US) 4–6 6–2 6–3 9–7

1902

Pairs	Semi-final	Final
P. de Borman (B) & W. Lemaire (B) F. L. Riseley & S. H. Smith	Riseley & Smith 6–4 6–3 6–3	F. L. Riseley & S. H. Smith 7–5 2–6 6–8 6–3 6–1
G. C. Ball-Greene & H. Roper Barrett C. H. L. Cazalet & G. W. Hillyard	Cazalet & Hillyard 6–2 4–6 9–7 6–2	

Challenge Round **F. L. Riseley & S. H. Smith** d H. L. Doherty & R. F. Doherty 4–6 8–6 6–3 4–6 11–9

1903

Pairs	Semi-final	Final
G. C. Ball-Greene & W. V. Eaves H. L. Doherty & R. F. Doherty	Doherty & Doherty 6–2 6–1 6–1	H. L. Doherty & R. F. Doherty 8–6 6–2 6–2
H. S. Mahony & M. J. G. Ritchie G. R. Mewburn & F. J. Plaskitt	Mahony & Ritchie 6–3 6–4 6–4	

Challenge Round **H. L. Doherty & R. F. Doherty** d F. L. Riseley & S. H. Smith 6–4 6–4 6–4

1904

Pairs	Semi-final	Final
P. de Borman (B) & W. Lemaire (B) G. A. Caridia & A. W. Gore	Caridia & Gore 6–2 7–5 6–1	F. L. Riseley & S. H. Smith 6–3 6–4 6–3
G. Greville & M. J. G. Ritchie F. L. Riseley & S. H. Smith	Riseley & Smith 6–1 7–5 6–1	

Challenge Round **H. L. Doherty & R. F. Doherty** d F. L. Riseley & S. H. Smith 6–3 6–4 6–3

1905

Pairs	Semi-final	Final
N. E. Brookes (AUS) & A. W. Dunlop (AUS) W. J. Clothier (US) & W. A. Larned (US)	Brookes & Dunlop 6–4 6–0 2–6 6–1	F. L. Riseley & S. H. Smith 6–2 1–6 6–2 6–3
F. L. Riseley & S. H. Smith Holcombe Ward (US) & B. C. Wright (US)	Riseley & Smith 2–6 6–3 6–2 9–7	

Challenge Round **H. L. Doherty & R. F. Doherty** d F. L. Riseley & S. H. Smith 6–2 6–4 6–8 6–3

1906

Pairs	Semi-final	Final
F. L. Riseley & S. H. Smith M. J. G. Ritchie & A. F. Wilding (NZ)	Riseley & Smith 6–4 7–5 6–3	F. L. Riseley & S. H. Smith 6–2 6–2 5–7 6–4
C. H. L. Cazalet & G. M. Simond K. Collins (US) & R. D. Little (US)	Cazalet & Simond 2–6 7–9 6–3 6–4 6–4	

Challenge Round **F. L. Riseley & S. H. Smith** d H. L. Doherty & R. F. Doherty 6–8 6–4 5–7 6–3 6–3

1907

Pairs	Semi-final	Final
K. Behr (US) & B. C. Wright (US) R. J. McNair & G. A. Thomas	Behr & Wright 6–2 6–1 6–4	N. E. Brookes (AUS) & A. F. Wilding (NZ) 6–4 6–4 6–2
N. E. Brookes (AUS) & A. F. Wilding (NZ) X. A. Casdagli & M. J. G. Ritchie	Brookes & Wilding 6–1 6–3 6–1	

Challenge Round **N. E. Brookes (AUS) & A. F. Wilding (NZ)** (w.o.)

1908

Pairs	Semi-final	Final
C. P. Dixon & A. D. Prebble A. W. Gore & H. Roper Barrett	Gore & Roper Barrett 6–2 2–6 6–3 6–4	M. J. G. Ritchie & A. F. Wilding (NZ) 6–1 6–2 1–6 1–6 9–7
C. H. L. Cazalet & G. W. Hillyard M. J. G. Ritchie & A. F. Wilding (NZ)	Ritchie & Wilding 6–3 4–6 4–6 7–5 7–5	

Challenge Round **M. J. G. Ritchie & A. F. Wilding (NZ)** (w.o.)

1909

Pairs	Semi-final	Final
S. N. Doust (AUS) & H. A. Parker (AUS) K. Powell & R. B. Powell (CAN)	Doust & Parker 3–6 6–2 3–6 8–6 6–3	A. W. Gore & H. Roper Barrett 6–2 6–1 6–4
E. Gordon Cleather & C. Gordon Smith A. W. Gore & H. Roper Barrett	Gore & Roper Barrett 7–5 6–1 6–2	

Challenge Round **A. W. Gore & H. Roper Barrett** (w.o.)

1910

W. C. Crawley & J. C. Parke K. Powell & R. B. Powell (CAN)	Powell & Powell 6–3 6–4 6–3	M. J. G. Ritchie & A. F. Wilding (NZ) 9–7 6–0 6–4
S. N. Doust (AUS) & L. O. S. Poidevin (AUS) M. J. G. Ritchie & A. F. Wilding (NZ)	Ritchie & Wilding 4–6 6–3 6–4 1–6 6–3	

Challenge Round **M. J. G. Ritchie & A. F. Wilding (NZ)** d A. W. Gore & H. Roper Barrett 6–1 6–1 6–2

1911

M. Decugis (F) & A. H. Gobert (F) S. N. Doust (AUS) & E. O. Pockley (AUS)	Decugis & Gobert 4–6 4–6 6–3 7–5 6–4	M. Decugis (F) & A. H. Gobert (F) 6–2 6–1 6–2
A. W. Gore & H. Roper Barrett S. Hardy (US) & J. C. Parke	Hardy & Parke 3–6 6–3 7–9 retired	

Challenge Round **M. Decugis (F) & A. H. Gobert (F)** d M. J. G. Ritchie & A. F. Wilding (NZ) 9–7 5–7 6–3 2–6 6–2

1912

A. E. Beamish & J. C. Parke S. Hardy (US) & R. B. Powell (CAN)	Beamish & Parke 7–5 8–6 6–4	C. P. Dixon & H. Roper Barrett 6–8 6–4 3–6 6–3 6–4
C. P. Dixon & H. Roper Barrett A. D. Prebble & G. A. Thomas	Dixon & Roper Barrett 8–6 6–1 6–4	

Challenge Round **C. P. Dixon & H. Roper Barrett** d M. Decugis (F) & A. H. Gobert (F) 3–6 6–3 6–4 7–5

1913

A. E. Beamish & J. C. Parke A. H. Lowe & F. G. Lowe	Beamish & Parke 6–4 7–5 6–4	H. Kleinschroth (G) & F. W. Rahe (G) 6–3 6–2 6–4
W. C. Crawley & A. Hendriks H. Kleinschroth (G) & F. W. Rahe (G)	Kleinschroth & Rahe 6–0 6–1 6–3	

Challenge Round **C. P. Dixon & H. Roper Barrett** d H. Kleinschroth (G) & F. W. Rahe (G) 6–2 6–4 4–6 6–2

1914

N. E. Brookes (AUS) & A. F. Wilding (NZ) S. N. Doust (AUS) & T. M. Mavrogordato	Brookes & Wilding 6–1 6–2 3–6 6–3	N. E. Brookes (AUS) & A. F. Wilding (NZ) 6–2 8–6 6–1
H. Crisp & H. C. Eltringham A. H. Lowe & F. G. Lowe	Lowe & Lowe 2–6 6–2 8–6 4–6 6–3	

Challenge Round **N. E. Brookes (AUS) & A. F. Wilding (NZ)** d C. P. Dixon & H. Roper Barrett 6–1 6–1 5–7 8–6

1915–18 not held

1919

F. M. B. Fisher (NZ) & M. J. G. Ritchie R. W. Heath (AUS) & R. Lycett	Heath & Lycett 12–10 8–6 6–3	P. O'Hara Wood (AUS) & R. V. Thomas (AUS) 6–4 6–2 4–6 6–2
N. E. Brookes (AUS) & G. L. Patterson (AUS) P. O'Hara Wood (AUS) & R. V. Thomas (AUS)	O'Hara Wood & Thomas 6–4 6–4 3–6 6–3	

Challenge Round **P. O'Hara Wood (AUS) & R. V. Thomas (AUS)** (w.o.)

1920

C. S. Garland (US) & R. N. Williams (US) W. M. Johnston (US) & W. T. Tilden (US)	Garland & Williams 4–6 6–4 6–3 4–6 6–2	C. S. Garland (US) & R. N. Williams (US) 4–6 6–4 7–5 6–2
P. M. Davson & T. M. Mavrogordato A. R. F. Kingscote & J. C. Parke	Kingscote & Parke 6–4 6–4 6–1	

Challenge Round **C. S. Garland (US) & R. N. Williams (US)** (w.o.)

1921

L. S. Deane (IN) & S. M. Jacobs (IN) A. H. Lowe & F. G. Lowe	Lowe & Lowe 6–1 6–8 4–6 6–0 12–10	R. Lycett & M. Woosnam 6–3 6–0 7–5
R. Lycett & M. Woosnam B. I. C. Norton (SA) & H. Roper Barrett	Lycett & Woosnam 8–6 2–6 6–3 6–4	

Challenge Round **R. Lycett & M. Woosnam** (w.o.)

Challenge Round abolished

1922

B. I. C. Norton (SA) & H. Roper Barrett P. O'Hara Wood (AUS) & G. L. Patterson (AUS)	O'Hara Wood & Patterson 6–1 3–6 5–7 6–3 15–13	J. O. Anderson (AUS) & R. Lycett 3–6 7–9 6–4 6–3 11–9
J. O. Anderson (AUS) & R. Lycett G. C. Caner (US) & D. Mathey (US)	Anderson & Lycett 6–2 6–3 6–2	

1923

L. S. Deane (IN) & A. H. Fyzee (IN) L. A. Godfree & R. Lycett	Godfree & Lycett 8-6 6-4 6-3	L. A. Godfree & R. Lycett 6-3 6-4 3-6 6-3
J. Borotra (F) & R. Lacoste (F) E. Flaquer (SP) & Count de Gomar (SP)	Flaquer & de Gomar 11-9 4-6 6-4 3-6 7-5	

1924

L. A. Godfree & R. Lycett W. M. Washburn (US) & R. N. Williams (US)	Washburn & Williams 4-6 12-10 6-3 7-7 retired	F. T. Hunter (US) & V. Richards (US) 6-3 3-6 8-10 8-6 6-3
F. T. Hunter (US) & V. Richards (US) L. Raymond (SA) & P. D. B. Spence (SA)	Hunter & Richards 6-4 6-4 6-2	

1925

J. Brugnon (F) & H. Cochet (F) R. Casey (US) & J. Hennessey (US)	Casey & Hennessey 7-5 5-7 9-7 6-4	J. Borotra (F) & R. Lacoste (F) 6-4 11-9 4-6 1-6 6-3
J. Borotra (F) & R. Lacoste (F) H. L. de Morpurgo (IT) & B. von Kehrling (HU)	Borotra & Lacoste 11-9 7-9 6-1 6-1	

1926

J. Brugnon (F) & H. Cochet (F) B. von Kehrling (HU) & C. E. van Lennep (NTH)	Brugnon & Cochet 9-7 6-4 6-2	J. Brugnon (F) & H. Cochet (F) 7-5 4-6 6-3 6-2
H. W. Austin & R. Lycett H. Kinsey (US) & V. Richards (US)	Kinsey & Richards 7-5 6-4 6-4	

1927

H. W. Austin & R. Lycett F. T. Hunter (US) & W. T. Tilden (US)	Hunter & Tilden 6-0 10-8 6-4	F. T. Hunter (US) & W. T. Tilden (US) 1-6 4-6 8-6 6-3 6-4
J. Brugnon (F) & H. Cochet (F) J. Condon (SA) & L. Raymond (SA)	Brugnon & Cochet 6-1 6-2 7-5	

1928

J. B. Hawkes (AUS) & G. L. Patterson (AUS) F. T. Hunter (US) & W. T. Tilden (US)	Hawkes & Patterson 7-9 7-9 6-4 6-4 10-8	J. Brugnon (F) & H. Cochet (F) 13-11 6-4 6-4
J. Brugnon (F) & H. Cochet (F) J. Hennessey (US) & G. M. Lott (US)	Brugnon & Cochet 11-9 6-4 3-6 7-5	

1929

I. G. Collins & J. C. Gregory J. Hennessey (US) & G. M. Lott (US)	Collins & Gregory 4-6 7-5 6-1 4-6 7-5	W. L. Allison (US) & J. Van Ryn (US) 6-4 5-7 6-3 10-12 6-4
W. L. Allison (US) & J. Van Ryn (US) F. T. Hunter (US) & W. T. Tilden (US)	Allison & Van Ryn 6-3 12-10 6-3	

1930

J. Brugnon (F) & H. Cochet (F) J. H. Doeg (US) & G. M. Lott (US)	Doeg & Lott 8-6 3-6 6-3 6-1	W. L. Allison (US) & J. Van Ryn (US) 6-3 6-3 6-2
W. L. Allison (US) & J. Van Ryn (US) I. G. Collins & J. C. Gregory	Allison & Van Ryn 4-6 7-5 6-3 6-3	

1931

J. Brugnon (F) & H. Cochet (F) F. X. Shields (US) & S. B. Wood (US)	Brugnon & Cochet 6-4 7-5 6-2	G. M. Lott (US) & J. Van Ryn (US) 6-2 10-8 9-11 3-6 6-3
G. P. Hughes & F. J. Perry G. M. Lott (US) & J. Van Ryn (US)	Lott & Van Ryn 6-4 11-9 6-4	

1932

W. L. Allison (US) & J. Van Ryn (US) J. Borotra (F) & J. Brugnon (F)	Borotra & Brugnon 6-3 6-2 6-4	J. Borotra (F) & J. Brugnon (F) 6-0 4-6 3-6 7-5 7-5
C. Boussus (F) & A. Merlin (F) G. P. Hughes & F. J. Perry	Hughes & Perry 8-6 6-1 6-3	

1933

E. Nourney (G) & G. von Cramm (G) R. Nunoi (J) & J. Satoh (J)	Nunoi & Satoh 7-5 3-6 6-4 6-1	J. Borotra (F) & J. Brugnon (F) 4-6 6-3 6-3 7-5
J. Borotra (F) & J. Brugnon (F) N. G. Farquharson (SA) & V. G. Kirby (SA)	Borotra & Brugnon 5-7 3-6 6-4 6-3 6-4	

1934			
	H. C. Hopman (AUS) & D. Prenn (G) G. M. Lott (US) & L. R. Stoefen (US)	Lott & Stoefen 6-4 4-6 6-3 8-6	G. M. Lott (US) & L. R. Stoefen (US) 6-2 6-3 6-4
	J. Borotra (F) & J. Brugnon (F) I. G. Collins & F. H. D. Wilde	Borotra & Brugnon 7-5 3-6 6-2 6-4	
1935			
	W. L. Allison (US) & J. Van Ryn (US) G. P. Hughes & C. R. D. Tuckey	Allison & Van Ryn 4-6 6-4 6-2 6-2	J. H. Crawford (AUS) & A. K. Quist (AUS) 6-3 5-7 6-2 5-7 7-5
	J. D. Budge (US) & G. Mako (US) J. H. Crawford (AUS) & A. K. Quist (AUS)	Crawford & Quist 6-2 13-11 6-3	
1936			
	J. Borotra (F) & J. Brugnon (F) C. E. Hare & F. H. D. Wilde	Hare & Wilde 6-1 4-6 6-1 6-4	G. P. Hughes & C. R. D. Tuckey 6-4 3-6 7-9 6-1 6-4
	W. L. Allison (US) & J. Van Ryn (US) G. P. Hughes & C. R. D. Tuckey	Hughes & Tuckey 7-5 6-4 3-6 11-9	
1937			
	L. Hecht (CZ) & R. Menzel (CZ) G. P. Hughes & C. R. D. Tuckey	Hughes & Tuckey 6-2 6-2 6-4	J. D. Budge (US) & G. Mako (US) 6-0 6-4 6-8 6-1
	J. D. Budge (US) & G. Mako (US) H. Henkel (G) & G. von Cramm (G)	Budge & Mako 4-6 4-6 6-2 6-4 6-3	
1938			
	J. D. Budge (US) & G. Mako (US) G. P. Hughes & F. H. D. Wilde	Budge & Mako 6-2 6-4 12-10	J. D. Budge (US) & G. Mako (US) 6-4 3-6 6-3 8-6
	H. Henkel (G) & G. von Metaxa (G) F. Kukuljevic (YU) & J. Pallada (YU)	Henkel & von Metaxa 7-5 6-2 6-4	
1939			
	C. E. Hare & F. H. D. Wilde J. S. Olliff & R. A. Shayes	Hare & Wilde 6-2 6-4 6-4	E. T. Cooke (US) & R. L. Riggs (US) 6-3 3-6 6-3 9-7
	J. Borotra (F) & J. Brugnon (F) E. T. Cooke (US) & R. L. Riggs (US)	Cooke & Riggs 6-4 3-6 6-2 6-3	
1940-5 not held			
1946			
	G. E. Brown (AUS) & D. Pails (AUS) D. Mitic (YU) & J. Pallada (YU)	Brown & Pails 6-2 6-4 6-3	T. Brown (US) & J. A. Kramer (US) 6-4 6-4 6-2
	T. Brown (US) & J. A. Kramer (US) J. E. Patty (US) & F. Segura (Ecuador)	Brown & Kramer 6-3 6-3 6-3	
1947			
	G. E. Brown (AUS) & C. F. Long (AUS) R. Falkenburg (US) & J. A. Kramer (US)	Falkenburg & Kramer 10-8 6-4 6-4	R. Falkenburg (US) & J. A. Kramer (US) 8-6 6-3 6-3
	J. E. Bromwich (AUS) & D. Pails (AUS) A. J. Mottram & O. W. Sidwell (AUS)	Mottram & Sidwell 6-3 6-3 7-5	
1948			
	L. Bergelin (SWE) & J. E. Harper (AUS) T. Brown (US) & G. Mulloy (US)	Brown & Mulloy 1-6 6-3 4-6 6-4 8-6	J. E. Bromwich (AUS) & F. A. Sedgman (AUS) 5-7 7-5 7-5 9-7
	J. E. Bromwich (AUS) & F. A. Sedgman (AUS) R. Falkenburg (US) & F. A. Parker (US)	Bromwich & Sedgman 6-2 6-8 4-6 6-4 6-1	
1949			
	R. A. Gonzales (US) & F. A. Parker (US) J. E. Patty (US) & E. W. Sturgess (SA)	Gonzales & Parker 6-3 6-1 3-6 5-7 7-5	R. A. Gonzales (US) & F. A. Parker (US) 6-4 6-4 6-2
	G. E. Brown (AUS) & O. W. Sidwell (AUS) G. Mulloy (US) & F. R. Schroeder (US)	Mulloy & Schroeder 6-4 3-6 6-8 6-3 9-7	
1950			
	J. E. Bromwich (AUS) & A. K. Quist (AUS) J. Drobny (EG) & E. W. Sturgess (SA)	Bromwich & Quist 6-4 3-6 6-3 6-4	J. E. Bromwich (AUS) & A. K. Quist (AUS) 7-5 3-6 6-3 3-6 6-2
	G. E. Brown (AUS) & O. W. Sidwell (AUS) J. E. Patty (US) & M. A. Trabert (US)	Brown & Sidwell 6-4 6-4 6-3	

Year	Semi-finals	Result	Final
1951	K. McGregor (AUS) & F. A. Sedgman (AUS) J. E. Patty (US) & H. Richardson (US)	McGregor & Sedgman 6-4 6-2 6-3	K. McGregor (AUS) & F. A. Sedgman (AUS) 3-6 6-2 6-3 3-6 6-3
	J. Drobny (EG) & E. W. Sturgess (SA) G. Mulloy (US) & R. Savitt (US)	Drobny & Sturgess 4-6 6-4 6-3 6-4	
1952	J. Drobny (EG) & J. E. Patty (US) K. McGregor (AUS) & F. A. Sedgman (AUS)	McGregor & Sedgman 6-3 6-4 7-9 6-4	K. McGregor (AUS) & F. A. Sedgman (AUS) 6-3 7-5 6-4
	L. A. Hoad (AUS) & K. R. Rosewall (AUS) E. V. Seixas (US) & E. W. Sturgess (SA)	Seixas & Sturgess 6-4 8-6 6-8 7-5	
1953	J. Brichant (B) & P. Washer (B) L. A. Hoad (AUS) & K. R. Rosewall (AUS)	Hoad & Rosewall 4-6 6-0 6-4 3-6 6-1	L. A. Hoad (AUS) & K. R. Rosewall (AUS) 6-4 7-5 4-6 7-5
	R. N. Hartwig (AUS) & M. G. Rose (AUS) G. Mulloy (US) & E. V. Seixas (US)	Hartwig & Rose 14-16 6-3 6-3 6-4	
1954	L. A. Hoad (AUS) & K. R. Rosewall (AUS) E. V. Seixas (US) & M. A. Trabert (US)	Seixas & Trabert 6-3 7-5 3-6 4-6 8-6	R. N. Hartwig (AUS) & M. G. Rose (AUS) 6-4 6-4 3-6 6-4
	R. N. Hartwig (AUS) & M. G. Rose (AUS) G. Mulloy (US) & J. E. Patty (US)	Hartwig & Rose 4-6 6-4 6-2 6-1	
1955	R. N. Hartwig (AUS) & L. A. Hoad (AUS) M. G. Rose (AUS) & G. A. Worthington (AUS)	Hartwig & Hoad 7-9 6-4 6-4 2-6 6-1	R. N. Hartwig (AUS) & L. A. Hoad (AUS) 7-5 6-4 6-3
	N. A. Fraser (AUS) & K. R. Rosewall (AUS) E. V. Seixas (US) & M. A. Trabert (US)	Fraser & Rosewall 6-2 1-6 6-1 4-6 6-3	
1956	L. A. Hoad (AUS) & K. R. Rosewall (AUS) R. N. Howe (AUS) & A. Larsen (US)	Hoad & Rosewall 4-6 6-2 7-5 6-3	L. A. Hoad (AUS) & K. R. Rosewall (AUS) 7-5 6-2 6-1
	A. J. Cooper (AUS) & N. A. Fraser (AUS) N. Pietrangeli (IT) & O. Sirola (IT)	Pietrangeli & Sirola 6-4 6-4 8-6	
1957	N. A. Fraser (AUS) & L. A. Hoad (AUS) N. Pietrangeli (IT) & O. Sirola (IT)	Fraser & Hoad 14-12 1-6 8-6 6-3	G. Mulloy (US) & J. E. Patty (US) 8-10 6-4 6-4 6-4
	R. Becker & R. N. Howe (AUS) G. Mulloy (US) & J. E. Patty (US)	Mulloy & Patty 9-7 7-5 6-3	
1958	S. Davidson (SWE) & U. Schmidt (SWE) N. Pietrangeli (IT) & O. Sirola (IT)	Davidson & Schmidt 8-6 3-6 6-3 7-5	S. Davidson (SWE) & U. Schmidt (SWE) 6-4 6-4 8-6
	A. J. Cooper (AUS) & N. A. Fraser (AUS) B. MacKay (US) & M. G. Rose (AUS)	Cooper & Fraser 3-6 8-6 7-5 7-5	
1959	R. G. Laver (AUS) & R. Mark (AUS) N. Pietrangeli (IT) & O. Sirola (IT)	Laver & Mark 6-4 6-4 6-3	R. S. Emerson (AUS) & N. A. Fraser (AUS) 8-6 6-3 14-16 9-7
	R. S. Emerson (AUS) & N. A. Fraser (AUS) L. Legensein (Stateless) & T. Ulrich (DEN)	Emerson & Fraser 6-3 8-6 6-4	
1960	R. G. Laver (AUS) & R. Mark (AUS) R. H. Osuna (MEX) & R. D. Ralston (US)	Osuna & Ralston 4-6 10-8 15-13 4-6 11-9	R. H. Osuna (MEX) & R. D. Ralston (US) 7-5 6-3 10-8
	M. G. Davies & R. K. Wilson R. A. J. Hewitt (AUS) & M. F. Mulligan (AUS)	Davies & Wilson 3-6 6-3 6-2 6-4	
1961	R. A. J. Hewitt (AUS) & F. S. Stolle (AUS) R. G. Laver (AUS) & R. Mark (AUS)	Hewitt & Stolle 4-6 10-8 6-3 6-4	R. S. Emerson (AUS) & N. A. Fraser (AUS) 6-4 6-8 6-4 6-8 8-6
	R. S. Emerson (AUS) & N. A. Fraser (AUS) K. N. Fletcher (AUS) & J. D. Newcombe (AUS)	Emerson & Fraser 10-8 11-9 6-1	

1962

Semi-finals		Final
R. S. Emerson (AUS) & N. A. Fraser (AUS) B. Jovanovic (YU) & N. Pilic (YU)	Jovanovic & Pilic 4–6 6–3 6–4 6–4	R. A. J. Hewitt (AUS) & F. S. Stolle (AUS) 6–2 5–7 6–2 6–4
J. G. Fraser (AUS) & R. G. Laver (AUS) R. A. J. Hewitt (AUS) & F. S. Stolle (AUS)	Hewitt & Stolle 8–6 5–7 7–5 6–2	

1963

Semi-finals		Final
G. L. Forbes (SA) & A. A. Segal (SA) R. H. Osuna (MEX) & A. Palafox (MEX)	Osuna & Palafox 6–3 5–7 6–4 6–4	R. H. Osuna (MEX) & A. Palafox (MEX) 4–6 6–2 6–2 6–2
J. C. Barclay (F) & P. Darmon (F) R. S. Emerson (AUS) & M. Santana (SP)	Barclay & Darmon 6–2 7–5 3–6 6–3	

1964

Semi-finals		Final
I. S. Crookenden (NZ) & L. A. Gerard (NZ) R. S. Emerson (AUS) & K. N. Fletcher (AUS)	Emerson & Fletcher 14–12 6–2 6–1	R. A. J. Hewitt (AUS) & F. S. Stolle (AUS) 7–5 11–9 6–4
R. A. J. Hewitt (AUS) & F. S. Stolle (AUS) R. H. Osuna (MEX) & A. Palafox (MEX)	Hewitt & Stolle 6–2 6–2 6–3	

1965

Semi-finals		Final
K. N. Fletcher (AUS) & R. A. J. Hewitt (AUS) C. E. Graebner (US) & M. C. Riessen (US)	Fletcher & Hewitt 7–5 6–4 6–4	J. D. Newcombe (AUS) & A. D. Roche (AUS) 7–5 6–3 6–4
J. D. Newcombe (AUS) & A. D. Roche (AUS) R. D. Ralston (US) & H. Richardson (US)	Newcombe & Roche 5–7 14–12 6–8 7–5 6–4	

1966

Semi-finals		Final
W. W. Bowrey (AUS) & O. K. Davidson (AUS) M. Cox & A. R. Mills	Bowrey & Davidson 6–2 6–4 9–7	K. N. Fletcher (AUS) & J. D. Newcombe (AUS) 6–3 6–4 3–6 6–3
K. N. Fletcher (AUS) & J. D. Newcombe (AUS) C. E. Graebner (US) & M. C. Riessen (US)	Fletcher & Newcombe 6–3 7–5 6–1	

1967

Semi-finals		Final
P. W. Curtis & G. R. Stilwell R. S. Emerson (AUS) & K. N. Fletcher (AUS)	Emerson & Fletcher 6–4 8–6 4–6 5–7 9–7	R. A. J. Hewitt (SA) & F. D. McMillan (SA) 6–2 6–3 6–4
W. W. Bowrey (AUS) & O. K. Davidson (AUS) R. A. J. Hewitt (SA)* & F. D. McMillan (SA)	Hewitt & McMillan 6–2 10–8 6–2	

* R. A. J. Hewitt adopted South African allegiance on residential qualification.

1968

Semi-finals		Final
R. S. Emerson (AUS) & R. G. Laver (AUS) J. D. Newcombe (AUS) & A. D. Roche (AUS)	Newcombe & Roche 6–3 8–6 2–6 7–5	J. D. Newcombe (AUS) & A. D. Roche (AUS) 3–6 8–6 5–7 14–12 6–3
R. A. J. Hewitt (SA) & F. D. McMillan (SA) K. R. Rosewall (AUS) & F. S. Stolle (AUS)	Rosewall & Stolle 6–2 6–3 6–4	

1969

Semi-finals		Final
R. A. J. Hewitt (SA) & F. D. McMillan (SA) J. D. Newcombe (AUS) & A. D. Roche (AUS)	Newcombe & Roche 3–6 6–3 14–12 6–2	J. D. Newcombe (AUS) & A. D. Roche (AUS) 7–5 11–9 6–3
R. S. Emerson (AUS) & R. G. Laver (AUS) T. S. Okker (NTH) & M. C. Riessen (US)	Okker & Riessen 6–3 3–6 6–3 6–4	

1970

Semi-finals		Final
R. A. J. Hewitt (SA) & F. D. McMillan (SA) J. D. Newcombe (AUS) & A. D. Roche (AUS)	Newcombe & Roche 7–5 8–6 5–7 5–7 6–4	J. D. Newcombe (AUS) & A. D. Roche (AUS) 10–8 6–3 6–1
I. Nastase (ROM) & I. Tiriac (ROM) K. R. Rosewall (AUS) & F. S. Stolle (AUS)	Rosewall & Stolle 6–4 3–6 10–8 0–6 6–3	

1971

Semi-finals		Final
J. G. Alexander (AUS) & P. C. Dent (AUS) R. S. Emerson (AUS) & R. G. Laver (AUS)	Emerson & Laver 6–4 3–6 6–3 6–4	R. S. Emerson (AUS) & R. G. Laver (AUS) 4–6 9–7 6–8 6–4 6–4
A. R. Ashe (US) & R. D. Ralston (US) C. E. Graebner (US) & T. Koch (BRA)	Ashe & Ralston 8–9* 6–3 8–6 6–4	

* Tie break

1972

Semi-finals		Final
J. R. Cooper (AUS) & N. A. Fraser (AUS) R. A. J. Hewitt (SA) & F. D. McMillan (SA)	Hewitt & McMillan 8–6 4–6 9–8 6–2	R. A. J. Hewitt (SA) & F. D. McMillan (SA) 6–2 6–2 9–7
P. Cornejo (Chile) & J. Fillol (Chile) S. R. Smith (US) & E. J. van Dillen (US)	Smith & van Dillen 9–7 6–1 6–4	

1973

Pairs	Semi-final	Final
J. S. Connors (US) & I. Nastase (ROM) J. Fassbender (G) & K. Meiler (G)	Connors & Nastase 9–7 3–6 6–4 6–3	J. S. Connors (US) & I. Nastase (ROM) 3–6 6–3 6–4 8–9 6–1
J. R. Cooper (AUS) & N. A. Fraser (AUS) D. A. Lloyd & J. G. Paish	Cooper & Fraser 3–6 6–3 6–2 6–4	

1974

Pairs	Semi-final	Final
J. S. Connors (US) & I. Nastase (ROM) J. D. Newcombe (AUS) & A. D. Roche (AUS)	Newcombe & Roche 3–6 4–6 6–3 6–2 6–4	J. D. Newcombe (AUS) & A. D. Roche (AUS) 8–6 6–4 6–4
E. C. Drysdale (SA) & T. S. Okker (NTH) R. C. Lutz (US) & S. R. Smith (US)	Lutz & Smith 3–6 6–1 7–5 9–7	

1975

Pairs	Semi-final	Final
J. Fassbender (G) & H. J. Pohmann (G) V. Gerulaitis (US) & A. Mayer (US)	Gerulaitis & Mayer 8–9 3–6 6–3 6–3 6–3	V. Gerulaitis (US) & A. Mayer (US) 7–5 8–6 6–4
R. D. Crealy (AUS) & N. Pilic (YU) C. Dowdeswell (RHOD) & A. J. Stone (AUS)	Dowdeswell & Stone 9–8 3–6 4–6 9–8 6–3	

1976

Pairs	Semi-final	Final
B. E. Gottfried (US) & R. Ramirez (MEX) A. Amritraj (IN) & V. Amritraj (IN)	Gottfried & Ramirez 6–3 7–5 8–6	B. E. Gottfried (US) & R. Ramirez (MEX) 3–6 6–3 8–6 2–6 7–5
R. L. Case (AUS) & G. Masters (AUS) R. C. Lutz (US) & S. R. Smith (US)	Case & Masters 6–4 6–3 6–4	

WOMEN'S DOUBLES

A women's doubles event was first staged in 1899, though without the status of a championship event. It was abandoned after 1907. It's revival in 1913 was as one of the five 'World Championships on Grass'.

1899

Pairs	Semi-final	Final
Miss E. J. Bromfield & Mrs Kirby Mrs G. W. Hillyard & Miss B. Steedman	Mrs Hillyard & Miss Steedman 6–1 6–0	Mrs G. W. Hillyard & Miss B. Steedman 6–4 2–6 6–4
Miss L. Austin & Miss C. Cooper Mrs N. Durlacher & Mrs W. H. Pickering	Mrs Durlacher & Mrs Pickering 2–6 6–3 6–3	

1900

Pairs	Semi-final	Final
Mrs G. Greville & Miss B. Tulloch Mrs W. H. Pickering & Miss M. E. Robb	Mrs Pickering & Miss Robb 6–2 6–3	Mrs W. H. Pickering & Miss M. E. Robb 2–6 6–4 6–4
Miss E. J. Bromfield & Miss D. K. Douglass Mrs G. W. Hillyard & Miss L. Martin	Mrs Hillyard & Miss Martin 4–6 6–4 7–5	

1901

Pairs	Semi-final	Final
Miss Adams & Mrs W. H. Pickering Mrs G. E. Evered & Miss E. M. Stawell-Brown	Miss Adams & Mrs Pickering 6–3 6–2	Mrs G. W. Hillyard & Mrs A. Sterry 6–3 6–0
Mrs G. W. Hillyard & Mrs A. Sterry Miss T. Lowther & Miss M. E. Robb	Mrs Hillyard & Mrs Sterry 5–7 6–3 6–3	

1902

Pairs	Semi-final	Final
Mrs G. W. Hillyard & Miss B. Steedman Miss A. M. Morton & Mrs A. Sterry	Miss Morton & Mrs Sterry 7–5 6–3	Miss A. M. Morton & Mrs A. Sterry w.o.
Mrs G. Greville & Miss E. W. Thomson Miss H. Lane & Miss C. M. Wilson	Miss Lane & Miss Wilson 4–6 7–5 10–8	

1903

Pairs	Semi-final	Final
Miss E. J. Bromfield & Miss A. M. Morton Miss H. Lane & Miss C. M. Wilson	Miss Lane & Miss Wilson 6–1 6–8 6–3	Miss D. K. Douglass & Mrs W. H. Pickering 6–2 6–1
Miss D. K. Douglass & Mrs W. H. Pickering Miss A. N. G. Greene & Miss E. R. Morgan	Miss Douglass & Mrs Pickering 6–1 1–6 6–3	

1904

Pairs	Semi-final	Final
Miss A. Farrington & Miss M. B. Squire Miss W. A. Longhurst & Miss E. W. Thomson	Miss Longhurst & Miss Thomson 6–0 6–2	Miss W. A. Longhurst & Miss E. W. Thomson 6–4 3–6 7–5
Miss D. K. Douglass & Mrs A. Sterry Mrs G. Greville & Mrs R. J. Winch	Miss Douglass & Mrs Sterry 6–2 6–4	

1905

Pairs	Semi-final	Final
Miss D. P. Boothby & Miss E. M. Stawell-Brown Miss A. M. Morton & Miss M. Sutton (US)	Miss Morton & Miss Sutton 6–4 6–1	Miss W. A. Longhurst & Miss E. W. Thomson 6–3 6–3
Miss H. Lane & Miss C. M. Wilson Miss W. A. Longhurst & Miss E. W. Thomson	Miss Longhurst & Miss Thomson 6–3 9–7	

1906

Pairs	Semi-final	Final
Mrs G. W. Hillyard & Miss M. Sutton (US) Miss W. A. Longhurst & Miss E. W. Thomson	Mrs Hillyard & Miss Sutton 3–6 6–2 6–4	Mrs G. W. Hillyard & Miss M. Sutton (US) 10–8 6–4
Miss M. E. Brown & Miss V. M. Pinckney Miss A. M. Morton & Mrs A. Sterry	Miss Morton & Mrs Sterry 6–4 6–3	

1907

Pairs	Semi-final	Final
Miss M. Coles & Miss W. M. Slocock Mrs R. Lambert Chambers & Miss C. M. Wilson	Mrs Lambert Chambers & Miss Wilson w.o.	Mrs R. Lambert Chambers & Miss C. M. Wilson 7–9 6–3 6–2
Miss D. P. Boothby & Miss C. H. E. Meyer Miss A. M. Morton & Mrs A. Sterry	Miss Morton & Mrs Sterry 6–4 3–6 6–4	

Full Championship Event

1913

Pairs	Semi-final	Final
Mrs Armstrong & Miss O. B. Manser Mrs A. Sterry & Mrs R. Lambert Chambers	Mrs Sterry & Mrs Lambert Chambers 6–3 2–6 6–3	Mrs R. J. McNair & Miss D. P. Boothby 4–6 2–4 retired
Mrs D. R. Larcombe & Mrs E. G. Parton Mrs R. J. McNair & Miss D. P. Boothby	Mrs McNair & Miss Boothby 6–3 6–4	

1914

Mrs D. R. Larcombe & Mrs G. Hannam
Miss V. Pinckney & Mlle M. Broquedis (F)
Mrs Larcombe & Mrs Hannam
6-2 6-0

Mrs R. Lambert Chambers & Mrs A. Sterry
Miss A. M. Morton & Miss E. Ryan (US)
Miss Morton & Miss Ryan
6-4 6-1

Miss A. M. Morton &
Miss E. Ryan (US)
6-1 6-3

1915-18 not held

1919

Mlle S. Lenglen (F) & Miss E. Ryan (US)
Mrs R. J. McNair & Mrs E. G. Parton
Mlle Lenglen & Miss Ryan
6-2 6-1

Mrs A. Hall & Miss E. D. Holman
Mrs R. Lambert Chambers & Mrs D. R. Larcombe
Mrs Lambert Chambers & Mrs Larcombe
6-1 6-2

Mlle S. Lenglen (F) &
Miss E. Ryan (US)
4-6 7-5 6-3

1920

Mrs Armstrong & Miss O. B. Manser
Mlle S. Lenglen (F) & Miss E. Ryan (US)
Mlle Lenglen & Miss Ryan
6-1 6-0

Mrs A. E. Beamish & Miss H. Hogarth
Mrs R. Lambert Chambers & Mrs D. R. Larcombe
Mrs Lambert Chambers & Mrs Larcombe
6-1 6-1

Mlle S. Lenglen (F) &
Miss E. Ryan (US)
6-4 6-0

1921

Mrs A. E. Beamish & Mrs G. Peacock (SA)
Mrs Craddock & Miss M. McKane
Mrs Beamish & Mrs Peacock
6-2 6-1

Miss P. L. Howkins & Miss D. C. Shepherd
Mlle S. Lenglen (F) & Miss E. Ryan (US)
Mlle Lenglen & Miss Ryan
6-2 6-0

Mlle S. Lenglen (F) &
Miss E. Ryan (US)
6-1 6-2

1922

Mrs A. C. Geen & Mrs R. J. McNair
Mlle S. Lenglen (F) & Miss E. Ryan (US)
Mlle Lenglen & Miss Ryan
6-0 6-1

Miss E. D. Holman & Mrs J. L. Leisk
Miss K. McKane & Mrs A. D. Stocks
Miss McKane & Mrs Stocks w.o.

Mlle S. Lenglen (F) &
Miss E. Ryan (US)
6-0 6-4

1923

Mrs R. Lambert Chambers & Miss K. McKane
Mlle S. Lenglen (F) & Miss E. Ryan (US)
Mlle Lenglen & Miss Ryan
6-1 6-2

Miss J. Austin & Miss E. L. Colyer
Miss E. F. Rose & Mrs J. S. Youle
Miss Austin & Miss Colyer
8-6 6-4

Mlle S. Lenglen (F) &
Miss E. Ryan (US)
6-3 6-1

1924

Mrs B. C. Covell & Miss K. McKane
Mrs R. Lambert Chambers &
Mrs D. C. Shepherd-Barron
Mrs Covell & Miss McKane
6-4 3-6 6-4

Miss E. Goss (US) & Mrs M. Jessup (US)
Mrs G. Wightman (US) & Miss H. N. Wills (US)
Mrs Wightman & Miss Wills
8-6 6-4

Mrs G. Wightman (US) &
Miss H. N. Wills (US)
6-4 6-4

1925

Mrs A. E. Beamish & Miss E. R. Clarke
Mlle S. Lenglen (F) & Miss E. Ryan (US)
Mlle Lenglen & Miss Ryan
6-0 6-2

Mrs A. V. Bridge & Mrs C. G. McIlquham
Mrs R. Lambert Chambers & Miss E. H. Harvey
Mrs Bridge & Mrs McIlquham
6-1 2-6 6-4

Mlle S. Lenglen (F) &
Miss E. Ryan (US)
6-2 6-2

1926

Mrs A. E. Beamish & Miss E. R. Clarke
Miss M. K. Browne (US) & Miss E. Ryan (US)
Miss Browne & Miss Ryan
6-2 6-3

Mrs L. A. Godfree & Miss E. L. Colyer
Mrs Jackson Fielden & Miss N. Welch
Mrs Godfree & Miss Colyer
6-2 6-3

Miss M. K. Browne (US) &
Miss E. Ryan (US)
6-1 6-1

1927

Miss E. H. Harvey & Mrs C. G. McIlquham
Miss E. L. Heine (SA) & Mrs G. Peacock (SA)
Miss Heine & Mrs Peacock
5-7 6-2 6-1

Mrs L. A. Godfree & Miss B. Nuthall
Miss H. N. Wills (US) & Miss E. Ryan (US)
Miss Wills & Miss Ryan
6-2 6-2

Miss H. N. Wills (US) &
Miss E. Ryan (US)
6-3 6-2

1928

Miss D. Akhurst (AUS) & Miss E. Boyd (AUS)
Miss E. Bennett & Miss E. H. Harvey
Miss Bennett & Miss Harvey
6-8 6-3 6-2

Mrs R. Lycett & Miss E. Ryan (US)
Mrs M. Watson & Miss P. Saunders
Mrs Watson & Miss Saunders
6-3 6-1

Mrs M. Watson &
Miss P. Saunders
6-2 6-3

Semi-finals	Final	Winners
1929		
Miss E. H. Harvey & Mrs C. G. McIlquham Mrs M. Watson & Mrs L. R. C. Michell	Mrs Watson & Mrs Michell 6–4 5–7 6–2	Mrs M. Watson & Mrs L. R. C. Michell 6–4 8–6
Mrs B. C. Covell & Mrs D. C. Shepherd-Barron Miss B. Nuthall & Miss E. Ryan (US)	Mrs Covell & Mrs Shepherd-Barron 6–4 3–6 9–7	
1930		
Miss E. Cross (US) & Miss S. Palfrey (US) Miss B. Feltham & Miss M. Heeley	Miss Cross & Miss Palfrey 8–6 6–2	Mrs F. S. Moody (US) & Miss E. Ryan (US) 6–2 9–7
Mrs F. S. Moody (US) & Miss E. Ryan (US) Mlle J. Sigart (B) & Mme S. Henrotin (F)	Mrs Moody & Miss Ryan 6–2 6–0	
1931		
Mlle D. Metaxa (F) & Mlle J. Sigart (B) Mrs F. Whittingstall & Miss B. Nuthall	Mlle Metaxa & Mlle Sigart 4–6 8–6 6–4	Mrs D. C. Shepherd-Barron & Miss P. E. Mudford 3–6 6–3 6–4
Mrs L. A. Godfree & Miss D. E. Round Mrs D. C. Shepherd-Barron & Miss P. E. Mudford	Mrs Shepherd-Barron & Miss Mudford 7–5 3–6 6–3	
1932		
Miss H. H. Jacobs (US) & Miss E. Ryan (US) Mlle L. Payot (SWI) & Miss M. A. Thomas	Miss Jacobs & Miss Ryan 6–1 6–2	Mlle D. Metaxa (F) & Mlle J. Sigart (B) 6–4 6–3
Mrs P. Holcroft-Watson & Miss E. H. Harvey Mlle D. Metaxa (F) & Mlle J. Sigart (B)	Mlle D. Metaxa & Mlle Sigart 7–5 6–2	
1933		
Mrs L. A. Godfree & Mrs L. R. C. Michell Miss F. James & Miss A. M. Yorke	Miss James & Miss Yorke 5–7 6–0 6–4	Mme R. Mathieu (F) & Miss E. Ryan (US) 6–2 9–11 6–4
Mme R. Mathieu (F) & Miss E. Ryan (US) Mrs J. B. Pittman & Miss J. C. Ridley	Mme Mathieu & Miss Ryan 6–1 4–6 6–4	
1934		
Mme R. Mathieu (F) & Miss E. Ryan (US) Mlle L. Payot (SWI) & Miss M. A. Thomas	Mme Mathieu & Miss Ryan 7–5 6–0	Mme R. Mathieu (F) & Miss E. Ryan (US) 6–3 6–3
Mrs D. B. Andrus (US) & Mme S. Henrotin (F) Mrs L. A. Godfree & Miss M. C. Scriven	Mrs Andrus & Mme Henrotin 6–3 12–10	
1935		
Mme R. Mathieu (F) & Fru S. Sperling (DEN) Mme J. de Meulemeester (B) & Mrs P. D. Howard (F)	Mme Mathieu & Fru Sperling 6–4 8–6	Miss F. James & Miss K. E. Stammers 6–1 6–4
Mrs R. E. Haylock & Mrs J. S. Kirk Miss F. James & Miss K. E. Stammers	Miss James & Miss Stammers 6–3 6–0	
1936		
Mrs M. Fabyan (US) & Miss H. H. Jacobs (US) Miss J. Ingram & Mrs M. R. King	Mrs Fabyan & Miss Jacobs 6–4 6–3	Miss F. James & Miss K. E. Stammers 6–2 6–1
Mrs D. B. Andrus (US) & Mme S. Henrotin (F) Miss F. James & Miss K. E. Stammers	Miss James & Miss Stammers 6–0 6–4	
1937		
Miss E. M. Dearman & Miss J. Ingram Mme R. Mathieu (F) & Miss A. M. Yorke	Mme Mathieu & Miss Yorke 7–5 6–3	Mme R. Mathieu (F) & Miss A. M. Yorke 6–3 6–3
Mrs D. B. Andrus (US) & Mme S. Henrotin (F) Mrs M. R. King & Mrs J. B. Pittman	Mrs King & Mrs Pittman 6–3 6–4	
1938		
Mrs E. L. Heine Miller (SA) & Miss M. Morphew (SA) Miss A. Marble (US) & Mrs M. Fabyan (US)	Miss Marble & Mrs Fabyan 7–5 6–4	Miss A. Marble (US) & Mrs M. Fabyan (US) 6–2 6–3
Mrs D. B. Andrus (US) & Mme S. Henrotin (F) Mme R. Mathieu (F) & Miss A. M. Yorke	Mme Mathieu & Miss Yorke 3–6 6–3 6–4	
1939		
Mrs S. H. Hammersley & Miss K. E. Stammers Miss A. Marble (US) & Mrs M. Fabyan (US)	Miss Marble & Mrs Fabyan 8–6 6–3	Miss A. Marble (US) & Mrs M. Fabyan (US) 6–1 6–0
Miss H. H. Jacobs (US) & Miss A. M. Yorke Miss J. Nicoll & Miss B. Nuthall	Miss Jacobs & Miss Yorke 5–7 6–4 11–9	

1940–5 not held

Year	Semi-finalists	Semi-final results	Final
1946	Miss P. M. Betz (US) & Miss D. J. Hart (US) Mrs E. W. A. Bostock & Mrs M. Menzies	Miss Betz & Miss Hart 3–6 6–3 6–4	Miss A. L. Brough (US) & Miss M. E. Osborne (US) 6–3 2–6 6–3
	Miss A. L. Brough (US) & Miss M. E. Osborne (US) Mrs P. C. Todd (US) & Miss D. Bundy (US)	Miss Brough & Miss Osborne 6–4 6–2	
1947	Mrs E. W. A. Bostock & Mrs B. E. Hilton Miss D. J. Hart (US) & Mrs P. C. Todd (US)	Miss Hart & Mrs Todd 6–0 6–1	Miss D. J. Hart (US) & Mrs P. C. Todd (US) 3–6 6–4 7–5
	Mrs N. W. Blair & Mrs M. Menzies Miss A. L. Brough (US) & Miss M. E. Osborne (US)	Miss Brough & Miss Osborne 6–2 6–1	
1948	Miss A. L. Brough (US) & Mrs W. du Pont (US) Mrs H. P. Rihbany (US) & Miss B. Scofield (US)	Miss Brough & Mrs du Pont 7–5 6–0	Miss A. L. Brough (US) & Mrs W. du Pont (US) 6–3 3–6 6–3
	Mrs N. W. Blair & Mrs E. W. A. Bostock Miss D. J. Hart (US) & Mrs P. C. Todd (US)	Miss Hart & Mrs Todd 6–4 8–6	
1949	Miss A. L. Brough (US) & Mrs W. du Pont (US) Miss J. Gannon & Mrs B. E. Hilton	Miss Brough & Mrs du Pont 6–2 6–2	Miss A. L. Brough (US) & Mrs W. du Pont (US) 8–6 7–5
	Miss S. J. Fry (US) & Mrs H. P. Rihbany (US) Miss G. Moran (US) & Mrs P. C. Todd (US)	Miss Moran & Mrs Todd 6–0 7–5	
1950	Miss S. J. Fry (US) & Miss D. J. Hart (US) Mrs T. D. Long (AUS) & Mrs A. J. Mottram	Miss Fry & Miss Hart 6–0 6–2	Miss A. L. Brough (US) & Mrs W. du Pont (US) 6–4 5–7 6–1
	Miss A. L. Brough (US) & Mrs W. du Pont (US) Mrs M. Buck (US) & Miss N. Chaffee (US)	Miss Brough & Mrs du Pont 6–1 6–3	
1951	Miss A. L. Brough (US) & Mrs W. du Pont (US) Mrs G. Davidson (US) & Miss B. Rosenquest (US)	Miss Brough & Mrs du Pont 6–1 6–3	Miss S. J. Fry (US) & Miss D. J. Hart (US) 6–3 13–11
	Miss B. Baker (US) & Miss N. Chaffee (US) Miss S. J. Fry (US) & Miss D. J. Hart (US)	Miss Fry & Miss Hart 6–0 6–2	
1952	Miss A. L. Brough (US) & Miss M. Connolly (US) Mrs T. D. Long (AUS) & Mrs P. C. Todd (US)	Miss Brough & Miss Connolly 5–7 6–1 6–4	Miss S. J. Fry (US) & Miss D. J. Hart (US) 8–6 6–3
	Miss S. J. Fry (US) & Miss D. J. Hart (US) Miss J. S. V. Partridge & Mrs J. Rinkel-Quertier	Miss Fry & Miss Hart 7–5 6–3	
1953	Miss H. Fletcher & Mrs J. Rinkel-Quertier Miss S. J. Fry (US) & Miss D. J. Hart (US)	Miss Fry & Miss Hart 6–0 6–0	Miss S. J. Fry (US) & Miss D. J. Hart (US) 6–0 6–0
	Miss M. Connolly (US) & Miss J. Sampson (US) Miss A. Mortimer & Miss J. A. Shilcock	Miss Connolly & Miss Sampson 6–2 6–3	
1954	Miss S. J. Fry (US) & Miss D. J. Hart (US) Miss A. Mortimer & Miss J. A. Shilcock	Miss Fry & Miss Hart 6–2 6–1	Miss A. L. Brough (US) & Mrs W. du Pont (US) 4–6 9–7 6–3
	Mrs W. Brewer (BERM) & Miss K. Hubble (US) Miss A. L. Brough (US) & Mrs W. du Pont (US)	Miss Brough & Mrs du Pont 6–1 6–1	
1955	Miss S. J. Bloomer & Miss P. E. Ward Mrs J. Fleitz (US) & Miss D. R. Hard (US)	Miss Bloomer & Miss Ward 6–3 9–7	Miss A. Mortimer & Miss J. A. Shilcock 7–5 6–1
	Miss A. Mortimer & Miss J. A. Shilcock Miss F. Muller (AUS) & Mrs L. A. Hoad (AUS)	Miss Mortimer & Miss Shilcock 6–2 6–1	
1956	Miss A. Mortimer & Miss J. A. Shilcock Miss F. Muller (AUS) & Miss D. G. Seeney (AUS)	Miss Muller & Miss Seeney 6–4 6–2	Miss A. Buxton & Miss A. Gibson (US) 6–1 8–6
	Miss A. L. Brough (US) & Miss S. J. Fry (US) Miss A. Buxton & Miss A. Gibson (US)	Miss Buxton & Miss Gibson 7–5 6–4	

Year	Semi-finalists	Semi-final result	Final result
1957	Mrs K. Hawton (AUS) & Mrs T. D. Long (AUS) Miss Y. Ramirez (MEX) & Miss R. M. Reyes (MEX)	Mrs Hawton & Mrs Long 7–5 6–2	Miss A. Gibson (US) & Miss D. R. Hard (US) 6–1 6–2
	Miss A. Gibson (US) & Miss D. R. Hard (US) Miss S. Reynolds (SA) & Miss R. Schuurman (SA)	Miss Gibson & Miss Hard 6–2 6–2	
1958	Mrs W. du Pont (US) & Miss M. Varner (US) Miss Y. Ramirez (MEX) & Miss R. M. Reyes (MEX)	Mrs du Pont & Miss Varner 6–2 6–3	Miss M. E. Bueno (BRA) & Miss A. Gibson (US) 6–3 7–5
	Miss M. E. Bueno (BRA) & Miss A. Gibson (US) Mrs K. Hawton (AUS) & Mrs T. D. Long (AUS)	Miss Bueno & Miss Gibson 6–3 6–2	
1959	Miss J. Arth (US) & Miss D. R. Hard (US) Miss S. Reynolds (SA) & Miss R. Schuurman (SA)	Miss Arth & Miss Hard 6–0 6–2	Miss J. Arth (US) & Miss D. R. Hard (US) 2–6 6–2 6–3
	Mrs J. Fleitz (US) & Miss C. C. Truman Miss Y. Ramirez (MEX) & Miss R. M. Reyes (MEX)	Mrs Fleitz & Miss Truman 8–6 6–1	
1960	Mrs K. Hawton (AUS) & Miss J. Lehane (AUS) Miss S. Reynolds (SA) & Miss R. Schuurman (SA)	Miss Reynolds & Miss Schuurman 7–5 6–1	Miss M. E. Bueno (BRA) & Miss D. R. Hard (US) 6–4 6–0
	Miss M. E. Bueno (BRA) & Miss D. R. Hard (US) Miss K. Hantze (US) & Miss J. S. Hopps (US)	Miss Bueno & Miss Hard 3–6 6–1 6–4	
1961	Miss M. L. Hunt (SA) & Miss L. M. Hutchings (SA) Miss J. Lehane (AUS) & Miss M. Smith (AUS)	Miss Lehane & Miss Smith 6–1 6–1	Miss K. Hantze (US) & Miss B. J. Moffitt (US) 6–3 6–4
	Miss K. Hantze (US) & Miss B. J. Moffitt (US) Miss S. M. Moore (US) & Miss L. Turner (AUS)	Miss Hantze & Miss Moffitt 6–3 6–0	
1962	Miss M. E. Bueno (BRA) & Miss D. R. Hard (US) Mrs L. E. G. Price (SA) & Miss R. Schuurman (SA)	Mrs Price & Miss Schuurman 6–3 6–3	Miss B. J. Moffitt (US) & Mrs J. R. Susman (US) 5–7 6–3 7–5
	Miss J. Bricka (US) & Miss M. Smith (AUS) Miss B. J. Moffitt (US) & Mrs J. R. Susman (US)	Miss Moffitt & Mrs Susman 6–3 6–4	
1963	Miss R. A. Ebbern (AUS) & Miss M. Smith (AUS) Mrs P. F. Jones & Miss R. Schuurman (SA)	Miss Ebbern & Miss Smith 7–5 3–6 6–3	Miss M. E. Bueno (BRA) & Miss D. R. Hard (US) 8–6 9–7
	Miss M. E. Bueno (BRA) & Miss D. R. Hard (US) Miss A. Dmitrieva (USSR) & Miss J. A. M. Tegart (AUS)	Miss Bueno & Miss Hard 6–4 9–7	
1964	Mrs P. Haygarth (SA) & Mrs P. F. Jones Miss M. Smith (AUS) & Miss L. R. Turner (AUS)	Miss Smith & Miss Turner 6–3 6–2	Miss M. Smith (AUS) & Miss L. R. Turner (AUS) 7–5 6–2
	Miss M. E. Bueno (BRA) & Miss R. A. Ebbern (AUS) Miss B. J. Moffitt (US) & Mrs J. R. Susman (US)	Miss Moffitt & Miss Susman 4–6 6–2 6–3	

Year / Semi-finalists	Semi-final	Final
1965		
Frl E. Buding (G) & Frl H. Schultze (G) Mlle F. Durr (F) & Mlle J. Lieffrig (F)	Mlle Durr & Mlle Lieffrig 6–4 7–5	Miss M. E. Bueno (BRA) & Miss B. J. Moffitt (US) 6–2 7–5
Miss M. E. Bueno (BRA) & Miss B. J. Moffitt (US) Mrs C. E. Graebner (US) & Miss N. Richey (US)	Miss Bueno & Miss Moffitt 6–4 6–2	
1966		
Mrs P. F. Jones & Miss S. V. Wade Miss M. Smith (AUS) & Miss J. A. M. Tegart (AUS)	Miss Smith & Miss Tegart 10–8 6–4	Miss M. E. Bueno (BRA) & Miss N. Richey (US) 6–3 4–6 6–4
Miss M. E. Bueno (BRA) & Miss N. Richey (US) Miss K. M. Krantzcke (AUS) & Miss K. A. Melville (AUS)	Miss Bueno & Miss Richey 6–2 6–3	
1967		
Miss M. E. Bueno (BRA) & Miss N. Richey (US) Miss J. A. M. Tegart (AUS) & Miss L. R. Turner (AUS)	Miss Bueno & Miss Richey 4–6 6–4 6–4	Miss R. Casals (US) & Mrs L. W. King (US) 9–11 6–4 6–2
Miss R. Casals (US) & Mrs L. W. King (US) Mrs P. F. Jones & Miss S. V. Wade	Miss Casals & Mrs King 6–1 6–4	
1968		
Mrs W. W. Bowrey (AUS) & Miss J. A. M. Tegart (AUS) Miss R. Casals (US) & Mrs L. W. King (US)	Miss Casals & Mrs King 1–6 6–1 10–8	Miss R. Casals (US) & Mrs L. W. King (US) 3–6 6–4 7–5
Mlle F. Durr (F) & Mrs P. F. Jones Mrs J. A. G. Lloyd & Miss F. V. MacLennan	Mlle Durr & Mrs Jones 6–1 6–0	
1969		
Mrs B. M. Court (AUS) & Miss J. A. M. Tegart (AUS) Mrs P. W. Curtis (US) & Miss V. J. Ziegenfuss (US)	Mrs Court & Miss Tegart 6–4 6–4	Mrs B. M. Court (AUS) & Miss J. A. M. Tegart (AUS) 9–7 6–2
Miss P. S. A. Hogan (US) & Miss M. Michel (US) Miss K. M. Krantzcke (AUS) & Miss K. A. Melville (AUS)	Miss Hogan & Miss Michel 4–6 6–2 7–5	
1970		
Miss R. Casals (US) & Mrs L. W. King (US) Miss K. M. Krantzcke (AUS) & Miss K. A. Melville (AUS)	Miss Casals & Mrs King 6–2 8–6	Miss R. Casals (US) & Mrs L. W. King (US) 6–2 6–3
Mlle F. Durr (F) & Miss S. V. Wade Miss H. F. Gourlay (AUS) & Miss P. M. Walkden (SA)	Mlle Durr & Miss Wade 6–4 0–6 6–3	
1971		
Miss R. Casals (US) & Mrs L. W. King (US) Mme J. B. Chanfreau (F) & Mlle F. Durr (F)	Miss Casals & Mrs King 4–6 6–4 6–4	Miss R. Casals (US) & Mrs L. W. King (US) 6–3 6–2
Mrs B. M. Court (AUS) & Miss E. F. Goolagong (AUS) Mrs P. W. Curtis (US) & Miss V. J. Ziegenfuss (US)	Mrs Court & Miss Goolagong 6–2 6–4	
1972		
Mrs L. W. King (US) & Miss B. F. Stove (NTH) Miss W. M. Shaw & Mrs G. M. Williams	Mrs King & Miss Stove 7–5 3–6 6–3	Mrs L. W. King (US) & Miss B. F. Stove (NTH) 6–2 4–6 6–3
Miss R. Casals (US) & Miss S. V. Wade Mrs D. E. Dalton (AUS) & Mlle F. Durr (F)	Mrs Dalton & Mlle Durr 6–4 6–1	
1973		
Miss R. Casals (US) & Mrs L. W. King (US) Miss E. F. Goolagong (AUS) & Miss J. A. Young (AUS)	Miss Casals & Mrs King 7–5 7–5	Miss R. Casals (US) & Mrs L. W. King (US) 6–1 4–6 7–5
Miss F. Binicelli (Uruguay) & Miss I. Fernandez (COL) Mlle F. Durr (F) & Miss B. F. Stove (NTH)	Mlle Durr & Miss Stove 7–5 8–6	

1974

Miss J. Anthony (US) & Miss M. Schallau (US) Miss H. F. Gourlay (AUS) & Miss K. M. Krantzcke (AUS)	Miss Gourlay & Miss Krantzcke 9-8* 6-2	Miss E. F. Goolagong (AUS) & Miss M. Michel (US) 2-6 6-4 6-3
Miss C. M. Evert (US) & Mrs O. Morozova (USSR) Miss E. F. Goolagong (AUS) & Miss M. Michel (US)	Miss Goolagong & Miss Michel 7-5 6-2	

* Tie break

1975

Mme J. B. Chanfreau (F) & Miss H. F. Gourlay (AUS) Miss A. K. Kiyomura (US) & Miss K. Sawamatsu (J)	Miss Kiyomura & Miss Sawamatsu 8-6 6-8 6-2	Miss A. K. Kiyomura (US) & Miss K. Sawamatsu (J) 7-5 1-6 7-5
Miss R. Casals (US) & Mrs L. W. King (US) Mlle F. Durr (F) & Miss B. F. Stove (NTH)	Mlle Durr & Miss Stove 2-6 8-6 6-2	

1976

Miss L. J. Charles & Miss S. Mappin Mrs L. W. King (US) & Miss B. Stove (NTH)	Mrs King & Miss Stove 6-4 6-3	Miss C. M. Evert (US) & Miss M. Navratilova (CZ) 6-1 3-6 7-5
Miss D. A. Boshoff (SA) & Miss I. S. Kloss (SA) Miss C. M. Evert (US) & Miss M. Navratilova (CZ)	Miss Evert & Miss Navratilova 8-6 8-6	

MIXED DOUBLES

A mixed doubles as a non-championship event was first staged in 1900. Unlike the women's doubles it had continuity until 1913 when it became one of the 'World Championships on Grass' events.

1900

Pairs	Semi-final	Final
C. H. L. Cazalet & Miss M. E. Robb H. A. Nisbet & Mrs W. H. Pickering	Nisbet & Mrs Pickering 7–5 6–8 6–3	H. A. Nisbet & Mrs W. H. Pickering 8–6 6–3
E. D. Black & Miss C. Cooper H. Roper Barrett & Miss E. J. Bromfield	Roper Barrett & Miss Bromfield 6–3 6–2	

1901

Pairs	Semi-final	Final
W. V. Eaves & Mrs N. Durlacher G. Greville & Mrs G. Greville	Eaves & Mrs Durlacher w.o.	H. L. Doherty & Mrs A. Sterry 6–2 6–3
H. L. Doherty & Mrs A. Sterry G. W. Hillyard & Mrs G. W. Hillyard	Doherty & Mrs Sterry 3–6 7–5 6–1	

1902

Pairs	Semi-final	Final
C. H. L. Cazalet & Miss M. E. Robb C. H. Martin & Miss D. K. Douglass	Cazalet & Miss Robb 6–2 6–1	H. L. Doherty & Mrs A. Sterry 6–4 6–3
H. L. Doherty & Mrs A. Sterry R. F. Doherty & Miss B. Steedman	Doherty & Mrs Sterry 0–1 (sets) retired	

1903

Pairs	Semi-final	Final
E. D. Robinson & Miss M. Stonham S. H. Smith & Miss E. W. Thomson	Smith & Miss Thomson 6–2 6–3	S. H. Smith & Miss E. W. Thomson 6–2 6–3
C. Hobart (US) & Miss E. J. Bromfield F. L. Riseley & Miss D. K. Douglass	Hobart & Miss Bromfield w.o.	

1904

Pairs	Semi-final	Final
H. N. Marrett & Miss H. Lane S. H. Smith & Miss E. W. Thomson	Smith & Miss Thomson 6–2 6–2	S. H. Smith & Miss E. W. Thomson 7–5 12–10
W. V. Eaves & Mrs R. J. Winch G. Greville & Mrs G. Greville	Eaves & Mrs Winch 6–4 2–6 6–4	

1905

Pairs	Semi-final	Final
S. H. Adams & Miss D. P. Boothby A. F. Wilding (NZ) & Miss E. W. Thomson	Wilding & Miss Thomson 6–0 6–0	A. W. Gore & Miss C. M. Wilson 8–6 6–4
R. F. Doherty & Miss G. S. Eastlake Smith A. W. Gore & Miss C. M. Wilson	Gore & Miss Wilson 6–3 4–6 6–3	

1906

Pairs	Semi-final	Final
A. W. Gore & Miss E. W. Thomson G. W. Hillyard & Miss M. Sutton (US)	Gore & Miss Thomson 6–3 3–6 8–6	A. F. Wilding (NZ) & Miss D. K. Douglass 4–6 6–2 6–3
R. F. Doherty & Miss G. S. Eastlake Smith A. F. Wilding (NZ) & Miss D. K. Douglass	Wilding & Miss Douglass 4–6 6–2 7–5	

1907

Pairs	Semi-final	Final
N. Durlacher & Miss A. M. Morton B. C. Wright (US) & Miss M. Sutton (US)	Wright & Miss Sutton w.o.	B. C. Wright (US) & Miss M. Sutton (US) 6–1 6–3
W. V. Eaves & Miss T. Lowther A. D. Prebble & Miss D. P. Boothby	Prebble & Miss Boothby 6–3 7–5	

1908

Pairs	Semi-final	Final
A. W. Gore & Mrs J. F. Luard H. Roper Barrett & Mrs A. Sterry	Roper Barrett & Mrs Sterry 5–7 6–4 6–3	A. F. Wilding (NZ) & Mrs R. Lambert Chambers 6–4 6–3
A. D. Prebble & Miss D. P. Boothby A. F. Wilding (NZ) & Mrs R. Lambert Chambers	Wilding & Mrs Lambert Chambers 6–1 6–0	

1909

Pairs	Semi-final	Final
A. D. Prebble & Miss D. P. Boothby J. B. Ward & Miss M. Coles	Prebble & Miss Boothby 6–1 7–5	H. Roper Barrett & Miss A. M. Morton 6–2 7–5
C. P. Dixon & Miss A. N. G. Greene H. Roper Barrett & Miss A. M. Morton	Roper Barrett & Miss Morton 11–9 6–3	

1910

S. N. Doust (AUS) & Mrs R. Lambert Chambers E. Gwynne Evans & Miss A. G. Ransome	Doust & Mrs Lambert Chambers 6–1 6–2	S. N. Doust (AUS) & Mrs R. Lambert Chambers 6–2 7–5
R. B. Powell (CAN) & Mrs A. Sterry H. Roper Barrett & Mrs E. S. Lamplough	Powell & Mrs Sterry 6–1 6–4	

1911

T. M. Mavrogordato & Mrs E. G. Parton R. B. Powell (CAN) & Mrs A. Sterry	Mavrogordato & Mrs Parton 7–5 6–1	T. M. Mavrogordato & Mrs E. G. Parton 6–2 6–4
S. N. Doust (AUS) & Mrs R. Lambert Chambers J. B. Ward & Miss M. Coles	Doust & Mrs Lambert Chambers 6–1 6–2	

1912

S. N. Doust (AUS) & Mrs G. W. Hillyard A. D. Prebble & Miss D. P. Boothby	Prebble & Miss Boothby 7–5 6–2	J. C. Parke & Mrs D. R. Larcombe 6–4 6–2
T. M. Mavrogordato & Mrs E. G. Parton J. C. Parke & Mrs D. R. Larcombe	Parke & Mrs Larcombe 8–6 6–2	

Full Championship Event

1913

Hope Crisp & Mrs C. O. Tuckey N. S. B. Kidson & Mrs O'Neill	Crisp & Mrs Tuckey 6–2 6–3	Hope Crisp & Mrs C. O. Tuckey 3–6 5–3 retired
T. M. Mavrogordato & Mrs E. G. Parton J. C. Parke & Mrs D. R. Larcombe	Parke & Mrs Larcombe 6–3 6–4	

1914

H, Aitken & Mrs G. Hannam A. F. Wilding (NZ) & Mlle M. Broquedis (F)	Wilding & Mlle Broquedis 6–3 4–6 6–3	J. C. Parke & Mrs D. R. Larcombe 4–6 6–4 6–2
Hope Crisp & Mrs C. O. Tuckey J. C. Parke & Mrs D. R. Larcombe	Parke & Mrs Larcombe 4–6 6–2 6–2	

1915–18 not held

1919

R. Lycett & Miss E. Ryan (US) R. V. Thomas (AUS) & Mrs D. R. Larcombe	Lycett & Miss Ryan 6–2 6–3	R. Lycett & Miss E. Ryan (US) 6–0 6–0
M. Decugis (F) & Miss L. Addison A. D. Prebble & Mrs R. Lambert Chambers	Prebble & Mrs Lambert Chambers 6–1 6–0	

1920

A. E. Beamish & Mrs A. E. Beamish G. L. Patterson (AUS) & Mlle S. Lenglen (F)	Patterson & Mlle Lenglen 6–1 6–4	G. L. Patterson (AUS) & Mlle S. Lenglen (F) 7–5 6–3
R. Lycett & Miss E. Ryan (US) B. I. C. Norton (SA) & Mrs D. R. Larcombe	Lycett & Miss Ryan 6–3 6–4	

1921

A. E. Beamish & Mrs D. R. Larcombe R. Lycett & Miss E. Ryan (US)	Lycett & Miss Ryan 6–4 6–1	R. Lycett & Miss E. Ryan (US) 6–3 6–1
M. Alonso (SP) & Mrs R. J. McNair M. Woosnam & Miss P. L. Howkins	Woosnam & Miss Howkins 6–1 6–4	

1922

J. B. Gilbert & Mrs R. J. McNair R. Lycett & Miss E. Ryan (US)	Lycett & Miss Ryan 6–2 6–1	P. O'Hara Wood (AUS) & Mlle S. Lenglen (F) 6–4 6–3
P. O'Hara Wood (AUS) & Mlle S. Lenglen (F) C. J. Tindell Green & Mrs J. S. Youle	O'Hara Wood & Mlle Lenglen 6–2 6–2	

1923

L. S. Deane (IN) & Mrs D. C. Shepherd-Barron V. Richards (US) & Mrs F. I. Mallory (US)	Deane & Mrs Shepherd-Barron 5–7 6–3 6–4	R. Lycett & Miss E. Ryan (US) 6–4 7–5
R. Lycett & Miss E. Ryan (US) J. Washer (B) & Mlle S. Lenglen (F)	Lycett & Miss Ryan 7–5 6–3	

Year	Semi-finals	Semi-final winners	Final
1924	L. A. Godfree & Mrs D. C. Shepherd-Barron M. Woosnam & Mrs B. C. Covell	Godfree & Mrs Shepherd-Barron 6–4 4–6 6–4	J. B. Gilbert & Miss K. McKane 6–3 3–6 6–3
	J. B. Gilbert & Miss K. McKane E. T. Lamb & Miss E. H. Harvey	Gilbert & Miss McKane 6–2 6–4	
1925	H. L. de Morpurgo (IT) & Miss E. Ryan (US) J. D. P. Wheatley & Mrs R. Lambert Chambers	de Morpurgo & Miss Ryan 9–7 6–4	J. Borotra (F) & Mlle S. Lenglen (F) 6–3 6–3
	J. Borotra (F) & Mlle S. Lenglen (F) R. Lycett & Mrs R. Lycett	Borotra & Mlle Lenglen 6–4 5–7 6–3	
1926	L. A. Godfree & Mrs L. A. Godfree V. Richards (US) & Miss E. Ryan (US)	Godfree & Mrs Godfree 7–5 6–4	L. A. Godfree & Mrs L. A. Godfree 6–3 6–4
	A. Berger & Mrs F. Strawson H. O. Kinsey (US) & Miss M. K. Browne (US)	Kinsey & Miss Browne 5–7 6–4 6–0	
1927	L. A. Godfree & Mrs L. A. Godfree D. M. Greig & Mrs M. Watson	Godfree & Mrs Godfree 6–3 6–4	F. T. Hunter (US) & Miss E. Ryan (US) 8–6 6–0
	F. T. Hunter (US) & Miss E. Ryan (US) L. Raymond (SA) & Miss E. L. Heine (SA)	Hunter & Miss Ryan 6–3 6–4	
1928	F. T. Hunter (US) & Miss H. N. Wills (US) P. D. B. Spence (SA) & Miss E. Ryan (US)	Spence & Miss Ryan 4–6 6–4 6–3	P. D. B. Spence (SA) & Miss E. Ryan (US) 7–5 6–4
	J. H. Crawford (AUS) & Miss D. Akhurst (AUS) E. F. Moon (AUS) & Mrs P. O'Hara Wood (AUS)	Crawford & Miss Akhurst 6–3 7–5	
1929	I. G. Collins & Miss J. Fry J. C. Gregory & Miss E. Ryan (US)	Collins & Miss Fry 6–2 6–3	F. T. Hunter (US) & Miss H. N. Wills (US) 6–1 6–4
	N. G. Farquharson (SA) & Miss E. L. Heine (SA) F. T. Hunter (US) & Miss H. N. Wills (US)	Hunter & Miss Wills 6–8 6–2 6–3	
1930	H. Cochet (F) & Mrs F. Whittingstall J. H. Crawford (AUS) & Miss E. Ryan (US)	Crawford & Miss Ryan 6–3 7–9 6–4	J. H. Crawford (AUS) & Miss E. Ryan (US) 6–1 6–3
	G. R. O. Crole-Rees & Miss P. E. Mudford D. Prenn (G) & Frl H. Krahwinkel (G)	Prenn & Frl Krahwinkel 4–6 6–3 6–3	
1931	I. G. Collins & Miss J. C. Ridley P. D. B. Spence (SA) & Miss B. Nuthall	Collins & Miss Ridley 4–6 6–4 6–4	G. M. Lott (US) & Mrs L. A. Harper (US) 6–3 1–6 6–1
	G. M. Lott (US) & Mrs L. A. Harper (US) F. J. Perry & Miss M. Heeley	Lott & Mrs Harper 1–6 3–4 retired	
1932	J. Brugnon (F) & Mme R. Mathieu (F) H. C. Hopman (AUS) & Mlle J. Sigart (B)	Hopman & Mlle Sigart 6–4 6–4	E. Maier (SP) & Miss E. Ryan (US) 7–5 6–2
	H. Cochet (F) & Mrs F. Whittingstall E. Maier (SP) & Miss E. Ryan (US)	Maier & Miss Ryan 7–5 3–6 6–1	
1933	J. Borotra (F) & Miss B. Nuthall N. G. Farquharson (SA) & Miss M. Heeley	Farquharson & Miss Heeley 8–6 11–9	G. von Cramm (G) & Frl H. Krahwinkel (G) 7–5 8–6
	C. H. Kingsley & Mrs L. A. Godfree G. von Cramm (G) & Frl H. Krahwinkel (G)	von Cramm & Frl Krahwinkel 6–3 8–6	
1934	H. G. N. Lee & Miss F. James R. Miki (J) & Miss D. E. Round	Miki & Miss Round 6–3 6–2	R. Miki (J) & Miss D. E. Round 3–6 6–4 6–0
	H. W. Austin & Mrs D. C. Shepherd-Barron J. S. Olliff & Miss J. Ingram	Austin & Mrs Shepherd-Barron 6–4 6–1	

Semi-finalists	Semi-final result	Final
1935		
H. C. Hopman (AUS) & Mrs H. C. Hopman (AUS) G. von Cramm & Fru S. Sperling (DEN)	Hopman & Mrs Hopman 6–4 6–4	F. J. Perry & Miss D. E. Round 7–5 4–6 6–2
F. J. Perry & Miss D. E. Round A. K. Quist (AUS) & Miss J. Jedrzejowska (POL)	Perry & Miss Round 6–1 6–3	
1936		
J. D. Budge (US) & Mrs M. Fabyan (US) C. E. Malfroy (NZ) & Fru S. Sperling (DEN)	Budge & Mrs Fabyan 6–4 6–3	F. J. Perry & Miss D. E. Round 7–9 7–5 6–4
F. J. Perry & Miss D. E. Round F. H. D. Wilde & Miss M. Whitmarsh	Perry & Miss Round 6–4 1–6 6–3	
1937		
J. D. Budge (US) & Miss A. Marble (US) G. Mako (US) & Miss J. Jedrzejowska (POL)	Budge & Miss Marble 6–3 6–2	J. D. Budge (US) & Miss A. Marble (US) 6–4 6–1
Y. Petra (F) & Mme R. Mathieu (F) D. Prenn (G) & Miss E. M. Dearman	Petra & Mathieu 6–2 6–4	
1938		
H. Henkel (G) & Mrs M. Fabyan (US) A. D. Russell (ARG) & Miss F. James	Henkel & Mrs Fabyan 6–3 1–6 6–3	J. D. Budge (US) & Miss A. Marble (US) 6–1 6–4
J. D. Budge (US) & Miss A. Marble (US) R. A. Shayes & Miss J. Saunders	Budge & Miss Marble 6–4 6–2	
1939		
C. E. Malfroy (NZ) & Miss B. Nuthall R. L. Riggs (US) & Miss A. Marble (US)	Riggs & Miss Marble 3–6 6–2 6–4	R. L. Riggs (US) & Miss A. Marble (US) 9–7 6–1
E. T. Cooke (US) & Mrs M. Fabyan (US) F. H. D. Wilde & Miss N. B. Brown	Wilde & Miss Brown 6–3 7–5	
1940–5 not held		
1946		
T. Brown (US) & Miss A. L. Brough (US) H. C. Hopman (AUS) & Miss M. E. Osborne (US)	T. Brown & Miss Brough 6–3 6–3	T. Brown (US) & Miss A. L. Brough (US) 6–4 6–4
G. E. Brown (AUS) & Miss D. Bundy (US) J. E. Patty (US) & Miss P. M. Betz (US)	G. E. Brown & Miss Bundy 12–10 6–2	
1947		
T. Brown (US) & Miss M. E. Osborne (US) C. F. Long (AUS) & Mrs N. W. Bolton (AUS)	Long & Mrs Bolton 7–5 6–2	J. E. Bromwich (AUS) & Miss A. L. Brough (US) 1–6 6–4 6–2
L. Bergelin (SWE) & Miss D. J. Hart (US) J. E. Bromwich (AUS) & Miss A. L. Brough (US)	Bromwich & Miss Brough 6–4 6–2	
1948		
T. Brown (US) & Mrs W. du Pont (US) F. A. Sedgman (AUS) & Miss D. J. Hart (US)	Sedgman & Miss Hart 6–4 3–6 6–3	J. E. Bromwich (AUS) & Miss A. L. Brough (US) 6–2 3–6 6–3
J. E. Bromwich (AUS) & Miss A. L. Brough (US) J. Drobny (CZ) & Mrs P. C. Todd (US)	Bromwich & Miss Brough 5–7 6–1 8–6	
1949		
J. E. Bromwich (AUS) & Miss A. L. Brough (US) G. A. Worthington (AUS) & Mrs T. D. Long (AUS)	Bromwich & Miss Brough 6–1 6–2	E. W. Sturgess (SA) & Mrs S. P. Summers (SA) 9–7 9–11 7–5
O. W. Sidwell (AUS) & Mrs W. du Pont (US) E. W. Sturgess (SA) & Mrs S. P. Summers (SA)	Sturgess & Mrs Summers 6–4 7–9 6–3	
1950		
G. E. Brown (AUS) & Mrs P. C. Todd (US) G. A. Worthington (AUS) & Mrs T. D. Long (AUS)	Brown & Mrs Todd 9–7 6–4	E. W. Sturgess (SA) & Miss A. L. Brough (US) 11–9 6–1 6–4
F. A. Sedgman (AUS) & Miss D. J. Hart (US) E. W. Sturgess (SA) & Miss A. L. Brough (US)	Sturgess & Miss Brough 6–2 9–7	

Year	Semi-finalists	Semi-final winners	Final
1951	M. G. Rose (AUS) & Mrs N. W. Bolton (AUS) E. W. Sturgess (SA) & Miss A. L. Brough (US)	Rose & Mrs Bolton 7–5 6–2	F. A. Sedgman (AUS) & Miss D. J. Hart (US) 7–5 6–2
	K. McGregor (AUS) & Mrs W. du Pont (US) F. A. Sedgman (AUS) & Miss D. J. Hart (US)	Sedgman & Miss Hart 6–2 4–6 6–3	
1952	D. W. Candy (AUS) & Mrs P. C. Todd (US) F. A. Sedgman (AUS) & Miss D. J. Hart (US)	Sedgman & Miss Hart 6–2 6–3	F. A. Sedgman (AUS) & Miss D. J. Hart (US) 4–6 6–3 6–4
	K. McGregor (AUS) & Miss A. L. Brough (US) E. Morea (ARG) & Mrs T. D. Long (AUS)	Morea & Mrs Long 6–3 7–5	
1953	E. Morea (ARG) & Miss S. J. Fry (US) G. A. Worthington (AUS) & Miss P. E. Ward	Morea & Miss Fry 6–2 6–2	E. V. Seixas (US) & Miss D. J. Hart (US) 9–7 7–5
	L. A. Hoad (AUS) & Miss J. Sampson (US) E. V. Seixas (US) & Miss D. J. Hart (US)	Seixas & Miss Hart 6–3 7–5	
1954	M. A. Otway (NZ) & Miss J. F. Burke (NZ) E. V. Seixas (US) & Miss D. J. Hart (US)	Seixas & Miss Hart 6–4 6–1	E. V. Seixas (US) & Miss D. J. Hart (US) 5–7 6–4 6–3
	L. A. Hoad (AUS) & Miss M. Connolly (US) K. R. Rosewall (AUS) & Mrs W. du Pont (US)	Rosewall & Mrs du Pont 6–8 6–4 6–4	
1955	N. A. Fraser (AUS) & Miss B. Penrose (AUS) E. Morea (ARG) & Miss A. L. Brough (US)	Morea & Miss Brough 7–9 6–4 6–4	E. V. Seixas (US) & Miss D. J. Hart (US) 8–6 2–6 6–3
	L. A. Hoad (AUS) & Mrs L. A. Hoad (AUS) E. V. Seixas (US) & Miss D. J. Hart (US)	Seixas & Miss Hart 6–3 9–7	
1956	R. N. Howe (AUS) & Miss D. R. Hard (US) E. V. Seixas (US) & Miss S. J. Fry (US)	Seixas & Miss Fry 6–3 7–5	E. V. Seixas (US) & Miss S. J. Fry (US) 2–6 6–2 7–5
	T. T. Fancutt (SA) & Miss D. G. Seeney (AUS) G. Mulloy (US) & Miss A. Gibson (US)	Mulloy & Miss Gibson 6–4 6–4	
1957	L. Ayala (Chile) & Mrs T. D. Long (AUS) M. G. Rose (AUS) & Miss D. R. Hard (US)	Rose & Miss Hard 3–6 6–3 6–2	M. G. Rose (AUS) & Miss D. R. Hard (US) 6–4 7–5
	R. S. Emerson (AUS) & Miss M. Hellyer (AUS) N. A. Fraser (AUS) & Miss A. Gibson (US)	Fraser & Miss Gibson 6–4 6–4	
1958	F. Contreras (MEX) & Miss R. M. Reyes (MEX) R. N. Howe (AUS) & Miss L. Coghlan (AUS)	Howe & Miss Coghlan 6–4 6–4	R. N. Howe (AUS) & Miss L. Coghlan (AUS) 6–3 13–11
	W. A. Knight & Miss S. J. Bloomer K. Nielsen (DEN) & Miss A. Gibson (US)	Nielsen & Miss Gibson 7–5 6–3	
1959	W. A. Knight & Miss Y. Ramirez (MEX) R. G. Laver (AUS) & Miss D. R. Hard (US)	Laver & Miss Hard 6–2 5–7 6–2	R. G. Laver (AUS) & Miss D. R. Hard (US) 6–4 6–3
	N. A. Fraser (AUS) & Miss M. E. Bueno (BRA) R. Mark (AUS) & Miss J. Arth (US)	Fraser & Miss Bueno 6–3 6–2	
1960	R. G. Laver (AUS) & Miss D. R. Hard (US) R. Mark (AUS) & Miss J. S. Hopps (US)	Laver & Miss Hard 4–6 6–1 6–2	R. G. Laver (AUS) & Miss D. R. Hard (US) 13–11 3–6 8–6
	R. N. Howe (AUS) & Miss M. E. Bueno (BRA) J. Javorsky (CZ) & Miss V. Puzejova (CZ)	Howe & Miss Bueno 6–1 2–6 6–4	
1961	J. Javorsky (CZ) & Mrs V. Sukova (CZ) F. S. Stolle (AUS) & Miss L. R. Turner (AUS)	Stolle & Miss Turner 7–5 6–3	F. S. Stolle (AUS) & Miss L. R. Turner (AUS) 11–9 6–2
	R. N. Howe (AUS) & Frl E. Buding (G) E. Morea (ARG) & Miss M. Smith (AUS)	Howe & Frl Buding 6–3 6–2	

Year	Semi-finalists	Semi-final results	Final
1962	R. N. Howe (AUS) & Miss M. E. Bueno (BRA) R. D. Ralston (US) & Miss A. S. Haydon	Ralston & Miss Haydon 6–3 8–10 6–4	N. A. Fraser (AUS) & Mrs W. du Pont (US) 2–6 6–3 13–11
	N. A. Fraser (AUS) & Mrs W. du Pont (US) F. S. Stolle (AUS) & Miss L. R. Turner (AUS)	Fraser & Mrs du Pont 4–6 6–3 6–4	
1963	R. A. J. Hewitt (AUS) & Miss D. R. Hard (US) F. S. Stolle (AUS) & Miss L. R. Turner (AUS)	Hewitt & Miss Hard 5–7 6–2 6–2	K. N. Fletcher (AUS) & Miss M. Smith (AUS) 11–9 6–4
	K. N. Fletcher (AUS) & Miss M. Smith (AUS) R. D. Ralston (US) & Mrs P. F. Jones	Fletcher & Miss Smith 6–1 7–5	
1964	K. N. Fletcher (AUS) & Miss M. Smith (AUS) F. A. Froehling (US) & Miss J. Bricka (US)	Fletcher & Miss Smith 7–5 6–3	F. S. Stolle (AUS) & Miss L. R. Turner (AUS) 6–4 6–4
	T. S. Okker (NTH) & Miss T. Groenman (NTH) F. S. Stolle (AUS) & Miss L. R. Turner (AUS)	Stolle & Miss Turner 2–6 6–2 6–3	
1965	A. D. Roche (AUS) & Miss J. A. M. Tegart (AUS) F. S. Stolle (AUS) & Miss L. R. Turner (AUS)	Roche & Miss Tegart 6–3 11–9	K. N. Fletcher (AUS) & Miss M. Smith (AUS) 12–10 6–3
	K. N. Fletcher (AUS) & Miss M. Smith (AUS) R. D. Ralston (US) & Miss M. E. Bueno (BRA)	Fletcher & Miss Smith 7–5 6–4	
1966	K. N. Fletcher (AUS) & Miss M. Smith (AUS) F. S. Stolle (AUS) & Mlle F. Durr (F)	Fletcher & Miss Smith 6–1 7–5	K. N. Fletcher (AUS) & Miss M. Smith (AUS) 4–6 6–3 6–3
	F. D. McMillan (SA) & Miss A. M. van Zyl (SA) R. D. Ralston (US) & Mrs L. W. King (US)	Ralston & Mrs King 6–4 6–4	
1967	O. K. Davidson (AUS) & Mrs L. W. King (US) F. D. McMillan (SA) & Miss A. M. van Zyl (SA)	Davidson & Mrs King 6–3 3–6 6–1	O. K. Davidson (AUS) & Mrs L. W. King (US) 7–5 6–2
	K. N. Fletcher (AUS) & Miss M. E. Bueno (BRA) R. O. Ruffels (AUS) & Miss K. M. Krantzcke (AUS)	Fletcher & Miss Bueno 6–3 6–1	
1968	O. K. Davidson (AUS) & Mrs L. W. King (US) K. N. Fletcher (AUS) & Mrs B. M. Court (AUS)	Fletcher & Mrs Court 6–4 9–7	K. N. Fletcher (AUS) & Mrs B. M. Court (AUS) 6–1 14–12
	A. Metreveli (USSR) & Miss O. Morozova (USSR) F. S. Stolle (AUS) & Mrs P. F. Jones	Metreveli & Miss Morozova 6–3 12–10	
1969	K. N. Fletcher (AUS) & Mrs B. M. Court (AUS) F. S. Stolle (AUS) & Mrs P. F. Jones	Stolle & Mrs Jones 11–9 11–9	F. S. Stolle (AUS) & Mrs P. F. Jones 6–3 6–2
	A. D. Roche (AUS) & Miss J. A. M. Tegart (AUS) R. O. Ruffels (AUS) & Miss K. M. Krantzcke (AUS)	Roche & Miss Tegart 6–4 7–5	
1970	D. Irvine (RHOD) & Miss H. F. Gourlay (AUS) A. Metreveli (USSR) & Miss O. Morozova (USSR)	Metreveli & Miss Morozova 9–11 6–3 6–4	I. Nastase (ROM) & Miss R. Casals (US) 6–3 4–6 9–7
	F. D. McMillan (SA) & Mrs D. E. Dalton (AUS) I. Nastase (ROM) & Miss R. Casals (US)	Nastase & Miss Casals 5–7 6–2 6–4	

1971

F. D. McMillan (SA) & Mrs D. E. Dalton (AUS) M. C. Riessen (US) & Mrs B. M. Court (AUS)	Riessen & Mrs Court 7–5 6–3	O. K. Davidson (AUS) & Mrs L. W. King (US) 3–6 6–2 15–13
O. K. Davidson (AUS) & Mrs L. W. King (US) I. Nastase (ROM) & Miss R. Casals (US)	Davidson & Mrs King 6–4 6–1	

1972

P. J. Cramer (SA) & Mrs Q. C. Pretorius (SA) K. G. Warwick (AUS) & Miss E. F. Goolagong (AUS)	Warwick & Miss Goolagong 6–4 6–3	I. Nastase (ROM) & Miss R. Casals (US) 6–4 6–4
C. E. Graebner (US) & Mrs L. W. King (US) I. Nastase (ROM) & Miss R. Casals (US)	Nastase & Miss Casals 9–8* 7–5	

* Tie break

1973

J. R. Cooper (AUS) & Miss K. M. Krantzcke (AUS) R. Ramirez (MEX) & Miss J. S. Newberry (US)	Ramirez & Miss Newberry 6–1 6–4	O. K. Davidson (AUS) & Mrs L. W. King (US) 6–3 6–2
O. K. Davidson (AUS) & Mrs L. W. King (US) A. Metreveli (USSR) & Mrs O. Morozova (USSR)	Davidson & Mrs King 5–7 7–5 6–1	

1974

O. K. Davidson (AUS) & Mrs L. W. King (US) A. D. Roche (AUS) & Mlle F. Durr (F)	Davidson & Mrs King 3–6 6–3 6–4	O. K. Davidson (AUS) & Mrs L. W. King (US) 6–3 9–7
M. J. Farrell & Miss L. J. Charles N. A. Fraser (AUS) & Miss H. F. Gourlay (AUS)	Farrell & Miss Charles 7–9 8–6 6–2	

1975

J. Kodes (CZ) & Miss M. Navratilova (CZ) M. C. Riessen (US) & Mrs B. M. Court (AUS)	Riessen & Mrs Court 5–7 6–3 6–2	M. C. Riessen (US) & Mrs B. M. Court (AUS) 6–4 7–5
A. Metreveli (USSR) & Mrs O. Morozova (USSR) A. J. Stone (AUS) & Miss B. F. Stove (NTH)	Stone & Miss Stove 2–6 6–4 6–4	

1976

A. D. Roche (AUS) & Miss F. Durr (F) F. D. McMillan (SA) & Miss B. F. Stove (NTH)	Roche & Miss Durr 6–3 6–3	A. D. Roche (AUS) & Miss F. Durr (F) 6–3 2–6 7–5
R. A. J. Hewitt (SA) & Miss G. R. Stevens (SA) R. L. Stockton (US) & Miss R. Casals (US)	Stockton & Miss Casals 6–3 9–8	

MEN'S SINGLES PLATE

	Winner	*Finalist*	*Score*
1896	A. W. Gore	H. L. Doherty	1–6 6–2 7–5
1897	H. Baddeley	A. E. Crawley	6–1 6–3 5–7 6–2
1898	G. W. Hillyard	A. C. Pearson	6–3 8–6
1899	W. V. Eaves	G. W. Hillyard	w.o.
1900	G. Greville	E. D. Black	6–2 4–6 6–3
1901	P. G. Pearson	H. W. Davies	6–1 4–6 6–2 7–5
1902	B. Hillyard	C. R. D. Pritchett	8–6 6–1
1903	A. W. Gore	C. Hobart	7–5 6–3
1904	G. Greville	B. Hillyard	6–3 6–0
1905	W. V. Eaves	B. Murphy	6–3 6–2
1906	G. W. Hillyard	T. M. Mavrogordato	6–2 6–4
1907	A. F. Wilding (NZ)	C. von Wesseley (AU)	6–3 6–4
1908	O. Kreuzer (G)	V. R. Gauntlett (SA)	6–3 6–4
1909	R. B. Powell (CAN)	H. A. Parker (NZ)	3–6 6–3 6–1
1910	A. H. Gobert (F)	P. M. Davson	6–4 6–4
1911	A. H. Lowe	J. C. Parke	6–0 8–6
1912	F. M. Pearson	F. E. Barritt (AUS)	6–0 10–8
1913	F. G. Lowe	F. F. Roe	8–10 6–3 6–3
1914	C. P. Dixon	R. W. F. Harding	6–1 6–2
1915–18	not held		
1919	F. R. L. Crawford	M. Woosnam	6–3 5–7 7–5
1920	F. G. Lowe	C. P. Dixon	1–6 8–6 6–3
1921	J. B. Gilbert	F. M. B. Fisher (NZ)	7–5 4–6 6–0
1922	B. I. C. Norton (SA)	R. C. Wertheim (AUS)	6–2 6–2
1923	J. Washer (B)	M. J. G. Ritchie	6–3 6–4
1924	J. Condon (SA)	J. M. Hillyard	7–5 6–2
1925	B. von Kehrling (HU)	R. George (F)	6–3 6–4
1926	J. B. Gilbert	F. R. L. Crawford	10–8 6–2
1927	A. Gentien (F)	O. G. N. Turnbull	1–6 6–2 6–0
1928	M. Sleem (IN)	J. B. Gilbert	6–3 6–3
1929	E. G. Chandler (US)	W. H. Powell	6–4 6–1
1930	E. du Plaix (F)	C. E. Malfroy (NZ)	6–1 8–6
1931	V. G. Kirby (SA)	G. E. L. Rogers (IRE)	2–6 6–3 6–3
1932	H. Cochet (F)	T. Kuwabara (J)	6–2 6–4
1933	F. H. D. Wilde	J. D. P. Wheatley	6–4 6–4
1934	H. W. Artens (AU)	C. R. D. Tuckey	5–7 7–5 6–1
1935	J. Yamagishi (J)	J. Lesueur (F)	6–2 6–2
1936	D. N. Jones (US)	I. G. Collins	6–0 6–2
1937	W. Sabin (US)	N. G. Farquharson (SA)	2–6 6–0 6–3
1938	D. W. Butler	O. Szigeti (HU)	6–1 8–10 6–3
1939	D. McNeill (US)	J. van den Eynde (B)	8–6 6–2
1940–5	not held		
1946	R. Abdesselam (F)	C. Spychala (POL)	7–5 6–3
1947	E. W. Sturgess (SA)	A. J. Mottram	6–3 6–3
1948	F. Ampon (Philippines)	H. Weiss (ARG)	11–9 6–4
1949	E. H. Cochell (US)	G. P. Jackson (IRE)	4–6 6–3 6–1
1950	G. L. Paish	J. Brichant (B)	6–4 6–4
1951	N. M. Cockburn (SA)	K. H. Ip (HK)	7–5 5–7 10–8
1952	L. Ayala (Chile)	N. Kumar (IN)	8–6 6–2
1953	G. L. Paish	J. W. Ager (US)	4–6 6–0 7–5
1954	H. W. Stewart (US)	A. Vieira (BRA)	8–6 6–4
1955	N. A. Fraser (AUS)	R. N. Howe (AUS)	6–2 7–5
1956	H. W. Stewart (US)	G. Mulloy (US)	4–6 6–4 6–4
1957	G. L. Forbes (SA)	A. Segal (SA)	10–8 11–13 6–3
1958	P. Remy (F)	J. N. Grinda (F)	6–3 11–9
1959	J. Javorsky (CZ)	M. Fox (US)	6–3 6–2
1960	T. Ulrich (DEN)	O. Sirola (IT)	6–4 7–5
1961	J. Ulrich (DEN)	N. Kumar (IN)	6–4 10–12 6–3
1962	J. A. Douglas (US)	A. Segal (SA)	3–6 6–2 6–3
1963	E. L. Scott (US)	I. S. Crookenden (NZ)	w.o.
1964	R. K. Wilson	W. W. Bowrey (AUS)	6–4 6–3
1965	O. K. Davidson (AUS)	T. S. Okker (NTH)	6–3 8–6
1966	R. Taylor	R. N. Howe	6–4 2–6 7–5
1967	J. H. McManus (US)	E. L. Scott (US)	6–3 6–2
1968	G. Battrick	H. S. Fitzgibbon (US)	6–4 3–6 7–5
1969	T. Koch (BRA)	R. O. Ruffels (AUS)	6–1 6–3
1970	R. R. Maud (SA)	R. R. Barth (US)	6–4 6–3
1971	R. D. Crealy (AUS)	P. Cornejo (Chile)	6–3 6–4
1972	K. G. Warwick (AUS)	I. Molina (COL)/ N. Kalogeropoulos (GRE)	w.o.
1973	J. G. Clifton	S. G. Messmer (US)	6–4 4–6 6–1
1974	T. I. Kakulia (USSR)	P. C. Kronk (AUS)	6–3 7–5
1975	T. Koch (BRA)	V. Gerulaitis (US)	6–3 6–2
1976	B. E. Fairlie (NZ)	R. Taylor	4–6 6–3 6–4

WOMEN'S SINGLES PLATE

	Winner	*Finalist*	*Score*
1933	Miss C. Rosambert (F)	Miss J. Goldschmidt (F)	6–4 6–1
1934	Miss L. Valerio (IT)	Miss J. Saunders	7–5 6–3
1935	Miss L. Valerio (IT)	Miss A. E. L. McOstrich	6–2 1–6 6–0
1936	Miss F. S. Ford	Miss M. Riddell	6–4 6–4
1937	Miss F. James	Miss M. E. Lumb	6–0 7–5
1938	Miss D. Stevenson (AUS)	Miss J. Hartigan (AUS)	6–4 6–4
1939	Mrs R. D. McKelvie	Miss A. Weiwers (LUX)	6–4 4–6 6–2
1940–5	not held		
1946	Miss J. Jedrzejowska (POL)	Miss P. A. O'Connell	6–4 7–5
1947	Miss J. Jedrzejowska (POL)	Mrs N. W. Blair	6–2 7–5
1948	Mrs H. Weiss (ARG)	Miss E. M. Wilford	6–1 5–7 7–5
1949	Mrs A. Bossi (IT)	Miss B. Gullbrandson (SWE)	6–0 7–5
1950	Miss K. L. A. Tuckey	Miss B. Rosenquest (US)	6–4 6–1
1951	Mrs F. Bartlett (SA)	Miss G. E. Woodgate	3–6 6–1 6–2
1952	Mrs B. Abbas (EG)	Miss G. C. Hoahing	0–6 6–4 6–3
1953	Miss M. P. Harrison	Miss E. F. Lombard (IRE)	1–6 6–3 6–3
1954	Miss R. Walsh	Miss P. A. Hird	6–2 7–5
1955	Miss F. Muller (AUS)	Miss L. L. Felix (US)	6–4 6–4
1956	Mrs T. D. Long (AUS)	Frl I. Buding (G)	6–3 6–4
1957	Miss M. B. Hellyer (AUS)	Miss R. Schuurman (SA)	6–4 6–4
1958	Miss S. Reynolds (SA)	Miss M. B. Hellyer (AUS)	6–2 6–2
1959	Mrs C. Brasher	Mrs M. Sladek (CAN)	3–6 6–3 7–5
1960	Miss D. M. Catt	Mrs J. W. Cawthorn	6–3 6–2
1961	Miss R. H. Bentley	Miss A. Dmitrieva (USSR)	6–4 3–6 6–3
1962	Miss M. L. Gerson (SA)	Miss M. B. Hellyer (AUS)	6–2 6–1
1963	Miss F. Durr (F)	Miss A. Dmitrieva (USSR)	6–1 6–3
1964	Mrs V. Sukova (CZ)	Miss J. Bricka (US)	0–6 6–3 6–3
1965	Miss A. Dmitrieva (USSR)	Miss F. E. Truman	6–1 6–2
1966	Miss P. M. Walkden (RHOD)	Mrs J. G. A. Lloyd	6–4 6–0
1967	Miss P. S. A. Hogan (US)	Miss G. V. Sheriff (AUS)	6–2 9–7
1968	Miss S. V. Wade	Miss K. M. Harter (US)	6–2 12–10
1969	Miss B. A. Grubb (US)	Miss L. A. Rossouw (SA)	6–3 4–6 6–4
1970	Miss E. F. Goolagong (AUS)	Miss L. Liem (INDO)	6–2 6–1
1971	Mrs M. R. Wainwright	Miss B. F. Stove (NTH)	6–4 0–6 6–2
1972	Miss K. M. Krantzcke (AUS)	Miss S. A. Walsh (US)	6–4 6–1
1973	Miss H. F. Gourlay (AUS)	Miss V. A. Burton	6–1 4–6 6–1
1974	Miss M. V. Kroschina (USSR)	Miss L. J. Beaven	6–3 8–6
1975	Miss D. L. Fromholtz (AUS)	Miss V. A. Burton	6–4 6–2
1976	Miss M. Wikstedt (SWE)	Miss B. Bruning (US)	4–6 6–3 6–3

INVITATION JUNIOR TOURNAMENT

BOY'S SINGLES

	Winner	*Finalist*
1947	K. Nielsen (DEN)	(Played as round-robin)
1948	S. Stockenberg (SWE)	D. Vad (HU)
1949	S. Stockenberg (SWE)	J. A. T. Horn
1950	J. A. T. Horn	K. Moubarek (EG)
1951	J. Kupferburger (SA)	K. Moubarek (EG)
1952	R. K. Wilson	T. Fancutt (SA)
1953	W. A. Knight	R. Krishnan (IN)
1954	R. Krishnan (IN)	A. J. Cooper (AUS)
1955	M. P. Hann	J. E. Lundquist (SWE)
1956	R. Holmberg (US)	R. G. Laver (AUS)
1957	J. I. Tattersall	I. Ribiero (BRA)
1958	E. Buchholz (US)	P. J. Lall (IN)
1959	T. Lejus (USSR)	R. W. Barnes (BRA)
1960	A. R. Mandelstam (SA)	J. Mukerjea (IN)
1961	C. E. Graebner (US)	E. Blanke (AUS)
1962	S. J. Matthews	A. Metreveli (USSR)
1963	N. Kalogeropoulos (GRE)	I. El Shafei (EG)
1964	I. El Shafei (EG)	V. Korotkov (USSR)
1965	V. Korotkov (USSR)	G. Goven (F)
1966	V. Korotkov (USSR)	B. Fairlier (NZ)
1967	M. Orantes (SP)	M. Estep (US)
1968	J. D. Alexander (AUS)	J. Thamin (F)
1969	B. Bertram (SA)	J. D. Alexander (AUS)
1970	B. Bertram (SA)	F. Gebert (GRE)
1971	R. Kreiss (US)	S. A. Warboys
1972	B. Borg (SWE)	C. J. Mottram
1973	W. Martin (US)	C. Dowdeswell (RHOD)
1974	W. Martin (US)	Ashok Amritraj (IN)
1975	C. J. Lewis (NZ)	R. Ycaza (Ecuador)
1976	H. Guenthardt (SWI)	P. Elter (G)

GIRL'S SINGLES

	Winner	*Finalist*
1948	O. Miskova (CZ)	V. Rigollet (SWI)
1949	C. Mercellis (B)	S. Partridge
1950	L. Cornell	A. Winther (NOR)
1951	L. Cornell	S. Lazzarino (IT)
1952	F. ten Bosch (NTH)	R. Davar (IN)
1953	D. Kilian (SA)	V. A. Pitt
1954	V. A. Pitt	C. Monnot (F)
1955	S. M. Armstrong	B. de Chambre (F)
1956	A. S. Haydon	I. Buding (G)
1957	M. Arnold (US)	R. M. Reyes (MEX)
1958	S. M. Moore (US)	A. Dmitrieva (USSR)
1959	J. Cross (SA)	D. Schuster (AU)
1960	K. Hantze (US)	L. M. Hutchings (SA)
1961	G. Baksheeva (USSR)	K. D. Chabit (US)
1962	G. Baksheeva (USSR)	E. P. Terry (NZ)
1963	D. M. Salfati (F)	K. Dening (AUS)
1964	J. Bartkowicz (US)	E. Subirats (MEX)
1965	O. Morozova (USSR)	R. Giscafre (ARG)
1966	B. Lindstrom (FIN)	J. Congdon
1967	J. Salome (NTH)	M. Strandberg (SWE)
1968	K. Pigeon (US)	L. Hunt (AUS)
1969	K. Sawamatsu (J)	B. Kirk (SA)
1970	S. M. Walsh (US)	M. V. Kroschina (USSR)
1971	M. V. Kroschina (USSR)	S. Minford (IRE)
1972	I. Kloss (SA)	G. L. Coles
1973	A. Kiyomura (US)	M. Navratilova (CZ)
1974	M. Jausovec (YU)	M. Simionescu (ROM)
1975	N. Y. Chmyriova (USSR)	R. Marsikova (CZ)
1976	N. Y. Chmyriova (USSR)	M. Kruger (SA)

VETERANS' MEN'S DOUBLES

	Winners	*Finalists*
1964	B. Destremau & W. F. Talbert	G. R. MacCall & A. V. Martini
1965	G. Mulloy & W. F. Talbert	G. R. MacCall & A. V. Martini
1966	G. Mulloy & W. F. Talbert	R. J. Freedman & R. V. Sherman
1967	J. Drobny & A. V. Martini	R. J. Freedman & R. V. Sherman
1968	J. Drobny & A. V. Martini	S. Match & G. Mulloy
1969	J. Drobny & E. V. Seixas	E. G. Slack & R. C. Sorlein
1970	J. Drobny & R. L. Riggs	G. R. MacCall & F. Segura
1971	G. Mulloy & A. Vincent	L. S. Clark & E. V. Seixas
1972	L. S. Clark & E. V. Seixas	G. Mulloy & A. Vincent
1973	L. Bergelin & J. Drobny	J. D. Budge & F. A. Sedgman
1974	J. Dunas & G. Mulloy	H. K. Richards & R. C. Sorlein
1975	L. Bergelin & J. E. Patty	J. D. Budge & G. Mulloy
1976	L. Bergelin & J. E. Patty	H. K. Richards & R. C. Sorlein

MARRIED NAMES

The following women in the championship records are included under two identities.

Mme M. Billout	Mlle M. Broquedis
Mrs E. W. A. Bostock	Miss J. Nicoll
Mrs W. W. Bowrey	Miss L. R. Turner
Mrs N. W. Bolton	Miss N. Wynne
Mrs C. Brasher	Miss S. J. Bloomer
Mrs T. S. Bundy	Miss M. G. Sutton
Mrs R. Cawley	Miss E. F. Goolagong
Mrs R. Lambert Chambers	Miss D. K. Douglass
Mrs B. M. Court	Miss M. Smith
Mrs B. C. Covell	Miss P. L. Howkins
Mrs D. E. Dalton	Miss J. A. M. Tegart
Mrs G. Davidson	Miss B. Scofield
Mrs W. du Pont	Miss M. E. Osborne
Mrs M. Fabyan	Miss S. Palfrey
Mrs J. Fleitz	Miss B. Baker
Mrs A. C. Geen	Miss D. P. Boothby
Mrs P. F. Glover	Miss N. Lyle
Mrs L. A. Godfree	Miss K. McKane
Mrs G. Greville	Miss L. Austin
Mrs K. S. Gunter	Miss N. Richey
Mrs C. Harrison	(Mrs) B. E. Hilton
Mrs P. Haygarth	Miss R. Schuurman
Mrs E. L. Heine Miller	Miss E. L. Heine
Mrs G. W. Hillyard	Miss B. Bingley
Mrs P. D. Howard	Mlle D. Metaxa
Mrs P. F. Jones	Miss A. S. Haydon
Mrs L. W. King	Miss B. J. Moffitt
Mrs M. R. King	Miss P. E. Mudford
Mrs G. Lamplough	Miss G. Eastlake Smith
Mrs D. R. Larcombe	Miss E. W. Thomson
Mrs J. L. Leisk	Miss H. Aitchison
Mrs R. D. Little	Miss D. E. Round
Mrs J. F. Luard	Miss C. M. Wilson
Mrs R. Lycett	Miss J. Austin
Frau H. Masthoff	Frl H. Niessen
Mrs M. Menzies	Miss K. E. Stammers
Mme J. de Meulemeester	Mlle J. Sigart
Mrs L. R. C. Michel	Miss P. Saunders
Mrs F. S. Moody	Miss H. N. Wills
Mrs A. J. Mottram	Miss J. Gannon
Mme H. Nicolopoulo	Mlle H. Contoslavlos
Mrs E. G. Parton	Miss M. B. Squire
Mrs B. Pratt	Miss B. Rosenquest
Mrs Q. C. Pretorius	Miss P. M. Walkden
Mrs L. E. G. Price	Miss S. Reynolds
Mrs G. E. Reid	Miss K. Melville
Mrs J. Rinkel-Quertier	Miss J. Quertier
Mrs O. C. Shepherd Barron	Miss D. C. Shepherd
Fru S. Sperling	Frl H. Krahwinkel
Mrs A. Sterry	Miss C. Cooper
Mrs A. D. Stocks	Miss M. McKane
Mrs V. Sukova	Miss V. Puzejova
Mrs J. R. Susman	Miss K. Hantze
Mrs F. Whittingstall	Miss E. Bennett

BIOGRAPHIES

The following is a brief biographical record of those who were full Wimbledon champions.

Some of the basic facts have been elusive. In this context the diligence and research of Alan Little are gratefully acknowledged. The results of his research in the field of basic biographical data have been freely borrowed.

MEN

ALLISON, Wilmer Lawson

Born 8 December 1904, San Antonio, Texas, USA.
Doubles 1929, 1930.
Other successes:
US Championships, singles 1935; doubles 1931, 1935; mixed 1930.
Member US Davis Cup team 1929–35. First-ranking US player 1934, 1935.

A volleyer of exceptional daring.

ANDERSON, James Outram

Born 17 September 1895, Enfield, NSW, Australia.
Died 22 December 1973, Sydney, NSW, Australia.
Doubles 1922.
Other successes:
Australian Championships, singles 1922, 1924, 1925; doubles 1924.
Member Australasian/Australian Davis Cup team 1919–25.

He became a professional in December 1926.

ASHE, Arthur Robert

Born 10 July 1943, Richmond, Virginia, USA.
Singles 1975.
Other successes:
US Championships, singles 1968.
French Championships, doubles 1971.
Australian Championships, singles 1970.
WCT singles champion, Dallas, 1975.
Member of US Davis Cup team first in 1963.

The first black American male to have success at the highest level of the game. Having, as a black player, been denied entry in 1970 he was in 1973 singles runner-up and doubles winner, with Tom Okker of the Netherlands, in the South African Championships.

BADDELEY, Herbert

Born 11 January 1872, Bromley, Kent, England.
Died 20 July 1931, Cannes, France.
Doubles 1891, 1894, 1895, 1896.
Other successes:
Irish Championships, doubles, 1896, 1897.

The younger of twin sons of a London solicitor.

BADDELEY, Wilfred

Born 11 January 1872, Bromley, Kent, England.
Died 24 January 1929, Mentone, France.
Singles 1891, 1892, 1895.
Doubles 1891, 1894, 1895, 1896.
Other successes:
Irish Championships, singles 1896; doubles 1896, 1897.

The elder twin of the above. He was, in 1891, the youngest men's singles champion at the age of 19 years 5 months 23 days.

BARLOW, Harry Sibthorpe

Born 5 April 1860, Hammersmith, London, England.
Died 16 July 1917, Kennington, London, England.
Doubles 1892.
Other successes:
Welsh Championships, singles 1891, 1892.

A Middlesex county cricketer.

BARRETT, Herbert Roper

Born 24 November 1873, Upton, Essex, England.
Died 27 July 1943, Horsham, Sussex, England.
Doubles 1909, 1912, 1913.
Other successes:
Member of the British Isles Davis Cup team 1900–19; non-playing captain 1924–39.
Olympic gold medalist 1908.
Men's singles winner in the Saxmundham tournament 1898, 1899, 1902, 1904–14, 1919–21, seventeen times in all.

Chairman of the Lawn Tennis Association 1924.

His pseudonymous entry to the Championships in 1898 was as 'A. L. Gydear', in 1900 as 'J. Verne' and in 1901 as 'D'Agger'.

Played football for Corinthian Casuals and Weybridge. Chief Commoner of the City of London 1924; Master of the Worshipful Company of Farriers, London, 1921, 1933. Commander of the Crown of Italy; Commander of the Star of Romania. A solicitor. Educated Merchant Taylors' School.

BORG, Bjorn Rune

Born 6 June 1956, Sodertalje, nr Stockholm, Sweden.
Singles 1976.
Other successes:
French Championships, singles 1974, 1975.
Italian Championships, singles 1974.
WCT Championship, singles 1976.

Double handed on the backhand.

BOROTRA, Jean

Born 13 August 1898, Arbonne, Basses-Pyrénées, France.
Singles 1924, 1926.
Doubles 1925, 1932, 1933.
Mixed 1925.
Other successes:
US Championships, mixed 1926.
French Championships, singles 1931; doubles 1925, 1928, 1929, 1934, 1936; mixed 1927, 1934.
Australian Championships, singles 1928; doubles 1928; mixed 1928.
Member of the French Davis Cup team 1922–47; 11 times British Covered Court singles champion 1926–49; 12 times French Covered Court champion 1922–47.

Notable for the acrobatic exuberance of his volleying and the strength of his personality. Affectionately known as 'The Bounding Basque' and, with Jacques Brugnon, Henri Cochet and René Lacoste, one of the 'Four Musketeers'.

His playing record at Wimbledon, comprising all events, was unequalled:

1922–1976

	Matches		
	Won	*Lost*	*Total*
Singles	55	10	65
Doubles	57	31	88
Mixed	40	28	68
Veterans' doubles	2	12	14
Total	154	81	235

He was Minister of Sport in France from 1940 to 1942, being subsequently imprisoned by the Germans. Chevalier de la Légion d'honneur.

BOWES-LYON, Patrick

Born 5 March 1863, Belgravia, Middlesex, England.
Died 5 October 1946, Westerham, Kent, England.
Doubles 1887.
Other successes:
Scottish Championships, singles 1885, 1886, 1888.
Cambridge blue 1884–6.

Younger brother of the 14th Earl of Strathmore; Lieutenant, RN, 1877–80; Major, Essex Regiment; Barrister-at-law; managing director of the Boy Messengers Company.

BROMWICH, John Edward

Born 14 November 1918, Sydney, NSW, Australia.
Doubles 1948, 1950.
Mixed 1947, 1948.
Other successes:
US Championships, doubles 1939, 1949, 1950; mixed 1947.
Australian Championships, singles 1939, 1946; doubles 1938, 1939, 1940, 1946, 1947, 1948, 1949, 1950; mixed 1938.
Member Australian Davis Cup team 1937–50.

A gentle and exquisite craftsman on the court; he used an exceptionally lightweight racket with a narrow grip; double fisted on the forehand.

BROOKES, (Sir) Norman Everard

Born 14 November 1877, Melbourne, Victoria, Australia.
Died 28 September 1968, Melbourne, Victoria, Australia.
Singles 1907, 1914.
Doubles 1907, 1914.
Other successes:
US Championships, doubles 1919.
Australian Championships, singles 1911; doubles 1924.
Member Australasian Davis Cup team 1905–20.

The first man from overseas to win a Wimbledon championship; a left hander; a first-class cricketer, a medium left-handed bowler for the St Kilda CC; a near-scratch golfer.

He was knighted in 1939.

BROWN, Thomas Pollock

Born 26 September 1922, Washington, DC, USA.
Doubles 1946.
Mixed 1946.
Other successes:
US Championships, mixed 1948.
Member US Davis Cup team 1950–3.

BRUGNON, Jacques (Toto)

Born 11 May 1895, Paris, France.
Doubles 1926, 1928, 1932, 1933.
Other successes:
French Championships, doubles 1927, 1928, 1930, 1932, 1934; mixed 1925, 1926.
Australian Championships, doubles 1928.
Member French Davis Cup team 1921–34.

The doubles expert among the 'Four Musketeers', pairing equally well with Jean Borotra, Henri Cochet and Rene Lacoste. Chevalier de la Légion d'honneur.

BUDGE, John Donald (Don)

Born 13 June 1915, Oakland, California, USA.
Singles 1937, 1938.
Doubles 1937, 1938.
Mixed 1937, 1938.
Other successes:
US Championships, singles 1937, 1938; doubles 1936, 1938; mixed 1937, 1938.
French Championships, singles 1938.
Australian Championships, singles 1938.
Member US Davis Cup team 1935–8.

The first 'Grand Slam' singles winner; uniquely triple champion at Wimbledon in two successive years; notable for his heavy, rolled backhand and one of the outstanding players of all time. He became a professional in 1938.

COCHET, Henri Jean

Born 14 December 1901, Villeurbanne, nr Lyons, France.
Singles 1927, 1929.
Doubles 1926, 1928.
Othersuccesses:
US Championships, singles 1928; mixed 1927.
French Championships, singles 1926, 1928, 1930, 1932; doubles 1927, 1930, 1932; mixed 1928, 1929.
Member French Davis Cup team 1922–33.
Relinquished amateur status 1933, reinstated 1942.

One of the 'Four Musketeers' and famous for his half volleying. He was the only Wimbledon singles winner to recover from the loss of the first two sets in the quarter-final, semi-final and final. He reached the final of the singles in the British Hard Court Championships at Bournemouth in 1949 at the age of 47.

CONNORS, James Scott

Born 2 September 1952, East St Louis, Illinois, USA.
Singles 1974.
Doubles 1973.
Other successes:
US Championships, singles 1974, 1976; doubles 1975.
Australian Championships, singles 1974.
Member US Davis Cup team 1975.

A left hander, with double-fisted grip on the backhand. His prize-money earnings in 1975 were computed to be US $600 273, a record.

COOKE, Elwood Thomas

Born 4 July 1914, Ogden, Utah, USA.
Doubles 1939.
Other success:
French Championships, mixed 1939.

COOPER, Ashley John

Born 15 September 1936, Melbourne, Victoria, Australia.
Singles 1958.
Other successes:
US Championships, singles 1958; doubles 1957.
French Championships, doubles 1957, 1958.
Australian Championships, singles 1957, 1958; doubles 1958.
Member Australian Davis Cup team 1957–8.
Became a professional in 1958.

CRAWFORD, John Herbert, OBE (Jack)

Born 22 March 1908, Albury, NSW, Australia.
Singles 1933.
Doubles 1935.
Mixed 1930.
Other successes:
French Championships, singles 1933; doubles 1935; mixed 1933.
Australian Championships, singles 1931, 1932,

1933, 1935; doubles 1929, 1930, 1932, 1935; mixed 1931, 1932, 1933.
Member Australian Davis Cup team 1928–37.

Notable for his classic 'purety' of style, his use of a square-topped racket and 'old-fashioned' air.

CRISP, Hope

Born 6 February 1884, Highgate, Middlesex, England.
Died 25 March 1950, Roehampton, London, England.
Mixed 1913.
Other successes:
Cambridge blue 1911–13.

Played soccer for Cambridge. In 1919 and 1920 he played good-class lawn tennis despite his artificial leg.

DAVIDSON, Owen Keir

Born 4 October 1943, Melbourne, Victoria, Australia.
Mixed 1967, 1971, 1973, 1974.
Other successes:
US Championships, doubles 1973; mixed 1966, 1967, 1971, 1973.
French Championships, mixed 1967.
Australian Championships, doubles 1972; mixed 1967.

A left hander. British Davis Cup coach 1967–70.

DAVIDSON, Sven Viktor

Born 13 July 1928, Boras, Sweden.
Doubles 1958.
Other successes:
French Championships, singles 1957.
Member Swedish Davis Cup team 1950–60.

DECUGIS, Max

Born 24 September 1882, Paris, France.
Doubles 1911.
Other successes:
Olympic gold medallist 1912.
Member French Davis Cup team 1904–19.

DIXON, Charles Percy

Born 7 February 1873, Grantham, Lincolnshire, England.
Died 29 April 1939, West Norwood, London, England.
Doubles 1912, 1913.
Other successes:
Olympic gold medallist 1912.
Member British Isles Davis Cup team 1909–13.

Educated Haileybury and Cambridge. Rackets blue 1892. A solicitor.

DOHERTY, Hugh Laurence

Born 8 October 1875, Wimbledon, Surrey, England.
Died 21 August 1919, Broadstairs, Kent, England.
Singles 1902, 1903, 1904, 1905, 1906.
Doubles 1897, 1898, 1899, 1900, 1901, 1903, 1904, 1905.
Other successes:
US Championships, singles 1903; doubles 1902, 1903.
Irish Championships, singles 1902; doubles 1898, 1899, 1900, 1901, 1902; mixed 1901, 1902.
Olympic gold medals (2) 1900.
Member British Isles Davis Cup team 1902–6, winning 12 from 12 rubbers.
Cambridge blue 1896–8.

Educated Westminster and Cambridge.

DOHERTY, Reginald Frank

Born 14 October 1872, Wimbledon, Surrey, England.
Died 29 December 1910, Kensington, London, England.
Singles 1897, 1898, 1899, 1900.
Doubles 1897, 1898, 1899, 1900, 1901, 1903, 1904, 1905.
Other successes:
US Championship, doubles 1902, 1903.
Irish Championships, singles 1899, 1900, 1901; doubles 1898, 1899, 1900, 1901, 1902; mixed 1899, 1900.
Olympic gold medals 1900 (2), 1908.
Member British Isles Davis Cup team 1902–6.
Cambridge blue 1895–6.

Educated Westminster and Cambridge.

DROBNY, Jaroslav
Born 12 October 1921, Prague, Czechoslovakia.
Singles 1954.
Other successes:
French Championships, singles 1951, 1952; doubles 1948; mixed 1948.
Italian Championships, singles 1950, 1951, 1953; doubles 1951, 1952, 1954, 1956.
Member Czech Davis Cup team 1946–9.

Left handed. Played ice hockey for Czechoslovakia. Became a refugee in 1949; naturalised Egyptian in 1950; naturalised British in 1960.

EMERSON, Roy Stanley
Born 3 November 1936, Blackbutt, Queensland, Australia.
Singles 1964, 1965.
Doubles 1959, 1961, 1971.
Other successes:
US Championships, singles 1961, 1964; doubles 1959, 1960, 1965, 1966.
French Championships, singles 1963, 1967; doubles 1960, 1961, 1962, 1963, 1964, 1965.
Australian Championships, singles 1961, 1963, 1964, 1965, 1966, 1967; doubles 1962, 1966, 1969.
Italian Championships, doubles 1959, 1961, 1966; mixed 1961.
Member Australian Davis Cup team 1959–67.

Revealed precocious athletic skill at the age of 14 by running 100 yards *91·44 m* in 10·6 seconds and long jumping 21 ft 6 in *6·55 m*.

FALKENBURG, Robert
Born 29 January 1926, New York, NY, USA.
Singles 1948.
Doubles 1947.
Other success:
US Championships, doubles 1944.

Member Brazil's Davis Cup team 1954, 1955, his qualification being residential. He learned and played much of his lawn tennis in Los Angeles.

FLETCHER, Kenneth Norman
Born 15 June 1940, Brisbane, Queensland, Australia.
Doubles 1966.
Mixed 1963, 1965, 1966, 1968.
Other successes:
US Championships, mixed 1963.
French Championships, doubles 1964; mixed 1963, 1964, 1965.
Australian Championships, mixed 1963, 1964.

Achieved the 'Grand Slam' in mixed doubles with Margaret Smith in 1963.

FRASER, Neale Andrew
Born 3 October 1933, St Kilda, Melbourne, Victoria, Australia.
Singles 1960.
Doubles 1959, 1961.
Mixed 1962.
Other successes:
US Championships, singles 1959, 1960; doubles 1957, 1959, 1960; mixed 1958, 1959, 1960.
French Championships, doubles 1958, 1960, 1962.
Australian Championships, doubles 1957, 1958, 1962; mixed 1956.
Italian Championships, doubles 1957, 1959, 1961.
Member Australian Davis Cup team 1958–63.

Left handed.

GARLAND, Charles Stedman
Born 29 October 1898, Pittsburgh, Pennsylvania, USA.
Died 28 January 1971, Baltimore, Maryland, USA.
Doubles 1920.

Secretary USLTA 1921–2.

GERULAITIS, Vitas
Born 26 July 1954, Brooklyn, NY, USA.
Doubles 1975.

GILBERT, John Brian
Born 17 July 1887, Barnes, Surrey, England.
Died 28 June 1974, Roehampton, London, England.
Mixed 1924.
Other success:
Member British Davis Cup team 1923–5.

A left hander.

GOBERT, André Henri
Born 30 September 1890, Paris, France.
Died 6 December 1951, Paris, France.
Doubles 1911.
Other successes:
Olympic gold medals (2) 1912.
Member French Davis Cup team 1912–22.

GODFREE, Leslie Allison, MC
Born 27 April 1885, Brighton, Sussex, England.
Died 17 November 1971, Richmond, London, England.
Doubles 1923.
Mixed 1926.
Other success:
Member British Davis Cup team 1923–7.

GONZALES, Ricardo Alonzo (Pancho)
Born 9 May 1928, Los Angeles, California, USA.
Doubles 1949.
Other successes:
US Championships, singles 1948, 1949.
French Championships, doubles 1949.
Member US Davis Cup team 1949.

Turning professional in 1949 he was denied participation in the traditional events until open lawn tennis came about in 1968. Even so he established himself as one of the most powerful players of all time. His 112 games singles in 1969 in the first round against Charles Pasarell is, with the institution of the tie break, unlikely to be surpassed for the duration of its drama.

GORE, Arthur William Charles (Wentworth)
Born 2 January 1868, Lyndhurst, Hampshire, England.

Died 1 December 1928, Kensington, London, England.
Singles 1901, 1908, 1909.
Doubles 1909.
Other successes:
Olympic gold medals (2) 1908.
Member British Isles Davis Cup team 1900–12.

The most assiduous British player, competing first in 1888 and last in 1927, the year before his death. His statistical record for all events was:

	Matches		
	Won	*Lost*	*Total*
Singles	64	26	90
Doubles	32	26	58
Mixed	14	8	22
Plate singles	11	1	12
Total	121	61	182

He was the last of the Old Harrovian singles champions.

GORE, Spencer William

Born 10 March 1850, Wimbledon, Surrey, England.
Died 19 April 1906, Ramsgate, Kent, England.
Singles 1877.

The first champion. Son of the Hon C. A. Gore and Lady Augusta L. P. Ponsonby, Dowager Countess of Kerry. Educated Harrow 1863–9. Captain of cricket 1869. Rackets player 1869. Became land agent and surveyor. His brother became, in 1905, the first Bishop of Birmingham. Did not play in the Championships after his unsuccessful challenge-round defence in 1878.

GOTTFRIED, Brian Edward

Born 27 January 1952, Baltimore, Maryland, USA.
Doubles 1976.
Other successes:
French Championships, doubles 1975.
Italian Championships, doubles 1974, 1975, 1976.
Member US Davis Cup team 1975.

HADOW, Patrick Francis

Born 24 January 1855, Regent's Park, Middlesex, England.
Died 29 June 1946, Bridgwater, Somerset, England.
Singles 1878.

Educated Harrow 1868–73. Winner of Public School Rackets Championship 1873. Cricket for Harrow 1872–3. Played cricket for Middlesex 1873–4. Tea planter in Ceylon. A big-game hunter in India, central Asia and Africa. Returned to Wimbledon only in 1926 to receive Jubilee Medal as a former champion.

HAMILTON, Willoby (Willoughby James)

Born 9 December 1864, Monasterevin, Co Kildare, Ireland.
Died 27 September 1943, Dundrum, Dublin, Ireland.
Singles 1890.
Other successes:
Irish Championships, singles 1889; doubles 1886, 1887, 1888; mixed 1889.
Soccer international for Ireland.

HARTLEY, Rev. John Thorneycroft

Born 9 January 1849, Tong, Shifnal, Shropshire, England.
Died 21 August 1935, Knaresborough, Yorkshire, England.
Singles 1879, 1880.

Educated Harrow 1862–6 and Oxford. Won Oxford University Rackets Championship 1869 and Tennis 1870. Curate of Christ Church, Southwark, 1872–4. Vicar of Burmeston, Bedale, 1874–1919. Rural Dean of Catterick East 1891–1917. Hon. Canon of Ripon 1905.

HARTWIG, Rex Noel

Born 2 September 1929, Culcairn, NSW, Australia.
Doubles 1954, 1955.
Other successes:
US Championships, doubles 1953.
Australian Championships, doubles 1954; mixed 1953, 1954.
Member Australian Davis Cup team 1953–5.
Became a professional in 1955.

HEWITT, Robert Anthony John

Born 12 January 1940, Sydney, NSW, Australia.
Doubles 1962, 1964, 1967, 1972.
Other successes:
French Championships, doubles 1972; mixed 1970.
Australian Championships, doubles 1963, 1964; mixed 1961.
Member South African Davis Cup team 1967–74.
Adopted South African affiliation on residential qualification 1967.

HOAD, Lewis Alan (Lew)
Born 23 November 1934, Glebe, NSW, Australia.
Singles 1956, 1957.
Doubles 1953, 1955, 1956.
Other successes:
US Championships, doubles 1956.
French Championships, singles 1956; doubles 1953; mixed 1954.
Australian Championships, singles 1956; doubles 1953, 1956, 1957.
Italian Championships, singles 1956; doubles 1956, 1957.
Member Australian Davis Cup team 1953–6.
Became a professional in 1957.

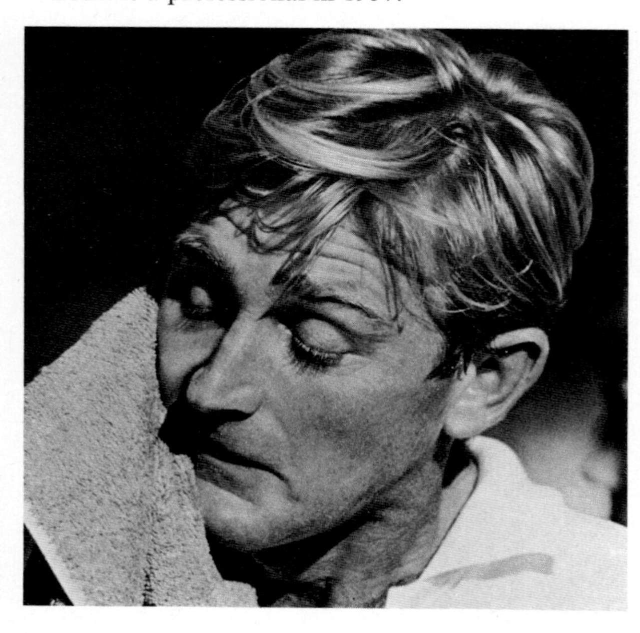

HOWE, Robert Neville
Born 3 August 1925, Sydney, NSW, Australia.
Mixed 1958.
Other successes:
French Championships, mixed 1960, 1962.
Australian Championships, mixed 1958.

HUGHES, George Patrick
Born 21 December 1902, Sutton Coldfield, Warwickshire, England.
Doubles 1936.
Other successes:
French Championships, doubles 1933.
Australian Championships, doubles 1934.
Italian Championships, singles 1931; doubles 1931, 1932; mixed 1931.
Member British Davis Cup team 1929–36.

HUNTER, Francis Townsend
Born 28 June 1894, New York, NY, USA.
Doubles 1924, 1927.
Mixed 1927, 1929.
Other successes:
US Championships, doubles 1927.
Olympic gold medal 1924.
Member US Davis Cup team 1927–9.
Became a professional in 1930.

JOHNSTON, William (W. M.)
Born 2 November 1894, San Francisco, California, USA.
Died 1 May 1946, San Francisco, California, USA.
Singles 1923.
Other successes:
US Championships, singles 1919; doubles 1915, 1916, 1920; mixed 1921.
World Hard Court Championships, singles 1923.
Member US Davis Cup team 1920–7.
Nicknamed 'Little Bill'.

KODES, Jan
Born 1 March 1946, Prague, Czechoslovakia.
Singles 1973.
Other successes:
French Championships, singles 1970, 1971.
Member Czech Davis Cup team 1966–76.
Graduated in economics at Prague University.

KRAMER, John Albert (Jack)
Born 1 August 1921, Las Vegas, Nevada, USA.
Singles 1947.
Doubles 1946, 1947.
Other successes:
US Championships, singles 1946, 1947; doubles 1940, 1941, 1943, 1947; mixed 1941.
Member US Davis Cup team 1939, 1946, 1947.

Became a professional in 1947. Subsequently a leading promoter of the professional game. Executive director of the Association of Tennis Professionals from its foundation in 1972.

LACOSTE, Jean René
Born 2 July 1904, Paris, France.
Singles 1925, 1928.
Doubles 1925.
Other successes:
US Championships, singles 1926, 1927.
French Championships, singles 1925, 1927, 1929; doubles 1925, 1929.
Member French Davis Cup team 1923–8.

Retired because of ill health in 1929, making a brief competitive reappearance in the French championships 1932. An outstanding tactician of the game and his *Lacoste on Tennis* (London, 1928) is among the most notable works on the game.

LAVER, Rodney George, MBE (Rod)
Born 9 August 1938, Rockhampton, Queensland, Australia.
Singles 1961, 1962, 1968, 1969.
Doubles 1971.
Mixed 1959, 1960.
Other successes:
US Championships, singles 1962, 1969.

French Championships, singles 1962, 1969; doubles 1961; mixed 1961
Australian Championships, singles 1960, 1962, 1969; doubles 1959, 1960, 1961, 1969.
Italian Championships, singles 1962, 1971; doubles 1962.
Member Australian Davis Cup team 1959–62, 1973.

Unique as twice winner of the 'Grand Slam' in 1962 and 1969. A left hander.

LAWFORD, Herbert Fortescue

Born 15 May 1851, Bayswater, Middlesex, England.
Died 20 April 1925, Dess, Aberdeenshire, Scotland.
Singles 1887.
Other successes:
Irish Championships, singles 1884, 1885, 1886.
Oxford Doubles Championship 1879.

Educated Repton and Edinburgh. Noted for a famous forehand, known as the 'Lawford stroke'.

LEWIS, Ernest Wool

Born 5 April 1867, Hammersmith, Middlesex, England.
Died 19 April 1930, Plymouth, Devon, England.
Doubles 1892.
Other successes:
Irish Championships, singles 1890, 1891; doubles 1889, 1892; mixed 1888.

Educated Godolphin School, Hammersmith.

LOTT, George Martin

Born 16 October 1906, Springfield, Illinois, USA.
Doubles 1931, 1934.
Mixed 1931.
Other successes:
US Championships, doubles 1928, 1929, 1930, 1933, 1934; mixed 1929, 1931, 1934.
Member US Davis Cup team 1928–34.

Turned professional 1934.

LYCETT, Randolph

Born 27 August 1886, Birmingham, England.
Died 9 February 1935, Jersey, Channel Islands.
Doubles 1921, 1922, 1923.
Mixed 1919, 1921, 1923.
Other successes:
Australian Championships, doubles 1905, 1911.
Member British Davis Cup team 1921–3.

Learned his lawn tennis in Australia and declined an offer of Davis Cup selection for Australasia in November 1911. Notable for winning the Wimbledon doubles championship for three successive years with three different partners, Max Woosnam, James Anderson and Leslie Godfree.

McGREGOR, Kenneth Bruce

Born 2 June 1929, Adelaide, SA, Australia.
Doubles 1951, 1952.
Other successes:
US Championships, doubles 1951; mixed 1950.
French Championships, doubles 1951, 1952.
Australian Championships, singles 1952; doubles 1951, 1952.
Member Australian Davis Cup team 1950–2.

Became a professional in 1953. A good footballer (Australian rules).

McKINLEY, Charles Robert (Chuck)

Born 5 January 1941, St Louis, Missouri, USA.
Singles 1963.
Other successes:
US Championships, doubles 1961, 1963, 1964.
Member US Davis Cup team 1960–5.

McMILLAN, Frew Donald

Born 20 May 1942, Springs, Transvaal, South Africa.
Doubles 1967, 1972.
Other successes:
French Championships, doubles 1972; mixed 1966.
Member South African Davis Cup team 1965–76.

Distinguished for his double-fisted strokes on both forehand and backhand and wearing a white cloth cap.

MAHONY, Harold Segerson

Born 13 February 1867, Edinburgh, Scotland.
Died 27 June 1905, Caragh Hill, nr Killorglin, Co Kerry, Ireland.
Singles 1896.
Other successes:
Irish Championships, singles 1898; mixed 1895, 1896.

Despite his birthplace, an Irish player. He was killed when thrown from his bicycle at the foot of an Irish hill.

MAIER, Enrique Gerardo

Born 31 December 1910, Barcelona, Spain.
Mixed 1932.
Other successes:
US Championships, mixed 1935.
Member Spanish Davis Cup team 1929–34.

Fought with General Franco's forces in the Spanish Civil War.

MAKO, Constantine Gene
Born 24 January 1916, Budapest, Hungary.
Doubles 1937, 1938.
Other successes:
US Championships, doubles 1936, 1938; mixed 1936.
Member US Davis Cup team 1935–8.

Most notable as the doubles partner of Don Budge. He learned and played his lawn tennis as a Californian.

MAYER, Alexander
Born 5 April 1952, New York, NY, USA.
Doubles 1975.

Graduate Stanford University.

MIKI, Tatsuyoshi (Ryuki)
Born 11 February 1904, Takamotsu, Japan.
Died 9 January 1967, Tokyo, Japan.
Mixed 1934.
Other success:
Captained Japanese Davis Cup team 1934.

Graduate Osaka University of Commerce.

MULLOY, Gardnar Putnam
Born 22 November 1913, Washington, DC, USA.
Doubles 1957.
Other successes:
US Championships, doubles 1942, 1945, 1946, 1948.
Member US Davis Cup team 1946–57.

At 43 years 7 months the oldest player to win a Wimbledon championship. He appeared fourteen times in the top ten of the US ranking list from 1939 to 1954, being first in 1952.

NASTASE, Ilie
Born 19 July 1946, Bucharest, Romania.
Doubles 1973.
Mixed 1970, 1972.
Other successes:
US Championships, singles 1972; doubles 1975.
French Championships, singles 1973; doubles 1970.
Italian Championships, singles 1970, 1973; doubles 1970, 1972.
Grand Prix Masters', singles 1971, 1972, 1973, 1975.
Member Romanian Davis Cup team 1966–76.

Outstandingly the best player to come from Eastern Europe with a delicacy of touch and repertoire of shots that was inspired by Manuel Santana of Spain.

NEWCOMBE, John David
Born 23 May 1944, Sydney, NSW, Australia.
Singles 1967, 1970, 1971.
Doubles 1965, 1966, 1968, 1969, 1970, 1974.
Other successes:
US Championships, singles 1967, 1973; doubles 1967, 1971, 1973; mixed 1964.
French Championships, doubles 1967, 1969, 1973.
Australian Championships, singles 1973, 1975; doubles 1965, 1967, 1971, 1973, 1976.
Italian Championships, singles 1969; doubles 1971, 1973; mixed 1964.
Member Australian Davis Cup team 1963–76.

OLMEDO, Alejandro Rodriguez (Alex)
Born 24 March 1936, Arequipa, Peru.
Singles 1959.
Other successes:
US Championships, doubles 1958.
Australian Championships, singles 1959.
Member US Davis Cup team 1958–9.

Educated USC, Los Angeles, California. Turned professional 1959.

OSUNA, Rafael Herrera
Born 15 September 1938, Mexico City, Mexico.
Died 4 June 1969, nr Monterrey, Mexico.
Doubles 1960, 1963.
Other successes:
US Championships, singles 1963; doubles 1962.
Member Mexican Davis Cup team 1958–69.

He met his death in an air crash.

PALAFOX, Antonio
Born 28 April 1936, Guadalja, Mexico.
Doubles 1963.
Other successes:
US Championships, doubles 1962.
Member Mexican Davis Cup team 1956–65.

PARKE, James Cecil
Born 26 July 1881, Clones, Co Monaghan, Ireland.
Died 27 February 1946, Llandudno, North Wales.
Mixed 1914.
Other successes:
Australian Championships, singles 1912; doubles 1912.
Member British Davis Cup team 1908–20.

Irish rugby international 1903–7, thrice captain, twenty caps in all. A scratch golfer. Educated Lurgan College and Dublin University. Gazetted Major in Leinster Regiment 1917.

PARKER, Frank Andrew (*née* **Franciszek Andzej Paikowski)**
Born 31 January 1916, Milwaukee, Wisconsin, USA.
Doubles 1949.
Other successes:
US Championships, singles 1944, 1945; doubles 1943.
French Championships, singles 1948, 1949; doubles 1949.
Member US Davis Cup team 1937–48.

Became a professional in 1949.

PATTERSON, Gerald Leighton, MC
Born 17 December 1895, Melbourne, Victoria, Australia.
Died 13 June 1967, Melbourne, Victoria, Australia.
Singles 1919, 1922.
Mixed 1920.
Other successes:
US Championships, doubles 1919.
Australian Championships, singles 1927; doubles 1914, 1922, 1925, 1926, 1927.

Member Australasian/Australian Davis Cup team 1919–28.

He was the nephew of Dame Nellie Melba.

PATTY, John Edward (Budge)

Born 11 February 1924, Fort Smith, Arkansas, USA.
Singles 1950.
Doubles 1957.
Other successes:
French Championships, singles 1950; mixed 1946.
Italian Championships, singles 1954.
Member US Davis Cup team 1951.

Took up residence in Europe following service in US army in the Second World War.

PERRY, Frederick John

Born 18 May 1909, Stockport, Cheshire, England.
Singles 1934, 1935, 1936.
Mixed 1935, 1936.
Other successes:
US Championships, singles 1933, 1934, 1936; mixed 1932.
French Championships, singles 1935; doubles 1933; mixed 1932.
Australian Championships, singles 1934; doubles 1934.
Member British Davis Cup team 1931–6.
World table tennis singles champion 1929.

Educated Ealing County School. Became a professional in 1936. The first player to become champion of America, Australia, France and Wimbledon. Later became US citizen.

PETRA, Yvon François Marie

Born 8 March 1916, Cholon, Indo-China.
Singles 1946.
Other successes:
French Championships, doubles 1938, 1946; mixed 1937.
Member French Davis Cup team 1937–47.

Became a professional in 1948.

PIM, Joshua

Born 20 May 1869, Bray, Co Wicklow, Ireland.
Died 15 April 1942, Dublin, Ireland.
Singles 1893, 1894.
Doubles 1890, 1893.
Other successes:
Irish Championships, singles 1893, 1894, 1895; doubles 1890, 1891, 1893, 1894, 1895.
British Isles Davis Cup team member 1902.

FRCS (Dublin).

QUIST, Adrian Karl

Born 23 January 1913, Medindie, SA, Australia.
Doubles 1935, 1950.
Other successes:
US Championships, doubles 1939.
French Championships, doubles 1935.
Australian Championships, singles 1936, 1940, 1948; doubles 1936, 1937, 1938, 1939, 1940, 1946, 1947, 1948, 1949, 1950.
Italian Championships, mixed 1950.
Member Australian Davis Cup team 1933–48.

His tenure as Australian doubles champion was unique, holding the title without a break from 1936 to 1950, the first two years with Don Turnbull and subsequently with John Bromwich. The championship was not held between 1940 and 1946. When Quist and Bromwich lost in 1951 to Frank Sedgman and Ken McGregor it was Quist's eleventh successive final.

RALSTON, Richard Dennis

Born 27 July 1942, Bakersfield, California, USA.
Doubles 1960.
Other successes:
US Championships, doubles 1961, 1963, 1964.
French Championships, doubles 1966
Member US Davis Cup team 1960–6; non-playing captain 1972–4.

Became a professional in 1966. He was, at 17 years 11 months, the youngest male champion of Wimbledon in 1960.

RAMIREZ, Raul Carlos

Born 20 June 1953, Ensenada, Mexico.
Doubles 1976.
Other successes:
French Championships, doubles 1975.
Italian Championships, singles 1975; doubles 1974, 1975, 1976.
Member Mexican Davis Cup team 1971–6.

RENSHAW, James Ernest

Born 3 January 1861, Leamington, Warwickshire, England.
Died 2 September 1899, Twyford, Berkshire, England.
Singles 1888.
Doubles 1884, 1885, 1886, 1888, 1889.
Other successes:
Irish Championships, singles 1883, 1887, 1888, 1892; doubles 1881, 1883, 1884, 1885.
Oxford Doubles Championship 1880, 1881.

Educated Cheltenham. The younger of twin brothers. With his brother the creator of modern lawn tennis.

RENSHAW, William Charles

Born 3 January 1861, Leamington, Warwickshire, England.
Died 12 August 1904, Swanage, Dorset, England.
Singles 1881, 1882, 1883, 1884, 1885, 1886, 1889.
Doubles 1884, 1885, 1886, 1888, 1889.
Other successes:
Irish Championships, singles 1880, 1881, 1882; doubles 1881, 1883, 1884, 1885; mixed 1884, 1885.
Oxford Doubles Championship 1880, 1881.

Educated Cheltenham. The elder of twin brothers and the main creator of modern lawn-tennis technique. Unequalled among men in winning seven singles championships at Wimbledon.

RICHARDS, Vincent

Born 20 March 1903, New York, NY, USA.
Died 28 September 1959, New York, NY, USA.
Doubles 1924.
Other successes:
US Championships, doubles 1918, 1921, 1922, 1926; mixed 1919, 1924.
Olympic gold medals (2) 1924.
Member US Davis Cup team 1922–6.

Became a professional in 1926.

RIESSEN, Martin Claire (Marty)

Born 4 December 1941, Hinsdale, Illinois, USA.
Mixed 1975.
Other successes:
US Championships, doubles 1976; mixed 1969, 1970, 1972.
French Championships, doubles 1971; mixed 1969.
Italian Championships, doubles 1968; mixed 1968.
Member US Davis Cup team 1963–73.

RIGGS, Robert Larimore

Born 25 February 1918, Los Angeles, California, USA.
Singles 1939.
Doubles 1939.
Mixed 1939.
Other successes:
US Championships, singles 1939, 1941; mixed 1940.
Member US Davis Cup team 1938–9.

Became a professional in 1941. Unique in winning all three events at his only challenge in the Wimbledon Championships. Played two widely publicised matches against women in Las Vegas in 1974, beating Margaret Court but being beaten by Billie Jean King.

RISELEY, Frank Lorymer

Born 6 July 1877, Clifton, Bristol, England.
Died 6 February 1959, Torquay, Devon, England.
Doubles 1902, 1906.
Other successes:
Irish Championships, singles 1906; doubles 1906; mixed 1906.
Member British Davis Cup team 1904, 1922.

RITCHIE, Major Josiah George

Born 18 October 1870, Westminster, Middlesex, England.
Died 28 February 1955, Ashford, Middlesex, England.
Doubles 1908, 1910.
Other successes:
Irish Championships, singles 1907.
German Championships, singles 1903, 1904, 1905, 1906, 1908; doubles 1904, 1906.
Olympic gold medal 1908.
Member British Davis Cup team 1908.

ROCHE, Anthony Dalton (Tony)

Born 17 May 1945, Wagga Wagga, NSW, Australia.
Doubles 1965, 1968, 1969, 1970, 1974.
Mixed 1976.
Other successes:
US Championships, doubles 1967.
French Championships, singles 1966; doubles 1967, 1969.
Australian Championships, doubles 1965, 1967, 1971, 1976; mixed 1966.
Italian Championships, singles 1966; doubles 1965, 1971.
Member Australian Davis Cup team 1964–76.

A left hander.

ROSE, Mervyn Gordon

Born 23 January 1930, Coffs Harbour, NSW, Australia.
Doubles 1954.
Mixed 1957.
Other successes:
US Championships, doubles 1952, 1953.
French Championships, singles 1958.
Australian Championships, singles 1954; doubles 1954.
Italian Championships, singles 1958.
Member Australian Davis Cup team 1951, 1957.

Turned professional 1958. A left hander.

ROSEWALL, Kenneth Robert

Born 2 November 1934, Sydney, NSW, Australia.
Doubles 1953, 1956.
Other successes:
US Championships, singles 1956, 1970; doubles 1956, 1969; mixed 1956.
French Championships, singles 1953, 1968; doubles 1953, 1968.
Australian Championships, singles 1953, 1955, 1971, 1972; doubles 1953, 1956, 1972.
Italian Championships, doubles 1953.
Member Australian Davis Cup team 1953–6, 1973, 1975.

Famous for the classical purity of his strokes and the control and severity of his backhand. He was 18 when he won his first Australian title in 1953 and 37 when he also won in 1972! He was singles finalist at Wimbledon in 1954, 1956, 1970 and 1974.

SANTANA, Manuel Martinez

Born 10 May 1938, Madrid, Spain.
Singles 1966.
Other successes:
US Championships, singles 1965.
French Championships, singles 1961, 1964; doubles 1963.
Member Spanish Davis Cup team 1958–73, winning 91 out of 119 rubbers.

Notable for both his geniality and delicacy of touch. Outstandingly the best player from Spain.

SAVITT, Richard

Born 4 March 1927, Bayonne, New Jersey, USA.
Singles 1951.
Other successes:
Australian Championships, singles 1951.
Member US Davis Cup team 1951.

SCHMIDT, Ulf Christian Johan

Born 12 July 1934, Nacka, Stockholm, Sweden.
Doubles 1958.
Other success:
Member Swedish Davis Cup team 1954–64.

SCHROEDER, Frederick Rudolph

Born 20 July 1921, Newark, New Jersey, USA.
Singles 1949.
Other successes:
US Championships, singles 1942; doubles 1940, 1941, 1947; mixed 1942.
Member US Davis Cup team 1946–51.

He learned and played his lawn tennis as a Californian.

SEDGMAN, Frank Allan

Born 29 October 1927, Mount Albert, Victoria, Australia.
Singles 1952.
Doubles 1948, 1951, 1952.
Mixed 1951, 1952.
Other successes:
US Championships, singles 1951, 1952; doubles 1950, 1951; mixed 1951, 1952.
French Championships, doubles 1951, 1952; mixed 1951, 1952.
Australian Championships, singles 1949, 1950; doubles 1951, 1952; mixed 1949, 1950.
Italian Championships, singles 1952; doubles 1952.
Member Australian Davis Cup team 1949–52.

Became a professional in January 1953.

SEIXAS, Elias Victor (Vic)

Born 30 August 1923, Philadelphia, Pennsylvania, USA.
Singles 1953.
Mixed 1953, 1954, 1955, 1956.
Other successes:
US Championships, singles 1954; doubles 1952, 1954; mixed 1953, 1954, 1955.
French Championships, doubles 1954, 1955; mixed 1953.
Australian Championships, doubles 1955.
Member US Davis Cup team 1951–7.

SMITH, Stanley Roger (Stan)

Born 14 December 1946, Pasadena, California, USA.
Singles 1972.
Other successes:
US Championships, singles 1971; doubles 1968.
Australian Championships, doubles 1970.
Member US Davis Cup team 1968–76.

SMITH, Sydney Howard

Born 3 February 1872, Stroud, Gloucestershire, England.
Died 27 March 1947, Stroud, Gloucestershire, England.
Doubles 1902, 1906.
Other successes:
Welsh Championships, singles 1897, 1898, 1899, 1900, 1901, 1902, 1904, 1905, 1906.
Member British Davis Cup team 1905–6.
All England Badminton singles champion 1900.

He was famous for his fierce forehand drive. He wore a leg iron.

SPENCE, Patrick Dennis Benham

Born 11 February 1898, Queenstown, Cape Colony, South Africa.
Mixed 1928.
Other successes:
French Championships, mixed 1931.
Member South African Davis Cup team 1924–31.

Educated Edinburgh University. Medical doctor. Played rugby football for Edinburgh University and Guy's Hospital. As British resident played in many British tournaments.

STOEFEN, Lester Rollo

Born 30 March 1911, Des Moines, Iowa, USA.
Died 8 February 1970, La Jolla, California, USA.
Doubles 1934.
Other successes:
US Championships, doubles 1933, 1934.
Member US Davis Cup team 1934.

A notable server. Became a professional in 1934.

STOKER, Frank Owen

Born 29 May 1867, Dublin, Ireland.
Died 8 January 1939, Dublin, Ireland.
Doubles 1890, 1893.
Other successes:
Irish Championships, doubles 1890, 1891, 1893, 1894, 1895.

STOLLE, Fred Sidney

Born 8 October 1938, Hornsby, NSW, Australia.
Doubles 1962, 1964.
Mixed 1961, 1964, 1969.
Other successes:
US Championships, singles 1966; doubles 1965, 1966, 1969; mixed 1962, 1965.
French Championships, singles 1965; doubles 1965, 1968.
Australian Championships, doubles 1963, 1964, 1966; mixed 1962.
Italian Championships, doubles 1963, 1964, 1966; mixed 1962.
Member Australian Davis Cup team 1964–6.

Became a professional early in 1967.

STURGESS, Eric William

Born 10 May 1920, Johannesburg, South Africa.
Mixed 1949, 1950.
Other successes:
US Championships, mixed 1949.
French Championships, doubles 1947; mixed 1947, 1949.
South African Championships, singles 1939, 1940, 1946, 1948, 1949, 1950, 1951, 1952, 1953, 1954, 1957; doubles 1946, 1947, 1948, 1951, 1952, 1953, 1955, 1957; mixed 1940, 1946, 1947, 1948, 1951, 1953.
Member South African Davis Cup team 1947–51.

THOMAS, Ronald Victor

Born 1889, Hammond, SA, Australia.
Died December 1936, Adelaide, SA, Australia.
Doubles 1919.
Other successes:
Australian Championships, doubles 1919, 1920.

TILDEN, William Tatem (Bill)

Born 10 February 1893, Germantown, Pennsylvania, USA.
Died 5 June 1953, Los Angeles, California, USA.
Singles 1920, 1921, 1930.
Doubles 1927.
Other successes:
US Championships, singles 1920, 1921, 1922, 1923, 1924, 1925, 1929; doubles 1918, 1921, 1922, 1923, 1927; mixed 1913, 1914, 1922, 1923.
French Championships, mixed 1930.
Italian Championships, singles 1930; doubles 1930.
Member US Davis Cup team 1920–30, winning thirteen consecutive challenge round singles 1920–6.

Became a professional in December 1930. Generally acknowledged as one of the greatest players of all time. Author of several illuminating books on lawn tennis, including *The Art of Lawn Tennis* (London, 1920), *Match Play and the Spin of the Ball* (London, 1928) and *Aces, Places and Faults* (London, 1938).

TRABERT, Marion Anthony (Tony)
Born 16 August 1930, Cincinnati, Ohio, USA.
Singles 1955.
Other successes:
US Championships, singles 1953, 1955; doubles 1954.
French Championships, singles 1954, 1955; doubles 1950, 1954, 1955.
Italian Championships, doubles 1950.
Member US Davis Cup team 1951–5; captain 1976.

In neither of his singles wins in the US Championships nor in his singles title at Wimbledon did Trabert lose a set in any round. He became a professional in 1955.

TUCKEY, Charles Raymond Davys
Born 15 June 1910, Godalming, Surrey, England.
Doubles 1936.
Other successes:
Cambridge blue 1931.
British Davis Cup team 1935–7.

A regular British army officer. In 1931 and 1932 partnered his mother Mrs C. O. Tuckey, in the mixed doubles.

VAN RYN, John William
Born 30 June 1906, Newport News, Virginia, USA.
Doubles 1929, 1930, 1931.
Other successes:
US Championships, doubles 1931, 1935.
Member US Davis Cup team 1929–36.

VINES, Henry Ellsworth
Born 28 September 1911, Los Angeles, California, USA.
Singles 1932.
Other successes:
US Championships, singles 1931, 1932; doubles 1932; mixed 1933.
Australian Championships, doubles 1933.
Member US Davis Cup team 1932–3.

Became a professional in 1933. Subsequently played successfully as a professional golfer.

VON CRAMM, Baron Gottfried
Born 7 July 1909, Nettlingen, nr Hanover, Germany.
Died 9 November 1976, in car crash, near Cairo, Egypt.
Mixed 1933.
Other successes:
US Championships, doubles 1937.
French Championships, singles 1934, 1936; doubles 1937.
German Championships, singles 1932, 1933, 1934, 1935, 1948, 1949; doubles 1948, 1949; mixed 1932, 1933, 1934.
Member German Davis Cup team 1932–53, winning 82 out of 102 rubbers.

He was imprisoned by the Gestapo in 1938.

WILBERFORCE, (Sir) Herbert William Wrangham
Born 8 February 1864, Munich, Germany.
Died 28 March 1941, Kensington, London, England.
Doubles 1887.
Other successes:
Cambridge blue 1883, 1884, 1885 and 1886.

Knighted 1931. A barrister. Great grandson of the emancipator William Wilberforce. Secretary of the Championships 1889–90. All England Club President 1921–30, Chairman 1921–36. Author of *Lawn Tennis* (London, 1889).

WILDING, Anthony Frederick, MC
Born 31 October 1883, Christchurch, New Zealand.
Died 9 May 1915, Neuve Chapelle, France.
Singles 1910, 1911, 1912, 1913.
Doubles 1907, 1908, 1910, 1914.

Other successes:
Scottish Championships, singles 1904; mixed 1904.
Australian Championships, singles 1906, 1909; doubles 1906.
New Zealand Championships, singles 1906, 1908, 1909.
German Championships, mixed 1905.
Member Australasian Davis Cup team 1905–14.
Cambridge blue 1904–5.

Admitted as barrister 1906. Won motor reliability trial Land's End to John o' Groat's in 1907. Captain Royal Marines. Killed in action.

WILLIAMS, Richard Norris

Born 29 January 1891, Geneva, Switzerland.
Died 2 June 1968, Bryn Mawr, Pennsylvania, USA.
Doubles 1920.
Other successes:
US Championships, singles 1914, 1916; doubles 1926; mixed 1912.
Olympic gold medal 1924.
Member US Davis Cup team 1913–26.

Educated at Harvard. Survived the *Titanic* disaster 1912. Served in US Army First World War. Chevalier de la Légion d'honneur. Croix de Guerre.

WOOD, Patrick O'Hara

Born 30 April 1891, Melbourne, Victoria, Australia.
Died 3 December 1961, Melbourne, Victoria, Australia.
Doubles 1919.
Mixed 1922.
Other successes:
Australian Championships, singles 1920, 1923; doubles 1919, 1920, 1923, 1925.
Member Australasian Davis Cup team 1922, 1924.

Served as Staff Captain in Australian forces First World War.

WOOD, Sydney Burr Beardslee

Born 1 November 1911, Black Rock, Connecticut, USA.
Singles 1931.
Other successes:
Member US Davis Cup team 1931, 1934.

First competed at Wimbledon in 1927 when only 15. He is the only champion to have gained his title with a walkover.

WOOSNAM, Maxwell

Born 6 September 1892, Liverpool, England.
Died 14 July 1965, Westminster, London, England.
Doubles 1921.
Other successes:
Olympic gold medal 1912.
Member British Davis Cup team 1921, 1924.
Cambridge blue 1914, 1919.

A notable all-rounder. He was a Cambridge soccer blue 1912, 1913, 1914, a real tennis blue 1913, 1914 and a golf blue 1912, 1913. He played soccer for Manchester City and England.

Educated at Winchester and Trinity, Cambridge.

WOMEN

ARTH, Jeanne Marie

Born 21 July 1935, St Paul, Minnesota, USA.
Doubles 1959.
Other successes:
US Championships, doubles 1958, 1959.
Member US Wightman Cup team 1959.

A school teacher.

AUSSEM, Cilly

Later Contessa F. M. Della Corta Brae (married 1936).
Born 4 January 1909, Cologne, Germany.
Died 22 March 1963, Portafino, Genoa, Italy.
Singles 1931.
Other successes:
French Championships, singles 1931; mixed 1930.
German Championships, singles 1927, 1930, 1931; mixed 1928, 1935.

BETZ, Pauline May

Later Mrs R. Addie (married 1949).
Born 6 August 1919, Dayton, Ohio, USA.
Singles 1946.
Other successes:
US Championships, singles 1942, 1943, 1944, 1946.
French Championships, mixed 1946.
Member US Wightman Cup team 1946.

Became a professional in 1947. Graduate Colombia University.

BINGLEY, Blanche, *see* **HILLYARD, Mrs G. W.**

BOOTHBY, Penelope Dora Harvey

Later Mrs A. C. Geen (married 1914).
Born 2 August 1881, Finchley, Middlesex, England.
Died 22 February 1970, Hammersmith, London, England.
Singles 1909.
Doubles 1913.

All England Badminton mixed champion 1909.

BOWREY, Mrs W. W.

Formerly Lesley R. Turner (married 1968).
Born 16 August 1942, Sydney, NSW, Australia.
Doubles 1964.
Mixed 1961, 1964.
Other successes:
US Championships, doubles 1961.
French Championships, singles 1963, 1965; doubles 1964, 1965.
Australian Championships, doubles 1964, 1965, 1967; mixed 1962, 1967.
Italian Championships, singles 1967, 1968; doubles 1961, 1964, 1967; mixed 1962, 1967.
Member Australian Federation Cup team 1963–5.

BROUGH, Althea Louise

Later Mrs A. T. Clapp (married 1958).
Born 11 March 1923, Oklahoma City, Oklahoma, USA.

Singles 1948, 1949, 1950, 1955.
Doubles 1946, 1948, 1949, 1950, 1954.
Mixed 1946, 1947, 1948, 1950.
Other successes:
US Championships, singles 1947; doubles 1942, 1943, 1944, 1945, 1946, 1947, 1948, 1949, 1950, 1955, 1956, 1957; mixed 1942, 1947, 1948, 1949.
French Championships, doubles 1946, 1947, 1949.
Australian Championships, singles 1950; doubles 1950.
Member US Wightman Cup team 1946–57, winning 22 from 22 rubbers; captain 1956.

BROWNE, Mary Kendall
Later Mrs K. Kenneth-Smith (married 1958).
Born 3 June 1891, Santa Monica, California, USA.
Died 19 August 1971, Laguna Hills, California, USA.
Doubles 1926.
Other successes:
US Championships, singles 1912, 1913, 1914; doubles 1912, 1913, 1914, 1921, 1925; mixed 1912, 1913, 1914, 1921.
Member US Wightman Cup team 1925–6; captain 1925, 1926.

Became a professional in 1926 with Suzanne Lenglen.

BUENO, Maria Esther Andion
Born 11 October 1939, São Paulo, Brazil.
Singles 1959, 1960, 1964.
Doubles 1958, 1960, 1963, 1965, 1966.
Other successes:
US Championships, singles 1959, 1963, 1964, 1966; doubles 1960, 1962, 1966, 1968.
French Championships, doubles 1960; mixed 1960.
Australian Championships, doubles 1960.
Italian Championships, singles 1958, 1961, 1965; doubles 1962.

BUXTON, Angela
Later Mrs D. Silk (married 1959).
Born 16 August 1934, Liverpool, England.
Doubles 1956.
Other successes:
French Championships, doubles 1956.
Member British Wightman Cup team 1954–6.

CASALS, Rosemary
Born 16 September 1948, San Francisco, California, USA.
Doubles 1967, 1968, 1970, 1971, 1973.
Mixed 1970, 1972.
Other successes:
US Championships, doubles 1967, 1971, 1974; mixed 1975.
Italian Championships, doubles 1967, 1970.
Member US Wightman Cup team 1967, 1976; US Federation Cup team 1967.

CAWLEY, Mrs Roger
Formerly Evonne Fay Goolagong (married 1975).
Born 31 July 1951, Barellan, NSW, Australia.
Singles 1971.
Doubles 1974.
Other successes:
French Championships, singles 1971; mixed 1972.
Australian Championships, singles 1974, 1975, 1976; doubles 1971, 1974, 1975, 1976.
Italian Championships, singles 1973.
Member Australian Federation Cup team 1971–6.

CHAMBERS, Mrs Robert Lambert
Formerly Dorothea Katharine Douglass (married 1907).
Born 3 September 1878, Ealing, Middlesex, England.
Died 7 January 1960, Kensington, London, England.
Singles 1903, 1904, 1906, 1910, 1911, 1913, 1914.
Other successes:
Wimbledon non-championship doubles 1903, 1907.
Wimbledon non-championship mixed 1906, 1908, 1910.
Olympic gold medal 1908.
Member British Wightman Cup team 1925–6; captain British Wightman Cup team 1924, 1925, 1926.

All England Badminton doubles champion 1903; mixed champion 1904.

Middlesex hockey player. Became a professional in 1928.

COGHLAN, Lorraine Georgine
Later Mrs J. D. G. Robinson (married 1959).
Born 23 September 1937, Warrnambool, Victoria, Australia.
Mixed 1958.

CONNOLLY, Maureen Catherine
Later Mrs Norman Brinker (married 1955).
Born 17 September 1934, San Diego, California, USA.
Died 21 June 1969, Dallas, Texas, USA.
Singles 1952, 1953, 1954.

Other successes:
US Championships, singles 1951, 1952, 1953.
French Championships, singles 1953, 1954; doubles 1954; mixed 1954.
Australian Championships, singles 1953; doubles 1953.
Italian Championships, singles 1954.
Member US Wightman Cup team 1952–4, winning nine out of nine rubbers.

Became a professional in 1955, her amateur career having ended when she broke her leg while horse riding in 1954. She was the first woman to win the 'Grand Slam' and was never beaten in the singles at Wimbledon.

COOPER, Charlotte, *see* **STERRY, Mrs A.**

COURT, Mrs Barry M., MBE
Formerly Margaret Smith (married 1967).
Born 16 July 1942, Albury, NSW, Australia.
Singles 1963, 1965, 1970.
Doubles 1964, 1969.
Mixed 1963, 1965, 1966, 1968, 1975.
Other successes:
US Championships singles 1962, 1965, 1969, 1970, 1973; doubles 1963, 1968, 1970, 1973, 1975; mixed 1961, 1962, 1963, 1964, 1965, 1969, 1970, 1972.
French Championships, singles 1962, 1964, 1969, 1970, 1973; doubles 1964, 1965, 1966, 1973; mixed 1963, 1964, 1965, 1969.
Australian Championships, singles 1960, 1961, 1962, 1963, 1964, 1965, 1966, 1969, 1970, 1971, 1973; doubles 1961, 1962, 1963, 1965, 1969, 1970, 1971, 1973; mixed 1963, 1964.
Italian Championships, singles 1962, 1963, 1964; doubles 1963, 1964, 1968; mixed 1961, 1964, 1968.
German Championships, singles 1963, 1964, 1965; doubles 1964, 1965, 1966; mixed 1965, 1966.
South African Championships, singles 1968, 1970, 1971; doubles 1966, 1971; mixed 1966, 1970, 1971, 1974.
Member Australian Federation Cup team 1963–70, winning 20 out of 20 singles, 15 out of 20 doubles.

Unique in the number of major championships won. She won the 'Grand Slam' in singles in 1970, having performed the same feat in mixed doubles in 1963 with Ken Fletcher.

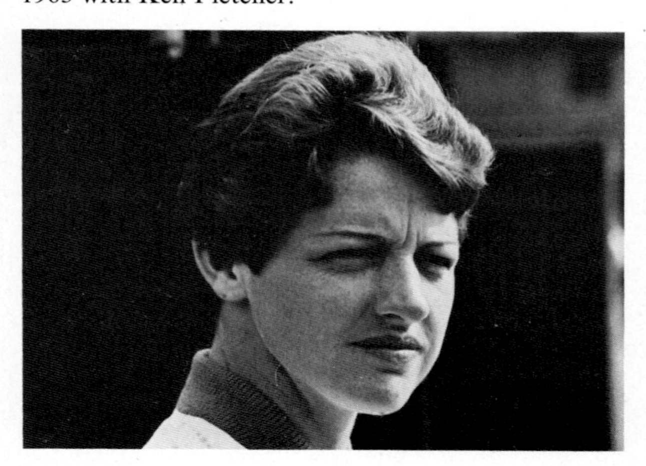

DALTON, Mrs David E.
Formerly Judith Anne Marshall Tegart (married 1969).
Born 12 December 1937, Melbourne, Victoria, Australia.
Doubles 1969.
Other successes:
US Championships, doubles 1970, 1971.
French Championships, doubles 1966.
Australian Championships, doubles 1964, 1967, 1969, 1970; mixed 1966.
Member Australian Federation Cup team 1965–70.

DOD, Charlotte (Lottie)
Born 24 September 1871, Bebington, Cheshire, England.
Died 27 June 1960, Sway, Hampshire, England.
Singles 1887, 1888, 1891, 1892, 1893.
Other successes:
Irish Championships, singles 1887; mixed 1887.

British women's golf champion 1904 (Troon).
English women's hockey international 1899, 1900.

She was never beaten at Wimbledon. The youngest champion in 1887 at the age of 15 years 10 months.

DOUGLASS, Dorothea Katharine, *see* **CHAMBERS, Mrs R. Lambert**

DU PONT, Mrs W.
Formerly Margaret Evelyn Osborne (married 1947).
Born 4 March 1918, Joseph, Oregon, USA.
Singles 1947.
Doubles 1946, 1948, 1949, 1950, 1954.
Mixed 1962.
Other successes:
US Championships, singles 1948, 1949, 1950; doubles 1941, 1942, 1943, 1944, 1945, 1946, 1947, 1948, 1949, 1950, 1955, 1956, 1957; mixed 1943, 1944, 1945, 1946, 1950, 1956, 1958, 1959, 1960.
French Championships, singles 1946, 1949; doubles 1946, 1947, 1949.
Member US Wightman Cup team 1946–62, winning 18 out of 18 rubbers; captain 1953–5, 1957, 1958, 1961–3, 1965.

DURR, Françoise
Mrs Boyd James Browning (married 1975).
Born 25 December 1942, Algiers, Algeria.
Mixed 1976.
Other successes:
US Championships, doubles 1969, 1972.
French Championships, singles 1967; doubles 1967, 1968, 1969, 1970, 1971; mixed 1968, 1971, 1973.
Italian Championships, doubles 1969.
German Championships, singles 1967.

EVERT, Christine Marie
Born 21 December 1954, Fort Lauderdale, Florida, USA.
Singles 1974, 1976.
Doubles 1976.
Other successes:
US Championships, singles 1975, 1976.
French Championships, singles 1974, 1975; doubles 1974, 1975.
Italian Championships, singles 1974, 1975; doubles 1974, 1975.
Member US Wightman Cup team 1971–6.

Double fisted on the backhand.

FABYAN, Mrs Marshall
Formerly Sarah Hammond Palfrey (married 1934); later Mrs E. T. Cooke (married 1940); later Mrs J. A. Danzig (married 1951).
Born 18 September 1912, Sharon, Massachusetts, USA.
Doubles 1938, 1939.
Other successes:
US Championships, singles 1941, 1945; doubles 1930, 1932, 1934, 1935, 1937, 1938, 1939, 1940, 1941; mixed 1932, 1935, 1937, 1941.
French Championships, mixed 1939.
Member US Wightman Cup team 1930–9.

Became a professional in 1946.

FRY, Shirley June
Later Mrs K. E. Irvin (married 1957).
Born 30 June 1927, Akron, Ohio, USA.
Singles 1956.
Doubles 1951, 1952, 1953.
Mixed 1956.
Other successes:
US Championships, singles 1956; doubles 1951, 1952, 1953, 1954.
French Championships, singles 1951; doubles 1950, 1951, 1952, 1953.
Australian Championships, singles 1957; doubles 1957.
Italian Championships, doubles 1951; mixed 1951.
Member US Wightman Cup team 1949–56.

GIBSON, Althea
Later Mrs W. A. Darben (married 1965).
Born 25 August 1927, Silver, South Carolina, USA.
Singles 1957, 1958.
Doubles 1956, 1957, 1958.
Other successes:
US Championships, 1957, 1958; mixed 1957.
French Championships, singles 1956; doubles 1956.
Australian Championships, doubles 1957.
Member US Wightman Cup team 1957–8.

The first black champion. Became a professional in 1958.

GODFREE, Mrs L. A.
Formerly Kathleen (Kitty) McKane (married 1926).
Born 7 May 1897, Bayswater, London, England.
Singles 1924, 1926.
Mixed 1924, 1926.
Other successes:
US Championships, doubles 1923, 1927; mixed 1925.
Olympic gold medallist 1920.
Member British Wightman Cup team 1923–34.

All England Badminton champion, singles 1920, 1921, 1922, 1924; doubles 1921, 1924; mixed 1924, 1925. In 1926 she and Leslie Godfree became the only married pair to win the Wimbledon mixed doubles championship.

GOOLAGONG, Evonne Fay, *see* **CAWLEY, Mrs Roger**

HANTZE, Karen J., *see* **SUSMAN, Mrs J. R.**

HARD, Darlene R.

Born 6 January 1936, Los Angeles, California, USA.
Doubles 1957, 1959, 1960, 1963.
Mixed 1957, 1959, 1960.
Other successes:
US Championships, singles 1960, 1961; doubles 1958, 1959, 1960, 1961, 1962, 1969.
French Championships, singles 1960; doubles 1955, 1957, 1960; mixed 1955, 1961.
Italian Championships, doubles 1962.
Member US Wightman Cup team 1957–60; US Federation Cup team 1963.

HARPER, Mrs L. A.

Formerly Anna Virginia McCune (married 1925).
Born 2 July 1902, Santa Barbara, California, USA.
Mixed 1931.
Other successes:
Member US Wightman Cup team 1931–2.

HART, Doris Jane

Born 20 June 1925, St Louis, Missouri, USA.
Singles 1951.
Doubles 1947, 1951, 1952, 1953.
Mixed 1951, 1952, 1953, 1954, 1955.
Other successes:
US Championships, singles 1954, 1955; doubles 1951, 1952, 1953, 1954; mixed 1951, 1952, 1953, 1954, 1955.
French Championships, singles 1950, 1952; doubles 1948, 1950, 1951, 1952, 1953; mixed 1951, 1952, 1953.
Australian Championships, singles 1949; doubles 1950; mixed 1949, 1950.
Member US Wightman Cup team 1946–55, winning 14 out of 14 singles, 8 out of 9 doubles.

Became a professional in 1955.

HILLYARD, Mrs George Whiteside

Formerly Blanche Bingley (married 1887).
Born 3 November 1863, Greenford, Middlesex, England.
Died 6 August 1946, Pulborough, Sussex, England.
Singles 1886, 1889, 1894, 1897, 1899, 1900.
Other successes:
Wimbledon non-championship doubles 1899, 1901, 1906.
German Championships, singles 1897, 1900.
Irish Championships, singles 1888, 1894, 1897; mixed 1894, 1897.
Welsh Championships, singles 1888.

Her husband, Commander (RN) Hillyard was secretary of the All England Club from 1907 to 1924. She competed 24 times in the Championships between 1884 and 1913.

JACOBS, Helen Hull

Born 6 August 1908, Globe, Arizona, USA.
Singles 1936.
Other successes:
US Championships, singles 1932, 1933, 1934, 1935; doubles 1932, 1934, 1935; mixed 1934.
Member US Wightman Cup team 1927–39.

JAMES, Winifred Alice (Freda)

Later Mrs S. H. Hammersley (married 1938).
Born 13 January 1911, Nottingham, England.
Doubles 1935, 1936.
Other successes:
US Championships, doubles 1933.
Member British Wightman Cup team 1933–9.

JONES, Mrs P. F. (Ann)

Formerly Adrianne Shirley Haydon (married 1962).
Born 7 October 1938, Birmingham, England.
Singles 1969.
Mixed 1969.
Other successes:
French Championships, singles 1961, 1966; doubles 1963, 1968, 1969.
Italian Championships, singles 1966; doubles 1969.
Member British Wightman Cup team 1957–70, 1975; captain 1971, 1972; British Federation Cup team 1963–7, 1971.
English women's table tennis international 1954–9; English women's doubles champion 1956, 1958.

A left hander.

KING, Mrs L. W. (Billie Jean)

Formerly Billie Jean Moffitt (married 1965).
Born 22 November 1943, Long Beach, California, USA.
Singles 1966, 1967, 1968, 1972, 1973, 1975.
Doubles 1961, 1962, 1965, 1967, 1968, 1970, 1971, 1972, 1973.
Mixed 1967, 1971, 1973, 1974.
Other successes:
US Championships, singles 1967, 1971, 1972, 1974; doubles 1964, 1967, 1974; mixed 1967, 1971, 1973, 1976.
French Championships, singles 1972; doubles 1972; mixed 1967, 1970.
Australian Championships, singles 1968; mixed 1968.
Italian Championships, singles 1970; doubles 1970.
German Championships, singles 1971; doubles 1971.

South African Championships, singles 1966, 1967, 1969; doubles 1967, 1970; mixed 1967.
Member US Wightman Cup team 1961–70; US Federation Cup team 1963–7, 1976; Federation Cup captain 1965, 1976.

KIYOMURA, Ann Kazuyo

Born 22 August 1955, San Mateo, California, USA.
Doubles 1975.

KRAHWINKEL, Hilde

Later Fru S. Sperling, Denmark (married 1933).
Born 26 March 1908, Essen, Germany.
Mixed 1933.
Other successes:
French Championships, singles 1935, 1936, 1937.
German Championships, singles 1933, 1934, 1935, 1937, 1939; doubles 1932, 1937; mixed 1932, 1933, 1934.

LARCOMBE, Mrs D. R.

Formerly Ethel Warneford Thomson (married 1906).
Born 8 June 1879, Islington, Middlesex, England.
Died 11 August 1965, Budleigh Salterton, Devon, England.
Singles 1912.
Mixed 1914.
Other successes:
Wimbledon non-championship doubles 1904, 1905; mixed 1903, 1904, 1912.
Irish Championships, singles 1912; mixed 1912.
Scottish Championships, singles 1910, 1911, 1912; doubles 1910, 1911, 1912; mixed 1910, 1912.
All England Badminton singles champion 1900, 1901, 1903, 1904, 1906; doubles champion 1902, 1904, 1905, 1906; mixed champion 1903, 1906.

Became a professional in 1922. Her husband, Major Dudley Larcombe, was secretary of the All England Club 1925–39.

LENGLEN, Suzanne Rachel Flore

Born 24 May 1899, Compiègne, France.
Died 4 July 1938, Paris, France.
Singles 1919, 1920, 1921, 1922, 1923, 1925.
Doubles 1919, 1920, 1921, 1922, 1923, 1925.
Mixed 1920, 1922, 1925.
Other successes:
French Championships, singles 1925, 1926; doubles 1925, 1926; mixed 1925, 1926.
World Hard Court Championships, singles 1914, 1921, 1922, 1923; doubles 1914, 1921, 1922; mixed 1921, 1922, 1923.
Olympic gold medals (2) 1920.

Became a professional in 1926. Except for her retirement against Molla Mallory at Forest Hills in 1921 she was invincible in singles anywhere from 1919 to 1926. Her standard of achievement was unique. She died of pernicious anaemia.

McKANE, Kathleen (Kitty), *see* **GODFREE, Mrs. L. A.**

McNAIR, Mrs R. J.

Formerly Winifred Margaret Slocock (married 1908).
Born 9 August 1877, Donnington, nr Newbury, Berkshire, England.
Died 28 March 1954, Kensington, London, England.
Doubles 1913.
Other success:
Olympic gold medal 1920.

Runner-up English Ladies Golf Championship 1921.

MARBLE, Alice

Born 28 September 1913, Plumas County, California, USA.
Singles 1939.
Doubles 1938, 1939.
Mixed 1937, 1938, 1939.
Other successes:
US Championships, singles 1936, 1938, 1939, 1940; doubles 1937, 1938, 1939, 1940; mixed 1936, 1938, 1939, 1940.
Member US Wightman Cup team 1933–9.
Became a professional in 1941.

MATHIEU, Mme Rene

Formerly Simone Passemard (married 1925).
Born 31 January 1908, Neuilly-sur-Seine, France.
Doubles 1933, 1934, 1937.
Other successes:
French Championships, singles 1938, 1939; doubles 1933, 1934, 1936, 1937, 1938, 1939; mixed 1937, 1938.

Officier de la Légion d'honneur. First-class bridge player.

METAXA, Doris Emille

Later Mrs P. D. Howard, Great Britain (married 1932).
Born 12 June 1911, Marseilles, France.
Doubles 1932.

A graduate in classics and philosophy.

MICHEL, Margaret (Peggy)

Born 2 February 1949, Santa Monica, California, USA.
Doubles 1974.
Other successes:
Australian Championships, doubles 1974, 1975.

MICHELL, Mrs L. R. C.

Formerly Margaret Amy (Peggy) Saunders (married 1928).
Born 28 January 1905, Chiswick, Middlesex, England.
Died 19 June 1941, Harrow, Middlesex, England.
Doubles 1928, 1929.
Other successes:
US Championships, doubles 1929.
Member British Wightman Cup team 1928, 1929, 1932.

MOFFITT, Billie Jean, *see* **KING, Mrs L. W.**

MOODY, Mrs F. S. (Helen Wills)

Formerly Helen Newington Wills (married 1929).
Later Mrs A. Roark (married 1939).
Born 6 October 1905, Berkeley, California, USA.
Singles 1927, 1928, 1929, 1930, 1932, 1933, 1935, 1938.
Doubles 1924, 1927, 1930.
Mixed 1929.
Other successes:
US Championships, singles 1923, 1924, 1925, 1927, 1928, 1929, 1931; doubles 1922, 1924, 1925, 1928; mixed 1924, 1928.
French Championships, singles 1928, 1929, 1930, 1932; doubles 1930, 1932.
Olympic gold medals (2) 1924.
Member US Wightman Cup team 1923–38; captain 1930, 1932.

MORTIMER, Florence Angela Margaret

Later Mrs J. E. Barrett (married 1967).
Born 21 April 1932, Plymouth, Devon, England.
Singles 1961.
Doubles 1955.
Other successes:
French Championships, singles 1955.
Australian Championships, singles 1958.
Member British Wightman Cup team 1953–61; captain 1964–70.

MORTON, Agnes Mary (Agatha)

Later Lady Hugh Stewart (married 1925).
Born 6 March 1872, Halstead, Essex, England.
Died 5 April 1952, Kensington, London, England.
Doubles 1914.
Other successes:
Wimbledon non-championship doubles 1902; mixed 1909.

MUDFORD, Phyllis Evelyn

Later Mrs M. R. King (married 1932).
Born 23 August 1905, Wallington, Surrey, England.
Doubles 1931.
Other successes:
Member British Wightman Cup team 1930–2, 1935; captain 1938.

NAVRATILOVA, Martina

Born 18 October 1956, Prague, Czechoslovakia.
Doubles 1976.
Other successes:
French Championships, doubles 1975; mixed 1974.
Italian Championships, doubles 1975.

Granted refugee status in USA in 1975. A left hander.

OSBORNE, Margaret Evelyn, *see* **DU PONT, Mrs W.**

RICE, Helena Bertha Grace (Lena)

Born 21 June 1866, Newinn, Co Tipperary, Ireland.
Died 21 June 1907, Newinn, Co Tipperary, Ireland.
Singles 1890.
Other success:
Irish Championships, mixed 1889.

RICHEY, Nancy Ann

Later Mrs K. S. Gunter (married 1970).
Born 23 August 1942, San Angelo, Texas, USA.

Doubles 1966.
Other successes:
US Championships, doubles 1965, 1966.
French Championships, singles 1968.
Australian Championships, singles 1967; doubles 1966.
Member US Wightman Cup team 1962–8; US Federation Cup team 1964–9.

ROBB, Muriel Evelyn
Born 13 May 1878, Newcastle upon Tyne, Northumberland, England.
Died 12 February 1907, Newcastle upon Tyne, Northumberland, England.
Singles 1902.
Other successes:
Wimbledon non-championship doubles 1902; mixed 1900.
Irish Championships, singles 1901.
Scottish Championships, singles 1901.
Welsh Championships, singles 1899.

ROUND, Dorothy Edith
Later Mrs D. L. Little (married 1937).
Born 13 July 1909, Dudley, Worcestershire, England.
Singles 1934, 1937.
Mixed 1934, 1935, 1936.
Other successes:
Australian Championships, singles 1935.
Member British Wightman Cup team 1931–6.

RYAN, Elizabeth Montague (Bunny)
Born 5 February 1892, Anaheim, Los Angeles, California, USA.
Doubles 1914, 1919, 1920, 1921, 1922, 1923, 1925, 1926, 1927, 1930, 1933, 1934.
Mixed 1919, 1921, 1923, 1927, 1928, 1930, 1932.
Other successes:
US Championships, doubles 1926; mixed 1926, 1933.
French Championships, doubles 1930, 1932, 1933, 1934.
World Hard Court Championships, doubles 1914, 1922; mixed 1913, 1914.
Italian Championships, singles 1933; doubles 1934; mixed 1934.
Member US Wightman Cup team 1926.
Became a professional in 1934. Lived mainly in England after 1912.

SAUNDERS, Margaret Amy (Peggy), *see* **MICHELL, Mrs L. R. C.**

SAWAMATSU, Kazuko
Later Mrs M. Yoshida (married 1976).
Born 5 January 1951, Nishinomiya, Japan.
Doubles 1975.
Member Japanese Federation Cup team 1970–5.

SHEPHERD-BARRON, Mrs D. C.
Properly Mrs W. P. Barron, formerly Dorothy Cunliffe Shepherd (married 1921).
Born 24 November 1897, Beighton, Norfolk, England.
Died 20 February 1953, Melbourn, nr Cambridge, England.
Doubles 1931.
Other successes:
Member British Wightman Cup team 1924, 1926, 1929; captain 1931, 1932, 1950, 1951.

SHILCOCK, Jacqueline Anne
Later Mrs J. K. Spann (married 1960).
Born 13 June 1932, Hartfield, Sussex, England.
Doubles 1955.
Other successes:
Member British Wightman Cup team 1953, 1954.

SIGART, Josane
Later Mrs J. de Meulemeester (married 1933).
Born 7 January 1909, Brussels, Belgium.
Doubles 1932.

SMITH, Margaret, *see* **COURT, Mrs Barry M.**

SPERLING, Fru S., *see* **KRAHWINKEL, Hilde**

STAMMERS, Katharine Esther
Later Mrs M. Menzies (married 1940). Later Mrs T. W. Bullitt (married 1975).
Born 3 April 1914, St Albans, Hertfordshire, England.
Doubles 1935, 1936.
Other successes:
French Championships, doubles 1935.
Member British Wightman Cup team 1935–9, 1946–8; captain 1948, 1949.
A left hander.

STERRY, Mrs A.
Formerly Charlotte Cooper (married 1901).
Born 22 September 1870, Ealing, Middlesex, England.
Died 10 October 1966, Helensburgh, Scotland.
Singles 1895, 1896, 1898, 1901, 1908.

Other successes:
Wimbledon non-championship doubles 1901, 1902; mixed 1901, 1902.
Olympic gold medals (2) 1900.
Irish Championships, singles 1895, 1898; mixed 1895, 1896, 1899, 1900.
Scottish Championships, singles 1899.
Played hockey for Surrey.

STOVE, Betty Flippina.
Born 24 June 1945, Rotterdam, Netherlands.
Doubles 1972.
Other successes:
US Championships, doubles 1972.
French Championships, doubles 1972.

SUMMERS, Mrs S. P.
Properly Mrs R. A. Summers, formerly Sheila Piercey (married 1943).
Born 18 March 1919, Johannesburg, South Africa.
Mixed 1949.
Other successes:
French Championships, mixed 1947, 1949.
South African Championships, singles 1948, 1949, 1951; doubles 1940, 1953; mixed 1940, 1946, 1947, 1948, 1951, 1953.

SUSMAN, Mrs J. R.
Formerly Karen J. Hantze (married 1961).
Born 11 December 1942, San Diego, California, USA.
Singles 1962.
Doubles 1961, 1962.
Other successes:
US Championships, doubles 1964
Member US Wightman Cup team 1960–2, 1965; Federation Cup team 1964.

SUTTON, May Godfray
Later Mrs T. C. Bundy (married 1912).
Born 25 September 1886, Plymouth, Devon, England.
Died 4 October 1975, Santa Monica, California, USA.
Singles 1905, 1907.
Other successes:
US Championships, singles 1904; doubles 1904.
Wimbledon non-championship doubles 1906; mixed 1907.
Welsh Championships, singles 1905.
Member US Wightman Cup team 1925.

She played as an American and was the first overseas challenger to become a Wimbledon champion.

TEGART, Judith Anne Marshall (Judy), *see* **DALTON, Mrs David E.**

TODD, Mrs P. C.
Properly Mrs R. B. Todd, formerly Mary Patricia Canning (married 1941).
Born 22 July 1922, San Francisco, California, USA.
Doubles 1947.
Other successes:
French Championships, singles 1947; doubles 1948; mixed 1948.
Member US Wightman Cup team 1947–51.

TUCKEY, Mrs C. O.
Formerly Agnes Katharine Raymond Daniell (married 1906).
Born 8 July 1877, Marylebone, Middlesex, England.
Died 13 May 1972, Winchester, Hampshire, England.
Mixed 1913.

Her son, Raymond Tuckey, was doubles champion in 1936. She played with him in the mixed doubles 1931, 1932. Raymond played for Great Britain in the Davis Cup 1935–7. Her daughter Kay played for Great Britain in the Wightman Cup 1949–51.

TURNER, Lesley Rosemary, *see* **BOWREY, Mrs. W. W.**

WATSON, Maud Edith Eleanor, MBE
Born 9 October 1864, Harrow, Middlesex, England.
Died 5 June 1946, Charmouth, Dorset, England.
Singles 1884, 1885.
Other successes:
Irish Championships, singles 1884, 1885; mixed 1884, 1885.
Welsh Championships, singles 1887.

WATSON, Mrs M. R.
Formerly Phoebe Catherine Holcroft (married 1925).
Later Mrs W. L. Blakstad (married 1933).
Born 7 October 1898, St Leonards-on-Sea, Sussex, England.
Doubles 1928, 1929.
Other successes:
US Championships, doubles 1929.
French Championships, doubles 1928.
Member British Wightman Cup team 1928–30.

WIGHTMAN, Mrs George W., CBE
Formerly Hazel Virginia Hotchkiss (married 1912).
Born 20 December 1886, Healdburg, California, USA.
Died 5 December 1974, Chestnut Hill, Massachusetts, USA.
Doubles 1924.
Other successes:
US Championships, singles 1909, 1910, 1911, 1919; doubles 1909, 1910, 1911, 1915, 1924, 1928; mixed 1909, 1910, 1911, 1915, 1918, 1920.
Olympic gold medallist (2) 1924.
Member US Wightman Cup team 1923–31; captain 1923, 1924, 1927, 1929, 1931, 1933, 1935, 1937–9, 1946–8.

The donor of the Wightman Cup. Awarded Honorary CBE at the Jubilee Wightman Cup match in Boston in 1973.

WILLS, Helen N., *see* **MOODY, Mrs F. S.**

YORKE, Adeline Maud (Billie)
Born 19 December 1910, Rawalpindi, Punjab, India.
Doubles 1937.
Other successes:
French Championships, doubles 1936, 1937, 1938; mixed 1936.

WIMBLEDON MISCELLANY

The All England Club and Open Lawn Tennis

Open lawn tennis came about in 1968 after a long political battle among the national associations of the world. The need for reform was blatantly evident for many years; the status as 'amateur' had, in the case of the more prominent players, become a technical definition and in the eyes of the world at large a hypocritical sham. In addition the constant move towards overt professionalism as amateurs won the leading championships diminished the stature of the traditional events.

The first direct attempt by the All England Club to exert its influence to bring reform was in the first year of the chairmanship of Herman David. He was as much concerned with the moral issue of calling players amateur, when obviously they were not, as with the desire to restore the Championships to their status as a tournament in which all the best players of the world participated. On 16 October 1959 a Special General Meeting of the club was convened at the Café Royal, London, and the following motion adopted by a wide majority:

> The members of the All England Lawn Tennis and Croquet Club hereby resolve that, in the interests of lawn tennis, the Lawn Tennis Association should consider recommending to the International Lawn Tennis Federation that the Championships held at Wimbledon should be open to all lawn tennis players throughout the world, and that the Committee of Management, in reviewing the conditions of entry for the Championships, should take into consideration the suggestion of the All England Club.

The next meeting of the International Federation was in July 1960 in Paris and there the British LTA, supported notably by the USA, France and Australia, moved for tournaments open to all players. This now historic meeting had elements of farce. Among delegates known to be in favour of reform one fell asleep. Another was absent at the toilet when the vote was taken. A third was arranging the evening's excursion for the delegates on the *bateaux mouche*. The total poll was 209. The proposal, needing a two-thirds majority to pass, failed by five votes.

The international pressure was maintained but without success. At the annual meeting of the LTA in December 1964 the All England Club delegates formally proposed:

> That, whilst appreciating the effort of the delegates of the Lawn Tennis Association at the meeting of the International Lawn Tennis Federation held in Vienna last July to obtain permission for the Championships in 1965 to be open to all lawn tennis players and taking note of the Federation's decision, the Association hereby give notice to the Federation that the Association will at once give permission to the Committee of Management that the Championships to be held at Wimbledon in 1965 be open to all lawn tennis players throughout the world.

Herman David was the leading speaker on behalf of the motion. It was a proposal for revolution, for the LTA directly to go counter to the rules of the ILTF. The debate was never on the need for lawn tennis reform, only on the expediency of the act of rebellion. It was defeated by 88 votes to 40.

When three years later, in 1967, the LTA did commit its act of revolution the All England Club was not directly involved as such. Even so the prime movers in getting the LTA to change its attitude were Herman David and another club member on the Management Committee, Ted Avory, who had spoken as a British representative for the original proposal in Paris in 1960. There were several events which gave momentum to the reform movement within the British ruling body.

The publication of articles about 'shamateurism' in the *Sunday Times* in March 1967 stirred wide feeling. It became more intense after the rejection of yet another reform proposal at the ILTF meeting in July. In August there was an upset with the British Davis Cup player Roger Taylor. He had undertaken to play in Austria but after his Wimbledon success as a semi-finalist he asked for better terms; in the end he went to Canada instead. At least that was so charged by the Austrians, who asked the British LTA to discipline Taylor. The LTA felt they had no power to act in any way against Taylor but were appalled at the situation with regard to a so-called amateur.

Eric Attewell was the LTA chairman at that time and he made a triumvirate with Derek Penman, chairman of the rules committee, and Derek Hardwick, then a vice-chairman, in urging the LTA to take unilateral action to reform the game. The outcome of their efforts was the LTA becoming an instrument of revolution.

In the meantime the All England Club broke its long tradition of rigid amateurism by staging, on 25, 26 and 28 August, the 'Wimbledon World Professional Lawn Tennis Championships'. This was the sort of tournament that had hitherto been staged at the Empire Pool, Wembley. It was promoted in conjunction with BBC 2 television and the committee of management was the same as that which had just steered the normal Wimbledon meeting to its successful conclusion. It was an eight-man tournament and played entirely on the Centre Court.

It was very successful. Rod Laver won the singles, his rivals being Fred Stolle, Andres Gimeno, Dennis Ralston, Lew Hoad, Ricardo Gonzales, Earl Buchholz and Ken Rosewall.

The full results were:

Singles
First round:
R. G. Laver d F. S. Stolle 6–4 6–2
A. Gimeno d R. D. Ralston 6–1 6–2
L. A. Hoad d R. A. Gonzales 3–6 11–9 8–6
K. R. Rosewall d E. Buchholz 5–7 6–2 6–3
Semi-final:
Laver d Gimeno 6–3 6–4
Rosewall d Hoad 6–2 6–2
Final:
Laver d Rosewall 6–2 6–2 12–10

Doubles
First round:
Laver & Stolle d Buchholz & Hoad 11–9 6–1
Gimeno & Gonzales d Ralston & Rosewall 6–4 7–9 6–4
Final:
Gimeno & Gonzales d Laver & Stolle 6–4 14–12

The singles winner received £3000 and the minimum earned, for the first round loser in both events, was £550 plus £200—£750 in all.

The LTA Council met on 5 October 1967 and agreed, by 61 votes to 6, that the following proposal be placed on the agenda of the Annual General Meeting of the LTA in December:

That all reference to amateurs and professionals be deleted from the Rules of the Lawn Tennis Association and that the Association itself should legislate only for players and take local autonomy to make such rules as they may require regarding the status of their own players and visitors when playing in this country.

In due course, on Thursday, 14 December, the Annual General Meeting debated the motion. It was a crowded occasion. An hour and 28 minutes was spent on the debate. The discussion was less on the merits of the change proposed than on the best time for it to take effect. In the event it was decreed to start, not on 1 January 1968, which would have been the normal procedure, but on 22 April 1968, the first day of the British Hard Court Championships at Bournemouth. The object was to give the International Lawn Tennis Federation time to take action. Only five delegates voted against this unilateral act of reform by the British LTA.

Faced with a *fait accompli* the ILTF yielded to the British pressure at a special meeting convened at the RAC in Paris on 3 March. The rules were changed to allow each nation its own choice of legislation regarding amateurs and professionals. Lawn tennis altered course and in Great Britain on 22 April 1968 the term amateur or professional ceased to have any meaning. The British action would almost certainly not have come about but for the pressure from the All England Club.

The prize money at Wimbledon increased steadily since it was first paid:

		Singles winners		First round losers	
	Total (£)	Men (£)	Women (£)	Men (£)	Women (£)
1968	26 150	2 000	750	50	25
1969	33 370	3 000	1 500	50	50
1970	41 650	3 000	1 500	100	75
1971	50 470	5 000	2 400	100	75
1972	50 330	5 000	2 400	100	75
1973	52 400	5 000	3 000	100	75
1974	97 100	10 000	7 000	150	150
1975	108 875	10 000	7 000	150	150
1976	157 740	12 500	10 000	150	150

The 1971 figure reflected a temporary change in the method of payment, one-third of the prize money going to the organisation under whose authority the competitor entered. In 1975 the two consolation singles events were allocated substantial prize money for the first time, this accounting for £8075 of the increase. The first round loser in both championship and plate singles had his or her earnings increased to £200.

In 1975 a meeting took place between Air Chief Marshal Sir Brian Burnett in his capacity as chairman of the Championships Committee and the Women's Tennis Association. Billie Jean King and the male executive of the WTA, Jerry Diamond, asked for a reduction in the differential between the men's and women's prize money. It was then agreed that in 1976 the women's ratio would be raised from 70 to 80 per cent.

Further discussions between Sir Brian Burnett and Jerry Diamond took place in June 1976. Subsequently Sir Brian issued the following announcement:

The Committee of Management of the Championships announce that their appointed representatives this morning met Mr J. Diamond and Miss Chris Evert, representing the Women's Tennis Association, to discuss their demand for parity with men players in the matter of prize-money at Wimbledon, as from 1977.

In the letter containing this demand, dated 19 May 1976, Mr Diamond says on behalf of the WTA that 'this will be the last year the women will play at Wimbledon unless complete and total equality in prize-money is guaranteed in both singles and doubles play'. The letter goes on to say that 'should a firm agreement not be reached by the conclusion of this year's Wimbledon event, the WTA will immediately begin negotiations for a women's event elsewhere in 1977 during the weeks of Wimbledon and establish strenuous sanctions against those players who participate in any other event that week'. This demand was made known by WTA to the Press this week even before the meeting, which had been arranged with the Championships Committee for this morning, and today it has been confirmed at our meeting with Mr Diamond and Miss Evert.

Having listened sympathetically to the WTA views and having then discussed them in full Committee this afternoon, the Committee of Management of the Championships have decided that they cannot submit to the WTAs ultimatum. This has been made known to Mr Diamond and the Committee have the following comments to make:

(*a*) Due to the smaller draw with the women (96 instead of 128 in the singles and 48 pairs instead of 64 pairs in the doubles) and to the fact that their matches are the best of three sets instead of five, the women play throughout the Championships approximately half the number of sets and are on court and providing entertainment for the public for approximately half the time. Therefore, on a strict basis of equal pay for equal amount of work, the women players should get approximately 50 per cent of the men's prize money. They are in fact getting 66 per cent overall despite their small numbers, and the better players are getting 80 per cent.

(*b*) On a basis of standard of play between the men and the women, there is no comparison.

(*c*) On a basis of crowd attraction, particularly on grass at Wimbledon, the Committee fully accept that a more equal distribution of prize-money is warranted and for this reason they agreed, following discussions with WTA last year, that the last eight in the women's singles and the finalists in the doubles this year should receive 80 per cent of the men's prize-money. They have never agreed or accepted, as published in certain sections of the Press, that there should be an automatic and gradual increase to full parity.

(*d*) The fact remains that in earlier rounds the standard of play of the women is such that they are nothing like such a great draw for the public as the men players, whose standard in depth is extremely high today.

(*e*) In no other major Championships outside the United States is the women's percentage of men's prize-money as high as it is already at Wimbledon.

Although the Championships Committee still feel that the women's percentage of prize-money is very fair and even generous on present standards of play, in order to help the WTA and to encourage the less good women players, the

Committee would be prepared next year to make the women's prize-money up to 80 per cent of the men's throughout and will continue to keep the matter of all prize-money under annual review. They believe that merit should be rewarded where it is due and are not prepared to give in to threats of any kind.

Finally the Committee of Management of the Championships would like to correct a misconception of many people, including the players, that The All England Club make enormous profits out of the Championships. The fact is that *all*, repeat *all*, the surplus from the Championships is passed to the LTA for the benefit of Lawn Tennis as a whole, including so-called 'grass roots' Tennis, in this country.

Friday, 25 June 1976.

Finances of Wimbledon

The Lawn Tennis Championships are run not by the All England Club, not by the Lawn Tennis Association but jointly by the two bodies. The controlling authority is the Management Committee of the Championships, made up by twelve nominations from the Club and six from the LTA. It is essentially an amateur concern. The secretary of the Management Committee is always the secretary of the All England Club and he is the only professional involved.

The preponderance of the club membership on the committee is two to one and to that extent control of the Championships is in the hands of the All England Club. The fact reflects the origins of the tournament, started by the All England Club in 1877 eleven years before the LTA came into existence. But it is not so simple as that. Should financial matters cause dispute between the two bodies then a new committee has to be brought into being, this special finance committee comprising six representatives from the LTA and three from the All England Club. The two to one balance is pushed the other way to give control to the LTA. It happens that this special committee has never been convened.

This interlocking control between the Club and the national Association was created in the first instance by a formal agreement in May 1920. It began to operate when the new site of the tournament became Church Road in 1922. It was replaced by a revised agreement in 1934 which, with a slight revision in 1966, has pertained since that time. In broad terms the agreement is simple. The Club maintains itself out of the Championship revenues. The surplus goes to the LTA. For more than 50 years such moneys have formed the main revenues by which the LTA has maintained itself and on which the British game at large is heavily dependent. The actual ground of the All England Club is owned in equal shares by the Club and the LTA. At the 'old' Wimbledon the profits belonged to the Club. At the 'new' Wimbledon they have belonged to the LTA.

The profit from the first meeting in 1877 was not, it seems, accurately and officially recorded. Tradition has it that it was of the order of £10.

The All England Club ran the Championships on its own until 1906. In that year two LTA representatives were appointed to the committee, the number increased to four in 1913 when the ruling body was allocated a share in the surplus.

With one exception the meeting has always flourished in financial terms. There was a surplus of £116 in 1879 and one of £306 a year later. With the Renshaw twins at their peak the meeting enjoyed a boom. The profit in 1883 was £732 and it increased to £800 in 1885. There were harder times in the 1890s. In 1895 there was actually a loss of £33. The rise of the Doherty brothers swung the balance back, though while the average surplus for the ten years 1881–90 was £500 that in the decade 1892–1901 was only £180.

Major David Mills, the All England Club Secretary at his desk with his two assistants, Chris Gorringe and Enid Stopka

There was a steady rise in the popularity, and profitability, of Wimbledon as a spectator event in the years leading up to the First World War. From 1902 to 1912 the profits that accrued were £14 000. By 1914 it was obvious that Wimbledon needed a more spacious venue to accommodate the crowds. The resumption of the meeting in 1919 made the need even more apparent and the upshot was the issue of Debenture Shares at £50 (the dividend being seats in the stand, not cash) and the investment of £140 000 in the new All England Club in Church Road.

The profitability of the 'new' Wimbledon, with its profit going to the LTA, has never been in doubt. The average surplus from 1922 up to the 1939 meeting was of the order of £10 000. The figure in 1933 was more than £16 000.

In the immediate post-war year of 1946 the LTA received its most meagre Wimbledon revenues of all time. It was but £750. That, though, was merely a nominal payment, since the first call on the money that year was to refill the reserve fund that had been depleted by six years without revenue.

The following are the five-year averages of the Wimbledon profits paid to the Lawn Tennis Association since 1946:

1946–50	£14 000
1951–5	£43 000
1956–60	£51 000
1961–5	£51 000
1966–70	£57 000
1971–5	£78 000

Seeding and the Draw

The principle of seeding was accepted at Wimbledon later than elsewhere. The US Nationals had a fully seeded men's singles in 1922. In that year Wimbledon abolished the challenge round that had been discarded in America ten years before. When it did come, the introduction of a draw that did not leave everything to chance was gradual.

National seeding, as distinct from merit seeding, was used in 1924. National associations nominated in each event up to four singles players and two doubles pairs to be placed in the draw so as to fall into different quarters or halves. This system, which prevented leading overseas players from clashing in an early round, was used until the inception of open lawn tennis in 1968. Nominated British players similarly had protection from each other.

Merit seeding was adopted in 1927. The first number one seed was René Lacoste, who failed to justify his status and lost in the semi-final. His French compatriot Henri Cochet, who achieved his incredible victory that year, was seeded only fourth. On the other hand, the official favourite for the women's singles proved a happy choice; it was Helen Wills who had the first of her eight victories.

The method of placing seeds remained the same in principle up to 1963. The first and second were drawn to make it a matter of chance into which half of the draw they fell. It was the same with the third and fourth seeds, the names being drawn by lot to make it fortuitous whether the top seed was likely to be confronted in a semi-final by a rival two or three places below in the merit standing. Similarly with the fifth, sixth, seventh and eighth selections, the prospective quarter-final opponents were picked by ballot. Seeds numbers nine to sixteen were on the same basis. Prestige was involved in the merit order but in practice there was equality in each group of seeds.

At the draw the first task was to settle the position of the merit seeds. The placing of nominated players followed. Often players fell into both categories. If the protection of national seeding conflicted with merit seeding adjustment was made giving the players of the same nationality maximum protection from one another. The merit seeds had fixed slots in which to go but the subsequent national placings could fall anywhere in the appropriate quarter. When all merit and national seeds were disposed of the rest of the field filled up the vacant places as drawn.

The Wimbledon draw became something of a ceremony in itself. An elaborate collection of numbered discs, plus four bags indicating the different quarters, was designed by H. Anthony Sabelli, secretary of the Lawn Tennis Association from 1912 to 1948, to ensure scrupulous fairness. It looked complicated to the uninitiated but was effective.

There was a slight change in 1932. Originally all the merit seeding slots were positioned at the top of the appropriate sections of the draw sheet. From that year the now familiar British pattern was adopted whereby the bottom half of the draw had its seeding slots at the base of each section; the two senior seeds neatly sandwiched the rest of the field. This in no way altered the principle by which chosen players were held apart from each other.

Until after the Second World War there was no question of having more than eight seeds in the men's singles, though the rules permitted up to sixteen in a field of 128. Four seeded pairs was the normal ration in the doubles, though in both 1932 and 1938 the mixed doubles had eight. The women's singles at no time varied from eight seeds. The men's singles was given sixteen in 1950. A year later there was the compromise figure of ten and an equally untidy twelve in 1952. It reverted to eight in 1953 but was twelve in 1954 when Jaroslav Drobny had the distinction of winning from as low as number eleven.

In 1963, following revision of the rules that was agreed without dissent—or, for that matter, without comment—at the annual meeting of the LTA the previous December, the Championships changed to what may be called the continental seeding method. It was the system used on the Continent and the logic of uniformity was cited as good reason for its adoption. In this method seeding position was fixed immutably. It mattered not whether the top seed was placed at the head or bottom of the draw—the practice in France was to have the number two at the top and the number one at the bottom—but the semi-final order was stipulated as number one versus number four, number two against number three. Similarly, the quarter-finals were such as to have one against eight, four against five, six against three and seven against two. There was a simple rule of thumb. If the numbering of the prospective semi-finalists be added it came to five. That of the quarter-finalists came to nine. In the case of the eighth-finalists, as they are called in France, the total was seventeen.

There is scope for a conflict of views about the merits of the method. Perhaps the major argument against it was that it left too little to chance. And in theory at any rate there might be a temptation by a seeding committee to bear in mind the outcome of its deliberations in the subsequent draw. Its task was to that degree made more invidious.

Having commenced in 1924 the placing of nominated players ended in 1968. The game was then open to all and many competitors were professionals unrecognised by their national associations. To have retained the placing of nominated players would manifestly have led to unfairness and the system was quietly abandoned.

In the same year the men's singles list was enlarged to the full quota of sixteen merit seeds, the men's doubles to eight. This number was maintained in 1969 and 1970 but reverted to eight for the singles and four for the doubles for the next three years. In 1974 the men's doubles went up to eight seeds, the singles to twelve. A year later the doubles remained at eight but the singles was again sixteen. Other events remained constant in their seeding quotas, eight for the women's singles, four for the women's doubles and four for the mixed.

The method of placing the seeds reverted in 1975 to that used prior to 1963. No change was made in the LTA rules governing the Championships but the meeting, as part of the global Grand Prix competition, found itself obliged to conform to Grand Prix regulations. The players themselves, through the Association of Tennis Professionals, had participated in the framing of them. Accordingly the system familiar from 1927 to 1962 was brought back, the seeds no longer having immutable positions *vis-à-vis* each other. There was a minor difference from the old method. The number one seed automatically headed the draw.

A further change in 1975, again made to conform with the Grand Prix, was the shape of the draw brought by the positioning of the byes. The byes were no longer divided into two neat bulk packages placed at the top and bottom of the draw. They were distributed throughout instead. The men's singles and men's doubles, with entries of 128 and 64, were not affected. It was different elsewhere. The women's singles, with 96 entries, needed 32 byes, the women's doubles with 48 needed 16 and the mixed with 80 required 48. The byes were drawn by lot but devised to fall evenly throughout.

The revision ended the familiar pattern in the women's singles whereby two of the most senior and two of the most junior seeds were inevitably required to play one round less than their rivals. The logic of the argument against unfairness could not be gainsaid even if in practice the presumed hardship had never seemed very evident.

It was not the novelty that may have been thought. The Bagnall-Wild system—so called after its inventor in the nineteenth century—by which all byes belonged to the first round and which were placed together had not always been in use. Much the same system of 1975 was tried in 1935, when it was known as the 'King' method (J. H. King propounded it) and designed to ensure that all seeded players had the same number of rounds. There were earlier examples, too. Wimbledon adopted the Bagnall-Wild method only in 1887. Up to 1884 byes fell in any round, including the semi-final. In 1885 and 1886 there was used a compromise system with the byes all falling in the first round but with their distribution made evenly throughout the draw. *Plus ça change!*

Seeding Positions of Finalists

	Singles				Doubles				Mixed Doubles	
	Men		Women		Men		Women			
Year	Winner	Runner-up	Winner	Runner-up	Winner	Runner-up	Winner	Runner-up	Winner	Runner-up
1927	4	3	1	4	3	1	1	2	4	1
1928	2	1	1	2	2	4	3	2	2	—
1929	1	2	1	5	—	4	2	3	2	—
1930	2	—	1	8	2	1	1	4	2	—
1931	7	3	1	4	1	2	—	4	—	—
1932	2	6	1	5	4	3	4	2	4	6
1933	2	1	1	2	1	—	1	—	—	4
1934	2	1	2	1	2	1	1	—	—	—
1935	1	2	4	3	2	1	3	2	3	—
1936	1	2	2	5	3	—	1	2	1	2
1937	1	2	7	4	2	1	2	—	1	2
1938	1	2	1	—	1	4	2	1	1	2
1939	2	6	1	6	2	4	1	2	2	—
1946	5	3	1	3	2	1	1	2	3	2
1947	1	3	1	3	1	—	2	1	1	3
1948	7	2	2	4	3	2	1	2	1	4
1949	1	6	1	2	3	1	1	2	4	1
1950	5	1	1	2	2	4	1	2	1	4
1951	6	7	3	4	1	4	2	1	2	—
1952	1	2	2	4	1	4	1	2	1	—
1953	2	—	1	2	1	3	1	2	1	4
1954	11	3	1	4	1	2	2	1	1	3

Year	Singles Men Winner	Singles Men Runner-up	Singles Women Winner	Singles Women Runner-up	Doubles Men Winner	Doubles Men Runner-up	Doubles Women Winner	Doubles Women Runner-up	Mixed Doubles Winner	Mixed Doubles Runner-up
1955	1	—	2	3	2	3	4	3	1	2
1956	1	2	5	6	1	—	3	—	1	3
1957	1	2	1	5	—	1	1	2	4	2
1958	1	4	1	—	—	1	1	—	4	2
1959	1	—	6	4	1	4	1	3	3	2
1960	1	3	1	8	—	—	1	4	1	2
1961	2	8	7	6	1	—	—	3	1	4
1962	1	—	8	—	2	—	2	4	3	—
1963	4	—	1	—	—	—	2	1	2	—
1964	1	6	2	1	3	4	1	2	2	1
1965	1	2	2	1	2	4	2	—	2	—
1966	4	6	4	2	—	4	2	1	1	3
1967	3	—	1	3	2	4	3	1	1	2
1968	1	15	1	7	4	2	1	3	4	—
1969	1	6	4	1	1	6	1	—	4	3
1970	2	5	1	2	1	6	2	4	—	—
1971	2	4	3	1	—	—	1	2	3	1
1972	1	2	2	1	1	2	1	3	2	1
1973	2	4	2	4	1	2	1	2	2	—
1974	3	9	2	8	4	3	—	—	1	—
1975	6	1	3	4	—	—	—	—	1	—
1976	4	3	1	2	1	—	2	1	—	—

(Note: seeding began in 1927.)

Size of Entry Year by Year

The following table records the number of entries received and accepted for the various events. The figures include the defending title holder standing out until the challenge round.

Year	Singles Men	Singles Women	Doubles Men	Doubles Women	Doubles Mixed
1877	22				
1878	35				
1879	45				
1880	61				
1881	49				
1882	29				
1883	24				
1884	29	13	10		
1885	24	10	11		
1886	24	9	8		
1887	17	6	10		
1888	25	7	13		
1889	25	6	10		
1890	31	4	7		
1891	22	9	5		
1892	28	8	6		
1893	28	8	11		
1894	24	11	11		
1895	18	9	7		
1896	32	7	15		
1897	32	8	15		
1898	38	18	15		
1899	38	18	16	7	
1900	35	17	15	8	14
1901	37	31	20	8	18
1902	43	23	21	12	19
1903	43	28	19	12	19
1904	63	42	28	19	27
1905	72	46	32	19	27
1906	70	49	29	19	33
1907	85	43	29	18	36
1908	70	30	35	—	29
1909	86	37	40	—	27
1910	93	32	40	—	31
1911	105	35	39	—	28
1912	82	34	35	—	29
1913	117	42	49	21	41
1914	103	52	45	20	39
1915–18 not held					
1919	129	44	55	21	42
1920	129	51	53	26	52
1921	129	57	64	23	64
1922	128	64	64	32	64
1923	133	70	64	38	64
1924	128	64	64	40	64
1925*	128	64	64	39	64
1926	128	64	64	41	64
1927	128	80	64	42	64
1928	128	80	64	40	64
1929	128	96	64	48	64
1930	128	96	64	48	67
1931–6	128	96	64	48	80
1937	128	97	64	48	80
1938	128	96	64	48	81

* Qualifying competition started.

Year	Singles		Doubles		
	Men	Women	Men	Women	Mixed
1939	128	96	64	48	80
1940–5 not held					
1946	128	96	64	48	80
1947	128	96	64	40	81
1948	128	96	64	40	80
1949–62	128	96	64	48	80
1963	128	96	68	48	80
1964–72	128	96	64	48	80
1973	128	96	64	50	80
1974	128	96	64	48	80
1975–6	128	96	64	48	64

Championship Records

Longest matches (in number of games)

Men's singles

1969 First round, R. A. Gonzales d C. Pasarell 22–24 1–6 16–14 6–3 11–9. Duration 5 hours 12 minutes, postponed overnight after first two sets. **Total 112 games**

Women's singles

1948 Second round, Miss A. Weiwers d Mrs O. Anderson 8–10 14–12 6–4. **Total 54 games**

Men's doubles

1966 First round, N. Pilic and E. L. Scott d C. Richey and T. Ulrich 19–21 12–10 6–4 4–6 9–7. **Total 98 games**

Women's doubles

1933 First round, Miss P. Brazier and Mrs I. H. Wheatcroft d Miss M. E. Nonweiler and Miss B. Soames 11–9 5–7 9–7. **Total 48 games**

Mixed doubles

1967 Quarter-finals, K. N. Fletcher and Miss M. E. Bueno d A. Metreveli and Miss A. Dmitrieva 6–8 7–5 16–14. **Total 56 games**

Longest finals (in number of games)

Men's singles

1954 J. Drobny d K. R. Rosewall 13–11 4–6 6–2 9–7. **Total 58 games**

Women's singles

1970 Mrs B. M. Court d Mrs L. W. King 14–12 11–9. **Total 46 games**
(In 1902 Miss M. E. Robb d Mrs A. Sterry 7–5 6–1 after abandoning overnight score of 4–6 13–11, an over-all total of 53 games.)

Men's doubles

1968 J. D. Newcombe and A. D. Roche d K. R. Rosewall and F. S. Stolle 3–6 8–6 5–7 14–12 6–3. **Total 70 games**

Women's doubles

1933 Mme R. Mathieu and Miss E. Ryan d Miss F. James and Miss A. M. Yorke 6–2 9–11 6–4

and in

1967 Miss R. Casals and Mrs L. W. King d Miss M. E. Bueno and Miss N. Richey 9–11 6–4 6–2. **Total 38 games**

Mixed doubles

1949 E. W. Sturgess and Mrs S. P. Summers d J. E. Bromwich and Miss A. L. Brough 9–7 9–11 7–5. **Total 48 games**

Longest set

1968 men's doubles, second round, A. Olmedo and F. Segura d G. L. Forbes and A. Segal **32–30** 5–7 6–4 6–4.

Longest set in final

1959 men's doubles, R. S. Emerson and N. A. Fraser d R. G. Laver and R. Mark 8–6 6–3 **14–16** 9–7.

Shortest finals

Men's singles

1881 W. Renshaw d J. T. Hartley 6–0 6–1 6–1 (duration 37 minutes).
and in
1936 F. J. Perry d G. Von Cramm 6–1 6–1 6–0. **Total 20 games**

Women's singles

1911 Mrs R. Lambert Chambers d Miss D. P. Boothby 6–0 6–0. **Total 12 games**

Men's doubles

1910 M. J. G. Ritchie and A. F. Wilding d A. W. Gore and H. Roper Barrett 6–1 6–1 6–2. **Total 22 games**

Women's doubles

1953 Miss S. J. Fry and Miss D. J. Hart d Miss M. C. Connolly and Miss J. Sampson 6–0 6–0. **Total 12 games**

Mixed doubles

1919 R. Lycett and Miss E. Ryan d A. D. Prebble and Mrs R. Lambert Chambers 6–0 6–0. **Total 12 games**

Most one-sided championship winners

Men singles

1903 H. L. Doherty won his challenge round defence against F. L. Riseley 7–5 6–3 6–0, taking the title by an over-all 19 games to 8.

Easiest victors, playing through, were
J. A. Kramer, 1947, won 21 sets to 1, 130 games to 37.
J. D. Budge, 1938, won 21 sets to 0, 129 games to 48.
M. A. Trabert, 1955, won 21 sets to 0, 131 games to 60.
C. R. McKinley, 1963, won 21 sets to 0, 140 games to 82.
B. Borg, 1976, won 21 sets to 0, 133 games to 70.

Women's singles

1911 As above in shortest finals, Mrs Lambert Chambers winning challenge round 6–0 6–0, taking the title by an over-all 12 games to 0.

Easiest victor, playing through, was Mlle S. Lenglen, 1925, 10 sets to 0, 60 games to 5.

Men's doubles

1947 R. Falkenburg and J. A. Kramer won 18 sets to 0, 115 games to 59
but
1946 T. Brown and J. A. Kramer won 18 sets to 1, 111 games to 47, a better winning percentage of games.

Women's doubles

1953 Miss D. J. Hart and Miss S. J. Fry won 8 sets to 0, 48 games to 4.

Mixed doubles

1922 P. O'Hara Wood and Mlle S. Lenglen won 12 sets to 0, 72 games to 25.

Most extended championship winners

Men's singles

1949 F. R. Schroeder won 21 sets to 8, 172 games to 119, losing more sets than Cochet
but
1927 H. Cochet won 21 sets to 7, 146 games to 114, losing a higher percentage of games than Schroeder (43 per cent to 40 per cent).

Women's singles

1934 Miss D. E. Round won 14 sets to 3, 96 games to 49.

Men's doubles

1963 R. H. Osuna and A. Palafox won 18 sets to 8, 154 games to 124.

Women's doubles

1975 Miss A. Kiyomura and Miss K. Sawamatsu won 10 sets to 3, 79 games to 66.

Mixed doubles

1931 G. M. Lott and Mrs L. A. Harper won 10 sets to 4, 77 games to 56.

Longest tie break

(The tie break, not used in the deciding set and operating at eight games all, was first used at Wimbledon in 1971.)

1973, men's singles, first round, B. Borg d P. Lall 6–3 6–4 9–8, the third set tie break extending to 20–18.

Youngest champion

Miss C. Dod
15 years 10 months when she won the women's singles in 1887.

Youngest male champion

R. D. Ralston
17 years 11 months when he won the men's doubles with R. H. Osuna in 1960.

Youngest men's singles champion

W. Baddeley
19 years 5 months when he won in 1891.

Oldest champion

Mrs W. du Pont
44 years 4 months when she won the mixed with N. A. Fraser in 1962.

Oldest male champion

G. Mulloy
43 years 7 months when he won the men's doubles with J. E. Petty in 1957.

Oldest men's singles champion

A. W. Gore
41 years 6 months when he won in 1909.

Oldest women's singles champion

Mrs A. Sterry
37 years 7 months when she won in 1908.

Oldest competitor

J. Borotra
65 years 10 months when he played in the men's and mixed doubles 1964.

Oldest singles competitor

A. W. Gore
54 years 5 months in 1922.

Oldest woman competitor

Mrs C. O. Tuckey
54 years 11 months when she played in the mixed doubles with her son C. R. D. Tuckey in 1932.

Singles winners at first attempt

1877	S. W. Gore (inaugural year)	
1878	P. F. Hadow	
1879	J. T. Hartley	
1884		Miss M. E. E. Watson (inaugural year)
1887		Miss C. Dod
1905		Miss M. G. Sutton
1919	G. L. Patterson	Mlle S. Lenglen
1920	W. T. Tilden	
1932	H. E. Vines	
1939	R. L. Riggs	
1946		Miss P. M. Betz
1949	F. R. Schroeder	
1951	R. Savitt	
1952		Miss M. C. Connolly

Of those listed in the table at the foot of the previous page the following were never beaten in singles at any time.

Men	Women	Winning years
Hadow*		1878
	Miss Dod	1887, 1888, 1891, 1892, 1893
	Mlle Lenglen†	1919, 1920, 1921, 1922, 1923, 1925
Riggs		1939
	Miss Betz*	1946
Schroeder		1949
	Miss Connolly	1952, 1953, 1954

* Neither Hadow nor Miss Betz lost a set. † Mlle Lenglen retired sick in 1924 and 1926.

The triple champions

		Matches	Sets		Games		
		Won	Won	Lost	Won	Lost	Partner
1920 Mlle S. Lenglen	Singles	1	2	0	12	3	
	Doubles	5	10	0	60	13	Miss E. Ryan
	Mixed	6	12	0	74	29	G. L. Patterson
		12	24	0	146	45	
							Average loss of games per set **1·875**
1922 Mlle S. Lenglen	Singles	6	12	0	75	20	
	Doubles	5	10	0	61	14	Miss E. Ryan
	Mixed	6	12	0	72	25	P. O'Hara Wood
		17	34	0	208	59	
							Average loss of games per set **1·735**
1925 Mlle S. Lenglen	Singles	5	10	0	60	5	
	Doubles	6	12	0	72	16	Miss E. Ryan
	Mixed	6	12	1	77	31	J. Borotra
		17	34	1	209	52	
							Average loss of games per set **1·485**
1937 J. D. Budge	Singles	7	21	1	140	68	
	Doubles	6	18	4	135	81	G. Mako
	Mixed	6	12	2	78	35	Miss A. Marble
		19	51	7	353	184	
							Average loss of games per set **3·172**
1938 J. D. Budge	Singles	7	21	0	129	48	
	Doubles	6	18	1	120	64	G. Mako
	Mixed	6	12	0	74	30	Miss A. Marble
		19	51	1	323	142	
							Average loss of games per set **2·730**
1939 Miss A. Marble	Singles	6	12	0	72	21	
	Doubles	5	10	1	66	23	Mrs M. Fabyan
	Mixed	6	12	2	83	42	R. L. Riggs
		17	34	3	221	86	
							Average loss of games per set **2·324**
1939 R. L. Riggs	Singles	7	21	3	147	92	
	Doubles	6	18	4	131	86	E. T. Cooke
	Mixed	6	12	2	83	42	Miss A. Marble
		19	51	9	361	220	
							Average loss of games per set **3·666**
1948 Miss A. L. Brough	Singles	6	*10	1	70	29	
	Doubles	5	10	1	64	26	Mrs W. du Pont
	Mixed	6	12	2	82	42	J. E. Bromwich
		17	32	4	216	97	
							Average loss of games per set **2·694**

* In one match, the quarter-final, her opponent retired injured before the end of the first set.

Year	Player	Event	Matches Won	Sets Won	Sets Lost	Games Won	Games Lost	Partner
1950	Miss A. L. Brough	Singles	6	12	2	80	34	
		Doubles	5	10	1	67	30	Mrs W. du Pont
		Mixed	6	12	1	87	54	E. W. Sturgess
			17	34	4	234	118	
							Average loss of games per set **3·105**	
1951	Miss D. J. Hart	Singles	7	14	0	86	34	
		Doubles	5	10	0	67	23	Miss S. J. Fry
		Mixed	6	12	1	81	35	F. A. Sedgman
			18	36	1	234	92	
							Average loss of games per set **2·486**	
1952	F. A. Sedgman	Singles	7	21	2	136	57	
		Doubles	6	18	3	138	75	K. McGregor
		Mixed	6	12	1	77	35	Miss D. J. Hart
			19	51	6	251	167	
							Average loss of games per set **2·929**	
1967	Mrs L. W. King	Singles	5	10	0	63	28	
		Doubles	6	12	1	81	39	Miss R. Casals
		Mixed	5	10	1	64	28	O. Davidson
			16	32	2	208	95	
							Average loss of games per set **2·794**	
1973	Mrs L. W. King	Singles	6	12	2	83	50	
		Doubles	5	10	1	67	38	Miss R. Casals
		Mixed	6	12	1	81	38	O. Davidson
			17	34	4	231	126	
							Average loss of games per set **3·315**	

(1901 Mrs A. Sterry, with the women's doubles and mixed doubles not standing as championship events.

Event	Matches Won	Sets Won	Sets Lost	Games Won	Games Lost	Partner
Singles	6	12	0	72	25	
Doubles	3	6	2	43	29	Mrs G. W. Hillyard
Mixed	5	10	2	66	40	H. L. Doherty
	14	28	4	181	94	

Average loss of games per set **2·937)**

The ceaseless throng which forms a background accompaniment to every Wimbledon fortnight

OFFICIAL PROGRAMME
THE LAWN TENNIS CHAMPIONSHIPS
1965
THE LAWN TENNIS CHAMPIONSHIPS

Championships Won from Match Point Down

1889	Men's singles	W. Renshaw in All Comers' Final beat H. S. Barlow 3–6 5–7 8–6 10–8 8–6 after six match points in the fourth set at 2–5 and 6–7.
	Women's singles*	Mrs G. W. Hillyard in All Comers' Final beat Miss L. Rice 4–6 8–6 6–4 after three match points in the second set.
1895	Men's singles*	W. Baddeley in All Comers' Final beat W. V. Eaves 4–6 2–6 8–6 6–2 6–3 from 5–6, 30–40, in the third set.
1901	Men's singles	A. W. Gore beat G. W. Hillyard in the quarter-final by 6–1 2–6 4–6 8–6 6–2 after one match point in the fourth set.
1908	Men's doubles*	A. F. Wilding and M. J. G. Ritchie in All Comers' Final beat A. W. Gore and H. Roper Barrett 6–1 6–2 1–6 1–6 9–7 after match point in the fifth set.
1919	Women's singles*	Mlle S. Lenglen in the challenge round beat Mrs R. Lambert Chambers 10–8 4–6 9–7 after two match points in the third set at 5–6 15–40.
1921	Men's singles*	W. T. Tilden in the challenge round beat B. I. C. Norton 4–6 2–6 6–1 6–0 7–5 after two match points in the fifth set at 4–5.
1926	Women's doubles	Miss E. Ryan and Miss M. K. Browne in the second round beat Mlle S. Lenglen and Mlle D. Vlasto 3–6 9–7 6–2 after two match points in the second set.
1927	Men's singles*	H. Cochet in the final beat J. Borotra 4–6 4–6 6–3 6–4 7–5 after six match points in the fifth set, one at 2–5 and five at 3–5.
	Men's doubles*	F. T. Hunter and W. T. Tilden in the final beat J. Brugnon and H. Cochet 1–6 4–6 8–6 6–3 6–4 after two match points in the third set at 4–5.
1932	Women's doubles	Mlle D. Metaxa and Mlle J. Sigart beat Miss F. James and Miss M. Heeley in the first round 2–6 6–4 7–5 after three match points in the fifth set.
1935	Women's singles*	Mrs F. S. Moody in the final beat Miss H. H. Jacobs 6–3 3–6 7–5 after one match point in the third set at 3–5.
	Men's doubles*	J. H. Crawford and A. K. Quist beat W. L. Allison and J. Van Ryn in the final 6–3 5–7 6–2 5–7 7–5 after one match point in the third set.
1947	Women's doubles*	Miss D. J. Hart and Mrs P. C. Todd in the final beat Miss A. L. Brough and Miss M. E. Osborne 3–6 4–6 7–5 after three match points in the fifth set at 3–5 0–40.
1948	Men's singles*	R. Falkenburg in the final beat J. E. Bromwich 7–5 0–6 6–2 3–6 7–5 after three match points in the third set at 3–5, 15–40 and advantage Bromwich.
1949	Men's singles	F. R. Schroeder in the quarter-final beat F. A. Sedgman 3–6 6–8 6–3 6–2 9–7 after two match points in the fifth set at 4–5 and 5–6.
1954	Women's doubles*	Miss A. L. Brough and Mrs W. du Pont in the final beat Miss S. J. Fry and Miss D. J. Hart 4–6 9–7 6–3 after two match points in the second set at 3–5.
1960	Men's singles	N. A. Fraser in the quarter-final beat E. Buchholz 4–6 6–3 4–6 15–15 retired after six match points in the fourth set.
	Mixed doubles*	R. G. Laver and Miss D. R. Hard in the final beat R. N. Howe and Miss M. E. Bueno 13–11 3–6 8–6 after three match points in the third set at 4–5.
1976	Mixed doubles*	A. D. Roche and Miss F. Durr in the final beat R. L. Stockton and Miss R. Casals 6–3 2–6 7–5 after a match point at 4–5 in the third set.

* Matches in which the losers, had they won, would have taken the title.

Wimbledon Centurions and Other Stalwarts

The most assiduous competitor in the history of the Championships was Jean Borotra. Competing first in 1922 he played 221 matches between then and his last challenge in 1964 at the age of 65 (after which he continued his enthusiasm in the non-championship veterans' doubles).

The most successful centurion was Elizabeth Ryan. She won 189 matches between 1912 and 1934 in the course of taking nineteen championships but played three fewer matches than did Borotra.

The following table records winners of one hundred matches or more.

	Titles won	Matches Played	Lost	Won
Miss E. Ryan (1912–34)				
Singles	—	61	15	46
Doubles	12	77	4	73
Mixed	7	80	10	70
Total	19	218	29	**189**
Mrs. L. W. King (1961–76)				
Singles	6	81	9	72
Doubles	9	70	7	63
Mixed	4	51	8	43
	19	202	24	**178**
J. Borotra (1922–64)				
Singles	2	65	10	55
Doubles	3	88	31	57
Mixed	1	68	28	40
	6	221	69	**152**
Miss A. L. Brough (1946–57)				
Singles	4	63	7	56
Doubles	5	43	4	39
Mixed	4	49	5	44
	13	155	16	**139**
Mrs B. M. Court (1961–75)				
Singles	3	60	9	51
Doubles	2	45	8	37
Mixed	5	51	4	47
	10	156	21	**135**
R. S. Emerson (1954–71)				
Singles	2	74	14	60
Doubles	3	72	12	60
Mixed	—	8	2	6
	5	154	28	**126**
Miss D. J. Hart (1946–55)				
Singles	1	51	8	43
Doubles	4	42	6	36
Mixed	5	49	4	45
	10	142	18	**124**
Mrs R. Lambert Chambers (1900–27)				
Singles	7	40	8	32
Doubles*	2*	54	14	40
Mixed*	3*	67	15	52
	12	161	37	**124**
N. A. Fraser (1954–76)				
Singles	1	51	13	38
Doubles	2	57	11	46
Mixed	1	48	12	36
	4	156	36	**120**
Mrs P. F. Jones (1956–69)				
Singles	1	70	13	57
Doubles	—	45	13	32
Mixed	1	39	10	29
	2	154	36	**118**
Miss M. E. Bueno (1958–76)				
Singles	3	57	8	49
Doubles	5	42	5	37
Mixed	—	36	8	28
	8	135	21	**114**
Mrs L. A. Godfree (1919–34)				
Singles	2	49	11	38
Doubles	—	46	12	34
Mixed	2	52	12	40
	4	147	35	**112**

* Includes the event prior to 1913 before it was technically a 'championship'.

	Titles won	Matches Played	Lost	Won
A. W. Gore (1888–1927)				
Singles	3	90	26	64
Doubles	1	58	26	32
Mixed*	1*	22	8	14
Total	5	170	60	**110**
R. A. J. Hewitt (1959–76)				
Singles	—	49	17	32
Doubles	4	68	13	55
Mixed	—	25	8	17
	4	142	38	**104**
Mme R. Mathieu (1926–47)				
Singles	—	60	14	46
Doubles	3	47	12	35
Mixed	—	34	13	21
	3	141	39	**102**
H. Roper Barrett (1898–1924)				
Singles	—	47	11	36
Doubles	3	58	16	42
Mixed*	1*	33	11	22
	4	138	38	**100**

* Includes the event prior to 1913 before it was technically a 'championship'.

Elizabeth Ryan

The over-all record of Miss Ryan was remarkable apart from her achievements at Wimbledon.

She played first in Great Britain in 1912 when, as a Californian of 19, she appeared in the Surbiton tournament with her sister Miss A. Ryan. She was a winner of her first match in the open singles, beating Mrs Hall 6–3 6–3, and then lost to Mrs R. J. McNair 6–4 7–5.

Her next tournament was a handicap-event-only affair at Stratford-upon-Avon. Playing from scratch she reached the singles final where she was given a walkover from her sister at receive 1/6. Together they won the doubles from scratch and Elizabeth won the mixed with A. Herschell from owe 4/6.

Accordingly the indomitable Miss Ryan won all three events at her second tournament in Britain. It was a pattern frequently repeated over the next two decades.

In 1912 Miss Ryan also played in tournaments at Liverpool, Malton, Wimbledon, Warwick, Winchester, Nottingham, Edgbaston, Lincoln, Tunbridge Wells, Saxmundham, Felixstowe, Scarborough, Colchester, Chichester, Dinard, Eastbourne and Hythe—19 tournaments in all.

In 1934, her last competitive year, she also played 19 tournaments. In 1924 she was at her zenith as a persistent competitor. In that year she played in at least 35 tournaments. She won 75 titles from 88 finals in which she was engaged. In 17 tournaments she won 3 events and was a triple finalist on 25 occasions.

It would be difficult to make an accurate tally of Miss Ryan's record. In her career, which covered 19 playing years, she played in at least 365 tournaments. She won at least 662 events, 193 singles, 255 women's doubles and 214 mixed doubles. She was unbeaten in any of 3 events at least 92 times and was a triple finalist at least 164 times. Her last tournament success, before turning professional, was in the Pacific South-West Championships in Los Angeles when she and Caroline Babcock won the women's doubles final against Betty Nuthall and Freda James, 6–3 3–6 6–3, that being her 662nd tournament triumph.

Even without her nineteen Wimbledon Championships Miss Ryan would stand out in the game. One of her titles, at least, will never be matched. She was singles champion of Imperial Russia in 1914.

Suzanne Lenglen

Her invincible singles record at Wimbledon, from 1919 to 1926, was:

1919
1st round Mrs Cobb 6–0 6–1
2nd round Mrs D. R. Larcombe 6–2 6–1
3rd round Mrs D. Craddock 6–0 6–1
4th round Miss K. McKane 6–0 6–1
Semi-final Miss E. Ryan (US) 6–4 7–5
Final Mrs P. Satterthwaite 6–1 6–1
Challenge round Mrs R. Lambert Chambers 10–8 4–6 9–7

1920
Challenge round Mrs R. Lambert Chambers 6–3 6–0

1921
Challenge round Miss E. Ryan (US) 6–2 6–0

1922
1st round Mrs M. F. Ellis 6–0 6–0
2nd round Miss K. McKane 6–1 7–5
3rd round Miss E. L. Colyer 6–0 6–0
4th round Miss E. Ryan (US) 6–1 8–6
Semi-final Mrs G. Peacock (SA) 6–4 6–1
Final Mrs F. Mallory (US) 6–2 6–0

1923
2nd round Miss P. Ingram 6–0 6–0
3rd round Mrs B. C. Covell 6–0 6–3
4th round Mlle D. Vlasto (F) 6–1 6–0
5th round Mrs Hazel 6–2 6–1
Semi-final Mrs A. E. Beamish 6–0 6–0
Final Miss K. McKane 6–2 6–2

1924
1st round Miss S. C. Lumley-Ellis 6–0 6–0
2nd round Miss E. R. Clarke 6–0 6–0
3rd round Mrs G. Wightman (US) 6–0 6–0
4th round Miss E. Ryan (US) 6–2 6–8 6–4
Semi-final scratched

1925
1st round Mrs H. Edginton w.o.
2nd round Miss E. Ryan (US) 6–2 6–0
3rd round Miss E. Goldsack 6–1 6–0
4th round Mrs A. E. Beamish 6–0 6–0
Semi-final Miss K. McKane 6–0 6–0
Final Miss J. Fry 6–2 6–0

1926
1st round Miss M. K. Browne (US) 6–2 6–3
2nd round Miss E. Dewhurst 6–2 6–2
3rd round scratched

Her over-all record was:

	Titles won	Matches Played	Lost	Won
Singles	6	32	0	32
Doubles	6	31	1	30
Mixed	3	31	2	29
Total	15	94	3	**91**

Helen Wills Moody

Her singles record, comprising 1 defeat in 9 meetings, was as follows:

1924
1st round Miss L. Scharman 6–1 6–0
2nd round Miss P. H. Dransfield 6–0 6–2
3rd round Mrs H. Edgington 6–2 6–2
4th round Mrs Colegate 6–1 6–0
Semi-final Mrs P. Satterthwaite 6–2 6–1
Final **lost to** Miss K. McKane 6–4 4–6 4–6

1927
1st round Miss G. R. Sterry 6–3 3–6 6–3
2nd round Miss S. C. Lumley-Ellis 6–3 6–2
3rd round Miss E. Bennett 7–5 6–3
4th round Miss E. Goldsack 6–1 6–3
5th round Mrs G. Peacock (SA) 6–3 6–1
Semi-final Miss J. Fry 6–3 6–1
Final Snta E. de Alvarez (SP) 6–2 6–4

1928
2nd round Miss E. Goldsack 6–2 6–1
3rd round Mlle V. Gallay (F) 6–0 6–0
4th round Miss E. H. Harvey 6–2 6–3
5th round Mrs M. Watson 6–3 6–0
Semi-final Miss E. Ryan (US) 6–1 6–1
Final Snta E. de Alvarez (SP) 6–2 6–3

1929
2nd round Miss G. E. Tomblin 6–0 6–0
3rd round Frau I. Schomburgk (G) 6–0 6–0
4th round Mlle J. Sigart (B) 6–2 6–3
5th round Miss E. L. Heine (SA) 6–2 6–4
Semi-final Miss E. Goldsack 6–2 6–0
Final Miss H. H. Jacobs (US) 6–1 6–2

1930
2nd round Frl H. Krahwinkel (G) 6–2 6–1
3rd round Miss E. G. Goldsworth 6–1 6–2
4th round Miss M. Canters 6–0 6–1
5th round Miss P. E. Mudford 6–1 6–2
Semi-final Mme R. Mathieu (F) 6–3 6–2
Final Miss E. Ryan (US) 6–2 6–2

1932
2nd round Miss M. R. Couquerque (NTH) 6–1 6–1
3rd round Miss W. M. C. Bower 6–1 6–0
4th round Mrs L. A. Godfree 6–3 6–0
5th round Miss D. E. Round 6–0 6–1
Semi-final Miss M. Heeley 6–2 6–0
Final Miss H. H. Jacobs (US) 6–3 6–1

1933
2nd round Mrs E. Macready 6–0 6–0
3rd round Miss M. Heeley 6–2 6–1
4th round Mme S. Henrotin (F) 6–3 6–0
5th round Mlle L. Payot (SWI) 6–4 6–1
Semi-final Frl H. Krahwinkel (G) 6–4 6–3
Final Miss D. E. Round 6–4 6–8 6–3

1935
1st round Miss A. Baumgarten (HU) 6–0 6–1
2nd round Miss A. M. Yorke 6–3 6–1
3rd round Miss S. Noel 6–2 7–5
4th round Miss S. Cepkova (CZ) 3–6 6–4 6–2
5th round Mme R. Mathieu (F) 6–3 6–0
Semi-final Miss J. Hartigan (AUS) 6–3 6–3
Final Miss H. H. Jacobs (US) 6–3 3–6 7–5

1938
2nd round Mrs H. C. Hopman (AUS) 6–3 6–4
3rd round Mrs P. F. Glover 6–4 7–5
4th round Mrs E. L. Heine Miller (SA) 8–6 6–4
5th round Miss K. E. Stammers 6–2 6–1
Semi-final Fru S. Sperling (DEN) 12–10 6–4
Final Miss H. H. Jacobs 6–4 6–0

Her over-all record was:

	Titles won	Matches Played	Lost	Won
Singles	8	56	1	55
Doubles	3	16	0	16
Mixed	1	22	3	19
Total	12	94	4	**90**

Louise Brough

Louise Brough won 22 singles in sequence 1948–51.

1948
2nd round Miss E. F. Lombard (IRE) 6–1 6–1
3rd round Mrs M. A. Prentiss (US) 6–1 4–6 6–1
4th round Miss E. A. Middleton 6–0 6–1
5th round Miss S. J. Fry (US) 3–1 retired
Semi-final Mrs P. C. Todd (US) 6–3 7–5
Final Miss D. J. Hart (US) 6–3 8–6

1949
2nd round Miss E. A. Middleton 6–1 6–1
3rd round Mrs W. C. J. Halford 6–1 6–0
4th round Miss R. Walsh 6–1 6–2
5th round Mrs N. W. Blair 6–2 6–3
Semi-final Mrs P. C. Todd (US) 6–3 6–0
Final Mrs W. du Pont (US) 10–8 1–6 10–8

1950
2nd round Mrs A. C. Brighton 6–0 6–1
3rd round Mrs A. J. Mottram 9–7 6–2
4th round Miss E. M. S. Andrews 6–0 6–0
5th round Miss S. J. Fry (US) 2–6 6–3 6–0
Semi-final Miss D. J. Hart (US) 6–4 6–3
Final Mrs W. du Pont (US) 6–1 3–6 6–1

1951
2nd round Mrs R. L. Scott 6–1 6–2
3rd round Miss G. C. Hoahing 6–1 6–3
4th round Miss P. A. Lewis 6–1 6–0
5th round Miss K. L. A. Tuckey 5–7 6–0 6–3
Semi-final **lost to** Miss S. J. Fry (US) 4–6 2–6

Maureen Connolly

Never beaten in singles, Maureen Connolly won 18 consecutive matches 1952–4.

1952
2nd round Mrs C. G. Moeller 6–2 6–0
3rd round Miss A. Mortimer 6–4 6–3
4th round Miss J. S. V. Partridge 6–3 5–7 7–5
5th round Mrs T. D. Long (AUS) 5–7 6–2 6–0
Semi-final Miss S. J. Fry (US) 6–4 6–3
Final Miss A. L. Brough (US) 7–5 6–3

1953
2nd round Miss D. Kilian (SA) 6–0 6–0
3rd round Miss J. M. Petchell 6–1 6–1
4th round Miss J. A. Shilcock 6–0 6–1
5th round Frau E. Vollmer (G) 6–3 6–0
Semi-final Miss S. J. Fry (US) 6–1 6–1
Final Miss D. J. Hart (US) 8–6 7–5

1954
2nd round Miss J. Scott (SA) 6–0 6–3
3rd round Frl E. Buding (G) 6–2 6–3
4th round Miss A. Buxton 6–0 6–0
5th round Mrs W. du Pont (US) 6–1 6–1
Semi-final Mrs C. Pratt (US) 6–1 6–1
Final Miss A. L. Brough (US) 6–2 7–5

Her over-all record 1952–4 was:

	Titles	Matches		
	won	Played	Lost	Won
Singles	3	18	0	18
Doubles	—	9	2	7
Mixed	—	12	3	9
Total	3	39	5	**34**

Fred Perry

Uniquely, for a man, Fred Perry won the singles playing through in 3 successive years, 1934, 1935 and 1936. His 21 sequential victories were:

1934
1st round C. R. D. Tuckey (GB) 6–2 6–2 5–7 6–0
2nd round R. N. Williams (US) 6–2 6–2 6–0
3rd round R. Menzel (CZ) 0–6 6–3 5–7 6–4 6–2
4th round A. K. Quist (AUS) 6–2 6–3 6–4
Quarter-final G. M. Lott (US) 6–4 2–6 7–5 10–8
Semi-final S. B. Wood (US) 6–3 3–6 7–5 5–7 6–3
Final J. H. Crawford (AUS) 6–3 6–0 7–5

1935
1st round M. Rainville (CAN) 6–1 6–1 6–3
2nd round W. Hines (US) 6–1 7–5 6–3
3rd round J. Van Ryn (US) 4–6 6–1 6–3 10–8
4th round J. Pallada (YU) 6–2 6–2 0–6 6–2
Quarter-final R. Menzel (CZ) 9–7 6–1 6–1
Semi-final J. H. Crawford (AUS) 6–2 3–6 6–4 6–4
Final G. von Cramm (G) 6–2 6–4 6–4

1936
1st round G. D. Stratford (US) 6–4 6–3 6–1
2nd round K. Chartikavanij (Siam) 6–3 6–2 6–2
3rd round J. Van Ryn (US) 6–3 6–2 6–0
4th round C. E. Malfroy (NZ) 6–2 6–2 6–4
Quarter-final B. M. Grant (US) 6–4 6–3 6–1
Semi-final J. D. Budge (US) 5–7 6–4 6–3 6–4
Final G. von Cramm (G) 6–1 6–1 6–0

His over-all singles record, 1929–36, was: played 41, won 36, lost 5.

Rod Laver

Rod Laver had a continuity of success unequalled by any other man in the singles. Winning in 1961 and 1962 he was excluded, because of his professional status, until 1968. He won that year and also in 1969. In 1970 he lost in the fourth round to Roger Taylor, the Yorkshire left hander, having won no less than 31 Championship singles in sequence. His wins were:

1961
1st round T. Lejus (USSR) 6–4 6–1 6–1
2nd round P. Darmon (F) 8–6 2–6 6–3 6–4 6–4
3rd round W. Bungert (G) 6–3 6–1 8–10 4–6 6–3
4th round R. A. J. Hewitt (AUS) 6–4 6–4 6–2
Quarter-final L. Ayala (Chile) 6–1 6–3 6–2
Semi-final R. Krishnan (IN) 6–2 8–6 6–2
Final C. R. McKinley (US) 6–3 6–1 6–4

1962
1st round N. Kumar (IN) 7–5 6–1 6–2
2nd round J. A. Pickard (GB) 6–1 6–2 6–2
3rd round W. Reed (US) 6–4 6–1 6–4
4th round P. Darmon (F) 6–3 6–2 13–11
Quarter-final M. Santana (SP) 14–16 9–7 6–2 6–2
Semi-final N. A. Fraser (AUS) 10–8 6–1 7–5
Final M. F. Mulligan (AUS) 6–2 6–2 6–1

1968
1st round E. L. Scott (US) 6–3 4–6 6–3 6–2
2nd round S. R. Smith (US) 6–3 6–4 6–4
3rd round M. C. Riessen (US) 6–4 3–6 7–5 6–3
4th round M. Cox (GB) 9–7 5–7 6–2 6–0
Quarter-final R. D. Ralston (US) 4–6 6–3 6–1 4–6 6–2
Semi-final A. R. Ashe (US) 7–5 6–2 6–4
Final A. D. Roche (AUS) 6–3 6–4 6–2

1969
1st round N. Pietrangeli (IT) 6–1 6–2 6–2
2nd round P. Lall (IN) 3–6 4–6 6–3 6–0 6–0
3rd round J. Leschly (DEN) 6–3 6–3 6–3
4th round S. R. Smith (US) 6–4 6–2 7–9 3–6 6–3
Quarter-final E. C. Drysdale (SA) 6–4 6–2 6–3
Semi-final A. R. Ashe (US) 2–6 6–2 9–7 6–0
Final J. D. Newcombe (AUS) 6–4 5–7 6–4 6–4

1970
1st round G. Seewagen (US) 6–2 6–0 6–2
2nd round J. G. Alexander (AUS) 6–1 6–3 6–3
3rd round F. D. McMillan (SA) 6–2 3–6 6–0 6–2 (*31st consecutive win*)
4th round lost to R. Taylor (GB) 6–4 4–6 2–6 1–6

His over-all singles record, 1956–71, was: played 55, won 49, lost 6.

The redoubtable Louise Brough, winner of eight championships in three years, 1948–50, and of 22 singles in sequence, 1948–51, and Margaret du Pont, the singles winner of 1947

Fred Perry, singles champion 1934–6

Overseas Challengers before 1914

Year	Men	Women
1884	*USA* J. Dwight, R. D. Sears, A. L. Rives	
1885	*USA* J. Dwight, A. A. Thomson	
1890	*USA* D. Miller, E. A. Thomson	
1892	*USA* O. S. Campbell	
1894	*USA* J. F. Talmage	
1896	*USA* A. E. Foote, W. A. Larned	
1898	*USA* W. C. Grant, C. Hobart, J. P. Paret	
1899	*USA* C. Hobart	
1900		*USA* Miss M. Jones
1901	*New Zealand* H. A. Parker	
1902	*Belgium* P. de Borman, W. Lemaire	
1903	*USA* C. Hobart *Netherlands* A. B. van Groenon, T. F. Vreede	
1904	*Belgium* P. de Borman, W. Lemaire *Austria* R. Kinzl	
1905	*USA* W. A. Clothier, K. Doust, W. A. Larned, H. Ward, B. C. Wright *New Zealand* H. A. Parker, A. F. Wilding *Belgium* P. de Borman, W. Lemaire, F. Houget *Australia* N. E. Brookes, A. W. Dunlop, B. Murphy *South Africa* H. A. Kitson *Denmark* E. Larsen, T. Hillerup	*USA* Miss M. G. Sutton
1906	*USA* K. Collins, R. D. Little *New Zealand* A. F. Wilding *Germany* R. F. Lalberer, L. Kulenkampff, R. Schomburgk	*USA* Miss M. G. Sutton
1907	*USA* H. Behr, K. Behr, D. P. Rhodes, B. C. Wright	*USA* Miss M. G. Sutton

Year	Men	Women
	New Zealand A. F. Wilding	
	Austria R. Kinzl, C. van Wesseley	
	Australia S. N. Doust, N. E. Brookes	
	Germany O. Kreuzer	
	Canada R. B. Powell	*Canada* Miss V. Summerhayes
1908	*USA* W. C. Grant	
	New Zealand A. F. Wilding	
	Belgium P. de Borman, W. Lemaire	
	South Africa V. R. Gauntlett, H. A. Kitson, Rev J. Richardson	
	Germany E. von Bissing, O. Froitzheim, O. Kreuzer, F. W. Rahe	
	Canada J. F. Foulkes, R. B. Powell	
	France M. Germot	
	India Sirdah Nihal Singh	
1909	*USA* D. P. Rhodes	
	New Zealand H. A. Parker, T. R. Quill	
	Belgium P. de Borman, W. Lemaire, L. Trasenster, G. Watson	
	Australia S. N. Doust, L. O. S. Poidevin	
	Germany E. von Bissing, F. W. Rahe	
	Canada R. B. Powell	
	India Sirdar Nihal Singh	
	Argentina E. Knight, H. B. Knight	
		Norway Fru M. Bjurstedt
1910	*USA* S. Hardy, A. Holmes, G. H. Nettleton, B. C. Wright	
	New Zealand A. F. Wilding	
	Netherlands B. J. Pfleiderer, R. A. Pfleiderer	
	Australia S. N. Doust, L. O. S. Poidevin	
	Denmark O. Frederiksen, P. Grous-Petersen, L. Rovsing	*Denmark* Fru C. Castenschiold
	Germany O. Froitzheim, O. Kreuzer	
	Canada R. B. Powell	
	France A. H. Gobert	
	India A. A. Fyzee, A. H. Fyzee, Sirdar Nihal Singh	
1911	*USA* C. Biddle, S. Hardy, D. P. Rhodes	
	New Zealand A. F. Wilding	

Year	Men	Women
	Belgium	
	P. de Borman	
	Australia	
	A. W. Dunlop, R. W. Heath, S. N. Doust	
	South Africa	
	F. E. Cochran	
	Denmark	*Denmark*
	E. Larsen	Fru C. Castenschiold
	Canada	
	R. B. Powell	
	France	
	M. Decugis, A. H. Gobert	
	Germany	
	H. Kleinschroth, F. W. Rahe	
	Italy	
	C. de Martino	
1912		*USA*
		Miss E. Ryan
	New Zealand	
	A. F. Wilding	
	Belgium	*Belgium*
	P. de Borman	Mlle J. Liebrechts
	Australia	
	F. E. Barritt, S. N. Doust	
	Denmark	
	E. Larsen	
	Germany	
	C. Bergmann, E. von Bissing, O. Froitzheim, F. W. Rahe	
	Canada	
	R. B. Powell	
	France	*France*
	M. Decugis, M. Germot, A. H. Gobert	Mme M. Decugis
1913	*USA*	*USA*
	C. Biddle, M. McLoughlin, R. N. Williams	Miss E. Ryan
	New Zealand	
	A. F. Wilding	
	Belgium	
	P. de Borman	
	Australia	
	S. N. Doust, A. B. Jones, H. M. Rice	
	South Africa	
	V. R. Gauntlett, C. R. Leach, R. F. Le Sueur	
	Denmark	
	E. Larsen	
	Germany	*Germany*
	O. Froitzheim, H. Kleinschroth, O. Kreuzer, F. W. Rahe	Frl M. Rieck
	Canada	
	J. F. Foulkes, H. G. Mayers, R. B. Powell, B. P. Schwengers	
	France	
	M. Decugis	
	Switzerland	
	A. C. Simon	
1914	*USA*	*USA*
	C. Biddle	Miss E. Ryan
	New Zealand	
	A. F. Wilding	
	Belgium	
	P. de Borman	
	Australia	
	N. E. Brookes, S. N. Doust, A. W. Dunlop	
	Denmark	
	E. Larsen	
	Germany	
	O. Froitzheim, H. Kleinschroth	
	France	*France*
	M. Decugis, M. Germot	Mlle M. Broquedis

HRH Duchess of Kent talking to the ball-boys who contribute so much to the smooth running of the Championships

The grounds have to be tended at all times and in all weathers and are in the care of the head groundsman, *right*, Mr Jack Yardley

Above: The Championships have always attracted large crowds, seen here queueing for admission

Crests at Wimbledon: those of the Lawn Tennis Association (*above*) and the All England Club (*top*)

Above: Keen fans of the young Swedish player, Bjorn Borg, demonstrating a trend of the seventies

Playing their respective parts. *Right*: Ball-boy and lineswoman. *Below*: TV cameraman

Men's Doubles before 1884

It is a matter of historical nicety whether the men's doubles championship should be regarded as having begun in 1884, when it was staged for the first time at the All England Club, Wimbledon, or whether the point of origin should be 1879, the date ascribed in the records since the early days.

The first men's doubles event played in the world would seem to be that in the Scottish Championships in 1878. It was won by A. Graham Murray (Viscount Dunedin) and C. C. Maconochie. In 1879 the Oxford University LTC inaugurated at the 'new' Norham Gardens ground the 'Oxford University Challenge Cup for Pairs'. Fourteen *club* pairs took part, playing the best of seven sets, in a tournament lasting from 20 to 23 May.

In 1880 twelve pairs, again competing over the best of seven sets, took part, including the Renshaw twins, who won. Subsequently the distance was reduced to the best of five sets. Eight pairs participated in 1881 and 1882. In 1883 the number diminished to six but there were scratchings and three matches were sufficient to finish the tournament. In its last three years it was called the 'Oxford University Doubles Championship'.

The original cups were donated to the All England Club and have been played for ever since. To what degree, though, can the championships at Oxford and Wimbledon be regarded as the same? The All England Club can hardly be said to have gobbled up a thriving championship; rather by staging a doubles event of their own they seem to have saved two cups in danger of being without a home, the Oxford event apparently dying on its feet.

Even so surviving doubles winners from Oxford were awarded the commemorative champions' medals at the Jubilee celebrations at Wimbledon in 1926. What, then, is the tally of doubles titles won by the Renshaws? Five were at Wimbledon. The two gained at Oxford, even though the same cups were involved, do not quite have the same hallmark. In this context it should be noted that at no time was the term 'All England Championship' used in reference to the event at Oxford.

The Oxford doubles championship results were:

1879

Semi-finals G. E. Tabor and F. Durant d W. F. Wells Cole and E. B. Hill 6–4 6–2 6–1 6–3

L. R. Erskine and H. F. Lawford d L. H. Mulholland and A. J. Mulholland 5–6 6–5 6–2 6–4 6–5

Final Erskine and Lawford d Tabor and Durant 4–6 6–4 6–5 6–2 3–6 5–6 10–8

1880

Semi-finals E. Renshaw and W. Renshaw d J. Comber and R. W. Braddell 6–4 6–3 6–1 6–2

C. J. Cole and O. E. Woodhouse a bye

Final E. Renshaw and W. Renshaw d Cole and Woodhouse 6–1 6–4 6–0 6–8 6–3

1881

Semi-finals E. Renshaw and W. Renshaw d R. W. Braddell and J. Comber 4–6 6–1 6–2 6–4

W. J. Down and H. L. Vaughan d C. J. Cole and D. Stewart 8–10 6–0 0–6 6–2 6–1

Final E. Renshaw and W. Renshaw d Down and Vaughan 6–0 6–0 6–4

1882

Semi-finals J. G. Horn and C. B. Russell d A. S. Rashleigh and M. G. Lascelles 6–2 6–4 2–6 6–3

J. T. Hartley and R. T. Richardson d E. Renshaw and W. Renshaw 6–3 6–5 6–2

Final Hartley and Richardson d Horn and Russell 6–2 6–1 6–0

1883

Semi-finals C. B. Russell and R. T. Mitford d F. R. Pinhorn and T. R. Deykin 6–5 3–6 6–4 6–3

C. M. Grinstead and C. E. Weldon w.o. E. Renshaw and W. Renshaw

Final Grinstead and Weldon d Russell and Mitford 3–6 6–1 6–3 6–4

The Davis Cup at Wimbledon

The Davis Cup, first played for in a contest between the British Isles and America at the Longwood Cricket Club in 1900, originated in the rivalry between those two nations. A precursor of the competition took place at the All England Club in 1883. From the United States came two brothers, C. M. and J. S. Clark, with official USLTA blessing as a representative American pair. They played two challenge doubles matches against Ernest and William Renshaw. In the first, on 18 July, the Renshaws won 6–4 8–6 3–6 6–1. On 25 July they won more easily, 6–3 6–2 6–3, with the British tactics of playing both men up at the same time proving manifestly better than the American formation of one up, one back.

Of the Davis Cup ties staged at Wimbledon two rubbers at the Inter-Zone level stand out. In 1936 Australia met Germany on Court One to decide the challenger against Great Britain. In the singles Adrian Quist had a memorable struggle against Baron Gottfried von Cramm, with the latter eventually winning 4–6 6–4 4–6 6–4 11–9. Rarely has a match swayed so excitingly, with von Cramm in the first instance having two match points when 5–3 in the fifth set and three more when 5–4. Subsequently Quist had five match balls of his own at 8–7. At 10–9 the other way von Cramm was denied four more match points before winning his tenth. By that time spectators were standing on the seats, almost delirious with tension and excitement. Despite this Australia won the tie 4–1 to earn the right to make what was a vain challenge against the British holders.

The following year, 1937, which brought the end of British Davis Cup success, von Cramm was again involved in an historic contest, again in the Inter-Zone round. This time he was on the losing side of a dramatic conflict against Don Budge, who played one of his finest matches against him. The USA and Germany were level at two rubbers each when Budge played von Cramm in the deciding rubber. The setting this time was the Centre Court. Von Cramm, playing impeccably and with a fluency at which he excelled above all rivals, took the first two sets 8–6 5–7. Budge fought back to take the third and fourth 6–4 6–2 but the German reasserted his smooth authority. He broke service and led 4–1 and 5–2. 'Don't worry,' Budge said to his captain, Walter Pate, 'I won't let you down.' Nor did he. He did not lead until the thirteenth game but he won the set 8–6. The power and confidence of his performance left no doubt about the issue of the subsequent Challenge Round when Great Britain was without Fred Perry.

It is to be doubted if the Davis Cup reached greater heights at any time at Wimbledon than in these two rubbers, Quist against von Cramm in 1936 and Budge against von Cramm in 1937.

1904 Final Round, 27–29 June
Belgium d France 3–2 (P. de Borman lost to M. Decugis 4–6 3–5 retired; W. Lemaire d P. Aymé 6–1 6–0 6–1; de Borman and Lemaire lost to Decugis and Aymé 7–5 4–6 6–0 4–6 2–6; de Borman d Aymé 6–1 6–3 2–6 1–6 6–3; Lemaire d Decugis 5–7 8–6 0–6 6–4 6–2.)

Challenge Round, 2–5 July
British Isles d Belgium 5–0 (H. L. Doherty d P. de Borman 6–4 6–1 6–1; F. L. Riseley d W. Lemaire 6–1 6–4 6–2; R. F. and H. L. Doherty d de Borman and Lemaire 6–0 6–1 6–3; Riseley d de Borman 4–6 6–2 8–6 7–5; H. L. Doherty w.o. Lemaire.)

1905 Challenge Round, 21–24 July
British Isles d USA 5–0 (H. L. Doherty d H. Ward 7–9 4–6 6–1 6–2 6–0; S. H. Smith d W. A. Larned 6–4 6–4 5–7 6–4; R. F. and H. L. Doherty d Ward and B. C. Wright 8–10 6–2 6–2 4–6 8–6; H. L. Doherty d Larned 6–4 2–6 6–8 6–4 6–2; Smith d W. J. Clothier 6–1 6–4 6–3.)

1906 Challenge Round, 15–18 June
British Isles d USA 5–0 (S. H. Smith d R. D. Little 6–4 6–4 6–1; H. L. Doherty d H. Ward 6–1 6–0 6–4; R. F. and H. L. Doherty d Little and Ward 3–6 11–9 9–7 6–1; Smith d Ward 6–1 6–0 6–4; H. L. Doherty d Little 3–6 6–3 6–8 6–1 6–3.)

1907 Preliminary Tie, 13–16 July
Australasia d USA 3–2 (N. E. Brookes d B. C. Wright 6–4 6–4 6–2; A. F. Wilding d K. Behr 1–6 6–3 3–6 7–5 6–3; Brookes and Wilding lost to Behr and Wright 6–3 10–12 6–4 2–6 3–6; Wilding lost to Wright 8–6 3–6 3–6 5–7; Brookes d Behr 4–6 6–4 6–1 6–2.)

Challenge Round, 20–23 July
Australasia d British Isles 3–2 (N. E. Brookes d A. W. Gore 7–5 6–1 7–5; A. F. Wilding d H. Roper Barrett 1–6 6–4 6–3 7–5; Brookes and Wilding lost to Gore and Roper Barrett 6–3 6–4 5–7 2–6 11–13; Wilding lost to Gore 6–3 3–6 5–7 2–6; Brookes d Roper Barrett 6–2 6–0 6–3.)

1913 Final Round, 18–21 July
USA d Canada 3–0 (R. N. Williams d B. P. Schwengers 6–4 6–2 6–4; M. E. McLoughlin d R. B. Powell 10–8 6–1 6–4; H. H. Hackett and McLoughlin d Powell and Schwengers 6–3 6–3 12–10.)
Challenge Round, 25–28 July
USA d British Isles 3–2 (M. E. McLoughlin lost to J. C. Parke 10–8 5–7 4–6 6–1 5–7; R. N. Williams d C. P. Dixon 8–6 6–3 6–2; H. H. Hackett and McLoughlin d H. Roper Barrett and Dixon 5–7 6–1 2–6 7–5 6–4; McLoughlin d Dixon 8–6 6–3 6–2; Williams lost to Parke 2–6 7–5 7–5 4–6 2–6.)

1914 Second Round, 11–14 July
British Isles d France 4–1 (T. M. Mavrogordato d M. Germot 4–6 7–5 9–7 6–2; J. C. Parke d M. Decugis 6–2 4–6 3–6 6–3 6–3; H. Roper Barrett and Mavrogordato lost to Decugis and Germot 3–6 7–5 5–7 4–6; Mavrogordato d Decugis 6–1 7–5 7–5; Parke d Germot 7–5 6–1 6–3.)

1920 Second Round, 16–19 July
USA d British Isles 5–0 (W. M. Johnston d J. C. Parke 6–4 6–4 2–6 3–6 6–2; W. T. Tilden d A. R. F. Kingscote 4–6 6–1 6–3 6–1; Johnston and Tilden d Parke and Kingscote 8–6 4–6 4–6 6–3 6–2; Johnston d Kingscote 6–4 4–6 3–6 6–4 7–5; Tilden d Parke 6–2 6–3 7–5.)

1933 European Zone Final, 13–15 July, Centre Court
Great Britain d Australia 3–2 (H. W. Austin lost to J. H. Crawford 6–4 2–6 2–6 3–6; F. J. Perry d V. B. McGrath 6–2 6–4 6–2; G. P. Hughes and Perry d D. P. Turnbull and A. K. Quist 7–5 6–4 3–6 6–3; Austin d McGrath 6–4 7–5 6–3; H. G. N. Lee lost to Crawford 6–8 5–7 4–6.)

1934 Inter-Zone Final, 21–25 July, Court One
USA d Australia 3–2 (F. X. Shields lost to J. H. Crawford 1–6 2–6 10–12; S. B. Wood lost to V. B. McGrath 5–7 4–6 6–1 7–9; G. M. Lott and L. R. Stoefen d Crawford and A. K. Quist 6–4 6–4 2–6 6–4; Wood d Crawford 6–3 9–7 4–6 4–6 6–2; Shields d McGrath 6–4 6–2 6–4.)
Challenge Round, 28–31 July, Centre Court
Great Britain d USA 4–1 (F. J. Perry d S. B. Wood 6–1 4–6 5–7 6–0 6–3; H. W. Austin d F. X. Shields 6–4 6–4 6–1; G. P. Hughes and H. G. N. Lee lost to G. M. Lott and L. R. Stoefen 5–7 0–6 6–4 7–9; Perry d Shields 6–4 4–6 6–2 15–13; Austin d Wood 6–4 6–0 6–8 6–3.)

1935 Inter-Zone Final, 20–24 July, Court One
USA d Germany 4–1 (W. L. Allison lost to G. von Cramm 6–8 3–6 4–6; J. D. Budge d H. Henkel 7–5 11–9 6–8 6–1; Allison and J. Van Ryn d von Cramm and K. Lund 3–6 6–3 5–7 9–7 8–6; Allison d Henkel 6–1 7–5 11–9; Budge d von Cramm 0–6 9–7 8–6 6–3.)
Challenge Round, 27–30 July, Centre Court
Great Britain d USA 5–0 (F. J. Perry d J. D. Budge 6–0 6–8 6–3 6–4; H. W. Austin d W. L. Allison 6–2 2–6 4–6 6–3 7–5; G. P. Hughes and C. R. D. Tuckey d Allison and J. Van Ryn 6–2 1–6 6–8 6–3 6–3; Austin d Budge 6–2 6–4 6–8 7–5; Perry d Allison 4–6 6–4 7–5 6–3.)

1936 Inter-Zone Final, 18–21 July, Court One
Australia d Germany 4–1 (A. K. Quist lost to G. von Cramm 6–4 4–6 6–4 4–6 9–11; J. H. Crawford d H. Henkel 6–2 6–2 retired; Crawford and V. B. McGrath d von Cramm and Henkel 6–4 4–6 6–4 6–4; McGrath d Henkel 6–3 5–7 6–4 6–4; Crawford d H. Denker 6–3 6–1 6–4.)
Challenge Round, 25–28 July, Centre Court
Great Britain d Australia 3–2 (F. J. Perry d A. K. Quist 6–1 4–6 7–5 6–2; H. W. Austin d J. H. Crawford 4–6 6–3 6–1 6–1; G. P. Hughes and C. R. D. Tuckey lost to Crawford and Quist 4–6 6–2 5–7 8–10; Austin lost to Quist 4–6 6–3 5–7 2–6; Perry d Crawford 6–2 6–3 6–3.)

1937 Inter-Zone Final, 17–20 July, Centre Court
USA d Germany 3–2 (J. D. Budge d H. Henkel 6–2 6–1 6–3; B. M. Grant lost to G. von Cramm 3–6 4–6 2–6; Budge and C. G. Mako d von Cramm and Henkel 4–6 7–5 8–6 6–4; Grant lost to Henkel 5–7 6–2 3–6 4–6; Budge d von Cramm 6–8 5–7 6–4 6–2 8–6.)
Challenge Round, 24–27 July, Centre Court
USA d Great Britain 4–1 (J. D. Budge d C. E. Hare 15–13 6–1 6–2; F. Parker lost to H. W. Austin 3–6 2–6 5–7; Budge and C. G. Mako d C. R. D. Tuckey and F. H. D. Wilde 6–3 7–5 7–9 12–10; Parker d Hare 6–2 6–4 6–2; Budge d Austin 8–6 3–6 6–4 6–3.)

1939 European Zone, Third Round, Court One
Great Britain d France 3–2 (C. E. Hare d B. Destremeau 6–2 6–3 3–6 14–12; R. A. Shayes lost to C. Boussus 2–6 4–6 0–6; Hare and F. H. D. Wilde d Y. Petra and P. Pelizza 6–3 6–3 3–6 4–6 6–3; Shayes d Destremeau 6–3 4–6 6–4 7–5; L. Shaffi lost to Boussus 0–6 2–6 5–7.)

1949 European Zone, Second Round, Court One
Czechoslovakia d Great Britain 4–1 (J. Drobny d A. J. Mottram 6–4 6–3 8–6; V. Cernik d G. L. Paish 6–3 2–6 6–4 6–4; Drobny and Cernik d Mottram and Paish 6–3 6–3 6–1; Drobny d Paish 6–3 6–0 6–3; Cernik lost to Mottram 2–6 4–6 4–6.)

1951 European Zone, Second Round, Court One
Great Britain d France 3–2 (G. L. Paish lost to P. Remy 3–6 2–6 3–6; A. J. Mottram d B. Destremeau 6–3 1–6 6–8 6–2 6–3; Mottram and Paish d Remy and R. Abdesselam 7–5 6–3 6–8 6–4; Mottram d Remy 6–2 6–4 6–4; A. G. Roberts lost to Destremeau 5–7 2–6 8–6 6–3 3–6.)

1960 European Zone, Semi-final, Court One
Italy d Great Britain 4–1 (N. Pietrangeli d R. K. Wilson 6–4 6–3 4–6 7–5; O. Sirola d M. G. Davies 9–7 7–5 1–6 2–6 6–4; Pietrangeli and Sirola d Davis and Wilson 6–4 3–6 8–6 6–3; Pietrangeli d Davies 6–4 6–3 6–4; S. Tacchini lost to Wilson 6–3 3–6 6–8 2–6.)

1963 European Zone Final, Court One
Great Britain d Sweden 3–2 (M. J. Sangster d J. E. Lundquist 3–6 6–2 4–6 12–10 9–7; R. K. Wilson lost to U. Schmidt 4–6 6–4 4–6 6–4 4–6; Sangster and Wilson d Lundquist and Schmidt 22–20 6–4 6–3; Wilson lost to Lundquist 6–3 6–2 2–6 2–6 1–6; Sangster d Schmidt 7–5 6–2 9–11 3–6 6–3.)

1969 Inter-Zone Semi-final, Court One
Great Britain d Brazil 3–2 (G. R. Stilwell d J. E. Mandarino 6–3 8–6 8–6; M. Cox lost to T. Koch 6–4 13–11 3–6 6–8 6–8; Cox and P. W. Curtis lost to Koch and Mandarino 6–4 4–6 4–6 4–6; Stilwell d Koch 7–5 6–4 6–4; Cox d Mandarino 6–3 18–16 3–6 6–2.)

Inter-Zone Final, Court One
Romania d Great Britain 3–2 (I. Tiriac d M. Cox 6–4 6–4 6–3; I. Nastase lost to G. R. Stilwell 4–6 6–4 1–6 2–6; Nastase and Tiriac d Cox and Stilwell 10–8 3–6 6–3 6–4; Tiriac lost to Stilwell 3–6 2–6 2–6; Nastase d Cox 3–6 6–1 6–4 6–4.)

1976 European Zone Section B Final, Court One
Italy d Great Britain 4–1 (A. Zugarelli d R. Taylor 6–1 7–5 3–6 6–1; A. Panatta d J. M. Lloyd 5–7 6–3 6–3 2–6 6–4; Panatta and P. Bertolucci lost to J. M. and D. A. Lloyd 8–6 6–3 3–6 16–18 2–6; Panatta d Taylor 3–6 6–2 6–4 6–4; Zugarelli d J. M. Lloyd 4–6 6–8 6–1 6–1 6–1.)

The Wightman Cup

The annual team contest, comprising 5 singles and 2 doubles matches, between the women of Great Britain and the United States was staged first at the West Side Club, Forest Hills, New York, and then from 1924 to 1972 in alternate years at the All England Club.

	Winner	Score	Venue
1923	USA	7–0	Forest Hills
1924	GB	6–1	Wimbledon, Centre Court
1925	GB	4–3	Forest Hills
1926	USA	4–3	Wimbledon, Centre Court
1927	USA	5–2	Forest Hills
1928	GB	4–3	Wimbledon, Centre Court
1929	USA	4–3	Forest Hills
1930	GB	4–3	Wimbledon, Centre Court
1931	USA	5–2	Forest Hills
1932	USA	4–3	Wimbledon, Court One
1933	USA	4–3	Forest Hills
1934	USA	5–2	Wimbledon, Centre Court
1935	USA	4–3	Forest Hills
1936	USA	4–3	Wimbledon, Centre Court
1937	USA	6–1	Forest Hills
1938	USA	5–2	Wimbledon, Centre Court
1939	USA	5–2	Forest Hills
1940–5 not held			
1946	USA	7–0	Wimbledon, Court One
1947	USA	7–0	Forest Hills
1948	USA	6–1	Wimbledon, Court One

Hazel Wightman, donor of the famous cup now named after her

	Winner	Score	Venue
1949	USA	7–0	Merion Club, Philadelphia
1950	USA	7–0	Wimbledon, Court One
1951	USA	6–1	Brookline, Mass.
1952	USA	7–0	Wimbledon, Court One
1953	USA	7–0	Forest Hills
1954	USA	6–0*	Wimbledon, Court One
1955	USA	6–1	Rye, NY
1956	USA	5–2	Wimbledon, Court One
1957	USA	6–1	Pittsburgh
1958	GB	4–3	Wimbledon, Court One
1959	USA	4–3	Pittsburgh
1960	GB	4–3	Wimbledon, Court One
1961	USA	6–1	Chicago
1962	USA	4–3	Wimbledon, Court One
1963	USA	6–1	Cleveland
1964	USA	5–2	Wimbledon, Court One
1965	USA	5–2	Cleveland
1966	USA	4–3	Wimbledon, Court One
1967	USA	6–1	Cleveland
1968	GB	4–3	Wimbledon, Court One
1969	USA	5–2	Cleveland
1970	USA	4–3	Wimbledon, Court One
1971	USA	4–3	Cleveland
1972	USA	5–2	Wimbledon, Court One
1973	USA	5–2	Brookline, Mass.
1974	GB	6–1	Deeside, North Wales (Indoor Court)
1975	GB	5–2	Cleveland (Indoor Court)
1976	USA	5–2	Crystal Palace, London (Indoor Court)

* One match unplayed.

The Olympics

One of the by-ways in the history of Wimbledon is the Olympic event of 1908. There were two lawn tennis Olympics held for the London meeting, a tournament for covered courts which was staged at Queen's Club in May and the Olympic titles on grass staged at the All England Club in July after the end of the Championships.

Looked at from a distance it was a curious event. There was an entry of 45 for the men's singles from nine countries. There were twelve from Great Britain of whom five scratched, eight from Bohemia, of whom four scratched, five from Hungary of whom two scratched, five from Germany, of whom none scratched, four from Canada, with only one pulling out, two from France, with but just one absentee, and two from Holland, all of whom arrived. There were also four Austrians to add to the weight from mid Europe and three of these turned up.

With fourteen withdrawals, including Gore who had just won the Wimbledon Championship for the second time, and Roper Barrett, who had just lost the All Comers' Final to Gore, the men's singles can hardly be said to have gone with a dash. Major Ritchie beat the German Otto Froitzheim in the final. But it was a sparkling event indeed compared with the women's singles. Here the total entry was thirteen, including six overseas players from Hungary, Austria and France. None turned up. It left the seven British, at that stage not an unimpressive field. It included Mrs Lambert Chambers, at that time already three times singles champion of Wimbledon, Mrs Sterry, who had just won the title for the fifth time, Miss A. M. Morton, who had just lost the All Comers' Final, Dora Boothby, who had just been in the semi-final and was, in fact, a champion-to-be, and Mrs Hillyard, six times the champion. But Mrs Hillyard scratched, Miss Boothby scratched, Mrs Sterry scratched and in the end the whole event was decided on the outcome of four matches, one in each of four rounds. Mrs Lambert Chambers, playing in the last three of them, won comfortably.

Mrs Lambert Chambers got a gold medal by taking six sets for the total loss of thirteen games. Miss Boothby won an Olympic silver medal by playing just one match, the final, and losing it 6–1 7–5. Mrs Winch stands as a bronze medallist by reason of having two walkovers and losing 6–1 6–1 to Mrs Lambert Chambers.

There was a third event, the men's doubles. George Hillyard, the All England Club secretary and avid tournament player, won this in partnership with Reggie Doherty. Accordingly Great Britain emerged well from the event with four Olympic gold medallists, Major Ritchie, George Hillyard, Reggie Doherty and Dorothea Lambert Chambers. The prestige of lawn tennis had not, though, been heightened by the happenings. There should have been 76 matches decided on court. Instead of which there were actually 45.

Men's Singles

First round: C. P. Dixon (British Isles) d F. W. Rahe (Germany) 6–2 7–5 6–4
J. Cerny (Bohemia) w.o. O. Schmid (Hungary)
E. Zsigmondy (Hungary) w.o. L. Ivanka (Hungary)
Baron von Bissing (Germany) w.o. G. C. Ball-Greene (British Isles)
A. Zborzil (Austria) w.o. A. W. Gore (British Isles)
C. von Wesseley (Austria) w.o. H. Roper Barrett (British Isles)
W. V. Eaves (British Isles) d R. Kinzl (Austria) 6–3 6–1 6–0
E. Toth (Hungary) d J. Micovsky (Bohemia) 6–3 2–1 retired
J. C. Parke (British Isles) w.o. J. Roessler Orowsky (Bohemia)

O. Kreuzer (Germany) d F. Piepes (Austria) 6–3 6–1 6–4
O. Froitzheim (Germany) d K. Powell (British Isles) 6–3 6–1 6–4
R. B. Powell (Canada) d C. van Lennep (Netherlands) 6–4 6–1 6–2
E. Razny (Bohemia) w.o. H. L. Doherty (British Isles)

Second round: C. K. Vitous (Bohemia) w.o. H. M. Suckling (Canada)
M. Germot (France) d H. Schomburgh (Germany) 7–5 6–4 6–2
M. J. G. Ritchie (British Isles) d V. R. Gauntlett (S. Africa) 6–1 6–4 6–1
W. C. Crawley (British Isles) w.o. G. W. Hillyard (British Isles)
Dixon d D. Lauber (Hungary) 6–1 6–0 6–0
Cerny d Szigmondy 7–5 6–4 3–6 6–0
Von Bissing d Zborzil 6–1 6–4 6–4
Eaves w.o. von Wesseley
Parke d Toth 6–1 6–3 6–2
Froitzheim d Kreuzer 6–2 6–3 6–3
R. B. Powell d Razny 2–6 6–0 6–4 6–1
G. A. Caridia (British Isles) d H. A. Kitson (South Africa) 6–1 6–3 6–1
Capt J. F. Foulkes (Canada) d R. van Lennep (Netherlands) 6–2 6–4 6–3
Rev. J. Richardson (South Africa) w.o. M. Decugis (France)
D. Slava (Bohemia) w.o. J. Zemla (Bohemia)
Capt C. R. Brown (Canada) w.o. Z. Jansky (Bohemia)

Third round: Germot w.o. Vitous
Ritchie d Crawley 6–1 6–4 6–1
Dixon d Cerny 6–1 6–2 6–3
Eaves d von Bissing 8–6 7–5 7–5
Froitzheim d Parke 6–4 11–9 6–4
Caridia d Powell 6–4 3–6 6–4 6–2
Richardson d Foulkes 6–2 6–4 6–3
Brown d Slava 6–2 6–1 6–2

Fourth round: Ritchie d Germot 6–0 4–0 retired
Eaves d Dixon 6–3 7–5 6–3
Froitzheim d Caridia 6–4 6–1 5–7 6–1
Richardson d Brown 6–3 6–1 6–0

Semi-finals: Ritchie d Eaves 2–6 6–1 6–4 6–1
Froitzheim d Richardson 2–6 6–1 6–4 6–4

Final: Ritchie d Froitzheim 7–5 6–3 6–4

Gold Medal: M. J. G. Ritchie

Silver Medal: O. Froitzheim

Bronze Medal: W. V. Eaves

Women's Singles

First round: Miss A. M. Morton (British Isles) d Miss A. N. G. Greene (British Isles) 8–6 6–2
Miss de Czery (Hungary) w.o. Miss F. Pietrikowski (Austria)
Mrs Winch (British Isles) w.o. Miss E. Matouch (Austria)
Mme Fenwick (France) w.o. Miss M. Amende (Austria)
Mrs A. Sterry (British Isles) w.o. Miss de Madarasz (Hungary)

Second round: Mrs R. Lambert Chambers (British Isles) d Miss Morton 6–2 6–3
Mrs Winch w.o. Miss de Czery
Mme Fenwick w.o. Mrs Sterry
Miss D. P. Boothby (British Isles) w.o. Mrs G. W. Hillyard (British Isles)

Semi-finals: Mrs Lambert Chambers d Mrs Winch 6–1 6–1
Miss Boothby w.o. Mme Fenwick

Final: Mrs Lambert Chambers d Miss Boothby 6–1 7–5

Gold Medal: Mrs R. Lambert Chambers

Silver Medal: Miss D. P. Boothby

Bronze Medal: Mrs Winch

Men's Doubles

First round: C. H. L. Cazalet and C. P. Dixon (British Isles) w.o. R. Kinzl and C. von Wesseley (Austria)
H. Schomburgh and O. Froitzheim (Germany) d O. Kreuzer and F. W. Rahe (Germany) 6–1 6–3 6–3

	V. R. Gauntlett and H. A. Kitson (South Africa) d J. Cerny and D. Slava (Bohemia) 6–0 6–4 6–3 L. Ivanka and D. Lauber (Hungary) w.o. A. W. Gore and H. Roper Barrett (British Isles) A. Zborzil and F. Piepes (Austria) w.o. J. Micovsky and J. Roessler-Orowsky (Bohemia)
Second round:	W. C. Crawley and K. Powell (British Isles) d Capt J. F. Foulkes and R. B. Powell (Canada) 7–5 6–3 6–2 G. W. Hillyard and R. F. Doherty (British Isles) w.o. J. Zemla and C. K. Vitous (Bohemia) Cazalet and Dixon d C. and R. van Lennep (Netherlands) 6–4 6–0 3–6 6–2 Gauntlett and Kitson d Schomburgh and Froitzheim 3–6 6–2 7–5 6–3 Zborzil and Piepes w.o. Ivanka and Lauber M. J. G. Ritchie and J. G. Parke (British Isles) d E. Toth and E. Zsigmondy (Hungary) 6–1 6–0 6–3 Capt C. R. Brown and H. M. Suckling (Canada) w.o. Z. Jansky and Z. Razny (Bohemia) M. Germot and M. Decugis (France) w.o. W. V. Eaves and G. C. Ball-Greene (British Isles)
Third round:	Hillyard and R. F. Doherty d Crawley and Powell 10–8 6–1 7–9 7–5 Cazalet and Dixon d Gauntlett and Kitson 6–2 5–7 2–6 6–3 6–3 Ritchie and Parke d Zborzil and Piepes 7–5 6–4 6–2 Germot and Decugis w.o. Brown and Suckling
Semi-finals:	Hillyard and R. F. Doherty d Cazalet and Dixon 5–7 2–6 6–4 17–15 6–4 Ritchie and Parke w.o. Germot and Decugis
Final:	Hillyard and R. F. Doherty d Ritchie and Parke 9–7 7–5 9–7
Gold Medals:	G. W. Hillyard and R. F. Doherty
Silver Medals:	M. J. G. Ritchie and J. C. Parke
Bronze Medals:	C. H. L. Cazalet and C. P. Dixon

INDEX

Notes

1. Women are indexed under final playing names; previous names are listed on p. 192.
2. *Page numbers*: ordinary roman type denotes a reference to the historical section; italic, to the results section; bold, to 'Wimbledon Miscellany'.
3. Full champions have biographies on pp. 193–216; these pages are not given in the index.
4. Subject entries only are given for 'Wimbledon Miscellany'. Players' names are not generally included.
5. People with unknown initials are placed before others with the same surname.

* Two players with same name.